Contents

MILTON AND HERESY

EDITED BY

STEPHEN B. DOBRANSKI

AND

JOHN P. RUMRICH

CAMBRIDGE
UNIVERSITY PRESS

PUBLISHED BY THE PRESS SYNDICATE OF THE UNIVERSITY OF CAMBRIDGE
The Pitt Building, Trumpington Street, Cambridge CB2 1RP, United Kingdom

CAMBRIDGE UNIVERSITY PRESS
The Edinburgh Building, Cambridge CB2 2RU, United Kingdom
40 West 20th Street, New York, NY 10011–4211, USA
10 Stamford Road, Oakleigh, Melbourne 3166, Australia

First published 1998

Printed in the United Kingdom at the University Press, Cambridge

Typeset in Baskerville 11/12.5 pt [CP]

A catalogue record for this book is available from the British Library

Library of Congress cataloguing in publication data

Milton and Heresy / edited by Stephen B. Dobranski and
John P. Rumrich.
p. cm.
Includes bibliographical references and index.
ISBN 0 521 63065 7 (hardback)
1. Milton, John, 1608–1674 – Religion. 2. Christian literature,
English – History and criticism. 3. Heresies, Christian – History –
Modern period, 1500– . 4. England – Church history – 17th century.
5. Heresies, Christian, in literature. 6. Theology – History – 17th
century. 7. Heresy in literature. I. Dobranski, Stephen B.
II. Rumrich, John Peter, 1954–   .
PR3592.R4M55 1998
821′.4–dc21
97-35243 CIP
ISBN 0 521 63065 7 hardback

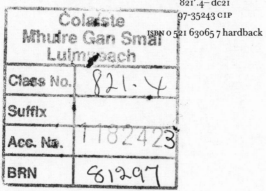

Contributors

JOAN S. BENNETT, *University of Delaware*

THOMAS N. CORNS, *University of Wales, Bangor*

STEPHEN B. DOBRANSKI, *Georgia State University*

STEPHEN M. FALLON, *University of Notre Dame*

JOHN K. HALE, *University of Otago, New Zealand*

WILLIAM KERRIGAN, *University of Massachusetts, Amherst*

BARBARA K. LEWALSKI, *Harvard University*

DAVID LOEWENSTEIN, *University of Wisconsin, Madison*

JANEL MUELLER, *University of Chicago*

JOHN P. RUMRICH, *University of Texas, Austin*

ELIZABETH SAUER, *Brock University, Canada*

JOSEPH WITTREICH, *The City University of New York*

Acknowledgments

The editors wish to thank the contributors to this volume for their patience, good will, and uncommon diligence. We are also grateful to our editor, Josie Dixon, and the anonymous readers for Cambridge University Press whose detailed, informed recommendations guided our revisions. The introduction further benefited from the advice of Lance Bertelsen, Stephen M. Fallon, and David Loewenstein. During the final stages of revision, Mark Womack and Gregory Chaplin were instrumental in bringing a diverse manuscript into consistent, publishable form. We secured their valuable assistance with the support of the Department of English, University of Texas, Austin – specifically through the good offices of James D. Garrison and Sally Gordon. A subsequent travel grant from the Department of English, Georgia State University allowed the editors to work side by side while finishing the manuscript. Finally, Stephen Dobranski wishes to thank Shannon L. Prosser for her many insights, abiding encouragement, and generosity.

This collection is intended to honor the monumental efforts of Maurice Kelley in establishing the textual history and antecedents of Milton's *de doctrina Christiana*.

Abbreviations

CP   *Complete Prose Works of John Milton*, gen. ed. Don M. Wolfe, 8 vols.
             (New Haven, 1953–82).

CW   *The Works of John Milton*, ed. Frank Allen Patterson, 18 vols.
             (New York, 1931–38).

References to the above are given in the form of a roman numeral to indicate volume number, followed by arabic numerals to indicate page numbers.

References to *Paradise Lost* are in the form of Book number, followed by line numbers.

Introduction: Heretical Milton

Stephen B. Dobranski and John P. Rumrich

> There are some irrational bigots who, by a perversion of justice,
> condemn anything they consider inconsistent with conventional
> beliefs and give it an invidious title – "heretic" or "heresy" – without
> consulting the evidence of the Bible upon the point. To their way of
> thinking, by branding anyone out of hand with this hateful name, they
> silence him with one word and need take no further trouble.
>
> John Milton, *de doctrina Christiana* (*CP* VI: 123)

Our understanding of Milton and heresy must begin with his theological
treatise, *de doctrina Christiana*. In what he described as his "dearest and best
possession," Milton rejects the Trinity, denies creation *ex nihilo*, and insists
on the common materiality and mortality of body and soul (*CP* VI: 590). It
seems absurd that the idiosyncratic Christian revealed by *de doctrina* – who
also opposed infant baptism, scorned paid clergy, renounced state interference in religious affairs, defended divorce, and approved of polygamy –
could be heard as a voice of orthodoxy. Yet twentieth-century scholars have
often understated, explained away, or otherwise soft-pedaled his heretical
beliefs. When efforts to mitigate Milton's heresies have met with resistance, some have tried to eradicate them at their most germane textual
source: witness the recent challenge to Milton's authorship of *de doctrina
Christiana*.

This collection investigates aspects of Milton's works "inconsistent with
conventional beliefs" – whether those conventional beliefs comprise standard dogmas of seventeenth-century theologians, or common assumptions of recent Milton scholars. Although we are stretching the meaning of
"heresy" by including chapters that dissent from modern critical orthodoxies, we are encouraged by Milton's own flexibility of usage. As Janel
Mueller notes in her chapter, "heresy" could indicate for the etymologically minded Milton "only the choise or following of any opinion good or
bad in religion or any other learning" (*CP* VII: 246). For Milton, heretics
were not only those who assert "traditions or opinions not probable by

I

scripture" (*CP*VII: 249), but also those who follow set doctrine without con-firmation of conscience (*CP* II: 543). The search for truth, according to Milton, inevitably entails "much arguing, much writing, many opinions; for opinion in good men is but knowledge in the making" (*CP* II: 554). In this dynamic, non-pejorative sense, "heresy" implies a rational process that ultimately produces conviction and instigates future inquiry. The process of heresy may provoke the formation of a new school of thought, or the deviation from an existing one, whether in religion or philosophy. Hence heresy evolves into orthodoxy, from which new heresies eventually depart. "On the New Forcers of Conscience under the Long Parliament" alludes to such a process as Milton complains that

> Men whose Life, Learning, Faith and pure intent
> Would have been held in high esteem with *Paul*,
> Must now be nam'd and printed Heretics
> By shallow *Edwards* and Scotch what d'ye call.   (lines 9–12)

The Presbyterians, now ascendant but once persecuted for opposing Episcopacy, defame as heretics those who challenge their own imposition of orthodoxy. Heresy and orthodoxy beget and define one another, as Milton explicitly recognized, and, at least in the non-pejorative sense of heresy, he accepted this process as inevitable and even desirable. For him, the relation of heresy to orthodoxy is always one of historical process within a manifold community of believers.

The history of Milton scholarship since the nineteenth century also exemplifies the process of heresy. In comparison to the ecclesiastical con-troversies of the 1640s, this critical history was unusually protracted. Yet it also involved critics' religious beliefs, sometimes explicitly. As Robert Adams has remarked, "the Christian humanist majority ... has [long] held the strong right-center position in Miltonic criticism ... against ... many antagonists."[1] We believe that in the second half of the twentieth century these conflicts ultimately produced an institutionally orthodox Milton and rendered certain previous opinions about the poet heretical in the static, pejorative sense of the term.[2]

The most obvious and venerable example of an opinion deemed hereti-cal in the ordinary sense, and the one most crucial to the establishment of critical orthodoxy, is the claim that Satan in *Paradise Lost* is a heroic victim deserving of readers' sympathy. Featuring a stunning refutation of that claim, Stanley Fish's *Surprised by Sin* (1967) deployed reader-response theory in a way that allowed characterization of Satan's sympathizers as will-ful, rebellious, and inept readers – i.e., critical heretics. Fish's dexterous use of theory thus enabled a decisive victory for the long-standing depiction of Milton as a champion of what critics like C. S. Lewis and C. A. Patrides described as Christianity's "great central tradition." Once Fish had refuted the romantic vision of Milton as a heroic rebel, religious and critical orthodoxies dovetailed. Scholars who identified and pondered Milton's religio-political heterodoxy left themselves open to charges of critical heresy from the newly consolidated school of thought.[3]

Although we find this critical orthodoxy inadequate, our collection does not attempt to resurrect the controversy over Satan's heroism, nor does it object to the designation of Milton as a Christian humanist. We are not, in other words, attempting to rejoin the lengthy battles that produced the present critical settlement. Rather than pursue a critical agenda nostalgic for the excesses of Romantic readers, we offer opinions that react against the limitations and occasional errors of the present orthodoxy. For the most part, each chapter in this book focuses on a dimension of Milton's career as poet and political activist that has been neglected or misconstrued in the drive to depict him as a poet of the timeless verities of Christianity.

The chapters in this book thus deviate from the theoretical preoccupations and formulaic historicisms that have diverted recent critical practice from its presumed goals of clarity and accuracy. Our contributors situate Milton and his writings within his specific historical circumstances, with special attention to his paradigmatic position within seventeenth-century religious controversy. For most seventeenth-century Protestants, study and teaching of scripture mediated divine grace and sustained theological inquiry. The Bible was the common field of knowledge to which many of the century's greatest minds devoted their best efforts – as if their eternal lives depended on it. Recent work on the place of theological controversy in the political and intellectual history of seventeenth-century England suggests three broad categories for these scripturally based disputes, vital to the development of modern interpretive methodology, philosophy, and political order. They follow a rough chronological order, succeeding one another as the central site of contention, though with considerable overlap and without a necessary causal link. It is within this historical framework that most of our contributors work.

The first category concerns God's grace and its operation as the effective means of salvation. Nicholas Tyacke has proposed that through 1640 the consolidation of an "anti-Calvinist" heterodoxy decisively influenced the course of political-religious events. Polemically identified with a quasi-papist belief in free will and labeled Arminian, this faction disrupted a broad Calvinist orthodoxy, and, gaining sway, polarized the English

church, galvanized the Puritans, and prepared the way for civil war.[4] Until
the early 1640s, as Barbara Lewalski's chapter indicates, the young Milton
aligned himself with the Calvinist or Puritan side, though with what realization or endorsement of predestinarian theology remains unclear. The
unmistakable Arminianism of the mature Milton, as Stephen Fallon's
chapter demonstrates, is somewhat complicated by Calvinist vestiges –
though these vestiges, as Fallon explains, are not without uncannily close
precedent in Arminius himself. We are tempted to speculate that during
the 1640s, the political and military defeat of the anti-Calvinists – or perhaps the rigid sanctimony of the Presbyterian victors – opened a space for
Milton to adopt an Arminian advocacy of free will and valorization of
rational choosing. These tendencies break through in Milton's divorce
tracts and become undeniably evident in *Areopagitica's* exaltation of
rational choice and advocacy of toleration.

After the downfall of Laud and Parliament's convocation of the
Westminster Assembly, the debate shifted from soteriology to church government – the second site of religious controversy in seventeenth-century
England. The crumbling of Laudian censorship cleared the way for
unprecedented and burgeoning debate, much of it touching the proper
organization of the church. By the mid-1640s, the central dialectic in that
debate had become toleration of sectarian heterodoxy versus rigorous
enforcement of church discipline. Parliament in August of 1645 moved to
institute Presbyterianism in London, an effort that persisted into 1646
along with continued exertions to squelch the sects' heterodox opinions. In
the common discourse of this dominant faction and indeed for most
Puritans of the time, "toleration" was a term of reproach, one that easily
segued into accusations of Arminianism and Socinianism.[5] Milton's early
support of the Presbyterians had subsisted mainly on his loathing of
Episcopacy and entrenched abuses of it, rather than on enthusiasm for the
upstart system, which, familiar grown, pleased less. Once the Presbyterians
took control of government and attempted to check the debate they had
helped to spawn, Milton became their outspoken opponent: "*New Presbyter*
is but *Old Priest* writ Large."

In relation to the course of politico-religious events in England, Milton's
biography neatly exemplifies the heretical process that we have posited – a
parabolic arc of increasing correlation followed by increasing deviation.
The point of near intersection occurs at mid-century. As Stephen
Dobranski observes, it has seemed odd to Milton's biographers that
this outraged critic of "the new forcers of conscience" and proponent of
toleration should so identify with the Cromwellian victors as to become a

government licenser. Yet, however seriously Milton played his part as guardian of the new orthodoxy, his activities could not have been too extensive; the new regime was by seventeenth-century standards remarkably tolerant. Freedom to publish under Cromwell's government, according to Tyacke, "was in fact almost unbounded, approaching very near to the ideal advanced by John Milton in his *Areopagitica* of 1644." The Cromwellian church, too, was notable for its inclusiveness: "a loose confederation of Presbyterians, Independents, and some Baptists, with a great variety of permitted sectarian activity beyond its fringes."[6]

The Presbyterians' identification of such loose church discipline and toleration with Arminianism and antitrinitarian heresy is not empirically unreasonable. The connection seemed real enough at mid-century. Although christology, the third category of seventeenth-century theological controversy, becomes most prominent after the Restoration – when the Clarendon Code obviated debate over ecclesiastical organization – the "effective birth" of antitrinitarian heresy into seventeenth-century religious discourse occurs in the 1640s.[7] Indeed Milton's licensing of the Socinian *Racovian Catechism* helped introduce antitrinitarianism into public discourse. Dobranski demonstrates how little we know about the circumstances surrounding the tract's licensing and publication or the subsequent parliamentary investigation, yet regardless of the reliability of the story as it appears in the anecdotal record, it is for our purposes truly illustrative.

Leo de Aitzema's report that Milton defended his action by appealing to his known tolerationist principles concentrates our three broad categories of controversy – soteriology, church government, christology – into a single representative moment. For Milton, the desirability of toleration followed from his authentically Protestant devotion to individual interpretation of scripture and an Arminian emphasis on the dignity of human will and reason. Advocacy of toleration on such grounds resulted in advocacy of a church organization capable of embracing any scripturally based sect, and thus any scripturally based departure from orthodoxy. Antitrinitarianism, in its Arian origins and seventeenth-century incarnation, based its heretical doctrine on scripture and reason. Because of its politically charged origins at the time when the heretical Christian sect became the orthodox state religion of imperial Rome, it has been described as the "archetypal heresy."[8] As John Rumrich observes in his chapter, late-century exponents of Arianism typically valued their own interpretations over those prescribed by clerical authority, which they disdained.

***

Within the community of Milton scholars, the recent debate that has animated discussions of the author's heretical theology concerns the provenance of *de doctrina Christiana*. In summer 1991 William Hunter raised the astonishing possibility that Milton did not write the theologically heterodox treatise long attributed to him.[9] Hunter's claim is in one sense heretical – "inconsistent with conventional beliefs." Yet Hunter's challenge to the customary attribution promotes the claim that Milton himself was not heretical, but instead espoused the commonplaces of traditional Christianity. As heresy evolves into orthodoxy, so Hunter's challenge appears to have been endorsed by the community of Milton scholars: in 1993 the Milton Society of America awarded Hunter the James Holly Hanford Prize for the outstanding article on Milton published during the previous year.

Because this challenge to Milton's authorship of *de doctrina* has been deemed substantial and credible, a collection concerned with the heretical Milton is bound to address it. Most of our chapters depend heavily on *de doctrina* for evidence. Yet a rebuttal of every argument that has been raised lies outside our compass and athwart our inclination. The debate has become dauntingly multiple and in places recondite. Beginning with panels and plenaries that generated articles and rebuttals, the controversy ultimately brought forth a committee of experts, which convened to scrutinize the proliferating problem and report its findings. (Two members of the committee responsible for the report make important contributions to this collection.) And report the committee has, regularly, at a half dozen international venues and in a lengthy electronic text, published in 1996. Finally, as this collection goes into production, a revised version of the committee's electronic text is set to appear in *Milton Quarterly*.[10]

To confront this many headed controversy at every point would therefore require more space than we can afford it. Nor would it be fitting to do so. The arguments that have thus far been put forward to challenge Milton's authorship do not, in the opinion of the editors of this collection, merit the extensive notice given them by the committee. No doubt it wished to produce a balanced report, and certainly we appreciate the committee's endorsement of the historical and bibliographical data painstakingly assembled by Maurice Kelley, whose contribution to our understanding of *de doctrina*, as the report handsomely acknowledges, "is a scholarly achievement unmatched by any other student of the treatise" (section 6). Yet the final report equivocates and by its very bulk encourages readers to indulge the tenuously grounded speculation that it sifts. Careful reading of the report confirms that Milton is the author of *de doctrina* in any sense of the term "author" that matters. Yet the report's stylometric analysis and ultimate conclusions – while acknowledging that Milton wrote at least significant portions of the treatise – ostensibly justify continued uncertainty regarding the provenance of the treatise. Worse, the report denies the relevance of *de doctrina* to our understanding of Milton and of his exemplary position within the history of seventeenth-century English religious controversies.

It may seem paradoxical for the editors of a collection that registers the inevitability of uncertainty and indeterminacy to advocate "set belief" in Milton's authorship of *de doctrina*. Our point, though, is that by ordinary standards of attribution – which none of the participants in the controversy has challenged – Milton's authorship of the treatise is practically indisputable. We cannot help but ask why the controversy has arisen when there is so little basis for it by conventional standards and when those conventional standards have not themselves come under scrutiny. Hence, the committee mostly retraces and confirms the history long ago worked out by David Masson, William Riley Parker, and, most substantially, Maurice Kelley: (1) various acquaintances of Milton's – including Edward Phillips, Cyriack Skinner, and John Aubrey – testify that Milton steadily worked on a system or body of divinity, perhaps beginning in the early 1640s; (2) the manuscript of *de doctrina* can be reliably dated as being in Milton's possession by 1658, from which time he reworked and revised it with the aid of several amanuenses, including Jeremy Picard and Daniel Skinner; (3) at the end of Milton's life, the manuscript was still not quite ready for the press; (4) Skinner, who copied rather sloppily much of the first half of the manuscript, attempted after Milton's death to publish it along with the poet's state papers; (5) Skinner represented the manuscript as being Milton's work. The committee adds that the author, supposing he were not Milton, was almost certainly an Englishman. Furthermore, the heavily revised manuscript in various hands is in a condition consistent with the supposition of a blind author.

Alternatives to Miltonic authorship, as proposed in section 6 of the committee's report, are purely speculative, and indeed inconsistent with the committee's own research:

The document may have been passed by its author to friends or associates for their comments or corrections. The document may have come into Milton's possession in this way, and he may have chosen to retain it, having comments inserted by a series of casual amanuenses. He may have received it already thus corrected or augmented. But if it were not Milton's, why, given how important it seems to have been to its author, did Milton retain it? Again there are a number of hypotheses. Possibly the author had tried to publish it and, after some discouragement, had abandoned it to the possession of someone who may have found it interesting or useful [i.e. Milton in 1658].

Admitting that *de doctrina* seems to have been "important . . . to its author," the report asks how the treatise left the author's control and came into Milton's hands. The committee can only know that the author valued his treatise from the prefatory epistle, which describes it as his "dearest and best possession." The committee infers, in other words, that the author of the prefatory epistle is, as he claims to be, the author of the treatise. Elsewhere in the report, the committee "most certainly concurs" with Barbara Lewalski's identification of Milton as the persona of the prefatory epistle – the style here is "close to the core of Miltonic practice," according to the report's multivariate statistical analysis (section 11).[11] And thus the report's speculation undoes itself: while mounting a purely conjectural case for uncertain provenance, the report assumes – it seems unavoidable – Miltonic authorship. The best reply to the question, "why did Milton retain it?" is that it belonged to him, "his dearest and best possession."

Leaving aside this telling inconsistency, we are otherwise left to conclude from the committee's findings that if Milton did not author the treatise, we must seek another mid-century Englishman, likely visually impaired – also a monist-materialist, mortalist, divorcer, opposed to tithing, mandatory sabbath observance, and civil interference in religious affairs. According to the arguments of Stephen Fallon and John Rumrich, in Part II of this volume, "Arminian" and "Arian" should be added to the list of undisputed qualifiers characterizing Milton as he appears even without the testimony of *de doctrina*. If the author were someone besides Milton, moreover, we would also have to acknowledge that Milton indulges in massive and intricately detailed dishonesty when in the prefatory epistle he claims the treatise as his own. It does not require great affection for Occam's razor to want to cut the apparently unnecessary multiplication of explanations that the assignment of *de doctrina* to someone besides Milton would require.

In concluding (section 12), the committee cites *Artis Logicae* as precedent for its claim that the provenance of *de doctrina* remains uncertain. Published under Milton's name, *Artis Logicae* derives primarily from a commentary on Ramus by George Downame, from whom Milton "lifted without acknowledgment" (section 12). Had Milton managed to publish *de doctrina* under his own name, the committee argues, he would have been following much the same practice, in this instance plagiarizing some as yet unidentified theological treatise(s) – the "ur text" to which the committee repeatedly refers. Although the report understates the extent of Milton's editorial work in *Artis Logicae*, we agree that Milton is not in the fullest modern sense the author of that work. The system of logic contained therein does not originate with him, nor did he write most of the explanations of that system. Milton admits as much in the preface, which forthrightly explains the book's genesis: "I have come to the conclusion that material from Ramus's own *Lectures on Dialectic* and from the commentaries by others necessary for the fuller understanding of the precepts of the art must be transferred to the body of the art proper and woven in there, except where I disagree with what these commentaries say" (*CP* VIII: 210). Milton nevertheless considered it appropriate to publish *Artis Logicae* under his own name because he chose the logic (Ramus's) and the commentaries (principally Downame's, though he does not name him), wove them together, and revised them according to his views. On these grounds, scholars have reasonably appealed to *Artis Logicae* for evidence of Milton's opinions on matters related to logic.

Unfortunately, the committee never defines what it means by the term "author." The presence of other voices within *Artis Logicae* or *de doctrina* does not preclude Milton's authorship of either work. Milton, of course, did not produce every word in *Artis Logicae* or *de doctrina* – but to hold any of his writings to this standard is to misunderstand seventeenth-century practices of authorship in general and Milton's method of writing in particular. Echoes and translations of previous poets and of scripture occur in all of Milton's poetry and prose, sometimes to the point of authorial self-effacement. Many memorable passages are of questionable origin, things formerly attempted in prose or rhyme. What is the provenance of divine oratory or of angels' hymns in *Paradise Lost*? According to Milton in *Areopagitica*, writing is a relational process that requires an author "to be inform'd in what he writes, as well as any that writ before him" (*CP* II: 532). The customary method of culling *loci communes* or commonplaces is part of this practice and has been historically situated by Walter Ong: "no one hesitated to use lines of thought or even quite specific wordings from another person without crediting the other person, for these were all taken to be – and most often were – part of the common tradition."[12] Mesmerized by the persona of the autonomous author that some of Milton's texts conjure, we fail to realize that all of his writings emerged from a "complex authorial genesis" (section 11). The notion that an author ought to initiate and control every detail of his work, from the subtlest nuances of language to the appearance of printed copies, is an unrealistic expectation at any time, and, as applied to Milton, a post-Romantic anachronism. Hence, although we also find the comparison to *Artis Logicae* instructive, it is not because, as the committee proposes, the Miltonic provenance of *de doctrina* seems roughly similar. *De doctrina* expresses Milton's thought and convictions more fully and centrally than the tract on logic, more fully and centrally than any other single work in the accepted canon of his writings.

The committee admits that the "ur text" that it postulates "may well have been a transcription of the system of divinity which had been assembled by the sighted Milton" (section 12). This likelihood, phrased so tentatively, has been the commonplace opinion of Milton scholars since the nineteenth century, an opinion based on solid evidence, especially that provided in the prefatory epistle "most certainly" of Miltonic provenance. Here, as in the preface to *Artis Logicae*, Milton explains the treatise's complex genesis:

> I made up my mind to puzzle out a religious creed for myself by my own exertions, and to acquaint myself with it thoroughly . . . I began by devoting myself when I was a boy to an earnest study of the Old and New Testaments in their original languages, and then proceeded to go carefully through some of the shorter systems of theologians. I also started, following the example of these writers, to list under general headings all passages from the scriptures which suggested themselves for quotation, so that I might have them ready at hand when necessary. At length, gaining confidence, I transferred my attention to more diffuse volumes of divinity, and to the conflicting arguments in controversies over certain heads of faith. (*CP* VI: 118–19)

Milton claims, characteristically, that he began preparing to become the author of *de doctrina* when he was still a boy, and what he says of his training agrees with what we already know about his education. He also acknowledges that he used antecedent systems of theology to establish general headings for his biblical research and to organize evidence on theologically controversial topics.

Admittedly, it helps to know that the prefatory epistle is statistically identifiable as authentically Miltonic in style. Yet stylometric analysis, however "multivariate," remains a limited and anachronistic tool for identifying the authorial distinctiveness of an early modern theological treatise, for it cannot be fine-tuned to factor in the meaning of the words it counts. For example, to prepare a sample of Milton's treatise for statistical analysis, the committee had to eliminate the strongest evidence of his authorial labor and, ironically, the single most important source for a sure grasp of Miltonic diction and phrasing: "Minimal pre-processing was carried out: ampersands were converted to 'et,' hyphenations were reformatted and quotations were removed. The last procedure changed the electronic version of *de doctrina Christiana* considerably as the resulting 60,000 words of text were derived from almost 90,000 words of original text" (section 11). Here the deletion of one-third of the sample – Milton's scriptural quotations – is noted in the same breath as the conversion of ampersands.

To appreciate the fundamental confusion implicit in the stylometric "minimal pre-processing," mark how Milton's prefatory epistle distinguishes his treatise from those by other authors:

> Most authors who have dealt with this subject at the greatest length in the past have been in the habit of filling their pages almost entirely with expositions of their own ideas . . . I, on the other hand, have striven to cram my pages even to overflowing, with quotations drawn from all parts of the Bible and to leave as little space as possible for my own words, even when they arise from the putting together of actual scriptural texts. (*CP* VI: 122)

In *A Scripture Index to John Milton's "de doctrina Christiana"*, Michael Bauman, a doctor of theology well versed in Protestant religious systematics, testifies to the accuracy of Milton's description: "After nearly twenty years of studying Christian doctrine, I have discovered no systematic theology, Protestant or other, that is even remotely as biblically grounded as Milton's. For page after page, the range and number of his biblical references easily outstrip those of every other comparable text."[13] According to Bauman's arithmetic, Milton quotes scripture 9,346 times in *de doctrina*. Calvin, by comparison, includes a mere 5,574 biblical quotations in the much lengthier *Institutes*.

The sophisticated stylometric analysis on which the committee relies for assessing the authorial genesis of *de doctrina* is thus incapable of registering Milton's most distinctive and significant authorial practice. No other major English poet is as adept or resourceful with scripture. From his earliest to his latest writings his subjects, narratives, style, prosody – all are deeply engaged with and reflective of biblical models. In this crucial regard, *de doctrina* stands at the dynamic center of Milton's authorial practice. Its pertinence to *Paradise Lost*, as Maurice Kelley has demonstrated, is especially pronounced and resonant, as one might expect of works whose subject matter and principal period of composition overlap.

Although our present intention is to address Milton and heresy in a broader context than the debate over the treatise's provenance, many of the chapters in this volume further support, either explicitly or implicitly, Milton's authorship of *de doctrina Christiana*. The collection moves from heresy in the specific sense of unorthodox religious belief to a more general examination of Milton's controversial ideas and actions; it concludes with a discussion of how Milton encouraged readers to reject, as he himself did, established doctrines in favor of personal convictions. We believe that this book appears at an important moment in Milton studies: as the dispute over *de doctrina* illustrates, the persistent desire to present Milton as an orthodox Christian threatens to undermine critical accomplishments of the past half century. Uniting the book's four parts is the shared premise that Milton as poet, thinker, and public servant shunned reliance on set beliefs and regarded indeterminacy and uncertainty as fundamental to human existence. Though he repudiated license, he consistently endorsed at least limited toleration and typically considered reasonable disagreement not only inevitable but desirable.

The first part of this book, entitled "Heretical theology," directly addresses Milton's tolerationist construction of the relation between Christian orthodoxy and heresy. Janel Mueller assesses Milton's engagement with and uses of the term "heresy," effectively establishing a field within which the rest of the book works. Demonstrating how Milton's application of this word changed over his career, Mueller examines Milton's attempts to fuse the pre-Christian sense of heresy (a free and principled personal choice to join a group) with its negative Christian connotation (a faction opposed to a unified church).

Mueller's emphasis on Milton's tolerationist construction of heresy is somewhat qualified and yet ultimately upheld in Thomas Corns's chapter, which discusses the notion of doctrinal toleration in Milton's antiprelatical pamphlets. Milton's attitude toward the sectaries between 1641 and 1642 is notoriously unstable, sometimes allowing that they manifest transitional errors, at other times valuing them as a dynamo of reformation. According to Corns, these diverse comments are unified by Milton's conviction that the sectaries' beliefs – though they may contain errors and heresies – cannot actually harm English Protestantism. Within Milton's reformed church, belief is left substantially free: heresies may come and go, but reason and conscience should never be made subject to prescription, Presbyterian or otherwise.

Barbara Lewalski links these characteristic Miltonic principles to the larger question of his early radicalism. She expands Corns's discussion of the antiprelatical controversy to survey all of Milton's prose and poetry through 1645. During his early career, Milton voiced blistering critiques of most contemporary institutions – the universities, the court, the church, the family, the censored press – and associated his role as poet with the inherently revolutionary power of prophecy and apocalyptic expectation.

Responding to the growing tendency to depict Milton as "confused elit-ist," Lewalski argues that his youthful political and religious attitudes were potentially heretical and, in many cases, were established at an earlier date than is generally supposed.

Like Lewalski's chapter, the three chapters in the next part, "Heresy and consequences," address tendencies within recent Milton criticism to downplay or eliminate the author's heretical opinions. Each chapter focuses on a single heresy – Arianism, Arminianism, and monism – and examines the ramifications of these unorthodox beliefs for Milton's life and art. Analyzing various arguments made since the 1960s for Milton's orthodoxy, for example, John Rumrich uses the controversy over the author's Arianism to illustrate the distorting bias of much twentieth-cen-tury Milton scholarship. He maintains that Milton was indeed an Arian, suggests that the author would have referred to his own beliefs with that polemical term, and re-evaluates the implications of Arianism in the seventeenth century.

Stephen Fallon also historicizes Milton's heretical beliefs, specifically his anti-Calvinist conception of predestination. Scrutinizing *de doctrina Christiana* and God's discourse on salvation in Book 3 of *Paradise Lost*, Fallon suggests that Milton's Arminian epic accommodates, as his theological treatise cannot, the poet's intimate wish to be chosen as one of Calvin's elect. Unsatisfied by a conception of election that would render him a pass-ive object of God's will, Milton contends that one merits election by freely accepting grace. He is reluctant, however, to relinquish the particular favor enjoyed by those receiving "peculiar grace." The individual Christian bears responsibility to choose God and so merit heavenly reward, but Milton also wants to be "elect above the rest," one whom God has specifi-cally chosen.

The final chapter in this part follows the thread laid down by Fallon's argument into the complexities of Miltonic inconsistency but shifts regis-ters to reflect on Milton's heretical conception of matter. Drawing on Rumrich and Fallon's work on this subject, William Kerrigan examines Milton's animist materialism as it affects the depiction of Adam and Eve's kisses in *Paradise Lost*. He views these tender moments from the perspective afforded by a literary tradition of lips touching in love, and contends that the famous kissing scene from Book 4 transcends the frustrations implicit in previous, dualistic representations of such embraces. For Milton, owing to his heretical materialism, kissing looks forward to consummation, concep-tion, and matrimony. He thus joins the luxuries of the lyric tradition with the spiritual dignity of marriage so as to create a new type of love poetry.

Although all our chapters allow for a historically informed understanding of Milton's heretical actions and writings, the third part in particular, "Heresy and community," focuses on Milton's mid-seventeenth-century milieu and the communities that define the shifting boundaries of orthodoxy and heterodoxy. A repeated theme of these chapters is Milton's struggle with individual identity versus group membership – groups such as the Commonwealth government, European humanists, Puritans and antinomians, and the interpretive community of Milton's heretical readers.

In the part's first chapter, Stephen Dobranski assesses Milton's work as licenser within Cromwell's government, specifically Milton's alleged approval of the heretical *Racovian Catechism*. Although scholars who wish to portray the author as an unswerving patron of toleration have emphasized this biographical episode, Dobranski demonstrates how little we actually know about what Milton accomplished as licenser – and how our desire for his constancy has skewed our understanding. In 1649, religious controversy in England was shifting from questions of ecclesiology to the corrosive issue of antitrinitarianism. It is within this context, Dobranski argues, that we need to interpret Milton's work as a government censor. Rather than positing an autonomous author who remained consistent in all things, we need to approach Milton's literary acts within their specific historical circumstances and especially respect the collaborative basis of textual production.

Milton's work as a government employee is also the subject of the next chapter, "Milton and the rationale of insulting," but John Hale instead concentrates on the disturbingly harsh polemical prose that Milton produced on behalf of the Commonwealth. Breaking with the usual apologies for and explanations of Milton's insults, Hale demonstrates that the author, far from composing unworthily or as a censorious preacher, works out of an established tradition. At moments in his *Defence of the English People*, Milton may seem dogmatic and shockingly rude, but in its original Latin the work delighted and thus persuaded – not bored or offended – its primary intended audience, the uncommitted humanists of Europe.

Complementing Hale's discussion of Milton's insults, David Loewenstein's chapter focuses on the author's use of "blasphemy." Though related to insult and heresy, blasphemy represented a more inflammatory issue in mid-seventeenth-century England. And yet, it was also an unusually flexible concept: used as a term of condemnation by orthodox Puritans, it also served radical sectarians who wished to condemn hirelings. Loewenstein investigates blasphemy in the politico-religious discourse of the 1640s and 1650s with specific attention to the prominence

given this offense in the unfolding action of Milton's theologically heterodox epic. Like Milton's use of insults, his treatment of blasphemy is highly
unorthodox: transforming the religious politics of blasphemy in his age,
Milton distinguishes between blasphemy as a radical "conscience in religion" and blasphemy as maliciously speaking evil against God.

Elizabeth Sauer's chapter concludes the third section of our collection
with a discussion of another type of community, Milton's seventeenth-
century readers. More specifically, she examines how *Samson Agonistes*
participates in the construction of a community of readers involved in
resisting conformity and oppressive authoritarian establishments. *Samson
Agonistes*, Sauer argues, is a Restoration closet drama – a play designed to be
read rather than staged – a genre that had served during the Civil War as a
medium for subversive discourse. Milton challenges the oppositional relationship between public and personal action by redefining heroic performance as internal conflict in the closet drama and by using this politically
edgy genre to transport the theater to the reader's private sphere.

Sauer's chapter thus looks forward to the book's final part, "Readers of
heresy," which focuses more exclusively on readers' reactions to the indeterminacy that pervades Milton's heretical thinking. Examining the
inconsistencies and surprising juxtapositions in Milton's three great long
poems, these chapters revisit in various ways the theoretical ground of
many contemporary constructions of Milton as a poet of orthodoxies – i.e.,
reader-response theory or reception aesthetics.

Joan Bennett begins with the observation that most modern readers
cannot imagine someone of Milton's deep religiosity and profound
humanism maintaining even a qualified political commitment. Turning to
present-day liberation theology, specifically its character as an indetermi-
nate theology in progress and one of social practice, she reminds us that in
his own time Milton's theological principles insistently precluded set doctrine and entailed political action. While she is not suggesting that Milton
was a "liberation theologian," she appeals to this developing and apparently inconsistent theology to address the ways Milton used his poetry to
help readers creatively interpret the liberating word of God. In *Paradise
Regained* and *Samson Agonistes*, Bennett argues, Milton is educating his readers about the hope and power behind the stories in the Bible so that they
can find a new way of living in history and the world.

Finally, Joseph Wittreich demonstrates the variety of early readers'
reactions to *Paradise Lost* and juxtaposes that variety against contemporary
readings of the poem, with special attention to the "sexual politics" of contemporary criticism. Wittreich views Milton's epic as an arena for conflict,

a battleground for warring values, contrary theologies, philosophies, and politics. Whether in the last decade of the twentieth century or in the first decade after Milton's death, readers who have perceived the radical implications of the epic's inconsistencies and contradictions have tended to repress them. This chapter compares previously neglected evidence concerning seventeenth-century readers of *Paradise Lost* with recent representations of Milton by all sides within the American culture wars. Despite efforts over three centuries to reaffirm Milton's allegiance to mainstream Protestant thought, *Paradise Lost* remains, above all, a testament to the lasting value of discussion, debate, and dissent.

We hope that this book, too, will help to demonstrate the value of dissent and encourage future readers of Milton to continue the process of discussion and debate that Wittreich describes. As Milton explains in *Areopagitica*, the pursuit of knowledge remains a collaborative project: like the building of a temple, it requires various kinds of workers, "some cutting, some squaring the marble, others hewing the cedars" (*CP* II: 555). We have thus assembled a diverse group of scholars – geographically, they represent Canada, New Zealand, the United States, and Wales; methodologically, they represent bibliographers, feminists, literary historians, Marxists, and psychoanalytic critics. Although we hope that this book will kindle enthusiasm for inquiries, and for styles of inquiry, currently out of favor, our goal is not to begin establishing a new orthodoxy within Milton studies. We instead want to help readers appreciate what it means to have one.

NOTES

1. Robert M. Adams, *Ikon: John Milton and the Modern Critics* (Ithaca, 1955), p. 71.
2. John P. Rumrich discusses the origin and nature of this orthodoxy in *Milton Unbound: Controversy and Reinterpretation* (Cambridge, 1996).
3. That the Milton Society of America posthumously honored William Empson as its Honored Scholar in 1995 suggests that Empson's contributions to Milton studies are gaining the recognition that they deserve.
4. Nicholas Tyacke, *Anti-Calvinists: The Rise of English Arminianism c. 1590–1640* (Oxford, 1987). Tyacke's analysis has been challenged as reductive and for exaggerating the disjunction between the anti-Calvinists and Elizabethan Calvinist orthodoxy. For a somewhat partisan discussion of this criticism, see Ann Hughes, *The Causes of the English Civil War* (London, 1991), pp. 98–101.
5. Blair Worden, "Toleration and the Cromwellian Protectorate," in W. J. Sheils, ed., *Persecution and Toleration* (Oxford, 1984), p. 200.
6. Nicholas Tyacke, "The Legalizing of Dissent, 1571–1719," in Ole Peter Grell, Jonathan I. Israel, and Nicholas Tyacke, eds., *From Persecution to Toleration* (Oxford, 1991), pp. 31, 30.

7. Ole Peter Grell, Jonathan I. Israel, and Nicholas Tyacke, "Introduction," *Persecution to Toleration*, p. 6. See H. J. McClachlan, *Socinianism in Seventeenth-Century England* (Oxford, 1951), pp. 162–74.
8. Maurice Wiles, *Archetypal Heresy* (Oxford, 1996), pp. 4–5. Wiles derives his title from the assessment of R. D. Williams, *Arian Heresy and Tradition* (London, 1987), p. 1.
9. William B. Hunter, "The Provenance of the *Christian Doctrine*," *Studies in English Literature* [hereafter, *SEL*] 32 (1992), 129–42. Responses by Barbara K. Lewalski and John T. Shawcross, as well as rebuttal by Hunter, follow Hunter's essay under the title, "Forum: Milton's *Christian Doctrine*," 143–66. Hunter added to his case with "The Provenance of the *Christian Doctrine*: Addenda from the Bishop of Salisbury," *SEL* 33 (1993), 191–207. Maurice Kelley and Christopher Hill responded to Hunter in, respectively, "The Provenance of John Milton's *Christian Doctrine*: A Reply to William B. Hunter," and "Professor William B. Hunter, Bishop Burgess, and John Milton," *SEL* 34 (1994), 153–63, 165–93. Hunter's reaction, "Animadversions upon the Remonstrants' Defenses against Burgess and Hunter," appears in the same issue, 195–203.
10. The editors wish to thank Roy Flannagan, editor of *Milton Quarterly*, who generously made available the final text of the committee's report, scheduled to appear in October 1997, entitled "The Provenance of *De Doctrina Christiana*." The committee comprises Gordon Campbell, Thomas N. Corns, John K. Hale, David I. Holmes, and Fiona J. Tweedie. References are to section numbers of the manuscript.
11. See Lewalski, "Forum."
12. Walter Ong, Introduction, *The Art of Logic*, *CP* VIII: 187.
13. Michael E. Bauman, *A Scripture Index to John Milton's "de doctrina Christiana"* (Binghamton, NY, 1989).

PART I

Heretical theology

CHAPTER I

Milton on heresy

Janel Mueller

In introducing his study, *Keywords*, which he calls "an inquiry into a vocabulary," Raymond Williams tells how his lexical items came to impress him
with a dual "significance." On the one hand, he says, they functioned as
"binding words in certain activities and their interpretation" and, on the
other, as "indicative words in certain forms of thought." As such, these
keywords posed "a problem of vocabulary, in two senses: the available and
developing meanings of known words, which needed to be set down; and
the explicit but as often implicit connections which people were making,
again and again, in . . . particular formations of meaning – ways not only of
discussing but, at another level, of seeing . . . central experiences." "Every
word which I have included," adds Williams, "has at some time, in the
course of some argument, virtually forced itself on my attention because
the problems of its meanings seemed to me inextricably bound up with the
problems it was being used to discuss."[1]

As with Williams's keywords generally, so too in particular, I want to
argue, with Milton's use of the word "heresy" and its derivatives ("heretic,"
"heretical," "heretically," and the like). I claim that this Miltonic term
yields exceptionally rich corroboration of an important fact about keywords in their historical and sociolinguistic contexts – namely, that apparently individualistic and idiosyncratic inflections like Milton's not only do
not resist, but indeed require the accrued polyvalence of cultural meanings
in order to achieve their special Miltonic force at strategic points in his
prose. In largest terms what this discussion of mine addresses is the necessary interdependence shown by early modern constructions of individual
identity and group membership, as they reach articulation as reciprocal
functions in language – a medium at once a common possession and a
resource made profoundly the writer's own.

A frequency count gives a quick sense of "heresy" and its derivatives as a
keyword for Milton: the computer-produced *Concordance to the English Prose*

lists a total of 108 instances clustered early, middle, and late, most conspicuously in the antiprelatical tracts, the divorce tracts and *Areopagitica*, in *Tenure of Kings and Magistrates* and *Eikonoklastes*, in *A Treatise of Civil Power*, and in *Of True Religion*. The presumably notecard-compiled index to the Columbia edition of Milton's works records an additional twenty-six instances of "haereses," "haereticus" and the like in the Latin tracts, especially the *First* and *Second Defences* and *de doctrina Christiana*.[2] Such abundance requires me to be selective, and I will accordingly concentrate on what I consider the single most revelatory site for the topic of Milton on heresy: the preface of *Civil Power*. Thereafter I will work out from this passage to remark significant developments in Milton's handling of this term, particularly in *The Reason of Church-Government* and *Areopagitica* among the earlier works, and in *Of True Religion* among the later.

Milton published *A Treatise of Civil Power in Ecclesiastical Causes: Shewing That it is not lawfull for any power on earth to compell in matters of Religon* as a public address in February 1659 to the newly convened Parliament of Richard Cromwell in which conservative and centrist Presbyterians held a majority. The tract gave new utterance to Milton's long-held conviction that English Protestants in the exercise of their religion should be free of regulation, whether by the state church or by the civil authority – the party immediately in question. The preface of *Civil Power* coolly undertakes to face down the increasingly influential Presbyterians who argued from their preoccupation with orthodoxy that the times required religion to be regulated. In this context Raymond Williams's observation proves directly pertinent. Milton forces the keyword "heresy" on his readers' attention because the problem of its meanings is inextricably bound up with the problems that he is using it to discuss. His specific tactic here is to track "heresy" back to its roots, to retrieve its colloquialism in former contexts. Thus Milton declares to his orthodoxy-minded opponents:

> Them I would first exhort not thus to terrifie and pose the people with a Greek word: but to teach them better what it is; [heresy] being a most usual and common word... They should first interpret to them, that heresie, by what it signifies in that language, is no word of evil note; meaning only the choise or following of any opinion good or bad in religion or any other learning: and thus not only in heathen authors, but in the New testament it self without censure or blame. *Acts* 15.5. *certain of the heresie of the Pharises which beleevd.* and 26.5. *after the exactest heresie of our religion I livd a Pharise.* In which sense Presbyterian or Independent may without reproach be calld a heresie. (*CP* VII: 246–47)

Twentieth-century lexicography has traced Greek *haíresis* to a literal root meaning a "seizing," a "taking hold," and thence to "choice" in the

general sense of an inclination. This sense in turn frequently extended to
the further meanings of a "resolve, enterprise, or effort directed at a goal,"
bringing *haíresis* close in the last instance to *proaíresis*, the Platonic and Aristotelian term for choice that leads to moral action.[3] The correctness of
Milton's basic definition of "heresy" as "the choise or following of any
opinion good or bad in religion or any other learning" thus finds ample
present-day etymological confirmation. But a pertinent further history
has also been traced for the chain of extended meanings of Greek *haíresis*.
Of this history Milton shows himself a sufficient master to undertake a
rewriting in the preface to *Civil Power*. The philologist Heinrich Schlier gives
the following sketch of these historical extensions of the meaning of "heresy":

There develops in Hellenism the predominant ... use of the term to denote a
"doctrine" and especially a "school." The *hairesis* of the philosopher, which in
antiquity always includes the choice of a distinctive *bios* [way of life] ... thus comes
to be the *hairesis* (teaching) of a particular *hairesis* (school) ... In the Septuagint [the
Greek-language version of the Old Testament] *hairesis* is found occasionally in the
general sense of "choice" ... or free choice ... More important is the signification
in Hellenistic and Rabbinic Judaism ... In Philo it denotes a Greek philosophical
school ... [while] Josephus sees all the Jewish religious schools in terms of the
Greek philosophical schools, the Essenes, Sadducees and Pharisees being the
"three *haireseis* among them" ... New Testament statements concerning *hairesis* are
to be understood against the Hellenistic and Jewish background. The usage in
Acts corresponds exactly to that of Josephus and the earlier Rabbis ...
Christianity, too, is called a *hairesis* by its opponents in [Acts] 24:5 ... In these passages the term has the neutral flavour of "school."[4]

It is only by specifically reinstating these Hellenistic and late antique
Jewish meanings of *hairesis* as a freely chosen school of philosophical or
religious thought that Milton in 1659 can invoke any "sense" in which
"Presbyterian or Independent may without reproach be calld a heresie."
The historical claim that he next makes for the term proves a great deal
more sweeping, however. He declares that the ancient meaning of
"heresy" has revived all at once with the advent of Protestantism, whose
"general maxim ... holds in religion that beleef or those opinions which ...
appeer with most evidence or probabilitie in the scripture" to the individual believer's "conscience and utmost understanding," itself "guided by
the Holy Spirit" (*CP* VI: 248–49). "To protestants therfore whose common
rule and touchstone is the scripture," Milton exults, "nothing can with
more conscience, more equitie, nothing more protestantly can be permitted
then a free and lawful debate at all times by writing, conference or disputation
of what opinion soever, disputable by scripture" (*CP* VII: 249).

Such sweeping etymological appropriation starkly exposes Milton at work on a particular formation of meaning, an alternative way of seeing a central experience – to revert to Williams's terminology. The preface to *Civil Power* reads the Reformation back into a late first-century context as a return to the origins of Christianity and thus, like it in that multicultural Greek-speaking context, a heresy. Having performed this conflation, Milton next reads "heresy" as a keyword both for his time and the former one in its neutral pagan and Jewish senses of a freely chosen, energetically arrived-at doctrine that in turn constitutes a school, whether of philosophy or religion. The word-wresting is both astonishing and typical of Milton. Little else could so well characterize, in such brief compass, the centrality of the inquiring reason to his understanding of Christianity than his eagerness here to establish that Protestantism is a heresy in the early, at once intellectualist and institutionalizing meanings of this term. As Milton defines it, "heresy" becomes a binding word that links certain activities – here, "a free and lawful debate at all times by writing, conference or disputation of what opinion soever, disputable by scripture" – with an interpretation of them as "heresy," here meaning a choice for oneself about the truth of scripture, which in turn entails and manifests one's membership in a group marked off from a more comprehensive religious or social totality by just that exercise of choice. Yet, for all the audacity and erudition with which Milton layers the contexts of his keyword, his etymologizing here bypasses the most arresting aspect of "heresy" in its late first-century context, what Schlier calls "the problem of the derivation of the special Christian sense" (*Th. Dict.*, vol. I, p. 182).

Heresy's strongly negative connotations comprise its special Christian sense, acquired under the authority of Paul. A neutral word – though one with some oppositional tonality – in Hellenism and Judaism,[5] "heresy" is never neutral in Pauline and post-Pauline Christianity. Schlier's careful account reviews key uses of the term in apostolic writings, chiefly Paul's epistles, and offers an unexpected reason for its negative charge. We expect to be told how "heresy" became one pole of the stark truth/error binarism that gives the word its conventional meaning both in Milton's time and ours. Schlier, however, explains that "the word seems to have been suspect in Christianity from the very first" for, when it is used there to designate either the Greek philosophical schools or the Jewish sects, it specifically marks these off as "societies outside Christianity and the Christian church." Accordingly, the terms "heresy" and "heretical" do not owe their meaning to "the development of an orthodoxy" but rather to "the new situation created by the introduction of the Christian *ekklesîa*" –

that is, the vision of the all-embracing church that would eventuate with the universal propagation of the gospel (*Th. Dict.*, vol. I, pp. 182–83). The binary that constitutes the term "heresy" in its first-century Christian sense is not truth/error but church/sect, with the further associated oppositions of wholeness versus divisiveness, community versus splitting into groups. When texts from the apostolic era repeatedly proclaim an incapacity to accept or accommodate heresy, they do so because of the Christian church's decisive claim simply to be the sole comprehensive assembly of God's people. A church so conceived and articulated can make no place for a word whose entire semantics turns on individual determinations of valid doctrine and principled affiliation. Thus in two separate contexts – in Galatians 5:20 and in 1 Corinthians 11:18 – Paul draws a link between *haíresis* and *skhîsma* or schism, since he cannot conceive of the operation of choice associated with the one without envisaging the unendurable rise of new societies alongside the *ekklesía* that the other betokens (*Th. Dict.*, vol. I, p. 183).[6]

How does Milton handle this apostolic Christian repudiation of "heresy," the term and the thing? In the first place, does he register its full force? Yes, he does; the preface to *Civil Power* explicitly addresses the negative charge of both of these Pauline texts. With Galatians 5:20 Milton's tactic is merely to be dismissive. "Heresie," he says, "is reck'nd among evil works *Gal. 5.20*: as if all evil works were to be punishd by the magistrate; wherof this place . . . reck'ns up besides heresie a sufficient number . . . not subject . . . to his cognisance and punishment": "*uncleanness, wantonness, enmitie, strife, emulations, animosities, contentions, envyings*" (*CP* VII: 250). But Milton's aim with 1 Corinthians 11:18, 19 is to explain – and indeed to explain away – the negative connotations of "heresy" as a species of linguistic contamination that occurred when Paul paired this term with another, "schism," which already had negative connotations in the New Testament. Milton says of the Pauline usage, "Where it is mentioned with blame, it seems to differ little from schism 1 *Cor.* 11.18, 19. *I hear that there be schisms among you* &c. *for there must also heresies be among you* &c;" and then characteristically etymologizes both "heresy" and "schism" to bring out the distinction that he finds so telling: "schism signifies division, and in the worst sense; heresie, choise only of one opinion before another, which may bee without discord" (*CP* VII: 247). Notwithstanding what he understands clearly as a weighted difference between the two terms, Milton notes what he represents as self-willed misunderstanding by unnamed others: "some who write of heresie after their own heads, would make it far worse then schism" (*CP* VII: 247).

Again by twentieth-century philological standards, Milton proves to be on solid ground in asserting that "schism" was a negatively charged term in the apostolic church where, according to Christian Maurer, it named those cleavages caused by factions attaching to individual leaders who competed for positions of authority, thus splitting the unity of the members of the body of Christ.[7] Because Milton does accurately register the paramount issue in the early Christian church to be that of compromised collectivity – in his words, "division, and in the worst sense," his assignment of that "worst sense" to schism and his differentiation of a benign sense for heresy – "choise only of one opinion before another, which may bee without discord" – may at first seem to engage frontally with Paul's anxiety in its socioreligious and linguistic context. But the difficulty with Milton's categorical distinction between heresy and schism lies in conceiving of the institutional ramifications of such language. What could it mean within the Christian church as an *ekklesîa* to have "choise . . . of one opinion before another . . . without discord"? In the at once unitary and universal collectivity that the primitive church purported to be, there could be no such choices of opinion without discord, in either the linguistic or the lived domain.

Milton's move at this point is boldest of all, in posing the ultimate issue of whether the individual or the institution grounds the faith and truth of Christianity. His move takes the form of a paradoxical equivocation that, in one application, makes "heresy" synonymous with "true religion" and, in another, returns "heresy" to its opprobrious ordinary sense. This equivocation results in paradox because Milton makes "heresy" function simultaneously in the two contrasted modes that Williams distinguishes for keywords: innovatively, as an indicative word for a certain form of thought, a new way of seeing a certain experience, and conventionally, as a set term, a binding word for a certain activity and its interpretation.

Milton does not simply argue that heresy, in the sense of personal and principled choice, can be countenanced by any church worthy of the name. He argues that any church worthy of the name cannot do without heresy in the sense of personal and principled choice, for such choice is the only genuine way of grounding the church among its adherents. If the church attempts to do without heresy, in this sense, at the individual level, it will confirm itself in heresy at the institutional level – understood in the latter instance as mortal spiritual error. In Milton's resonant words,

He then who to his best apprehension follows the scripture, though against any point of doctrine by the whole church receivd, is not the heretic; but he who follows the church against his conscience and perswasion grounded on the scripture . . . The inference of it self follows: if by the Protestant doctrine we beleeve the scripture not for the churches saying, but for its own as the word of God, then ought we to beleeve what in our conscience we apprehend the scripture to say, though the visible church with all her doctors gainsay; and being taught to beleeve them only for the scripture, they who so do are not heretics . . . No man in religion is properly a heretic at this day, but he who maintains traditions or opinions not probable by scripture; who, for aught I know, is the papist only; he is the only heretic, who counts all heretics but himself. (*CP* VII: 248–49)

Milton's paradoxical insistence that only an embrace of heresy in its pre-Christian sense will save the true Christian church from heresy in its Christian sense is no mere sleight of hand for a given polemical occasion. It is, rather, the articulation of a deeply held conviction for which the word "heresy" remains an index throughout his prose of the 1640s and 1650s. Yet the indexical function of this keyword does not begin with anything like such full paradoxical complexity; it develops this gradually by stages in Milton's writing. The process is worth tracking, if only in outline, in order to see how Miltonic usage collapses the relation of opposition that Raymond Williams theorizes as holding between binding words and indicative words – that is, between convention and innovation in language. Milton on "heresy" shows how any such opposition can undergo literary dissolution precisely where an innovative meaning successfully substitutes for a conventional one. Such a substitution proceeds first and minimally by being intelligible as a linguistic item, then by showing its utility as a term for what Williams calls "a way of looking at a certain experience," but lastly and literarily by proving indispensable for expressing that "way of looking at a certain experience" – in this case, a Miltonic apprehension of Christian faith and truth.

In Milton's prose "heresy" starts with its sense as a strongly negative term – its historical Christian sense – in ascendancy. He speaks confidently, for example, in *Animadversions* of heresy having its source either in "malice" that seeks to undermine the faith or in "weaknesse" too ignorant to tell truth from error (*CP* I: 691). Yet from early on, Milton also identifies a historical connection between "heresy" in its bad sense and the increasingly institutionalized character of the Christian church. When in his antiprelatical tracts Milton returns obsessively to ecclesiastical history in the patristic era, he does so to make the ironic, not yet paradoxical point that heresy was never repressed but always incited by authoritarian measures like the introduction of set forms of prayer, the appointment of bishops as spiritual overlords with the power of excommunication, and the exaltation of certain authors as fathers and doctors of the church.[8] In the next-to-last of these tracts, *The Reason of Church-Government*, published in early 1642 on the eve of civil war, Milton first comes to register a positive, even a divinely ordained purpose for the heresy that chronically besets the church in every age. It is there necessarily, to enable the true and faithful Christian to establish truth and faith by personal demonstration. However, in the actual wording of this portentous passage, the semantic element of choice that informs the etymology of "heresy" in pre-Christian Greek figures only by implication:

If God come to trie our constancy we ought not to shrink, or stand the lesse firmly for that, but passe on with more stedfast resolution to establish the truth though it were through a lane of sects and heresies on each side. Other things men do to the glory of God: but sects and errors it seems God suffers to be for the glory of good men, that the world may know and reverence their true fortitude and undaunted constancy in the truth . . . For if there were no opposition where were the triall . . . ? vertue that wavers is not vertue, but vice revolted from itselfe, and after a while returning. (*CP* I: 794–95)

The thematics of this less familiar passage in *The Reason of Church-Government* anticipate by slightly more than two years the famous and familiar passages in *Areopagitica* (November 1644) that punctuate Milton's appeal to the Long Parliament to lift its order for reinstating censorship prior to a work's printing and publication: "Since therefore the knowledge and survay of vice is in this world so necessary to the constituting of human vertue, and the scanning of error to the confirmation of truth, how can we more safely, and with lesse danger scout into the region of sin and falsity then by reading all manner of tractats, and hearing all manner of reason? And this is the benefit which may be had of books promiscuously read" (*CP* II: 516–17). "Well knows he," resumes Milton, "who uses to consider, that our faith and knowledge thrives by exercise, as well as our limbs and complexion . . . A man may be a heretick in the truth; and if he beleeve things only because his Pastor sayes so, or the Assembly so determins, without knowing their reason, though his belief be true, yet the very truth he holds, becomes his heresie" (*CP* II: 543).

Here in *Areopagitica* is the locus of the meaning exchange where linguistic convention is overtaken by Miltonic innovation, and with such a compelling paradoxical force that English has ever since possessed, as an idiom, the phrase "a heretick in the truth." But what does it mean? What of the antecedent tests of intelligibility and appropriateness that a candidate idiom must pass? In this phrase Milton uses "heretic" negatively, though neither in its conventional sense of damnable error nor in its earlier,

Pauline sense of one whose factional allegiance breaks the unity of the church. He uses it, rather, in a fusion of these generalized, Christian, negative connotations with the norms articulated by the term's pre-Christian, still more originary senses of a principled personal choice concerning a way of life that supplies one with a doctrine and aligns one with a school. Both components of meaning here are inherited, conventional, but their fusion has as its result a Miltonic neologism. His "heretick in the truth" is one who has arrived at a doctrinal position and some kind of church membership (as the references to following "his Pastor" or the Westminster "Assembly" of Divines indicate) – to this extent, this person manifestly accords with the dimension in the pre-Christian meaning of *haîresis* that registers external results and consequences, "a way of life," a "school." Yet this same "heretick in the truth" has failed to reason and determine for himself in the supremely vital matter of religious belief; hence he fails to satisfy what here becomes the more primary dimension of the pre-Christian sense of *haîresis*, that of free and principled individual choice.

Milton generates his paradox of "a heretick in the truth" by exemplifying how the originary dual senses of "heresy" can come to be opposed if the institutional sense does not remain radically contingent on the personal one. The distinction that he enforces by way of this paradox in *Areopagitica* is carried to the extreme of exalting the means of arriving at an end – one's own free seeking and choosing – above the end itself, even if this end proves to have been "the truth." For "a man may be a heretick in the truth . . . if he beleeve things . . . without knowing their reason"; "though his belief be true, yet the very truth he holds, becomes his heresie." Yet this tract in its context – the heady revolutionary ferment of London in the fall of 1644 – manages equally to sustain a vision of collectivity, of *ekklesîa*, as a grand, capacious, but eclectic temple of truth reared through the efforts of many. Although it remains implicit, there is a vital connection between the supreme emphasis laid on the means of personal and principled choice in Milton's "heretick in the truth" paradox and his defense, later in *Areopagitica*, of those who have recently been reviled as sectaries and schismatics:

Where there is much desire to learn, there of necessity will be much arguing, much writing, many opinions; for opinion in good men is but knowledge in the making. Under these fantastic terrors of sect and schism, we wrong the earnest and zealous thirst after knowledge and understanding which God hath stirr'd up in this City . . . A little generous prudence, a little forbearance of one another, and som grain of charity might win all these diligences to joyn, and unite into one generall and brotherly search after Truth . . . Yet these are the men cry'd out against for schismaticks and sectaries; as if while the Temple of the Lord was building . . . there should be a sort of irrationall men who could not consider there must be many schisms and many dissections made in the quarry and in the timber, ere the house of God can be built. And when every stone is laid artfully together, it cannot be united into a continuity, it can be but contiguous in this world; neither can every peece of the building be of one form; nay rather the perfection consists in this, that out of many moderat varieties and brotherly dissimilitudes that are not vastly disproportionall arises the goodly and the gracefull symmetry that commends the whole pile and structure. (*CP* II: 554–55)

   The Reason of Church-Government and *Areopagitica* witness the crucial semantic transactions that will make "heresy" a keyword for the Miltonic perspective on his and England's experience in subsequent prose tracts. Over the period 1644 to 1673, "heresy" continues to serve as a binding word infused with his own paradoxical but consistently construable and topical complexity. Oftenest and most straightforwardly, it is invoked in its conventional sense as a negative term, but one that requires to be distinguished from yet more negative terms for activities that look worse than heresy to Milton at various polemical junctures. The net effects are, gradually, to rehabilitate the term "heresy" by investing it with comparatively more innocuous meanings than other more opprobrious terms. Once again Williams's observation applies: the problems of this keyword's meaning are inseparable from the problems it is being used to discuss.

   In the divorce tracts, for example, Milton at first inclines but later strongly disinclines to equate idolatry with heresy, the more so as he notes in *Colasterion* that he himself has been denounced as "*Heretical*" for seeking to vindicate true marriage by arguing an explicit scriptural warrant for a principled, personal choice to divorce (*CP* II: 722). Thus *The Tenure of Kings and Magistrates* (January 1649) brands the plural benefices of the English Presbyterian ministers a worse "shame and scandal of Religion" than "Sects and Heresies" and later declares these ministers' "covetousness . . . and all kind of Simony" "worse then heresie" because such sins, unlike heresy, put Mammon in the place of God as their object of worship (*CP* III: 196, 241). Likewise, Milton in the *First Defence* (February 1651) terms "avarice and ambition – the two heresies that are most calamitous to the church" (*avaritiam et ambitionem, quae duae in ecclesia haereses perniciosissimae sunt*), but his tone and implications later deepen when, after detecting Salmasius in a major doctrinal error, Milton hesitates between calling this "ignorance or heresy" (*ignorantiam aut haeresin*) – as if the two might be nearly synonymous in certain troublous contexts like that of the Christian church in Europe and England in the late throes of the Thirty Years' War (*CW* VII: 60–61, 198–9).

The tonal ambivalence at this juncture in the *First Defence* proves prophetic of Milton's struggles with the keyword "heresy" in the next period of his Commonwealth writings. Here, as in the central case of the preface to *Civil Power*, he grapples with the hardest question posed by the term "heresy" within a Christian vocabulary and context – the one which the apostle Paul had answered unequivocally in the negative. Was there any meaningful place for *haîresis* as a principled personal choice of a religious or philosophical position within the linguistic and institutional context of the embracing religious body connoted by *ekklesîa?* Both the *Observations upon the Articles of Peace* and the *Second Defence* find Milton engaged in some basic ideological and semantic ground clearing to prepare for addressing this question. In roundly denouncing authoritarian measures for establishing religious conformity in the *Observations* (May 1649), for example, he represents these as not only futile attempts to counter heresy by "subduing . . . authors of hereticall opinions" but also inimical to "the power of truth."[9] The notable effect of these Miltonic binarisms in this context is to range authors of heretical opinions together with the power of truth, over against "the spirituall execution of Church discipline" (*CP*III: 324).

More notably still, the *Second Defence* turns back Alexander More's charge that the New Model Army is "the Lerna" – that is, the Hydra – "of all heresies" (*exercitus est omnium haeresewn lerna*) by portraying this species of *ekklesîa* or collectivity in exclusively spiritual terms that leave no room for coercion in religion and thus endow Christian militancy with a wholly new meaning. "Our army," asserts Milton, is in fact "most modest and religious," for its free time "is spent in the search of truth, in diligent attention to the holy scripture; nor is there any one who thinks it more honorable to smite the foe, than to instruct himself and others in the knowledge of heavenly things – more honorable to engage in the warfare of arms, than in the warfare of the gospel. And indeed," he continues, "if we consider the proper use of war, what can be more becoming in soldiers, who are enlisted and embodied for the express purpose of being the defenders of the laws, the guardians of justice in martial uniform, the champions of the church?" (*CW*VIII: 177, 179).[10] The dynamic of this passage conflates the champions of the church with the seekers for truth who attend diligently to the holy scripture in order to instruct themselves and others, thus effectually rendering "heretics" in the pre-Christian sense synonymous with *ekklesîa* in the early Christian sense. Milton effectually confutes the apostle Paul by making his contradiction between "heresy" and "church" vanish – vanish, at least, from the polemical context of this vindication of Cromwell's regime in May 1654.

The implications of equating truth-seekers with defenders of the faith remain salient for Milton throughout the 1650s. This equation reaches its climactic formulation in the prefatory letter to *de doctrina Christiana*, where he repeatedly uses "heresy" to characterize his own purposes in compiling a scriptural theology for himself, thus recasting his earlier portrayal of the New Model Army in the *Second Defence* into a resonantly paradoxical self-portrait of the true Christian as heretic. The passage begins by reciprocally constituting the Miltonic subject and the Christian religion by way of the pre-Christian sense of "heresy" as rational seeking and choosing of the truths by which one lives:

It has been my object to make it appear from the opinions I shall be found to have advanced . . . of how much consequence to the Christian religion is the liberty not only of winnowing and sifting every doctrine, but also of thinking and even writing respecting it, according to our individual faith and persuasion; an inference which will be stronger . . . in proportion to the authority of Scripture, on the abundant testimony of which they rest . . . I do not expect from candid and judicious readers a conduct so unworthy of them, that . . . they should stamp with the invidious name of heretic or heresy whatever appears to them to differ from received opinions, without trying the doctrine by a comparison with Scripture testimonies . . . Without this liberty there is neither religion nor gospel – force alone prevails – by which it is disgraceful for the Christian religion to be supported (*CW* XIV: 11, 13).[11]

In thus conjoining heresy and truth under the sign of free and rational determination, Milton makes a momentous substitution, however. "Christian religion" (*Christianam religionem*) has been put in place of *ekklesîa*, the all-embracing church envisioned in the Pauline epistles. This substitution proves to have extensive ramifications throughout *de doctrina Christiana* – a work which, as its title suggests, much more fully addresses religion, or doctrine, than it does ecclesiology, the explicit subject only of chapters 24, 29, 31–32 in the first book. Nevertheless Milton's heretical self-portrait in the prefatory letter closes with yet another effort – including a careful invocation of Paul as he speaks in Acts, not as he writes in his pastoral epistles – to secure the ever-problematic mediation between individual determination and church order attested by the tortuous history of the keyword "heresy": "For my own part, I adhere to the Holy Scriptures alone; I follow no other heresy or sect . . . If this be heresy, I confess with St. Paul, Acts xxiv.14 'that after the way which they call heresy, so worship I the God of my fathers, believing all things which are written in the law and the prophets'; to which I add whatever is written in the New Testament. Any other judges or paramount interpreters of the Christian belief, together with all implicit faith, as it is called, I, in common with the whole Protestant Church, refuse to recognize" (*CW* XIV: 15).[12]

Thus, toward the end of the Commonwealth era, Milton in his own often "heretical" *de doctrina Christiana* inscribes himself as the subject he portrays at fuller length in the preface to *Civil Power*: an individual with respect to whom the original Miltonic meaning of "a heretick in the truth" has been paradoxically transformed from negative to positive by now overtly stressing the pre-Christian personal sense of "heresy" as an individual's free, reasoned choice of a religious or philosophical doctrine that simultaneously entails a group affiliation. Having engineered this transformation, moreover, Milton continues to struggle mightily to retain comprehensiveness for the group affiliation that the pre-Christian institutional sense of "heresy" implies. Here, after hitting at Roman Catholicism in his dismissal of "implicit faith, as it is called," he specifies the institutional affiliation entailed by his own "heresy" as the *"universa Protestantium ecclesia,"* "the whole" – or universal – "Protestant Church." The phrasing is hugely revelatory. What makes universalist sense to Milton in the England of the late 1650s could only have registered with the apostle Paul in his era as oxymoron – or as nonsense. In Milton's last strenuous effort to keep *haîresis* and *ekklesîa* in meaningful conjunction, the ligature cannot be made to hold.

Milton's *Of True Religion, Haeresie, Schism, Toleration, And what best means may be us'd against the growth of popery* was published in 1673, the year before his death. This final prose tract bears striking witness to the dissolution of the double value that he had so long ascribed to his keyword "heresy" through paradoxical conflations of its discrete diachronic meanings – as (in the bad, distinctively Christian sense) that which makes true religious choice both meaningful and possible by standing in opposition to it and (in the neutral to good pre-Pauline sense) the exercise of that formative personal choice itself. While reechoing the Commonwealth-era formulation of *Civil Power* – namely, that "Popery is the only or the greatest Heresie: and he who is so forward to brand all others for Hereticks, the obstinate Papist, the only Heretick" (*CP* VIII: 421), *Of True Religion* makes a further move that goes far to confound both the cumulative sense of this Miltonic keyword and its Hellenistic pagan and Jewish prehistory. Milton suddenly voids the stable negative connotations of earlier terminology that he had put into varying relations with "heresy" in his earlier prose works. Now he defines "sects" and "schisms" as not necessarily injurious to the unity and integrity of the church. As he declares, "Sects may be in a true Church as well as in a false, when men follow the Doctrine too much for the Teachers sake . . . and this becomes through Infirmity, implicit Faith," and again,

Schism is a rent or division in the Church, when it comes to the separating of Congregations; and may also happen to a true Church, as well as to a false; yet in the true needs not tend to the breaking of Communion; if they can agree in the right administration of that wherein they Communicate, keeping their other Opinions to themselves, not being destructive to Faith (*CP* VIII: 422).

The positive definition of "sect" here appears to countenance "implicit Faith," a theological term of the period for beliefs embraced on the authority of an ordained spokesman for ecclesiastical orthodoxy. Milton thus makes nonsense of *Areopagitica's* sense of "a heretick in the truth" while also reducing to incoherence the repudiation of Catholicism that he had voiced as an objection to "implicit faith" as late as the preface to *de doctrina Christiana* – a repudiation that he sustains, moreover, in *Of True Religion*. The now positive definition of "schism" allows for the possibility of Christians uniting by procedural agreement while remaining divided on substantive doctrinal issues – a prospect for which the antiprelatical Milton had undisguised scorn when Joseph Hall advanced it as a means of sustaining the unity of the Church of England in the early 1640s.[13]

But the final surprise is what happens to the keyword "heresy" in *Of True Religion*: it undergoes redefinition to become a mere truism, a strongly negative term in its ordinary, later Christian sense. According to Milton's definition now, "Heresie is in the Will and choice profestly against Scripture; error is . . . in misunderstanding the Scripture after all sincere endeavours to understand it rightly: Hence it was said well by one of the Ancients [St. Augustine], *Err I may, but a Heretick I will not be*" (*CP* VIII: 423).[14] How is one to interpret such violent wrenchings of a long cultivated nexus of Miltonic meanings centered on the term "heresy"? One interesting symptom of the degree of wrenching entailed here is Milton's etymologically unwarranted move to dissociate from the faculty of reason the personal choice that for him was always the most vital sense of "heresy" and instead attach this to a wayward will, now that "heresy" is to become a negative term for him. This exempting of reason as choice from the newly negative connotations of "heresy" also indicates how deep his commitment was to the Hellenistic meanings of the term.

Apart from the saving of appearances, is everything distinctively Miltonic lost at this point? The answer seems to be yes. There is poignancy in the relevance here of Raymond Williams's observation that the problems of a keyword's meanings appear inextricably bound up with the problems it is used to discuss. When Milton argues against virtually the entire precedent of his prose works, with the notable and temporary exception of *Areopagitica*, that "sect" and "schism" are neutral to good terms and "heresy" alone is the bad term, the resulting semantic and rhetorical dislocations register the political costs of attempting to secure toleration for all Protestants and only for Protestants in 1673 under a restored Crown and Church of England.

To demarcate just that group, the English Protestants, and sustain a sense of their heterogeneity against any possible reassimilation within the so-called Church of England, the terminology of "sects" and "schisms" was both indispensable to Milton and available for positive signification within a vocabulary and conceptual system where "toleration" figured as a new keyword. This positive signification had indeed begun as early as the allusion in *Areopagitica* to Lord Brooke's "treating of sects and schisms . . . so full of meeknes and breathing charity" (*CP* II: 560–61), and accounts for that work's exceptional position in the patterns of Miltonic vocabulary that concern me here. But – and this point includes *Areopagitica* – Milton also remained as committed as ever to foreclosing the possibility of tolerating Catholicism in England. He never could regard Catholicism in any other light than as a conjoint abrogation of political safety and true religion founded in scripture and in unconstrained, individual choice. Such were the contextual exigencies and uncertainties in which Milton composed his last polemical tract that he jettisoned his long effort to affirm a meaningful connection between "heresy" and "church" against the influential precedent of strongly opposed opinion in Pauline and post-Pauline Christianity. In Milton's last piece of prose polemics the effort at connection gives way to the binarism between "true Religion," Protestantism, and "false Religion," Catholicism – one whose Augustinian origins in *De civitate Dei* Milton signals as he demotes "heresy" into a stock term of opprobrium.

However, he is also at pains to signal the un-Augustinian quotient of this binarism in the present context by remarking mordantly on how the term "Catholic," which once conveyed the force of *ekklesîa* – the church's claim to universality – now figures in the phrase "a Roman Catholick" as "a meer contradiction" or as that logical impossibility, a "universal particular." "For Catholic in Greek signifies universal: and the Christian Church was so call'd, as consisting of all Nations to whom the Gospel was to be preach't" (*CP* VIII: 422). These past- and past future-tense passives – "was so call'd," "was to be preach't" – register Milton's perception of unbridgeable historical distance as well as incommensurate institutional identity between the primitive Christian church and the sectarian England (and Europe) in which he lived. Yet when, as here, the locution "true Religion" replaces the universalist connotations of *ekklesîa*, Milton evokes a new

semantic context in which the pre-Christian senses of "heresy" could perhaps be returned to circulation. Doing so, however, would ostensibly
require dislodging rational inquiry from its central position in Milton's
understanding of what is "true." By his own accounting, the semantic context of a universal "true Religion" of the future would have to rate charity
more highly than verity, since the condition, "if they can agree in the right
administration," entails any prospective membership's "keeping other
Opinions to themselves, not being destructive to Faith." Would such a condition really have proven acceptable and feasible to Milton for any length
of time? On the showing of his whole corpus of prose, this hardly seems
likely.

Thus his sustained efforts to connect *haîresis* positively with *ekklesîa*
appear finally to crumble in the face of the imperative Milton saw of legiti-
mating the forms of Protestant sectarianism in Restoration England. His
paradigm for Christian community in *Of True Religion* no longer figures the
universal church but, to revert to Schlier's definition which I quoted to
begin discussion of this keyword, the "*haîresis* of the philosopher, which in
antiquity always includes the choice of a distinctive *bîos* [way of life], and
thus comes to be the *haîresis* (teaching) of a particular *haîresis* (school)." As
there were Pythagoreans, Platonists, Aristotelians, Stoics, and Epicureans
in antiquity, so Milton catalogues "Lutherans, Calvinists, Anabaptists,
Socinians, Arminians" in the present (*CP* VIII: 423). He also proceeds to
characterize their seeking and choosing in accordance with the range of
meanings encompassed by *haîresis* in its Hellenistic, pre-Pauline senses:
"So long as all these profess to set the Word of God only before them as the
Rule of faith and obedience; and use all diligence and sincerity of heart, by
reading, by learning, by study, by prayer for the Illumination of the holy
Spirit, to understand the Rule and obey it, they have done what man can
do" (*CP* VIII: 423–24). With the sectarian, schismatic paradigm to which he
has recourse to figure individual and institutional religion in and for his
early modern times, Milton does manage to sustain the positive root senses
of his keyword in Greek, as he had so long sought to do in his prose. But he
simultaneously confirms what he had also resisted so mightily and so long –
the apostle Paul's specifically Christian claim that a universal church and
heresy are mutually exclusive.

NOTES

I am grateful to Michael Lieb, David Loewenstein, Joshua Scodel, and Richard
Strier for helpful comments on an earlier version of this paper. Excerpts from it

were presented at the Fifth International Milton Symposium at the University of North Wales, Bangor, in July 1995, where I particularly benefited from Annabel Patterson's questions and criticisms.

1. Raymond Williams, *Keywords: A Vocabulary of Culture and Society*, rev. edn. (New York, 1983), p. 15.
2. Laurence Sterne and Harold H. Kollmeier, *A Concordance to the English Prose of John Milton* (Binghamton, NY, 1985), pp. 635–37; Frank A. Patterson and French R. Fogle, *An Index to the Columbia Edition of the Works of John Milton* (New York, 1940), vol. I, pp. 884–86.
3. I have discussed the centrality of "choice" and its relation to *proaîresis* in "The Mastery of Decorum: Politics as Poetry in Milton's Sonnets," in Robert von Hallberg, ed., *Politics and Poetic Value*, *Critical Inquiry* 13.2 (1987), 475–508; rpt. as Phoenix paperback (Chicago, 1987). My essay has also been reprinted in Harold Bloom, ed., *Milton: The Minor Poems – New Essays in Criticism* (Boston, 1990).
4. Heinrich Schlier, signed article on *haîresis*, in *Theological Dictionary of the New Testament*, ed. Gerhard Kittel, trans. Geoffrey W. Bromiley (10 vols., 1964–76, Grand Rapids and London) vol. I (1964), pp. 180–82, with references to Diogenes Laertius, Polybius, Dionysius of Halicarnassus, Sextus Empiricus, Philo, Josephus, and Acts 5:17, 15:5, 26:5, 24:5, 24:14, 28:22. It will be noted that two of these are the texts cited by Milton in *Civil Power*. Further references to Schlier's article are abbreviated *Th. Dict.* and incorporated parenthetically in my text.
5. Michael Lieb has kindly informed me (personal communication) that the sources of the Jewish conception of heresy lie in two forms: *min* and *n^edavah*. In rabbinical Judaism, heretics are known principally as *minim*. According to *A Hebrew and English Lexicon of the Old Testament based on the Lexicon of Wilhelm Gesenius*, trans. Edward Robinson, 30th edn. (Boston and New York, 1906), *min* denotes "kind" or "species" and is associated with God's creative acts in Genesis 1, while *n^edavah* denotes "voluntariness," frequently in reference to a free-will offering. Manifestly, *haîresis* connects with *min* in the correlation "way (of life)"/"kind," "species"; *haîresis* connects with *n^edavah* in the correlation "free choice"/"voluntariness."
6. Richard Strier (personal communication) has protested that Schlier and I overemphasize the difference between the church/schism and the truth/error distinctions since, as he puts it, "the second maps onto the first (the church's special and intrinsically universal status derives from its unique possession of saving truth)." But Strier's mapping regrettably fails to preserve the difference between freely sought and freely chosen belief that is central to the meaning of non-Christian *haîresis* and the authoritarian assertion that the church alone possesses and communicates true belief (*haîresis* in its Christian sense).
7. Christian Maurer, signed article on *skhîsma*, in *Theological Dictionary of the New Testament*, ed. Gerhard Friedrich, trans. Geoffrey W. Bromiley, 10 vols. (Grand Rapids and London, 1971), vol. VII, p. 964, which cites M. Meinertz, "*Schîsma*

und *Haîresis* im Neuen Testament," *Biblische Zeitschrift*, n. s. 1 (1957), 114–18, on the development of more specialized negative senses for both terms in patristic and later ecclesiastical history.

8. See, e.g., *Of Reformation* (*CP* I: 549–55), *Animadversions* (*CP* I: 685, 691), *The Reason of Church-Government* (*CP* I: 734–35, 781).

9. See the similar tactic in *Civil Power* where Milton retrospectively praises a parliamentary act of August 1650 for defining "blasphemie against God, as far as it is a crime belonging to civil judicature" while passing over in silence the same act's proscriptions against heresy, as presumably exceeding any civil – or, indeed, any human – power (*CP* VII: 246).

10. Milton's Latin reads: "*Exercitum nostrum . . . modestissimum ac religiosissimum es[t] . . . quod datur otii, disquirendae veritati impenditur, sacrae Scripturae invigilatur; nec quisquam pulchrius existimat hostem ferire, quam se atque alios coelestium cognitione rerum erudire, aut bellicam magis quam evangelicam militiam exercere. Et sane si proprium belli usum consideramus, quid aliud magis deceat milites? qui ideo constituti sunt atque conscripti, ut essent legum defensores, paludati justitiae satellites, ecclesiae propugnatores?*" (*CW* VIII: 176, 178).

11. Milton's Latin reads: "*Id denique ago, ut ex iis quae . . . attulisse censebor . . . pro scripturarum potius auctoritate quarum nituntur creberrimis testimoniis, intelligere omnes possint, quanti intersit religionis Christianae, concedi libertatem non excutiendae solum cuiuscunque doctrinae, palamque ventilandae, sed etiam de ea, prout cuique fide persuasum est, sentiendi atque etiam scribendi . . . Illud tamen ab hominibus ingenuis et cordatis, utpote indignum plane, non expecto, ut . . . quicquid abhorrere a doctrina vulgo tradita iudicaverint, id non scripturae testimoniis collatis, sed invidioso quolibet nomine vel haeretici vel haereseos impacto, per caluumniam damnent . . . sine qua libertate, religio nulla, Evangelium nullum est; sola vis viget; qua stare Christianam religionem, turpe et probrosum est*" (*CW* XIV: 10, 12). It will be obvious that I reject the arguments of William B. Hunter, who seeks to detach *de doctrina Christiana* from Milton's authorship. For references to the controversy over the treatise's provenance, see the introduction to this volume, n. 9.

12. Milton's Latin reads: "*De me, libris tantummodo sacris adhaeresco; haeresin aliam, sectam aliam sequor nullam . . . Hoc si haeresis est, fateor equidem cum Paulo, Act. xxiv.14.* me secundum viam illam quam haeresin dicunt, ita servire patrio Deo, ut qui credam omnibus quae in lege et in prophetis, *addo, quae in libris evangelicis etiam* scripta sunt: *alios fidei Christianae iudices aut summos interpretes fidemque omnem, quam vocant, implicitam, cum universa Protestantium ecclesia non agnosco*" (*CW* XIV: 14).

13. See Joseph Hall, *A Humble Remonstrance to the High Court of Parliament* (January 1641) and *A Defence of the Humble Remonstrance, against the Frivolous Exceptions of Smectymnuus* (April 1641) as well as the discussion by Ernest Sirluck, "Hall and the Smectymnuans," *CP* I: 76–86.

14. The editor, Keith W. F. Stavely, cites John Hales, *A Tract concerning Schisme*, p. 9, by way of elucidation: "*Heresie* is an act of the will, not of the reason, and is indeed a lye and not a mistake, else how could that of *Austen* [St. Augustine] go for true, *Errare possum, Haereticus esse nolo*" (*CP* VIII: 423 n.).

CHAPTER 2

Milton's antiprelatical tracts and the marginality of doctrine

Thomas N. Corns

The place of this essay in a book on Milton and heresy may seem super-ficially paradoxical, because I shall argue that Milton's earliest radical prose deflects the then crucial controversies about Laudian doctrinal innovation away from issues of belief and toward issues of practice, of discipline, in ways that seek to marginalize doctrine. However, my thesis is that this mar-ginalization is not because Milton is uninterested in doctrine, but because he probably subscribes, as early as 1641, to views deemed heretical by the middle ground of Puritan opinion. His silence is an attempt to win some space for heterodoxy from Presbyterian Calvinism and to site antiprelati-cism in anticlericalism.

Thus, the essay explores Milton's developing notion of what may be tol-erated, and re-appraises what he has to say about the characteristic prac-tices and beliefs of what is customarily termed Laudianism and, to a less extent, of the sects, in the context of recent historical discussions focused on the place of religious discord in the origins of the English Civil War.

John Morrill has forcefully argued that, of all the impulses driving oppo-sition to the personal rule of Charles I and precipitating open conflict, the determining factor was dissatisfaction with the Caroline church:

in the hectic early days of the Long Parliament, there were three quite distinct and separable perceptions of misgovernment or modes of opposition – what will be called the *localist*, the *legal-constitutionalist*, and the *religious*. One man could hold two or three of them; but many did not do so . . . the localist and the legal-constitution-alist perceptions of misgovernment lacked the momentum, the passion, to bring about the kind of civil war which England experienced after 1642. It was the force of religion that drove minorities to fight, and forced majorities to make reluctant choices.[1]

Milton, of course, was not a member of Parliament. Moreover, the life records for the period preceding his eruption into print in the early summer of 1641 give no indication of his personal view of the developing crisis. Gordon Campbell's new Milton chronology, a timely and immensely valuable

39

addition to the *Life Records* edited by J. Milton French, contains scarcely a trace of Milton for the period from 1639 to his earliest antiprelatical publications.[2] But most certainly, the early fixations of his political prose are wholly with religious concerns. Touchstones of legal-constitutionalist radicalism, matters like ship-money for example, go unmentioned. Though Milton emerges in 1649 and later as the most eloquent defender of the citizens' rights to call monarchs to account, in 1641–42 (and indeed in 1643–45) such issues do not surface in his prose.

I have for long been puzzled by Milton's slow start. When the Long Parliament convened in November 1640, matters of religion dominated the opening weeks.[3] Parliament received hundreds of petitions, most significantly the London petition for root-and-branch reform of the church, presented in mid-December 1640, and in January 1641 a digest of county petitions subscribed by 750 clergy and nineteen county root-and-branch petitions.[4] Milton's earliest contribution, if he is indeed the author of the postscript to the Smectymnuan *Answer to a Booke Entituled, An Humble Remonstrance*,[5] dates from March 1641 and *Of Reformation* from May, somewhat late in the campaign.

While Milton's initial reticence will probably remain unexplained, I have argued and still maintain that the principal tendency of his antiprelatical tracts is toward the devastation of the middle ground emerging in 1641–42 between moderate Presbyterians and anti-Laudian episcopalians and as such it constitutes a purposeful attempt to reanimate a flagging campaign that was entering a second and potentially unsuccessful phase.[6] Milton's tracts focus on prelatical malpractice from the early church to the age of William Laud, and in so doing they define (albeit polemically) what he deems unacceptable in Christian worship and observance.

Most distinctively Milton has almost nothing to say about the role of doctrine in dividing those associated with Laud from the advocates of a Puritan reformation. Accounts of the fissuring of the Anglican church have been deeply influenced by the argument of Nicholas Tyacke that the Arminian doctrine, espoused by Laud and his circle, broke a Calvinist consensus which had united Puritans and their enemies about matters of theory and, despite their arguments, about major aspects of ceremony.[7] Latterly, however, Kevin Sharpe and Julian Davies have argued rather differently against this recent historical orthodoxy. For Sharpe, the theoretical issue of Arminianism, which focuses on its doctrine of salvation, is subsumed within or rather overwhelmed by a populist, ignorant, and/or tendentious confusion of Arminianism with Catholicism: "The controversy over Arminianism and predestination was inextricably bound up with fears of Catholicism and the question of the Church of England's relations with Rome."[8] In Davies's view, "Religion became the major cause of the British Civil War not because of the bugbear of Arminianism but because Charles I was in conscious rebellion against lay and popular Protestantism – the very Reformation itself."[9] The case of Milton may seem pertinent to the Davies–Sharpe perspective, for he is almost silent on doctrinal divisions within the church.

Indeed, he has less to say about Arminianism than the root-and-branch London petition, *The First and Large Petition of the City of London and of other Inhabitants of London* (1641).[10] Among its twenty-eight clauses, several touch on doctrine. The second lists the Calvinist tenets allegedly silenced under "the Prelates":

The faint-heartednesse of Ministers to preach the truth of GOD, lest they should displease the Prelates as namely, *the Doctrine of Predestination, of Free-grace, of Perseverance, of Originall since [sic] remaining after Baptisme, of the Sabbith, the Doctrine against universall Grace, Election, for faith fare-seene, Free will, against Antichrist, Nonresidents, humane Inventions of GODS worship:* All which are generally with-held from the peoples knowledge, because not relishing to the Bishops. (*CP* I: 978)

Among the dissatisfactions with church discipline, there is evidence enough that the drafters of the petition understood full well what were the central doctrines of Calvinism, but before the Tyackean thesis may be endorsed from this evidence, those clauses dealing with Arminianism merit scrutiny. Quite simply, and much as Sharpe suggests, the term is used as a near-synonym for "Popery." Thus the petition protests against the suppression of almost all publication "which strikes either at Popery, or Arminianisme," and at the "publishing and venting of Popish, Arminian, and other dangerous Bookes and Tenets," and it asserts that "onely *Papists, Jesuits, Priests,* and such others as propagate Popery or *Arminianisme* are contenanced, spared, and have much libertie."[11] There is not much evidence here of an informed awareness of the doctrines of Jacobus Arminius.

But for Milton in his earliest tracts the issues do not advance even that far. Indeed, lamenting for an England which once took the lead in the Protestant reformation (through Wycliffe), he notes that discipline, not doctrine, severs his contemporary compatriots from those continental Protestants who have perfected that reformation:

yet me thinkes the *Precedencie* which GOD gave this *Iland*, to be the first *Restorer* of *buried Truth*, should have beene followed with more happy successe, and sooner attain'd Perfection; in which, as yet we are amongst the last: for, albeit in *purity* of *Doctrine* we agree with our Brethren; yet in Discipline, which is the *execution* and *applying* of *Doctrine* home, and laying the *salve* to the very *Orifice* of the *wound;* yea tenting and searching to the *Core*, without which *Pulpit Preaching* is but shooting at Rovers; in this we are no better then a *Schisme*, from all the *Reformation*, and a sore scandall to them. (*Of Reformation*, *CP* I: 526)

Of course, there is a merry game in calling English episcopalianism a "schism" from the Reformation, since the ability to suppress and control schism was among its favorite claims. Milton's more considered opinion will be addressed shortly. But the focus of Milton's critique of prelacy could not be clearer; it is on the delivery of doctrine, that is on discipline, and not on doctrine itself.

The issue recurs in *The Reason of Church-Government*, where Milton seems committed to a redefinition of the term "doctrine" so as to remove it from the theoretical to the practical level:

What is there in the world can measure[12] men but discipline? Our word ruling imports no lesse. Doctrine indeed is the measure, or at least the reason of the measure, tis true, but unlesse the measure be apply'd to that which it is to measure, how can it actually doe its proper worke. Whether therefore discipline be all one with doctrine, or the particular application thereof to this or that person, we all agree that doctrine must be such only as it commanded. (*CP* I: 760–61)

Milton is in weaseling mode, sliding away from doctrine onto the simpler ground of discipline. Doctrine is a constraint, or at least the justification of a constraint, but seemingly a constraint on action rather than belief. Moreover what constitutes doctrine is to be contracted into that which is firmly and finally demonstrable from scripture. There are two points. Firstly, Milton is withdrawing from doctrinal debate with the apologists of prelacy; secondly, he is asserting the simplicities of the core doctrine of Protestantism, leaving much of the intellectual territory of religion open, not to dogma, but to godly speculation.

I cannot find within the antiprelatical tracts evidence that Milton did indeed feel himself severed even from Laud by any central belief relating to that crucial area of denominational differentiation, salvation. Several possible explanations suggest themselves. Perhaps Sharpe and Davies are right: Arminianism is not a significant issue in 1640–41; thus, Milton may merely reflect the non-doctrinal focus of popular religious anxiety. However, it is surely significant that Milton does not attack Laudian "Arminianism" in even the tendentious, non-technical terms of *The First and Large Petition*. The doctrinal division within the Caroline church and its place in the origins of the Civil War constitute a fiercely disputed field among ecclesiastical and political historians. However the matter is finally resolved, Milton is unwilling to take the bishops to task for their (by Calvinist standards) heretical theories of salvation.

Possibly Milton recognized a new problem for anti-Arminians: Joseph Hall, his immediate adversary, was not an Arminian. However, a polemical strategy which, with exuberant disregard for church history, cheerfully lumps the errors of Protestant bishops with those of their Catholic predecessors, is unlikely to have acknowledged such niceties.

A likelier explanation rests in his own theory of salvation: Milton, who is certainly Arminian (in the technical, rather than the pejorative sense of the word) by the time he writes *Paradise Lost*, has already arrived at a theory of salvation that would distinguish him from at least double-predestination Calvinism.[13] The principal evidence for this hypothesis is to be found in the only early Miltonic document which deals at length with salvation, *Comus*.

The mature and explicit Arminianism of *Paradise Lost* internalizes the process of synergy between grace or the spirit and the soul struggling to choose the right course. As the Father explains to the Son:

> I will clear their senses dark,
> What may suffice, and soften stony hearts
> To pray, repent, and bring obedience due.
> To prayer, repentance, and obedience due,
> Though but endeavoured with sincere intent,
> Mine ear shall not be slow, mine eye not shut.
> And I will place within them as a guide
> My umpire conscience, whom if they will hear,
> Light after light well used they shall attain,
> And to the end persisting, safe arrive.
> This my long sufferance and my day of grace
> They who neglect and scorn, shall never taste;
> But hard be hardened, blind be blinded more,
> That they may stumble on, and deeper fall;
> And none but such from mercy I exclude   (3.188–202).[14]

Only the interiority of the process separates this theory of salvation from the thesis of *Comus*. There the hard who are hardened, the blind who are blinded more make up the rout of those wayfarers who have not striven against Comus's sensual temptations, and are excluded from mercy, left to "roll with pleasure in a sensual sty" (line 77). In contrast, divine intercession through the agency of the Attendant Spirit comes to those "that by due steps aspire / To lay their just hands on that golden key / That opes the palace of eternity" (lines 12–14). But just as the Father's argument in *Paradise*

Lost, while stressing that those who are saved chose to be saved, asserts that they are saved through God and not by their own will (3.173–74), so too the Lady is saved because she seeks her own salvation, but her will alone is not sufficient to ensure she will "safe arrive," in that telling spatial metaphor of *Paradise Lost* which links the epic with the journey of the masque.

Comus differs from *Paradise Lost* in the role it gives external agencies in catalyzing the synergy of the soul and grace. Only through the sacramental intervention of Sabrina, who sprinkles the Lady's lips, fingers, and the "venomed seat" (lines 910–17), can she be freed from bondage. The difference between the texts represents the difference between the Anglican Arminianism of the 1620s and 1630s and the radical Arminianism of the mature Milton. Two principal elements change. Radical Puritanism eliminates a role for priestly ceremonialism, and the radical valorization of the spirit within interiorizes the process of salvation. No doubt at least the former development would have occurred in Milton's theology by the late 1630s, since it is consonant with an anticlericalism already manifest in *Lycidas*.

Thus, Milton probably already had notions too distinctively Arminian for him to center his critique of episcopalianism in doctrine, even if that had been an urgent issue. Most pressingly, the theology of the ascendant Puritans of Presbyterian orientation was overwhelmingly Calvinist and their natural inclination was toward the suppression as heresy of more libertarian views such as Arminianism. For a radical Arminian the problem must have been an acute one; conscience had been liberated from the constraints of Laudian ceremonialism only to be enslaved by the dictates of Calvinist orthodoxy.

So Milton's apparent indifference to prelatical heresy strives to establish a *modus vivendi* between theological speculation and Presbyterian prescription. The definition of a rather minimalist doctrinal core to Protestantism serves to marginalize matters on which episcopalians had insisted. But it also offers a new Protestant communion. Hence that insistent polarizing of godly simplicity and the ungodly impulse to accrete unnecessary theory along with unnecessary ceremony:

we see again how Prelaty sayling in opposition to the main end and power of the Gospel doth not joyn in that misterious work of Christ, by lowlines to confound height, by simplicity of doctrin the wisdom of the world, but contrariwise hath made it self high in the world and the flesh to vanquish things by the world accounted low, and made it self wise in tradition and fleshly ceremony to confound the purity of doctrin which is the wisdom of God. (*The Reason of Church-Government*, *CP* I: 829–30)

On the one side stand ceremony and tradition; on the other a holy simplicity that asserts as a matter of faith only that which is made plain in the gospel. Thus, no doubt with a certain relish, he quotes church fathers Ignatius and Cyprian asserting the primacy of "the written doctrine of the Apostles, necessarily written for posterity" over tradition (*Of Reformation, CP* I: 563). In an image of considerable polemic power, the gospel simplicity is opposed to episcopal elaboration, both doctrinal and ceremonial: that "undeflour'd and unblemishable simplicity of the Gospell, nor she her selfe, for that could never be, but a false-whited, a lawnie resemblance of her . . . made by the sorcery of Prelats" (*The Reason of Church-Government*, I: 849).

But here, as so often in this group of tracts, Milton's criticism shifts from matters of specific religious controversy or of the history of the early church to an aesthetic of puritanical revulsion inscribed in gross images of emesis or grotesque sexuality. At the same time, though much more clearly in the concluding pamphlets of the series, a new antithesis emerges, homologous with that of ungodly complexity and simple godliness, between the perverted episcopalians and the honest wisdom of the ordinary believer: "there will not want divers plaine and solid men, that have learnt by the experience of a good conscience, what it is to be well taught, who will soone look through and through both the lofty nakednesse of your *Latinizing* Barbarian, and the finicall goosery of your neat Sermon-actor" (*Apology, CP* I: 935). Milton's antiprelatism persistently topples over into anticlericalism and the assertion of the rights of the laity to order their own religious beliefs according to their conscience.

Thus it is that Milton develops a perhaps grudging respect for the sectaries. In their church-outedness they share some characteristics of Milton's representation of his own exclusion from the clergy (*The Reason of Church-Government, CP* I: 823). For Milton in the 1630s (on his own account) the options had been either "blamelesse silence" or "the sacred office of speaking bought, and begun with servitude and forswearing" (*ibid.*). But the time for silence has passed, and Milton shares with those plain honest men an impulse to speak with a new confidence. Yet, while triumphalism and a sort of tipsy excitement are perhaps the preponderant tones, Milton nevertheless in 1641–42 is contemplating a new communion of English Protestant believers, which may embrace both episcopalians, Independents and sectaries. Of course, he rejoices that the bishops no longer have the physical punishment of dissenting voices within their power and indeed may themselves be open to presumably civil prosecution: "The punishing of that which you call our presumption and disobedience lies not now within the execution of your fangs, the mercifull God above and our just

Parliament will deliver us from your *Ephesian* beasts, your cruell *Nimrods*, with whom we shall be ever fearelesse to encounter" (*Animadversions, CP* I: 729). Of course, Milton may well be fearless henceforth (and his moral courage remains beyond question); the era of "blamelesse silence" is over. Indeed, in that famous apocalyptic vision that concludes *Of Reformation* (*CP* I: 614–17), and less sustainedly elsewhere, he anticipates an imminent last judgment and grim punishment for prelates. But also within the antiprelatical tracts prelates are occasionally acknowledged as a perverted manifestation of the English Protestant tradition which needs to be reclaimed. Episcopalians who have tangled with Catholicism in religious controversy have fared badly and they have let the English Protestant reformation down, but they are nevertheless coreligionists. "When any of our men of those that are wedded to antiquity come to dispute with a Papist, and leaving the Scriptures put themselves without appeale to the sentence of *Synods*, and Councells ... where they give the *Romanist* one buffe, they receive two counterbuffs" (*Prelatical Episcopacy, CP* I: 651): they may be an embarrassment, but they are still "our men."

It is not clear when Milton started to think of himself as an Independent (and indeed he never uses that term of himself, though his tolerationist tract, *Areopagitica*, is of course consonant with Independency). But he anticipates as early as February 1642 a reconfiguration of the church that would permit the return of separatists: "Noise it till ye be hoarse; that a rabble of Sects will come in, it will be answer'd ye, no rabble sir Priest, but a unanimous multitude of good Protestants will then joyne to the Church, which now because of you stand separated" (*The Reason of Church-Government, CP* I: 787–88). Exactly what he means by "unanimous" poses an enigma. The consensus between Brownists and Presbyterians could not extend over many issues of church-government, and certainly the former group permitted the entertainment of doctrinal heterodoxies the latter would not allow currency – as the events of the mid-1640s were to demonstrate. The reception of his own divorce tracts evidenced clearly enough the narrowing of the church the Presbyterians and their associates wished to effect.

But for Milton the characteristic gesture to fellow Protestants is one of inclusion. His position on sectaries in the antiprelatical tracts is notoriously unstable, sometimes regarding them as manifesting transitional errors, at other times valuing them as a dynamo of reformation.[15] But what does unite all his rather diverse comments in the period 1641–42 is the conviction that their beliefs, though they may indeed contain errors and perhaps heresies, cannot actually harm English Protestantism. Viewed most negatively, they are "fond errors and fanatick opinions, which when truth has the upper hand, and the reformation shall be perfeted, will easily be rid out of the way, or kept . . . low" (*The Reason of Church-Government, CP* I: 796). I do not think we can really know quite what Milton thought the end of the ructions of the early 1640s should have been; perhaps he did not know himself. Sometimes the desired outcome is a victory for "truth," as if there will be a unified and fresh-purged English Protestantism, to which all the godly subscribe electively. Elsewhere a process of constant questioning or of a victory which is won in the heart of the individual believer seems likelier; a Seeker subtext may sometimes be glimpsed. However, what is clear is that "truth," whether conceived as destination or process, cannot be harmed by heresy.

Indeed, heresy is too protean a thing easily to be trapped and tamed. Certainly set forms, for example for prayer, historically proved ineffectual in counteracting the spread of Arian and Pelagian heresies (*Animadversions, CP*I: 685). Indeed, the patristic period, whose nostrums are so touted by the episcopalians, was especially characterized by the profusion of heretical opinion: "Heresie begat heresie with a certain monstrous haste of pregnancy in her birth, at once borne and bringing forth" (*The Reason of Church-Government, CP*I: 781). At times, perhaps when most conscious of his mission of seconding the Smectymnuans, he may rehearse a very conservative case for the role of the state church in controlling and ordering English Protestantism. We cannot believe "that God would leave his fraile and feeble, though not lesse beloved Church here below to the perpetuall stumble of conjecture and disturbance in this our darke voyage without the card and compasse of Discipline" (*The Reason of Church-Government, CP*I: 753), a sentiment of Presbyterian orthodoxy. Yet a bolder, more inquisitive and more uncertain voice probably prevails. The heresy of Rome remains forever outside the pale, but as such it constitutes the most important shibboleth of Protestant godliness and is a way of defining the Protestant communion. To be against Catholicism is to be on the side of reason, scripture, and conscience.

I began by adapting John Morrill's three-part analysis to the case of Milton. The vigor of his "religious" mode of opposition scarcely needs demonstration. One could point with facility to the multitude of places in the antiprelatical tracts in which he inveighs against prelatical appetitiveness, speaks in furious indignation against the mutilations of the martyrs of 1637, berates the papistical trappings of episcopalian ceremony, ridicules vestments, condemns altar-rails and the altarwise orientation of the table of communion, and caricatures the Laudian clergy as ignorant, arrogant, guzzling grotesques. But on doctrinal distinctions within a very broadly defined Protestantism he is almost silent. Belief, within his reformed church, is to be left substantially free and beyond prescription; heresies may come and go, much as they did in the post-apostolic church, but reason and conscience and the spirit within matter more than any Presbyterian program for the installation of new tests of faith and ortho-doxy. Milton needs a society thus tolerant of heterodoxy and heresy in part because his own theory of salvation probably is, in Calvinist terms, a heresy, and he needs an intellectual environment permissive of innovation and deviancy as the prerequisite for the free operation of a mind and sensi-bility which are already pushing against the limitations imposed by those new forcers of conscience currently coming into their own.

NOTES

1. John Morrill, "The Religious Context of the English Civil War," *Transactions of the Royal Historical Society*, 5th series, 34 (1984); rpt. in John Morrill, *The Nature of the English Revolution* (London and New York, 1993), p. 47.
2. J. Milton French, ed., *The Life Records of John Milton*, 5 vols. (New Brunswick, 1949–58); Gordon Campbell, *A Milton Chronology* (Houndmills, Basingstoke, forthcoming). I am indebted to Professor Campbell for permission to read and cite his work before publication.
3. Morrill, "The Religious Context of the English Civil War," pp. 45–46.
4. John Morrill, "The Attack on the Church of England in the Long Parliament," in *The Nature of the English Revolution*, p. 77.
5. The evidence is augmented and reviewed by Don M. Wolfe, *CP* I: 961–65; it points at the least to a Miltonic collaboration.
6. Thomas N. Corns, *Uncloistered Virtue: English Political Literature 1640–1660* (Oxford, 1992), ch. 2.
7. Nicholas Tyacke, "Puritanism, Arminianism and Counter-Reformation," in Conrad Russell, ed., *The Origins of the English Civil War* (London and Basingstoke, 1973), pp. 119–43; *Anti-Calvinists: The Rise of English Arminianism, c. 1590–1640* (Oxford, 1987).
8. Kevin Sharpe, *The Personal Rule of Charles I* (New Haven, 1992), p. 301.
9. Julian Davies, *The Caroline Captivity of the Church: Charles I and the Remolding of Anglicanism 1625–1641* (Oxford, 1992), p. 17.
10. It is helpfully reprinted in *CP* I: 976–84.
11. *CP* I: 979, 983, clauses 9, 10, and 28.
12. That is, "regulate, moderate, restrain," as the Yale editor notes.
13. For my interpretation of Milton's mature theory of salvation, see my *Regaining "Paradise Lost"* (London and New York, 1994), pp. 78–86.
14. All references are to *The Poems of John Milton*, ed. John Carey and Alastair Fowler (London and Harlow, 1968).
15. Corns, *Uncloistered Virtue*, pp. 34–37.

CHAPTER 3

How radical was the young Milton?

Barbara K. Lewalski

Alongside George Sensabaugh's classic portrait of "That Grand Whig Milton" and Christopher Hill's leftist line-drawing of Milton the some-time associate of third culture radicals, a new sketch is taking form: Milton the confused elitist, divided against himself and inconsistent in his political ideas and allegiances.[1] The young Milton especially has been represented as inconsistent and even something of a Cavalier, given that at times he used genres, imagery, publication modes, and stances associated with the court, the Laudian church, the Cavalier poets, and even with Roman Catholicism.[2] But that image misrepresents Milton as badly as the engraving by William Marshall affixed to his 1645 *Poems*.

The new conception owes something to revisionist history, which reads the events of 1640–60 as a crisis touched off by political bungling and accident rather than as a revolution prompted by ideological conflict.[3] It owes something also to postmodernist attention to ambiguities and inconsistencies in Milton's texts, and New Historicist emphasis on his inevitable containment within his own culture. But the moment seems to have come for revising the revisionists, for again recognizing that the trial and execution of an anointed king was an awesome revolutionary act with ideological causes and consequences. Some historians are now reaching beyond Whiggish and Marxist categories to reconsider the place of religion, apocalyptic history, and republican political theory in an emergent revolutionary ideology.[4] And Miltonists like Michael Wilding, Cedric Brown, David Norbrook, and Sharon Achinstein have for some time been reclaiming and re-evaluating the reformist, republican, and radical elements in Milton's thought and his efforts to shape a revolutionary populace.[5]

I want to examine Milton's career up to the publication of his *Poems* in 1645, and to argue that almost from the outset he began to construct himself as a new kind of author, one who commands all the resources of learning and art but links them to radical politics, reformist poetics, and the inherently revolutionary power of prophecy. The question of Milton's

49

radicalism is not best addressed by invoking twentieth-century touchstones – class struggle, democratic egalitarianism, or feminism – since
Milton supposed the natural leaders of reform would be a virtuous, educated, and liberty-loving elite from the nobility and gentry (though judged
by merit, not blood). Nor was he ever a member of radical fringe groups –
Familists, Ranters, Fifth Monarchists, Levellers, or Diggers. Anyone who
objects to the term "radical" absent such criteria may consider it within
quotation marks: it is the meaning not the name I call, in proposing that
Milton's early self-constructions are radical in their own specific milieu.
The profusion of his early oppositional associations and attitudes is striking: he identifies with Puritan reformers, with zealous antipapists, and with
militants opposed to Stuart pacifism in the Thirty Years' War. He exhibits
a deep-rooted disposition to defy authority and think for himself. He
voices a blistering critique of many contemporary institutions (the universities, the court, the church, the family, the censored press). And he associates both his poetic and his polemic roles with prophecy and apocalyptic
expectation. Neither the nation nor Milton were set inexorably on a
course toward radical revolution in the 1620s, the 1630s, and the early
1640s, and Milton's politics developed in close relation to the changing
political and cultural scene during these years. Yet at every stage he took
up a reformist and oppositional stance which prepared him for the choice
he would ultimately make: to defend the regicide and undertake to model
anew the English church and state.

Milton's childhood prepared him to identify with the defining features
of oppositional politics in the 1620s: Puritan preaching, vehement
antipopery, support for Protestant internationalism and English militancy
in the Thirty Years' War, disaffection from the culture of the Stuart court
and criticism of Stuart political absolutism. His bourgeois scrivener father,
according to family lore, was cast out and disinherited by his Roman
Catholic father for reading an English Bible.[6] Young John Milton had a
Puritan pastor at All Hallows, Richard Stock, and a Puritan tutor at home,
Thomas Young. His literary mentor at St. Paul's School, Alexander Gil, Jr.
(son of the high master) wrote during Milton's tenure a militant Protestant
poem celebrating the destruction of nearly a hundred Catholics when
their chapel collapsed on Guy Fawkes Day.[7] In 1628 Gil was imprisoned
for toasting the assassination of the Duke of Buckingham and writing
brazenly injudicious verses terming Buckingham a Ganymede to King
James and King Charles, "the old fool and the young one."[8] Given such
influences, it is not surprising that Milton's first known poems – paraphrases of Psalms 114 and 136 written in 1623 at age fifteen – had political

resonance. Psalm 114 had been sung that same year at St. Paul's Cathedral, in thanksgiving for Prince Charles's return from Spain without wedding the Infanta. To both paraphrases Milton added original text emphasizing the people's hard won struggle for liberty and God's power over tyrants. In the *Book of Common Prayer* the first two lines of Psalm 114 simply record the Exodus event: "When Israel came out of Egypt, and the house of Jacob from among the strange people, / Judah was his sanctuary, and Israel his dominion." Milton adds the lines, "When the blest seed of *Terah's* faithful Son, / After long toil their liberty had won" (lines 1–2). His version of Psalm 136 echoes James Buchanan's politically charged expansion of the biblical phrase, "Lord of Lords": "O let us his praises tell, / That doth the wrathful tyrants quell" (lines 9–10).[9]

One of Milton's first poems as a university student at Cambridge was a satiric and militantly antipapist miniature epic on the Gunpowder Plot. He began that poem with an honorific description of King James as "pius" and "pacificus," but those epithets praise him specifically for unifying England and Scotland, and serve to magnify the evil of the papist conspirators. During his seven years at Cambridge (1625–32) Milton attacked his first institution and its authorities, offering a fierce critique of the university and its curriculum of scholastic disputation and rhetorical performance. Whether or not he was whipped or rusticated by his tutor William Chappell during his first year (as John Aubrey reports, citing Milton's brother),[10] the fact that he did change tutors points to some serious altercation. The problem may have been insubordination or too vociferous complaints about the curriculum. In his "Prolusions" Milton often inveighs against the set disputations on Aristotelian topics, taking the very occasions of his assigned exercises to denounce them as "empty quibbles" and as "ragged and tattered studies" that merely turn the student into "a more finished fool and cleverer contriver of conceits."[11] Later, in *The Reason of Church-Government* (1642) he insisted that such "monkish and miserable sophistry" produces dangerously ignorant ministers, lawyers, statesmen, and citizens, and in *Of Education* (1644) he proposed to do away altogether with university education for Arts students and prospective ministers, substituting inclusive academies (*CP* I: 854; II: 374–76).

Some of his university poems seem to reveal a very different cultural politics, but in fact present a young poet attempting to find a poetic voice consonant with his reformist views. Several sensuous Ovidian elegies (I, V, VII) revel in the beauty of women and the eroticism of nature in Springtime, but these poems in fact revise Ovid, as their Miltonic speaker avoids drink, feasting, and love-making, remaining (a bit wistfully) chaste. In Elegy VI to

Charles Diodati accompanying the *Nativity Ode* of December 1629, Milton playfully yet seriously rejects Ovid, as he assigns the Ovidian light elegy to lovers of wine, feasts, and festivities like Diodati, and associates his own austere life during the festive Christmas season with that of ascetic bards like Tiresias or Homer or Orpheus. In another mode, his funeral poems for Lancelot Andrewes, Bishop of Winchester, and Nicholas Felton, Bishop of Ely in 1626 indicate that at this point he was still willing to celebrate bishops who were generally recognized as good men and who had Cambridge connections as former fellows and college masters. But these poems also register Milton's reformist concerns. Felton was identified with opposition to the court over the university chancellorship: a few months before his death he spoke at Cambridge supporting the Earl of Berkshire against the King's nominee, his favorite Buckingham.[12] And Milton introduced into the Andrewes elegy a digressive lament for the lost Protestant heroes in the Thirty Years War – lines which seem an oblique protest of Stuart failure to support the embattled continental Protestants: "Then I remembered that glorious duke and his brother, whose bones were burned on untimely pyres; and I remembered the Heroes whom Belgia saw rapt into the skies – the lost leaders whom the whole nation mourned" (lines 9–12).[13] Later Milton praised Gil's poem on the Protestant victory at Hertogenbosch (September 1629), voicing his hope that Gil might soon celebrate comparable English deeds.[14] Milton's 1631 epitaph for twenty-three-year-old Jane Paulet, likely intended for a Cambridge volume honoring that kinswoman of the university chancellor, seems more problematic, since she was wife to the prominent Roman Catholic Marquess of Winchester. But Milton may well have believed the rumor reported by John Pory to Thomas Pickering, that "she was inclining to become a Protestant."[15] Milton was clearly willing to join in some university poetic tributes, perhaps hoping to call his talents to the attention of a worthy patron.

Yet in all his years at Cambridge Milton's muse entirely ignored the numerous royal and courtly occasions celebrated by other university poets: the death and funeral of James I, the coronation and wedding of Charles I, the visits of Charles and Buckingham to the University, the births and deaths of royal children. Unlike Donne and Herbert earlier, or his college friend and contemporary Edward King who wrote many such poems,[16] Milton seems never to have thought about courtiership. Though he was not yet a declared antiroyalist, this pointed disinclination to look to the court for patronage or imaginative stimulus registers some measure of disaffection. Most notably, in March, 1627, Milton contributed nothing to the lavish ceremonies and tributes offered to Buckingham at his visit to Cambridge, but in that very month he wrote Elegy IV to his Puritan tutor Thomas Young, then chaplain to the Merchant Adventurers at Hamburg. He constructs Young as the victim of a harsh regime, forced into exile because of his religious views: "O Fatherland, hard parent . . . do you drive them away thus with iron implacability to foreign soil . . . whom God himself in his providence has sent to you." More provocatively still, he compares Young to the prophet Elijah forced to flee from King Ahab and Queen Jezabel – inviting, it might well seem, application to Charles and his Roman Catholic Queen Henrietta Maria (lines 87–100).

William Laud's appointment as Bishop of London in 1628, Chancellor of Oxford University in 1629, and Archbishop of Canterbury in 1633 intensified Puritan fears that he would impose still more "popish idolatry" on the English church and would soon lead it back to Rome. While we cannot be sure when Milton considered himself definitively "church-outed by the prelates" (his phrase in 1642), it is significant that neither at Cambridge nor during his "studious retirement" at Hammersmith and Horton did he ever describe himself as a prospective minister, the vocation he had intended from childhood to undertake. This striking absence is no doubt explained in part by his growing commitment to poetry – he often presents himself as a present and future poet and scholar – but it registers as well his growing unease about the Laudian transformation of the church. In a letter of 1633, prompted by an unknown friend's criticism of his delay in taking orders, Milton insists that he is earnestly seeking to apply the parable of the talents to himself and jests that, having tired his addressee by preaching, he would surely tire a congregation. But he very pointedly declines to commit himself to the ministry, soon or later (*CP*I: 319–21). With this letter he enclosed the English sonnet, "How soon hath time," voicing profound anxieties about his calling.

Milton's major English poems of this period register his oppositional politics as well as his emerging conception of himself as a new kind of reformist poet. His command of all the resources of high culture sharply distinguishes him from a Puritan plain-style poet like George Wither.[17] But he departs as far from contemporary Cavalier lyricists, court masque writers, and Anglican devotional poets, critiquing their characteristic values as he offers "reformed" examples of several genres dominated by them. He also claims a poetic mode looking back to Dante and Spenser but shunned by the Cavaliers, prophecy.

The *Nativity Ode* (December 1629), with its cosmic reach from creation to doomsday and from the angel choirs on the first Christmas to the music of the spheres, is strikingly unlike the intimate, devotional Christmas lyrics of Southwell, or Donne, or Herbert, or Crashaw. Milton's reformist politics inform the very long catalogue of pagan idols expelled from their shrines, which suggests by a kind of formal mimesis the lengthy process of getting rid of all religious idols, as well lovely as hideous. Its great length registers heightened Puritan anxieties about the "Roman idolatry" fostered by Laud. In this poem also Milton formally claims a bardic/prophetic role as, with lips purified like another Isaiah, he associates his lofty hymn with the angels' alleluias: "And join thy voice unto the Angel Choir,/From out his secret Altar toucht with hallow'd fire" (lines 27–28).

L'Allegro and *Il Penseroso*, perhaps written in the summer of 1631,[18] appear to turn away from such lofty purposes. Some have seen affinities with the Cavalier poets in L'Allegro's pastoralism, his supposed elitist denial of rural labor, and his attendance at court masques and stage plays; and even affinities with the Laudians in Il Penseroso's fondness for cathedrals with "high embowed Roof," "storied Windows richly dight, / Casting a dim religious light," a "pealing Organ," and a "full voic'd Choir" engaged in "Service high and Anthems clear" (lines 157–62).[19] But that is to read too literally these very literary poems, which define lifestyles in terms of literary modes. Like Elegy VI, *L'Allegro* and *Il Penseroso* stage a choice of life defined in literary terms. On the one hand the life of youthful mirth, displayed in the activities and values of the pastoral mode and such literary genres as rural folk and fairy tales, court masques and pageants, Jonson's "learned comedy," Shakespeare's romantic comedies of the green world, and love songs in the Greek Lydian mode. And on the other hand, in the romance mode, the higher pleasures and values of the melancholy scholar-errant, delighting in esoteric philosophy, romances and allegories, Greek tragedies, Orphic and Christian hymns, and organ music producing ecstasy.

Milton does not repudiate pastoral, stage plays, or masques because he thinks Cavaliers have debased them, or church music and art because he thinks Laudians use them in the service of idolatry. Rather, these poems reclaim such art for innocent delight by excising any hint of licentiousness, or courtly neoplatonism, or idolatry. The coda to *Il Penseroso* makes Milton's poetic strategy clear. The speaker proposes to seek in old age a "peaceful hermitage" and a "Hairy Gown and mossy Cell" – not, obviously, because Milton has such plans for himself, but because they suit the medievalizing romance mode of the poem. He does, however, make these images figure his aspiration to prophetic poetry: "Till old experience do attain / To something like Prophetic strain" (lines 173–74).

Milton's concern to reform debased genres is more obvious in his 1632 entertainment, *Arcades,* for the Dowager Countess of Derby. He may have hoped to attract some settled patronage from the family: the Countess had been patron to a long line of reformist Protestant writers, notably Spenser. With this work Milton begins a critique of the pastoralism and neoplatonism associated in contemporary court masques with Henrietta Maria and her Catholicism,[20] linking his better aesthetics to the values of a soundly Protestant aristocracy. *Arcades* redirects pastoral myths associated with the Stuarts, and the neoplatonic identification of beauty and virtue in the masque praises of Queen Henrietta, to exalt the superior virtue of the seventy-three-year old Countess and her household. The entertainment makes tactful use of the Dowager Countess's role as a bulwark of strength and model of virtue to her family. She was supporting and educating several grandchildren at her Harefield estate and also (in a separate household) another daughter and grandaughter, both of whom had been subjected to outrageous sexual abuse at the hands of the daughter's husband, the Earl of Castlehaven, who was executed in May 1631.[21] In the *Arcades* device, the Countess's grandchildren and others have come from the "Arcadian" Stuart court to pay homage to a far superior queen of a better Arcadia: "Such a rural Queen / All *Arcadia* hath not seen" (lines 108–09). The text quite explicitly exalts her above Queen Henrietta Maria (who is Syrinx to King Charles's Pan): "Though *Syrinx* your *Pan's* mistress were, / Yet *Syrinx* well might wait on her" (lines 106–07). In the Trinity Manuscript these lines are added twice – to the second song and to the third – suggesting that Milton thought them important and debated where to place them for maximum effect.[22] In another revisionary move, the virtues of the Countess's Harewood estate are produced by the power of good art (the songs of Genius) as well as by the ruling lady. Genius nourishes all nature by his "puissant words" (line 60) and cures conditions that symbolize the evils of the fallen world – noisome winds, blasting vapors, evil dew. He also celebrates the power of music "To lull the daughters of *Necessity,* / And keep unsteady Nature to her law" (lines 69–70). His own songs participate in that function as they both celebrate and nurture the Countess's virtue.

In November 1632 the culture wars intensified sharply with the publication of William Prynne's *Histrio-mastix,*[23] which staked out the most extreme Puritan position. This passionate tirade of over 1,000 pages denounced stageplays, masques, queens who act in masques and plays, maypoles and rural festivals, country sports on the Sabbath, Laudian ritual, stained glass windows, and much more. Partly in response to Prynne, King Charles on October 18, 1633 reissued the *Book of Sports,*[24] prescribing the continuance of traditional holiday festivities and Sunday sports in every parish under the supervision of the clergy – activities denounced by Puritans as palpable occasions of sin and profanations of the Sabbath. Prynne's horrendous punishment in May 1634, testifies to the high stakes in these culture wars, in which both masques and country sports functioned as vehicles for Laudianism, political absolutism, and (it was often supposed) the Queen's Catholicism.[25] In his *Maske Presented at Ludlow Castle* (1634), celebrating the appointment of the Earl of Bridgewater as Lord President of Wales, Milton overtly claims his role as reformist poet. His use of the masque genre itself repudiates Prynne's wholesale prohibitions but he makes that genre carry a fierce critique of court politics and aesthetics. Bridgewater's character and Ludlow's distance from the court allowed Milton to create a reformed masque: though a friend and appointee of the King, Bridgewater seems to have been some species of Calvinist, a conscientious judge, and a political moderate who resisted the power of Laud's church courts in Wales.[26]

Milton's critique is directed to the fundamental values insinuated by the court masque. The tempter Comus and his bestial rout, with their "Tipsy dance and revelry," and their "Riot and ill-managed Merriment" (lines 104, 172), figure (on one level) Cavalier licentiousness, Laudian ritual, the depravities associated with court masques and feasts, and the unruly holiday festivities – maypoles, Morris dances, Whitsunales – promoted in the *Book of Sports*. In Milton's reformed masque Comus is the court masquer who weaves "dazzling Spells" and marvelous spectacles, but they are said "to cheat the eye with blear illusion" (lines 154–55).[27] By his shepherd disguise he deceitfully claims the world of pastoral, so often associated with Queen Henrietta. Then he leads the Lady to a decadent court where he seeks to make her his queen, offers her an elaborate banquet, and regales her with rhetoric that echoes countless Cavalier seduction poems on the themes of *Carpe Diem* and *Carpe floream:*

> List Lady, be not coy, and be not cozen'd
> With that same vaunted name Virginity . . .
>   . . .
> If you let slip time, like a neglected rose
> It withers on the stalk with languish't head.
> Beauty is nature's brag, and must be shown
> In courts, at feasts, and high solemnities
> Where most may wonder at the workmanship. (lines 737–47)

Comus is, as Cedric Brown has noted, the right tempter for the occasion, offering the noble Lady and her brothers the refined, dissolute, licentious, courtly, Cavalier ideal they must learn to resist.[28] In her response, the Lady denounces forcefully the profligate consumption Comus promotes (and court masques themselves so notoriously exhibit), urging the right of the worthy poor to share in the earth's bounty. Directly challenging the social vision of court masques that locate the evil of social disorder in the lower classes, Milton's Lady harshly censures the wasteful court and wealthy elites in a passage that has, for its time, remarkably egalitarian implications:

> If every just man that now pines with want
> Had but a moderate and beseeming share
> Of that which lewdly-pamper'd Luxury
> Now heaps upon some few with vast excess,
> Nature's full blessings would be well dispens't
> In unsuperfluous even proportion,
> And she no whit encumber'd with her store   (lines 768–74)

In Milton's *Maske* the court scene is not the locus of virtue and grace, as a masque audience would surely expect; it is Comus's own residence. Nor do rescue and renewal come from monarchs or courts, but from the songs and ritual of the river goddess Sabrina, as some instrument of divine grace from the region and as an embodiment of the transformative power of sublime song and poetry. The shepherds' dances at Ludlow Castle recuperate pastoral from its deceptive appropriation by the false masquer, Comus. Then the final masque dances display the pleasure, beauty, dance, and song that accord with the life of virtue, intimating that all these can best be nurtured in the households of the country aristocracy. If we compare *Coelum Britannicum*, Thomas Carew's sumptuous court masque of the same year (1634) in which the Caroline court provides a model for the reformation of Olympus itself, it will be evident how completely Milton has reversed the usual politics of masquing. When Henry Lawes published the work in 1637, Milton substituted for the truncated acting text a longer version that makes his central themes more explicit and more accessible to a wider audience.

In late 1637 Milton incorporated within his elegy for Edward King in the Cambridge commemorative volume a fierce apocalyptic diatribe that repudiates the Laudian church and sounds the insistent Puritan call for godly ministers. Even a cursory comparison of *Lycidas* to the other epitaphs and funeral poems in *Justa Edouardo King Naufrago* (1638) reveals its striking difference – in aesthetic quality of course, but also in conception. It is the only pastoral elegy and the only poem rising to prophecy and apocalyptic vision. The other contributors – chiefly clerics and often Cambridge fellows like King himself – focus on King and associate him closely with the church or the university he served. John Hayward's elegy, for example, descants on cathedrals, terms them "quires of angels in epitome / Maugre the blatant beast who cries them down / As savoring of superstition."[29] Milton, by contrast, focuses on his own anxieties about vocation, poetic and religious, and he dissociates King sharply from the corrupt Laudian church. Saint Peter is made to praise King as a single good minister among unnumbered "Blind Mouths" who only feed their own bellies, and whose wretched sermons leave their flocks famished and prey to the Roman Catholic wolf:[30]

> How well could I have spar'd for thee, young swain,
> Enough of such as for their bellies' sake,
> Creep and intrude and climb into the fold?
> Of other care they little reck'ning make,
> Than how to scramble at the shearers' feast,
> And shove away the worthy bidden guest;
> Blind mouths! that scarce themselves know how to hold
> A Sheep-hook, or have learn'd aught else the least
> That to the faithful Herdman's art belongs!
> What recks it them? What need they? They are sped;
> And when they list, their lean and flashy songs
> Grate on their scrannel Pipes of wretched straw,
> The hungry Sheep look up, and are not fed,
> But swoln with wind, and the rank mist they draw,
> Rot inwardly, and foul contagion spread:
> Besides what the grim Wolf with privy paw
> Daily devours apace, and [little] nothing said;
> But that two-handed engine at the door
> Stands ready to smite once, and smite no more   (lines 113–31).

The fact that the apostle Peter wears a mitre seems to indicate that Milton was not yet a root-and-branch man. But it is not clear whether this passage supports the prelatists' view that the apostles' ruling power derives to bishops, or the Presbyterian view that such power pertained only to the apostles. In the first published version of the poem the phrase "and little said" (line 129) refers to the King's inadequate response to a string of notorious recent conversions in the Queen's circle.[31] Christopher Hill's suggestion that Milton employed pastoral in *Lycidas* to disguise this furious apocalyptic diatribe from the censors seems dubious;[32] readers could hardly miss the point in 1638 – the reason, perhaps, that Milton signed with his initials only. The volume's compilers and Milton's Cambridge audience could hardly protest, since to do so might suggest that they thought Peter's Jeremiad applicable to themselves. *Ad Patrem,* written I believe about this time, also constructs the poet as Bard, emphasizing his high heroic and divine subjects and his kinship with various prophet figures – Orpheus, the Sibyl, and Apollo's priestesses.[33]

On the grand tour in 1638–39 Milton might seem to have set aside his bardic and reformist purposes as he revels in the praises of the Florentine academicians, the flattering notice of Manso the patron of Tasso, the new music of Monteverdi, the encounters with Galileo and Grotius, and even the hospitality of Cardinal Francisco Barbarini and the English Jesuits in Rome. But though he basked in the Italian sunshine and the afterglow of Florentine humanism he kept up his Protestant guard – especially in Rome and Naples. He was surprised and gratified by the attentions paid him by Cardinal Barbarini, to whom he was introduced by Lucas Holste, librarian of the Vatican collections. His letter of thanks to Holste[34] is lavish in praise of the Cardinal, but he constructs that praise carefully, eliding Barbarini's ecclesiastical role and portraying him rather as welcoming host and true heir to the great Italian Renaissance patrons of learning and the arts. Reporting these events later in his *Second Defence* (1654) Milton explained how he had tried to reconcile the responsibilities of a courteous guest with those of a zealous Protestant: he did not initiate quarrels about religion but "if questioned about my faith [I] would hide nothing, whatever the consequences" (*CP*IV: 619). This policy, he claimed, led the Jesuits in Rome to plot against his safety, though the fact that he returned to Rome for two months without incident suggests that later polemic considerations led him to exaggerate that danger.[35] But apparently not his Protestant apologetics. In 1653 the Dutch philologist and poet Nicholaas Heinsius, who travelled extensively in Italy, commented that Milton "was hated by the Italians . . . on account of his over-strict morals, [and] because he both disputed freely about religion, and on any occasion whatever prated very bitterly against the Roman Pontiff."[36] Milton also claimed in 1654 that he had cut short his Grand Tour because "I thought it base that I should travel abroad at my ease for the cultivation of my mind, while my fellow-citizens at home were fighting for liberty" (*CP*IV: 619).

They were not then yet actually in arms, nor did Milton immediately join in the ideological warfare at his return. In his remarkable Preface to *The Reason of Church-Government* (1642) he reports that he turned at first to his studies and his poetic plans, conscious of "an inward prompting [that] . . . now grew daily upon me, that by labour and intent study (which I take to be my portion in this life) joyn'd with the strong propensity of nature, I might perhaps leave something so written to aftertimes, as they should not willingly let it die" (*CP* I: 810). But when the controversy over the bishops intensified he felt a new call, to become a polemicist-prophet in the manner of Isaiah or Jeremiah: "when God commands to take the trumpet and blow a dolorous or a jarring blast, it lies not in mans will what he shall say, or what he shall conceal."[37]

Milton's five antiprelatical pamphlets of 1641–42 attack another institution, the established church. Associating himself with his former tutor Thomas Young and the other Smectymnuans, Milton formally supports the Presbyterians who were then leading the struggle to eradicate the "romish" liturgy and to remove the bishops – root and branch – from civil and ecclesiastical office. But he was already reaching toward more radical reformation. These tracts directly oppose Presbyterian precepts in condemning enforced tithes and the suppression of dissent, and in insisting that any worthy Christian can exercise any ministerial office, especially given the present "extraordinary effusion of *Gods* Spirit upon every age, and sexe" (I: 566, 591, 608). Often employing fiery rhetoric, furious invective, prophetic denunciations, and millenarian fervor, Milton now constructs himself as a prophet with an extra-ministerial call (*CP* I: 823). He also projects himself as a prophet-poet who hopes to herald the millennial kingdom of Christ the "shortly-expected King": "Then amidst the *Hymns*, and *Halleluiahs* of *Saints* some one may perhaps bee heard offering at high *strains* in new and lofty *Measures* to sing and celebrate thy *divine Mercies*, and *marvelous Judgements* in this Land throughout all AGES."[38]

At this juncture he portrays himself explicitly as a new kind of poet with a reformist agenda. Formalizing his earlier experiments in reforming genres and entertainments, in the *Reason of Church-Government* he dedicates himself to such a program, debating which of several literary genres and exemplary models might be "more doctrinal and examplary to a Nation" (*CP* I: 815). Also, recognizing that aristocratic entertainments like *Arcades* and *Comus* are no longer likely vehicles for reforming recreation, he now recommends "wise and artful recitations" in various public assemblies, expecting that such poetic performances will amend "our youth and gentry" who daily suck "corruption and bane . . . from the writings and interludes of libidinous and ignorant poetasters," and will entice the citizenry to the "love and practice of justice, temperance, and fortitude" (*CP* I: 819). In that tract also Milton formally covenants with his countrymen to become a national epic poet after the yoke of prelacy is removed, at which time he hopes to have the requisite qualifications: an inborn gift, arduous study, wide experience of life, and an Isaiah-like inspiration from "that eternall Spirit who can enrich with all utterance and knowledge, and sends out his Seraphim with the hallow'd fire of his Altar to touch and purify the lips of whom he pleases" (*CP*I: 820–1). In the *Apology for Smectymnuus* he constructs all his experience, including politics and polemics, as a vital part of that poetic preparation:

He who would not be frustrate of his hope to write well hereafter in laudable things, ought him selfe to bee a true Poem, that is, a composition, and patterne of the best and honourablest things; not presuming to sing high praises of heroick men, or famous Cities, unlesse he have in himselfe the experience and the practice of all that which is praise-worthy (*CP* I: 890).

In 1643–45 Milton's marital problems spurred him to demand root-and-branch reform in the most fundamental institution of society, the family. His proposal of divorce for incompatibility, argued in five divorce tracts, placed Milton among the most radical sectaries and heretics of the early 1640s. His position is consonant with Jewish law and has some scant precedent in Protestant discourse on marriage (as he notes) but was almost unheard of in England.[39] Accordingly, he saw himself taking on the whole establishment single-handed, as "the sole advocate of a discount'nanc't truth ... such as every seventh Son of a seventh Son does not venture on."[40] There were many calls for suppression of Milton's *Doctrine and Discipline of Divorce*, often linking it with two other works thought especially pernicious – notably Richard Overton's mortalist treatise and Roger Williams's argument for complete religious toleration.[41]

Milton's arguments for divorce are as radical as his proposal. He denies Christ's evident prohibition of divorce in Matthew 19:3–12 by appealing from the gospel's letter to its spirit – the overarching principles of reason, Christian liberty, and charity. Appealing to reason, he argues that "God hath not two wills, but one will, much lesse two contrary," and that, accordingly, Christ cannot possibly have meant to abrogate the Mosaic permission of divorce as he seemed to do in the Matthew text (*CP*II: 292). Liberty and charity, Milton insists, are so preeminently the essence of the gospel that "who so preferrs either Matrimony, or other Ordinance before the good of man and the plain exigence of Charity, let him professe Papist, or Protestant, or what he will, he is no better than a Pharise, and understands not the Gospel" (*CP*II: 233). Milton also explicates the biblical marriage texts by the same contract theory being used to justify taking up arms against a tyrannical king: "If they [the people] against any authority, Covenant, or Statute, may by the soveraign edict of charity, save not only their lives, but honest liberties from unworthy bondage, as well may he against any private Covnant . . . For no effect of tyranny can sit more heavy on the Common-wealth, then this houshold unhappines on the family" (*CP* II: 229).

Milton's definition of the primary end of marriage as fellowship of the mind and spirit (not procreation or the relief of lust) is unusual though not unique. But his passion in arguing that case is. So is his poignant and potentially very radical appeal to human experience as a basis for understanding God's intentions. The universal pain of loneliness and solitariness, a leitmotif in these tracts, testifies that the desire to join with "a fit conversing soul (which desire is properly call'd love)" was implanted by God himself. Also, the common experience that life with an unfit spouse threatens health, faith, and even life itself, producing misery, melancholy, and despair "in some degree like that which Reprobates feel," testifies that God cannot have intended the continuation of marriages so contrary to religion and human good.[42] As further evidence from experience he retells his own courtship story, barely concealed in an account of how easily an inexperienced chaste young man can be deluded in choosing a wife, given the social conventions of courtship and modest female behavior.

For all the warinesse can be us'd, it may yet befall a discreet man to be mistak'n in his choice . . . who knows not that the bashfull mutenes of a virgin may oft-times hide all the unlivelines & naturall sloth which is really unfit for conversation; nor is there that freedom of accesse granted or presum'd, as may suffice to a perfect discerning till too late: and where any indisposition is suspected, what more usuall then the perswasion of friends, that acquaintance, as it encreases, will amend all. And lastly, it is not strange though many who have spent their youth chastly, are in some things not so quick-sighted, while they hast too eagerly to light the nuptiall torch; nor is it therfore that for a modest error a man should forfeit so great a happines, and no charitable means to release him. Since they who have liv'd most loosely by reason of their bold accustoming, prove most successfull in their matches, because their wild affections unsetling at will, have been as so many divorces to teach them experience. When as the sober man honouring the apearance of modestie, and hoping well of every sociall vertue under that veile, may easily chance to meet, if not with a body impenetrable, yet often with a minde to all other due conversation inaccessible, and to all the more estimable and superior purposes of matrimony uselesse and almost liveles: and what a solace, what a fit help such a consort would be through the whole life of a man, is lesse paine to conjecture then to have experience (*CP* II: 249–50).

Milton's ideal of companionate marriage and of divorce as the necessary remedy for its failure are formulated from the man's perspective and in terms of gender hierarchy. He could not break free of the hierarchical world view to conceive of gender egalitarianism, which alone could realize his ideal. But his contract theory of marriage opens to the future, as does his recognition (appealing both to experience and meritocracy) of the occasional unusual case in which the woman is wiser than her husband and so by natural law should govern.[43]

Related to these radical arguments based on the authority of personal experience are the sweeping claims Milton makes in the divorce tracts, *Of Education*, and *Areopagitica* for the autonomy, authority, and originality proper to a scholar and author. In the domain of culture, this stance is also radical. No other English author before Milton assumed the role of author with such self-consciousness, such urgent insistence that authorship was his divinely authorized vocation, and such persistent claims of originality. As a polemicist he needed, on the one hand, to cite authorities who are in full or partial agreement with his positions, but on the other, he registers an almost visceral distaste for seeming to peddle others' ideas like a pedant or second-rate thinker. His resolution is to insist, again and again, that he arrived at his conclusions before seeing the arguments of others. In *Of Education* (1544) he declines to work out his exact debts to "old renowned Authors," and also asserts, implausibly, that he has not even read the famous treatises of the great modern educator and dean of the Hartlib Circle, Comenius: his observations are, he insists, his own, the offshoots "of many studious and contemplative yeers altogether spent in the search of religious and civil knowledge" (*CP* II: 364–66). The conflict is especially intense in Milton's preface to his translation of some chapters on marriage and divorce from Martin Bucer's *De Regno Christi*. He reports himself pleased to find support for his views in Grotius, Fagius, and Bucer, but he claims the role of a "collateral teacher" with them, since he came to his own views first, with only "the infallible grounds of Scripture to be my guide." He used Grotius only as an "able assistant," having found the *De Jure Naturali et Gentium* when the first edition of the *Doctrine and Discipline* was almost finished; Bucer he came upon three months after publication of his *Doctrine and Discipline*, and he found there "*the same reasons which in that publisht book without the help or imitation of any precedent Writer, I had labour'd out*" (*CP* II: 433–36). God, he supposes, "*intended to prove me, whether I durst alone take up a rightful cause against a world of disesteem, & found I durst*" (*CP* II: 434). In a postscript to *The Judgment of Martin Bucer* he somewhat truculently defends his method of selecting and epitomizing passages rather than translating exactly: "my mother bore me a speaker of what God made mine own, and not a translator" (*CP* II: 478).

In *Areopagitica* Milton famously rages against the demeaning constraints the process of censorship places on the autonomy and authority of an author, and attacks yet another institution, the government apparatus for the pre-publication censorship of books. An author, he insists, "summons up all his reason and deliberation" so as to be informed "as well as any that writ before him" and if he is subjected to a censor "in this most consummat act of his fidelity and ripeness ... it cannot be but a dishonor and dero-gation to the author, to the book, to the privilege and dignity of Learning" (*CP* II:532). He concludes angrily, "How can a man teach with autority, which is the life of teaching, how can he be a Doctor in his book as he ought to be, or else had better be silent, whenas all he teaches, all he delivers, is but under the tuition, under the correction of his patriarchal licencer to blot or alter" (*CP* II: 532–33). Significantly, however, Milton underscores his approval of the law's provision for author's copyright, "which preserves justly every mans Copy to himselfe" (*CP* II: 491). Echoes of these insistent authorial claims, forged in early controversy, resound throughout Milton's work. There may be no passage that so surely proclaims *The Christian Doctrine* to be Milton's as the author's insistent assertion of entire original-ity in his heresies: "I had not even studied any of the so-called heretical writers, when the blunders of those who are styled orthodox ... first taught me to agree with their opponents whenever these agreed with the Bible" (*CP* VI: 123–24).

In *Areopagitica* Milton develops a trenchant defense of intellectual liberty, adducing arguments which, as everyone knows, have become a corner-stone in the liberal defense of freedom of speech, press, and thought. He also supports, in opposition to the Presbyterians in power, Independent and Sectarian demands for broad religious toleration. Critics have prop-erly taken note of the qualifications and limitations of Milton's formu-lations: he allows that books may be prosecuted after publication for libel or other crimes (though not for heresy); and that toleration need not extend to open blasphemy (the Ranters) or to the open practice of idolatry (Roman Catholicism)[44] – though the latter exclusion is based chiefly on the political power of the Roman church and Milton's view of it as a tyranny binding the conscience to the Pope's authority. More important, however, is Milton's passionate articulation of principles that promote human free-dom: his belief in the potency and inestimable value of books – "as good almost kill a Man as kill a good Book"; his insistence that temptation and choice are of the essence of the human condition, the only means to find out the good and develop virtue in a fallen world; his optimistic faith in Truth's power to overcome falsehood through reasoned debate and con-test – "Who knows not that Truth is strong, next to the Almighty"; and his conception of truth as a process, not a doctrine, a dismembered Osiris whose parts are being but can never in this life be fully reassembled: "The light which we have gain'd, was giv'n us, not to be ever staring on, but by it to discover onward things more remote from our knowledge."[45] Most memorably, his ringing credo for the intellectual echoes down the centuries to protest every new tyranny: "Give me the liberty to know, to utter, and to argue freely according to conscience, above all liberties" (*CP* II: 560). In this tract Milton does not construct himself as a solitary prophet (his more usual stance) but as part of a community of authors, each working independently to recover lost truths and to test them by trial and contestation with one another. In 1644 Milton could find few contemporaries of whatever religious or political persuasion who shared his belief that such a clash of opinions would promote truth, and thereby hasten the utopian moment, "when not only our sev'nty Elders, but all the Lords people are become prophets":

> Behold now this vast City; a City of refuge, the mansion house of liberty . . . there be pens and heads there, sitting by their studious lamps, musing, searching, revolving new notions and idea's wherewith to present, as with their homage and their fealty the approaching Reformation: others as fast reading, trying all things, assenting to the force of reason and convincement. (*CP* II: 553–54)

The next year, 1645, Milton collected and published his *Poems*. That volume has been seen by some as a bid for respectability, in which Milton sought to distance himself from his recent polemics and to associate his book with contemporary Cavalier collections.[46] The prefatory matter invites such a reading, but that is chiefly the work of the bookseller Humphrey Moseley, who published most of the lyric collections of the 1640s – Fanshawe, Cartwright, Cowley, Davenant, Waller, Suckling, Vaughan, Crashaw – often in much the same format and with similar title-page assignment of the musical settings to Henry Lawes "of the Kings Chappell, and one of his Majesties Private Musick."[47] But since almost all of these volumes followed after Milton's, the fact that he published his poems with Moseley did not then place him in Cavalier company. Moseley's preface to Milton's poems points to the high "Commendations and Applause" accorded those poems by foreign and domestic academics, and invites the reader to compare them with "Mr. Wallers late choice Peeces" published a few months earlier. Yet Moseley's presentation of Milton is fraught with ambiguities. He allows that readers may prefer "more trivial Airs" than Milton's, whom he places in the tradition of "our famous Spencer."[48] He also commissioned William Marshall to provide an engraved portrait of Milton, and to Milton's evident dismay, published the notoriously distorted image as frontispiece: Richard Johnson notes that the visage is half that of a youthful poet, half of a crabbed controversialist.[49] Milton had his revenge by causing the unwitting Marshall to inscribe on the portrait a witty Greek epigram ridiculing his own – and by extension Moseley's – false representations of Milton.[50] More directly, by his title-page epigraph from Virgil's Eclogue VII Milton presents himself as predestined Bard (*vati . . . futuro*), explicitly refusing the construction laid upon him by Moseley's apparatus.[51]

Milton was responsible for the volume's contents, so we might wonder why he included commendations from now-declared royalists like Lawes and from Italian Catholic literati?[52] But why not? Poets do not usually see themselves tarred by the politics or religion of their commenders, and these introduce an as-yet-little-known poet to the world. The Ovidian love elegies and some funeral poems might also seem questionable – especially the elegy for Lancelot Andrewes, who was recently a target of Milton's anti-episcopal tracts. One explanation for their presence is that Milton is constructing here some record of his poetic growth, evident from his frequent if sometimes inaccurate notations of the age at which particular poems were written. As Thomas Corns notes, he leaves little out – not even the unfinished "Passion" which he describes as "above the years he had."[53] I have suggested above why Milton would not have thought the funeral poems for Felton, Andrewes, and Jane Paulet to be in any real conflict with his reformist agenda. The Ovidian love elegies he now presents as youthful folly – "These empty monuments to my idleness" – adding a recantation that stages his conversion from Ovid to Plato.[54]

By the organization of the volume Milton constructs himself as a reformist prophetic bard – *vates*, not Cavalier lyricist. A contemporary reader who made the comparison Moseley suggests would quickly see that Milton is no Waller. In his prefatory epistle Waller casts off poetry as a youthful toy, offering his *Poems* as "not onely all I have done, but all I ever mean to doe in this kind."[55] Milton offers his volume as an earnest of greater poems to come from the future bard. Waller's poems – all in English and haphazardly arranged – are mostly witty or elegant love songs, poems to or about patrons, and poems on royal personages or occasions. Milton's – in Italian, Latin, Greek, and Hebrew as well as English – emphasize his learning, his intellectual and poetic growth, and his self-construction as a reformist prophet-poet. His classical poems, chiefly *juvenalia*, are placed last: a book of Elegies ending with the recantation; and a book of *Sylvae* ending with a Latin dirge for Diodati that bids farewell to Italy, to Latin poetry, and to pastoral, and also reports a first attempt at epic. These classical books are preceded by *Comus*, again revised and expanded to underscore its critique of the court masque and court ethos. The (chiefly) English lyric "book" is placed first. Typical of the Cavaliers, Waller's lyric collection begins with several poems on King Charles, whereas Milton's begins with the Nativity Ode, a poem celebrating the birth of the Divine King and greeting the reader at the outset with Milton's dedication of himself as prophet-poet. His last English lyric, *Lycidas*, bears a new headnote pointing to the poem's prophecy, now fulfilled, of "the ruin of our corrupted Clergy, then in their height." Far from eliding his polemics Milton hereby formally links them to his poetry.

He continued that linkage. Soon after publication, Milton sent his volume of poems along with all his polemic tracts to date to John Rous, Librarian of the Bodleian, to preserve for the ages the work of both his right and left hands.[56] All this argues that Milton saw his 1645 *Poems*, not as a volume of would-be Cavalier poetry but as a worthy alternative – a volume of learned, delightful, reformist poems that would advance the project he began in several of his early poems and formally proposed in *The Reason of Church-Government*: to transform English culture through good art.

NOTES

1. George F. Sensabaugh, *That Grand Whig, Milton* (Stanford, 1952); and Christopher Hill, *Milton and the English Revolution* (London, 1977). For Milton's supposed elitism, confusion, or self-division, see, e.g., David Aers and Gunther Kress, "Historical Process, Individual and Communities in Milton's Early Prose," in Francis Barker, et al., eds., *1642: Literature and Power in the Seventeenth Century* (Colchester, 1981), pp. 283–300; and Andrew Milner, *John Milton and the English Revolution* (Totowa, NJ, 1981).
2. See, e.g., Louis L. Martz, "The Rising Poet, 1645," in Joseph Summers, ed., *The Lyric and Dramatic Milton* (New York, 1965) pp. 3–33; Annabel Patterson, "'Forc'd fingers': Milton's Early Poems and Ideological Constraint," in Claude J. Summers and Ted-Larry Pebworth, eds., *"The Muses Common-Weale": Poetry and Politics in the Seventeenth Century* (Columbia, 1988), pp. 9–22; Thomas N. Corns, "Milton's Quest for Respectability," *Modern Language Review* 77 (1982), 769–79.
3. See, e.g., Conrad Russell, ed., *The Origins of the English Civil War* (London and Basingstoke, 1973), and *The Causes of the English Civil War* (Oxford, 1990); John Morrill, *The Nature of the English Revolution* (London and New York, 1993); J. C. D. Clark, *Revolution and Rebellion: State and Society in England in the Seventeenth and Eighteenth Centuries* (Cambridge, 1981); and Mark Kishlansky, *Parliamentary Selection: Social and Political Choice in Early Modern England* (Cambridge, 1986).
4. See Derek Hirst, "'The Place of Principle," in "Revisionism Revised: Two Perspectives on Early Stuart Parliamentary History," *Past and Present* 92

68   BARBARA K. LEWALSKI

(August 1981), 55–99; William A. Hunt, *The Puritan Moment: The Coming of the Revolution in an English County* (Cambridge, MA, 1983); Thomas Cogswell, *The Blessed Revolution: English Politics and the Coming of War, 1621–1624* (Cambridge, 1989); and Richard Cust and Ann Hughes, eds., *Conflict in Early Stuart England: Studies in Religion and Politics 1603–1642* (London and New York, 1989).

5. See, e.g., Michael Wilding, *Dragon's Teeth: Literature in the English Revolution* (Oxford, 1987); David Norbrook, *Poetry and Politics in the English Renaissance* (London, 1984); Norbrook, "Lucan, Thomas May, and the Creation of a Republican Literary Culture," in Kevin Sharpe and Peter Lake, eds., *Culture and Politics in Early Stuart England* (London, 1994), pp. 45–66; Cedric C. Brown, *John Milton's Aristocratic Entertainments* (Cambridge, 1985); Sharon Achinstein, *Milton and the Revolutionary Reader* (Princeton, 1994); and David Armitage, Armand Himy, and Quentin Skinner, eds., *Milton and Republicanism* (Cambridge, 1995).

6. The story is reported by Milton's nephew Edward Phillips, and in more detail by John Aubrey. See Helen Darbishire, ed., *The Early Lives of Milton* (London, 1932), pp. 49–82, 1–15.

7. *"In ruinam camerae Papisticae,"* written in 1623, was later published in Gil's *Parerga, Sive Poetici Conatus, Alexandri* (London, 1632).

8. William Riley Parker, *Milton: A Biography*, 2 vols. (Oxford, 1968), vol. II, pp. 712–14.

9. All citations of Milton's poems are from *John Milton: Complete Poems and Major Prose*, ed. Merritt Y. Hughes (Indianapolis, 1981).

10. Darbishire, *Early Lives*, p. 10. Milton's Elegy I to Charles Diodati supplies some evidence for the rustication, with its references to a London "exile" and the threats of a "stern tutor" (lines 15–16). His new tutor was Nathaniel Tovey, a Ramist and Calvinist with ties to the Diodatis.

11. See especially Prolusions II and III, in *CP*1: 243, 245, 253.

12. The elections were hotly contested: the King backed Buckingham, who was at the time under indictment by the House of Commons, while the Commons and some younger Masters of Arts with Calvinist sympathies supported Thomas Howard, Earl of Berkshire. See James Bass Mullinger, *The University of Cambridge*, 3 vols. (Cambridge, 1873–1911), vol. I, pp. 157–59.

13. The two brothers are thought to be Christian of Brunswick and Ernest von Mansfield; the lost leaders include Maurice of Orange and several noble English volunteers killed in the fighting about Breda. Their loss threatened the collapse of Protestant military ventures in Europe.

14. Milton's letter to Gil is dated May 20, 1630 (*CP*1: 316–17). Gil's poem, *"In Silvam-Ducis,"* celebrates Protestant Henry of Nassau's capture of Hergogenbosch.

15. Pory's letter, dated April 21, 1631, is reprinted in R.F. Williams, ed., *Court and Times of Charles the First*, 2 vols. (London, 1848), vol. II, p. 106.

16. King wrote birthday poems in Latin for Princess Mary (1631), Prince James (1633), Princess Elizabeth (1635), and Princess Anne (1637); also congratulatory verses on the King's recovery from smallpox (1632), and on his safe return from Scotland (1633). See David Masson, *The Life of John Milton*, 7 vols. (London, 1877–96; rpt. Gloucester, MA, 1965), vol. I, pp. 648–49.

17. For Wither, see David Norbrook, "Levelling Poetry: George Wither and the English Revolution, 1642–1649," *English Literary Renaissance* 21 (1991), 217–56.

18. These poems have been dated as late as 1633–34 and as early as 1629, but the long vacation of 1631 seems most likely. In his Prolusion VII (1632) Milton refers to his "sweet intercourse with the Muses . . . amid rural scenes and woodland solitudes" the previous summer (*CP* I: 289).

19. See Patterson, "Forc'd fingers."

20. See Erica Veevers, *Images of Love and Religion: Queen Henrietta Maria and Court Entertainments* (Cambridge, 1989).

21. See Brown, *Aristocratic Entertainments*, pp. 7–26; and Barbara Breasted, "Milton and the Castlehaven Scandal," *Milton Studies* 3 (1971), 201–23.

22. See S. E. Sprott, ed., *John Milton: A Maske. The Earlier Versions* (Toronto, 1973). We cannot be certain whether the lines were added before the performance, or in the revision before publication.

23. William Prynne, *Histrio-mastix: or, The Players Scourge and Actors Tragedy* (London, 1633 [1632]).

24. Charles I, *The King's Majesty's declaration to his subjects concerning lawful sports to be used* (London, 1633). For the political issues see Leah Marcus, *The Politics of Mirth* (Chicago and London, 1986).

25. For the mutilation of Prynne's ears, see Masson, *Life*, vol. I, pp. 681–82; vol. II, p. 175.

26. He was also son-in-law to the Dowager Countess of Derby. See Marcus, *Politics of Mirth*, pp. 172–79; and Marcus, "The Milieu of Milton's *Comus*: Judicial Reform at Ludlow and the Problem of Sexual Assault," *Criticism* 25 (1983), 293–327.

27. See Maryann Cale McGuire, *Milton's Puritan Masque* (Athens, GA, 1983).

28. Brown, *Aristocratic Entertainments*, pp. 57–77.

29. Hayward's poem is printed among the English poems, "Obsequies to the Memory of Mr. Edward King," p. 17. This elegy was addressed to King's sister, Lady Margaret Lodor, associating her "reverent Church-like devotion" with his. Hayward was Chancellor of Lichfield Cathedral, and also author of one of the Latin poems. Four other elegies not included in the *Justa Edouardo King* also associate King with the Church or the university; they were edited by Norman Postlethwaite and Gordon Campbell and recently published in *Milton Quarterly* 28 (1994), 91–95.

30. Milton negotiates King's close family ties to the political and ecclesiastical establishment in Ireland by constructing him, Lawrence Lipking argues, as the "genius" of the Irish shore, inspiring those who will act to eradicate the still more dangerous popish "wolf" in that land. See Lawrence Lipking, "The Genius of the Shore: Lycidas, Adamastor, and the Poetics of Nationalism," *PMLA* III (1996), 1–221. King was son of John King, Privy Councilor for Ireland to Elizabeth, James, and Charles; his sister Margaret was wife of Gerard Lowther, Chief Justice of Ireland; the prelate Edward King, Bishop of Elphin, was his godfather.

31. Cedric C. Brown, "Milton and the Idolatrous Consort," *Criticism* 35 (1993), 419–39. Milton first wrote in the Trinity Manuscript "And nothing said," modified it in the manuscript and in the university volume to "And little said," (recognizing a tame royal proclamation on the matter in December, 1637), then reverted to "nothing" in 1645 – since nothing effective to stem the abuse had been said. The allusion takes in Catholic worship at Somerset House as well as the conversions among the Queen's ladies, most recently the Countess of Newport in October 1637.

32. Hill, *Milton and the English Revolution*, pp. 49–52.

33. Lines 24–30, 52–55. The poem has been dated as early as 1631–32, and as late as 1645, but many argue for 1637. For a review of the arguments, see *A Milton Encyclopedia*, ed. William B. Hunter, et al., 9 vols. (Lewisburg, 1978–83), vol. I, pp. 14–15.

34. March 29, 1639 (*CP* I: 333–36).

35. See Diana Trevino Benet, "The Escape from Rome: Milton's *Second Defense* and a Renaissance Genre," in Mario Di Cesare, ed., *Milton in Italy: Contexts, Images, Contradictions* (Birmingham, 1991), pp. 29–49.

36. Letter to Isaac Vossius (February 19, 1653), in J. Milton French, ed., *The Life Records of John Milton*, 5 vols. (New Brunswick, 1949–58), vol. III, p. 322.

37. *CP* I: 802–03. Cf. Isaiah 58:1 and Jeremiah 4:19ff. Milton also constructs himself as an English Jeremiah lamenting England's exiled Puritan children (*CP* I: 585).

38. *Of Reformation*, *CP* I: 616.

39. On such precedents see, e.g., Jason P. Rosenblatt, *Torah and Law in Paradise Lost* (Princeton, 1994), pp. 71–137; and James Grantham Turner, *One Flesh: Paradisal Marriage and Sexual Relations in the Age of Milton* (Oxford, 1987). Cf. "Introduction," *CP* II.

40. *CP* II: 224. Milton says that he made the anti-elitist decision to write in English rather than Latin because of "the esteem I have of my Countries judgement" (*CP* II: 233), though he came to regret that faith when he was so "lavishly traduc'd" (*CP* II: 436–37).

41. On August 9 the Commons ordered that Roger Williams's tract, *The Bloudy Tenant, of Persecution, for the Cause of Conscience Discussed* (London, 1644) be burned, and on August 13 Herbert Palmer's sermon to the two houses of Parliament raged against toleration and cited Milton's divorce tract as an audacious example of notorious wickedness that deserved burning (*The Glasse of Gods Providence* [London, 1644]). On August 24 the Stationers petitioned Parliament to enforce the laws against unlicensed blasphemous pamphlets, and two days later the Commons instructed its Committee on Printing to inquire out the authors, printers, and publishers of "the Pamphlets against the Immortality of the Soul [Richard Overton, *Mans Mortalitie* (Amsterdam, 1643)] and *Concerning Divorce*." On September 16 William Prynne denounced Roger Williams's "dangerous licentious work" defending liberty of conscience for all, a view which had promoted "the late dangerous increase of many Anabaptistical, Antinomian, Heretical, Atheistical opinions, as of *The Soul's Mortality, Divorce at Pleasure*, etc. . . . which I hope our Grand Council will speedily and carefully suppress" (*Twelve Considerable Serious Questions Touching Church Government* [London, 1644]).

42. *Doctrine and Discipline* (*CP* II: 246–53, 254, 258–60).
43. *Tetrachordon* (*CP* II: 589).
44. For critiques of Milton's restrictions see John Illo, "The Misreading of Milton," in Lee Baxandall, ed., *Radical Perspectives in the Arts* (Harmondsworth, 1972); and Abbe Blum, "The author's authority: *Areopagitica* and the Labour of Licensing," in Mary Nyquist and Margaret W. Ferguson, eds., *Re-membering Milton* (New York, 1988), pp. 74–96.
45. *CP* 2: 492, 549–50, 562–63.
46. See Louis L. Martz, *Poet of Exile: A Study of Milton's Poetry* (New Haven and London, 1980), pp. 31–59; Corns, "Milton's Quest for Respectability"; and Annabel Patterson, "Forc'd fingers."
47. The note on Milton's title page reads, "The Songs were set in Musick by Mr. Henry Lawes Gentleman of the Kings Chappel, and one of his Majesties Private Musick." Waller's reads, "All the Lyrick Poems in this Booke were sets by Mr. Henry lawes Gent. of the Kings Chappell, and one of his Majesties Private Musick."
48. He was right about reader preferences: Milton's volume took nearly fifteen years to sell out its first printing. See C. W. R. D. Moseley, *The Poetic Birth; Milton's Poems of 1645* (Aldershot, 1991).
49. Richard M. Johnson, "The Politics of Publication: Misrepresentation in Milton's 1645 *Poems*," *Criticism* 36 (1994), 45–71. Johnson argues that Moseley was complicit in creating this kind of portrait.
50. Moseley, *Poetic Birth*, p. 95, translates the epigram as follows: "When you look at the appearance of the original, you perhaps may say that this likeness was drawn by the hand of a novice. But, friends, since you do not recognize what is represented here, have a good laugh at this caricature by an artist who doesn't know his job."
51. The lines, "Baccare frontem / Cingite, ne vati noceat mala lingua futuro" (wreathe my brow with fragrant plants, lest an evil tongue harm your bard to be) are from Virgil's Eclogue VII, in which Thyrsis first introduces himself as "budding singer." See Moseley, *Poetic Birth*, p. 82.
52. The commendations preface the classical poems; they were offered to Milton during his Italian travels by Manso, Giovanni Salsilli, Carlo Dati, Antonio Francini, and one Selvaggi, as responses to some of his Latin poems here included.
53. Corns, "Milton's Quest for Respectability."
54. Lines 3–6: "harmful error led me wrong, and my unruly youth was an immoral teacher – until the shady Academy offered me the Socratic waters, and taught me to put off the yoke to which I had submitted," trans. C. Moseley, *Poetic Birth*, p. 231.
55. "To my Lady," in *Poems, &. Written by Mr. Ed. Waller* (London, 1645), sig. A2. Waller insists that poetry is the business of youth, not sober maturity: "These Nightingales sung only in the spring, it was the diversion of their youth . . . So that not so much to have made verses, as not to give over in time, leaves a man without excuse" (sig. A2v).

56. Stella Revard argues in "Ad Joannem Rousium: Elegiac Wit and Pindaric Mode," *Milton Studies* 19 (1984), 205–26, that in this ode Milton moves from self-construction as an elegiac poet to presenting himself as a Pindaric inspired poet divinely appointed to purge the land.

PART II

Heresy and consequences

CHAPTER 4

Milton's Arianism: why it matters

John P. Rumrich

In a preliminary report by the committee studying the provenance of *de doctrina Christiana*, Gordon Campbell stated that arguments based on the treatise's coherence with the accepted canon of Milton's works remind him of Fluellen's case for the resemblance between Henry V and Alexander the Great: "There is a river in Macedon, and there is also moreover a river at Monmouth ... and there is salmons in both."[1] Though Campbell assumed authorial responsibility, C. A. Patrides was the original wag. He quoted Fluellen a generation ago to deride Maurice Kelley's use of *de doctrina* as a theological guide to *Paradise Lost*.[2] Ironically, Patrides authored *Milton and the Christian Tradition*, a work that to characterize Milton's epic theology casts its nets into the boundless deep of more than fifteen centuries of Christian religious writing.[3] Kelley at least was fishing for trout in a peculiar river – one that he had, moreover, definitively charted.

Campbell's unacknowledged revival of Patrides's resile mockery indicates that the controversy over Milton's authorship of *de doctrina* springs in part from obscure sources. More than half a century ago, Kelley first argued systematically that the coherence of *Paradise Lost* and *de doctrina Christiana* is far-reaching, detailed, and, in their shared deviations from Christian orthodoxy, distinctive.[4] Perhaps Kelley's original description of the theology as a gloss on the poetry slights the integrity of distinct modes of discourse. But he did not overstate the broad intellectual coherence and large consistency of the poet-theologian who produced both. Others – Barbara Lewalski, William Kerrigan, and Stephen Fallon notable among them – have fortified Kelley's general claim through credible interpretation of Milton's poetry that rests substantially on reference to *de doctrina*. Such amplification by pertinent contextualization and discriminating comparison lies at the heart of philology and literary studies, including the assessment of provenance. Yet the committee's final report retains Campbell's skepticism "about argument arising from congruence or contradictions with works indisputably written by Milton" (section 10).

William Hunter, on the other hand, has repeatedly affirmed the vital part that "congruence or contradictions" plays in determining authorship: "The points of greatest interest ... are the heresies that *Paradise Lost* supposedly shares with the *Christian Doctrine*, a major part of both of Kelley's comparative studies of the two works."[5] Hunter candidly admits his stake in divorcing Milton from the treatise – so that we might see the poet as "closer to the great tradition of Christianity, no longer associated with a merely eccentric fringe."[6] His case against Milton's authorship rests largely on the claim that *Paradise Lost*, taken alone, seems orthodox, while *de doctrina* fairly bursts with heresies: "such heresies are not evident to the objective reader who limits himself to the poem and ignores the interpretations of it derived from ideas in the treatise."[7]

In support of this claim, Hunter repeats the familiar allegation, also more than half a century old, that prior to the discovery of *de doctrina* in 1825, readers found *Paradise Lost* "exemplary of Protestant dogma."[8] He acknowledges only two exceptions: Daniel Defoe's insistence that the epic offers an Arian representation of the Son and "another minor upheaval" caused by John Dennis's similar complaint in the early eighteenth century.[9] Michael Bauman has shown, however, that many more than two early readers thought the poem heretical, as John Toland indirectly testified in 1698: "As to the choice of his subject, or the particulars of his story, I shall say nothing in defence of them against those people who brand 'em with heresy and impiety." Similarly, in 1734, Jonathan Richardson, though defending the orthodoxy of Milton's epic, acknowledges "another Conjecture which some have made; I mean that Milton was an Arian." Antitrinitarianism seems indeed to have been early readers' common complaint. Charles Leslie in 1698 condemned Milton for making "the Angels ignorant of the blessed Trinity." The aforementioned John Dennis, commenting in 1704 on Book 3.383–95, claimed that "Milton was a little tainted with Socinianism, for by the first verse 'tis evident that he looked upon the Son of God as a created Being." When Bishop Charles Sumner published his translation of the treatise, he listed Newton, Trapp, Todd, Symmons, Warton, and Calton as previous readers who, without ever having seen *de doctrina*, regarded Milton's poetry as heretically Arian. Finally, Thomas Macaulay, commenting on Milton's Arianism just after the treatise was published, asserts that "we can scarcely conceive that any person could have read *Paradise Lost* without suspecting him of [it]."[10]

Far from supposing Milton's epic orthodox, early readers persistently suspected it of heresy, most often the "archetypal heresy" – Arianism –

which denies orthodox formulations of the trinity and in the late seventeenth century represented "the prime exemplar of heresy in general."[11] The focal power and overdetermined significance of this heresy, originally defined at the Council of Nicaea in 325, endures in Milton criticism of the present day. Not only in the essays questioning the provenance of *de doctrina*, but also in many earlier works over four decades, Hunter has doggedly contended that unlike the treatise, *Paradise Lost* presents an orthodox if subordinationist vision of the Son of God. Similarly, the committee's final report on the authorship controversy – despite its skepticism over "congruence or contradictions" – identifies a passage concerning the status of the Son of God as one of "a hard core of four points, all of them local, in which treatise and *Paradise Lost* are curiously and gratuitously at odds" (section 10). The local point it cites regarding the Son has also been raised previously in discussions of Milton's alleged Arianism – first by Patrides (1971) and then by committee member Campbell (1980). Michael Bauman answered their arguments (1987).[12] Yet the committee's report ignores previous controversy over this "local point."

In short, the evidence suggests that an unacknowledged critical history has predisposed current arguments, especially when the theological issue at stake is Milton's view of the Son of God. Hunter is moreover certainly correct to suggest that the reception history of *Paradise Lost* fairly cries out for explanation, though we must reverse his formulation: namely, how is it that so many early readers identified the epic as Arian, when most twentieth-century readers, despite the added evidence of *de doctrina*, have accepted the claim that *Paradise Lost* conforms to orthodoxy? The answer to this question is multiple and, as it concerns twentieth-century reception history, complicated by the quirky and competing agendas of Milton scholarship. The theological sensitivities of earlier readers, however, seem at this historical distance straightforward and relatively easy to explain.

Once a settlement of the ecclesiological battles of mid-century had been imposed, christology occupied the center stage of seventeenth-century English theological disputes. "Between 1687 and approximately 1700," notes John Marshall, "there was a major debate over the trinity in England which became known as the 'Unitarian Controversy.'"[13] The resurgence of antitrinitarianism featured an emphasis on the disciplined application of reason – purged of metaphysical complication – and preference for scriptural evidence over human authority. Milton's characterization of Arian and Socinian beliefs in *Of True Religion* (1673) is illustrative:

The Arian and Socinian are charg'd to dispute against the Trinity: They affirm to believe the Father, Son, and Holy Ghost, according to Scripture, and the Apostolic Creed; as for terms of Trinity, Triunity, Coessentiality, Tripersonality, and the like, they reject them as Scholastic Notions, not to be found in Scripture, which by a general Protestant Maxim is plain and perspicuous abundantly to explain its own meaning in the properest words, belonging to so high a Matter and so necessary to be known; a mystery indeed in their sophistic Subtilties, but in Scripture a plain Doctrin. (*CP* VIII: 424–25)

Milton here plainly states that Arians and Socinians reject orthodox trinitarian formulations as scholastic obscurities lacking scriptural warrant. The author of *de doctrina* rejects trinitarian orthodoxy on the same basis: "I shall state quite openly what seems to me much more clearly deducible from the text of scripture than the currently accepted doctrine" (*CP* VI: 201). The appeal for toleration of opinions based on scripture and the disciplined application of reason is a common theme in the mature Milton's writings.

Hunter also quotes the passage above, but contends that it endorses "the perspective of the Church of England," which in the late seventeenth century explicitly condemned antitrinitarian beliefs. To make the identification of Milton with this perspective seem plausible, Hunter recommends that we replace the final semi-colon with a period and indicate with a bracketed insertion – "[response]" – that the subsequent clause is Milton's judgment of the Arians and Socinians, rather than a description of the scholastic notions they forsook.[14] Extensive refutation of this modest editorial proposal is unnecessary, since the obvious contextual referent for "their sophistic Subtilties" is "Scholastic Notions." "Sophistic Subtilties" is, furthermore, diction that Milton typically reserves for criticism of scholasticism. Consider, for example, his condemnation of the "scholastick Sophistry" of "Canon iniquity" in *The Doctrine and Discipline of Divorce* – canon iniquity embraced by the Church of England, much to Milton's dismay (*CP* II: 351).

As with other antitrinitarians of the late seventeenth century, Milton's trust in human reason is deeply qualified in matters of religious knowledge; he, like Locke, insisted "on the impossibility of making significant deductions that take us beyond the expressions given in scriptural revelation."[15] Both of them firmly and consistently rejected what they regarded as excessive, speculative reasoning embodied in customary church doctrines like "the bizarre *troika* of Athanasius," as Hugh Trevor-Roper phrases it.[16] This methodological conviction confirmed for both Milton and Locke "long-standing anticlerical suspicions of clerical orthodoxy and ... support for toleration."[17] It has yet to be recognized how extensively Locke and other prominent late-century intellectuals recapitulate Milton's progression from anticlericalism and an Arminian tolerationist stance to serious consideration, if not endorsement, of antitrinitarian tenets. As the introduction to this volume suggests, Milton's paradigmatic religious development may be taken as a rough guide to the history of seventeenth-century theological controversy.

By the early eighteenth century so many had followed Milton's path that antitrinitarian deviations from orthodoxy "found widespread support in Britain."[18] Consciousness of antitrinitarian tendencies was unusually well developed, therefore, and the recorded responses of a reader with theological training – like Defoe, for example – ought to guide us as to what would register as unorthodox with a religiously informed reader of his time. As for later, relatively desensitized readers, it should not startle us that the Arianism of the epic has escaped notice. Though neither a whimsy put aside nor inept doctrine forsaken, the Arianism of the epic, as Balachandara Rajan has observed, is mixed in with the narrative fiction tactfully enough to avoid offending the orthodox, or, perhaps more to the point, to evade their ire.[19] The notorious Restoration Milton first published *Paradise Lost* in 1667, when the growing tendency toward toleration had suffered a shocking setback. Even when the tide of enforced conformity receded with the Toleration Act of 1689, antitrinitarians alone of Protestant sectaries suffered exclusion with the papists. At Glasgow in 1697 they hanged Thomas Aikenhead, aged eighteen, for denying the trinity.[20]

I use "Arian" rather than "antitrinitarian" to indicate Milton's beliefs concerning the Son of God. Part of England's theological vocabulary at least since the sixteenth century, "Arian" is the term Milton himself uses, almost exclusively, to describe antitrinitarian heresy (*CP* I: 533, 555, 557; VIII: 424). Though the term is vexed and has been polemically compromised for most of two millennia, "Arianism," as Maurice Wiles maintains, "has certainly existed as a powerful concept throughout Christian history."[21] As opposed to its cloudy origins in fourth-century church politics, the theological definition of Arianism is straightforward enough for summary in a few sentences. The foundation of the Arian position is the insistence that the essence of true Godhood is unique and unbegotten (*agenetos*). This unbegotten essence belongs only to the paternal God, not to the Son or to the Holy Spirit. As *de doctrina* insists, "really a God cannot be begotten at all," a blanket statment that covers figurative and literal meanings of begotten (*CP* VI: 211). From this perspective, even the standard Nicene formulation "begotten not made" registers the Son's real inferiority to the

Father. Arians deny the Son the essential divine attribute of unbegotten-
ness – or eternal existence – and also deny him related attributes such as
omnipotence, omniscience, and ubiquity. Inferior to the Father, the Son is
not "very" or "true" God, but instead, per the formulation in *de doctrina*, "a
God who is not self-existent, who did not beget but was begotten, is not
a first cause but an effect, and is therefore not a supreme God" (*CP* VI:
263–64).[22]

Long before launching the controversy over the treatise's provenance,
Professor Hunter argued that, unlike *de doctrina*, *Paradise Lost* offers an
orthodox, trinitarian depiction of God. In his view, the epic indicates that
Milton was not an Arian but instead a "subordinationist": "The poem
indeed has, as C. A. Patrides, J. H. Adamson, and I have shown, a subordi-
nationist underpinning: the Son is divine but subordinate to the Father as
Eve is human but subordinate to Adam."[23] Many have since followed
Hunter, Adamson, and Patrides in applying the term *subordinationist* to
Milton's epic presentation of the Son. The relevant entries from *A Milton
Encyclopedia* are revealing as to why:

On the basis of . . . highly competent theological analyses, what had earlier been
regarded by some as the Arian heresy is now generally recognized as a seventeenth-century expression of the "subordinationism" of early Fathers of the
Church up to the Council of Nicaea, a position that was held by many orthodox
writers.

Milton's view . . . has by some been identified with the Arian heresy, but this contention has been successfully questioned and corrected by meticulous and competent historical analysis.[24]

Part of the point seems to be that these theological affairs are complicated
enough to require extraordinary expertise and analytical powers, that
ordinary readers should submit to the authoritative judgment of the competent few. This attitude resembles that prevalent among civil and religious authorities concerned with heresy in the seventeenth century. It
also implies that readers like Defoe, Macaulay, David Masson, Rajan, and
Kelley, all of whom identified Milton as consistently Arian, are relatively
incompetent.

The excerpts quoted above do not exaggerate the general acceptance of
the term "subordinationism" among Milton scholars. Almost everyone
who has had occasion to discuss the Son's status uses it, though (or perhaps
because) no one seems to know what it signifies concerning Milton's relation to orthodoxy. Dennis Danielson, for example, warns that we should
not let Milton's subordinationism mislead us into underestimating "the

extent to which Milton is scriptural and orthodox in his presentation of the relationship between Father and Son."[25] Though the term was introduced in the defense of Milton's orthodoxy, Danielson clearly wishes to guard against the possibility that it implies unorthodoxy. The inclusiveness of "subordinationism" thus allows a convenient critical doublethink: (1) by using it, scholars acknowledge that Milton's representation of the Son differs significantly from customary representations of the Son; (2) by using it, scholars agree that Milton's version of the Son is nonetheless orthodox. For Milton scholarship "subordinationism" has in effect come to mean unorthodox orthodoxy.

If "subordinationism" already refers to orthodox doctrine, why should an exact scholar like Danielson need to qualify it as he does? I believe that its chief value to Milton criticism lies in its vagueness. Unlike the term "antitrinitarianism," which Kelley preferred, "subordinationism" does not explicitly deny the trinity. Instead, suggesting a grammatical model, it lumps together various ways in which the Son has been considered dependent on the main clause of paternal deity. Aside from the grammatological analogy it offers those disposed to parse the Godhead, "subordinationism" holds little descriptive value, bears no historical relevance to Milton's century (the *OED* records no usage of "subordinationism" before 1843), and indeed, outside of Milton studies is so obscure a piece of jargon that general encyclopedias (e.g., *Britannica, Americana*) ignore it, as do various specialized sources (e.g., *The Encyclopedia of Religion* edited by Mircea Eliade). *The New Catholic Encyclopedia* does include a short entry, but contrary to the definition of the term provided by Milton studies' theological experts, it begins, "the *heresy* . . . that admitted only the Father as truly God and taught the inferiority . . . of the Son" (italics mine). It never existed for condemnation as the name of a heresy until the nineteenth century, and even then only taxonomically, as a forbidden category. To say that something called subordinationism was "upheld by the early Christian writers to the Council of Nicaea," as Patrides would have it, is to perpetuate a grotesque anachronism.[26]

As Michael Bauman has argued, the depiction of the Son in *Paradise Lost* agrees with the doctrine presented in chapter 5 of *de doctrina*, which characterizes the Son as a limited, localized, mutable being, not eternal but derived in time from an eternal, substantially omnipresent Father.[27] During the course of the epic action, the Son increases in stature, authority, and power, all at the Father's pleasure – an augmentation of being that would not be possible or needed if he were unlimited, infinite, immutable, and eternal. The undeniable differences between the exposition of doctrine

and epic narration need not signal a difference in theology. The Arianism
of the epic is clear enough. As William Empson observed, "the poem
makes the Son and the Father about as unidentical as a terrier and a
camel." Empson even suggests that Milton discovered his Arianism as a
consequence of his epic composition, deciding "that what his imagination
had produced amounted to being an Arian."[28] Bauman presents the case
in compelling detail, addressing each relevant passage in the epic and con-
vincingly explicating its consistency with Arian belief. I do not have the
scope here to reiterate his arguments, but because they have been ignored
by Hunter and by most other Milton scholars, a sample seems warranted.

In a section entitled "Milton's Arian Angels," Bauman cites the
following hymn of praise:

> Thee next they sang of all creation first,
> Begotten Son, divine similitude,
> In whose conspicuous countenance, without cloud
> Made visible, the almighty Father shines.[29]

Bauman observes that the angels here, as always, address the Son after
praising the Father, "the only one who, in Milton's theology, is 'omnip-
otent, / Immutable, immortal, infinite' and 'eternal' " (3.372–4). The Son
is never addressed as possessing such traits, though on occasion he is
afforded access to them according to his Father's will.

In line 383, the phrase "of all creation first" alludes to Colossians 1:15;
Bauman cites the explication of this passage in *de doctrina*:

The first born of all created things . . . Here both the Greek accent and the verbal passive
protótomos show that the Son of God was *the first born of all created things* in the same
sense as the Son of man was the *protótomos* or *first born* of Mary, Matt. i. 25 . . . That
can only mean that he was the first of the things which God created. How, then,
can he be God himself? (*CP* VI: 302–03)

Bauman considers other Arian passages in the epic without adducing such
substantiating evidence from the treatise. This example is useful, however,
because it indicates how closely the poetry and theology correspond to
each other.

To describe Milton as an "orthodox subordinationist" is hardly more pre-
cise than simply to describe him as orthodox. Orthodox believers are all
subordinationist in that they posit an inequality of function, office, or sub-
sistence among the persons of the trinity. In the Nicene creed, the Father
begets the Son; the Son does not beget the Father. The Son sits at the right
hand of the Father, not the other way round, and so on. The theological
basis for Hunter's claim that Milton was an orthodox subordinationist is

that for Milton the Son derives from God's own substance ("one substance [*homoousia*] with the father," according to one translation of Nicene orthodoxy). For the monist materialist Milton, however, *all* creatures derive from God's own substance. By this criterion, to borrow the words of John Fry, an Arian supporter of Parliament present for Charles's trial, "I might be said to be God too, as well as Jesus Christ, and the like might be affirmed of all other creatures whatsoever."[30] Milton's cosmos begins with "one first matter all" and ends when "God shall be All in All" (*Paradise Lost* 5.472; 3.341). The Son's material being may originally be more refined and exalted than that of other creatures, but eventually parakeets and pachyderms would also qualify as participants in the Godhead.[31]

The import of Milton's monistic ontology should figure into any comparison with the strongly dualistic subordinationism of the Gnostics, who are cited by Hunter as historical precedent. Divinity of constituent substance is for Milton a universal condition of being, not a privilege in itself sufficient to warrant divine status. Another famous seventeenth-century Arian, Isaac Newton, criticized those Gnostics who thought it proper to worship Christ simply because he emanated from the substance of "the supreme God": "he that is of this opinion may believe Christ to be of one substance with the father without making him more then a meer man. Tis not cosubstantiality but power and dominion which gives a right to be worshipped."[32] The author of *de doctrina Christiana* is, like Newton, unmistakably explicit on the subject: "[God is] in a real sense Father of the Son, whom he made of his own substance. It does not follow, however, that the Son is of the same essence as the Father" (*CP* VI: 209). The treatise repeatedly insists that "the attributes of divinity belong to the Father alone," particularly the attribute of "supreme domination both in heaven and earth: the highest authority and highest power of making decisions according to his own absolutely free will" (*CP* VI: 227). God's eternal essence and thus his absolute causal priority qualify him alone as truly, unconditionally, divine.

When Hunter still acknowledged Milton's authorship of *de doctrina*, he elaborated his claim for Milton's orthodoxy by arguing that in the poet-theologian's opinion the Son is really eternal and absolute because, as the *Logos*, he has always existed in the mind of God. Hunter called this the "two-stage logos theory" and traced it, too, to Neoplatonic and Gnostic speculation within the early church.[33] Newton's meticulous knowledge of early church theological controversy is generally acknowledged to meet the highest standard of competence so that we can feel confident in turning to his writings for historical background: "The Gnosticks after the manner of

the Platonists and Cabbalists considered the thoughts or Ideas or intellectual objects seated in Gods mind as real Beings or substances." Newton
disparages this notion as crude and heathen, and as G. L. Prestige – an
authority often cited by Hunter – asserts, Christians "early opposed and
soon repudiated" the two-stage logos theory.[34] Ignoring Prestige on this
point, Hunter insists that the two-stage logos theory "entirely escaped condemnation by the early church."[35] True, as a theory it was too insignificant
to be condemned specifically at Nicaea. Yet it certainly falls under the
Nicene anathemas. For one thing, the transition between two states of
being entailed by the theory violates the Nicene insistence on the
immutability of the Son.

As Bauman observes, not only is the two-stage logos theory not orthodox; Milton never endorsed it.[36] Milton has no more patience than
Newton with the ontological premises of such a theory, insisting in the *Art
of Logic* that a thing that exists only in the mind of a subject does not in reality exist at all (*CP* VIII: 236). If, on the contrary, Milton had agreed that
divine consciousness of a phenomenon constitutes its existence, what
would become of the distinction he so carefully draws between foreknowledge and free will? Furthermore, supposing that Hunter were correct in
ascribing such arcane Gnostic notions to Milton, the idea of all creation –
indeed, of all possible creations – would also have eternally existed in the
mind of an omniscient God. Again the Son would enjoy no special ontological distinction from the rest of creation.

I have been appealing to the work of Isaac Newton because it contains
such detailed knowledge of the early church and because his arguments
are close to those presented in *de doctrina*. He is also, like Locke, a prime
example of the wave of antitrinitarian heresy that swept over late-seven-
teenth and early eighteenth-century England. For Newton as for the
author of *de doctrina*, trinitarianism confused causes and as a species of
polytheism, was an instance of the gravest sin, idolatry.[37] Both insisted on
the Arian position primarily because each viewed God as indivisibly one.
As the author of *de doctrina* wryly observes, "it would have been a waste of
time for God to thunder forth so repeatedly that first commandment
which said that he was the one and only God, if it could nevertheless be
maintained that another God existed as well" (*CP* VI: 212). (Carey's translation is fairly exact here, and the diction – e.g., *intonoare*, thunder forth –
strikes my ear as authentically Miltonic.) The Son, on the other hand,
according to Newton's theology, "had assumed and would assume many
shapes and forms ... a messenger, an agent, a vice-ruler under God, a
judge," and as "the one Mediator between God and Man."[38] Similarly,

de doctrina suggests that scripture calls the Son *only begotten* chiefly because he is the only mediator between God and man (*CP* VI: 210–11): "However the Son was begotten, it did not arise from natural necessity, as is usually maintained, but was just as much a result of the Father's decree and will as the Son's priesthood, kingship, and resurrection from the dead (*CP* VI: 208). It so happens that, as Milton, Newton, and most of their contemporary Arians agree, the Father chooses to do everything in creation through the Son.

Hence, in *Paradise Lost*, once the Father has determined to show humanity mercy, the Son volunteers to act as redeemer and rescue humankind from death and the Father enables him to do so: "all Power / I give thee" (3.317–18; see also 203–302). Similarly, the Father assigns him the task and provides the means of defeating the rebel angels: "Two days are therefore past, the third is thine; / For thee I have ordain'd it ... / ... Into thee such Virtue and Grace / Immense I have transfus'd" (6.699–704). Creation, too, occurs at the Father's pleasure, through the Son: "thou my Word, begotten Son, by thee / This I perform" (7.163–64). The angels sum up the unequal, complementary relationship between Father and Son quite explicitly:

> Hee Heav'n of Heavens and all the Powers therein
> By thee created, and by thee threw down
> Th' aspiring Dominations: thou that day
> Thy Father's dreadful Thunder didst not spare,
>
>   . . .
>
>   Son of thy Father's might,
> To execute fierce vengeance on his foes:
> Not so on Man; him though their malice fall'n,
> Father of Mercy and Grace, thou didst not doom
> So strictly, but much more to pity inclin'd,
> No sooner did thy dear and only Son
> Perceive thee purpos'd not to doom frail Man
> So strictly, but much more to pity inclin'd
> Hee to appease thy wrath ...
>
>   . . .
>
>   offer'd himself to die
> For man's offense.   (3.390–410)

Such power, knowledge, and position as the Son enjoys derive from the Father and are contingent on the Son's voluntary and therefore meritorious obedience. The Son's designation as judge of fallen humanity follows the same pattern: "Vicegerent Son, to thee I have transferr'd / All Judgment"; to which the Son replies, "Father Eternal, thine is to decree, /

Mine both in Heav'n and Earth to do thy will" (10.56–57, 68–69). Finally, when the Son acts as priest and intercessor on humanity's behalf, the Father observes that even here his own will preceded the Son's apparent agency: "all thy request was my Decree" (11.47).

In every guise, the contingent Son as represented in *Paradise Lost* acts to fulfill the will of the one absolute being. This exemplary obedience entitles him to divine honors and worship, but not to the status of true divinity. The demotion of the Son to finite if still divine status reflects again the insistently theodical point of Milton's theology. In *Paradise Lost*, the Son's freely made decisions to obey the Father's will function as a striking counter-example to the decisions of Satan and Adam, his angelic adversary and human predecessor, respectively. Through *voluntary* obedience both God's ways and the human race are justified.

Some might object that, regardless of Milton's own usage, the label "Arian," deriving from a fourth-century controversy, is as inappropriate to the seventeenth century as the nineteenth-century label "subordinationist." In the late seventeenth century, Arianism undoubtedly reflects a historically specific inclination on the part of individual believers to apply their own reason and logic to religious doctrine, and an associated tendency to scrutinize rigorously doctrinal and scriptural history. It also manifests the growing conviction among secular, educated men that the individual conscience alone must dictate in matters of faith. This distinctly early modern profile, retrospective though it may be, certainly fits figures like Newton, Locke, and the surprisingly large number of their intellectually eminent circle who held Arian opinions. Arguably, it is a profile that fits Milton as well. It does not of course fit fourth-century Arians, and in that respect the label "Arian" seems misleading.

Yet we should also consider another side to the intellectual–historical picture. Although for many scholars, seventeenth-century debates over the unity of God seem like irrelevant distractions from more pressing sociopolitical questions, such debates were not without much broader cultural ramifications. Nor was the theological position signified then and now by the term Arianism treated as a curious relic of fourth-century Christianity. Many different opinions of what was essential in Christian belief existed during Milton's time, but most included the trinity. Those in power in church and state, whether in London, Rome, or Geneva, were even in an intolerant age remarkably unyielding on the subject. In England, at least eight antitrinitarian heretics were burned at the stake from 1548 to 1612. One of the last was Bartholomew Legate. In a characteristic moment of personal involvement, the scholarly King James tried himself to convince the heretic of his error, but after listening to Legate, broke into "choler, spurn[ing] at him with his foot" and commanding him out of his presence.[39] That Legate was one of the last Arians burnt to death in England does not seem to have owed to a softening of official attitudes. As Thomas Fuller remarks, after Legate went up in flames, the King "politicly preferred that Heretics hereafter ... should silently and privately waste themselves away in Prison rather than to grace them and amuze others with the solemnity of a public Execution."[40] Perhaps the impulse toward demystification expressed in Arianism was dimly perceived as a threat to the ideological basis of monarchical power. If awe for the mystery of Christ's essential but unapparent divinity was lacking, what would become of the awe for kings as Christ's representatives, or indeed of any of the similarly unapparent ontological distinctions supposed to separate noble from common in a hierarchical society? Whatever it was that drove an outraged James to kick at Legate, the profession of Arian opinions provoked authorities across seventeenth-century Europe as no other heresy could.

Agents of the Enlightenment like Newton formed their consciously Arian opinions deliberately and knowledgeably in the vocabulary of fourth-century church history, a century for various reasons considered highly relevant by many educated and forward-looking men in seventeenth-century England, early and late. Newton corresponded with Locke about the trinity and at Locke's behest nearly allowed his arguments concerning the lack of scriptural evidence for the trinity to be published. Richard Westfall observes that a fairly wide circle of Arians was "connected with Newton"; Frank Manuel lists Edmund Halley, David Gregory, Fatio de Duillier, Hopton Haynes, and Samuel Clarke.[41] Newton's successor at Cambridge, William Whiston, was ejected from his chair when his Arian opinions became known.[42] Professional ruin is a far cry from incineration, yet there seems to have been sufficient reason even in the eighteenth century for an Arian to suppress his heretical belief. Though an Arian of deepest conviction, Newton, like Milton, "received a Church of England burial," which in Milton's case Hunter takes to mean, "that he had not voiced to anyone ... [his] heretical ideas."[43] Such public silence does not indicate that Milton was orthodox on the trinity, however, any more than Newton's public silence signals his orthodoxy. Unless he were seeking imprisonment or a martyr's death, certainly Milton, like Newton after him, would have kept his Arianism hidden from the authorities.

The nature of Newton's heretical beliefs was suppressed after his death, and his voluminous, unpublished, religious writings were, as Manuel again puts it, "bowdlerized, neglected, or sequestered."[44] It is a history that should not seem altogether strange to Milton scholars. By the early 1670s, Newton's massive and what would be sustained efforts in biblical and historical analysis centered on early church history, and especially on the trinitarian controversies of the fourth century. He repeatedly and variously builds the case for Arius while construing Athanasius as a vile politician symbolic of humanity's evil inclination to substitute man-made intricacy and superstition for the unity and singularity of divine truth. Newton convinced himself that "a universal corruption of Christianity had followed the central corruption of doctrine," according to Westfall, a corruption especially evident in church government, where the former polity was replaced by "concentration of ecclesiastical power in the hands of the hierarchy."[45] Like Milton, Newton refused to take orders in such a church – "accept ordination he could not" – though he became a fellow, ironically, of Trinity College.

For the author of *de doctrina*, too, Christianity had been "defiled with impurities for more than thirteen hundred years" – that is, since the time of Constantine and the institutionalization of Christianity as the state religion (*CP* VI: 117). Milton and Newton's opinions reflect the profound influence of the revisionist millenarian calculations of Joseph Mead, a tutor at Christ's College during Milton's time there. Presbyterians and Independents agreed that some apocalyptic history had passed, though more was to come. But while Presbyterians typically sought to institute an order defined by historical and legal precedent, Independents tended to see the imminent future as precipitating an ideal order, one that would transcend previous laws and institutions. Representative of Presbyterian belief on the subject, Richard Baxter supposed that the paradigm for the millennium had already occurred, under Constantine, and that Christians should work toward a return to the ideal represented by the Holy Roman Empire. Hence, amidst the many vacillations in Baxter's writings, one consistent theme, as William Lamont has shown, is his yearning for the reign of a godly prince, one who would use civil authority to promote the interests and discipline of true religion – under the guidance of divines like Baxter.[46] This ideal, and an associated adherence to preexisting forms of scriptural and national law, was the basis for Presbyterian allegiance to the monarchy and outrage at the regicide. Preferring Mead's interpretation of apocalyptic scripture, Independents like Milton looked back not to the first thousand years of the Holy Roman Empire, but forward to an unprecedented millennium when the true King, Christ, would return and rule.[47] The expectation of a new and just order – Augustine's invisible city of God made visible on Earth in real time – had the effect of rendering the institution of monarchy, as well as ecclesiastical policies and even civil law, less sacred and more open to question.

For Milton as for Newton, in line with Mead's chronology, the papal Antichrist originated in the fourth century, not the fourteenth, and was a product of the union of civil and ecclesiastical powers. Hence, as Newton would, Milton disapproved of the institution of Christianity as a state church and of the hierarchical exaltation of its clergy. Milton berated Constantine for promoting prelates to luxurious lives and giving them authority over matters better left to individual believers.[48] This early malediction of Constantine (1641) indicates that Milton's skeptical attitude toward supposedly sacred rulers and clerical authority preceded and perhaps prepared the way for his Arian convictions (*CP* I: 554–59; see also I: 420). The definition of Arianism at the Council of Nicaea indeed represented a crucial, politically charged moment in the establishment of a set doctrine for a unified state church.[49] Milton's aversion to such an alliance of civil authority and religious concerns, furthermore, is of a piece not only with his Arianism but also with the millenarian, tolerationist, historical perspective evinced by the opening argument of *Areopagitica*. For it was under the "Roman *Antichrist* . . . bred up by *Constantine*" that religious persecution, and with it pre-publication censorship, waxed strongest (*CP* I: 559).

Early readers recognized Arianism in *Paradise Lost* and, once *de doctrina Christiana* was discovered and published, various Milton scholars, Maurice Kelley most notably, recognized the consistency of its heretical theology with Milton's poetic fiction. Arianism is implicit, not effaced, in Milton's epic and consistent with his political ideology and view of apocalyptic history. An exemplary heresy in the seventeenth century, its adherents manifest an intellectual posture adopted by some of the best minds of the time, one for which they contended, sincerely if discreetly, in terms of fourth-century church history. The Arianism of *de doctrina Christiana* presents no obstacle to the assignment of the treatise to its author, John Milton. Is Milton scholarship so committed to the orthodoxy of *Paradise Lost* that it will continue in its refusal to acknowledge Milton's Arianism, even if it means denying the evident provenance of his theology?

NOTES

1. William Shakespeare, *King Henry V*, ed. Andrew Gurr (Cambridge, 1992), 4.7.20–25. The occasion for the report was the 1995 International Milton Symposium in Bangor, Wales.

2. C. A. Patrides, "Milton and the Arian Controversy," *Proceedings of the American Philosophical Society* 120 (1976), 245–52.

3. For more extensive criticism of Patrides's argument and method, see my *Milton Unbound: Controversy and Reinterpretation* (Cambridge, 1996), pp. 29–34.

4. Maurice Kelley, *This Great Argument* (Princeton, 1941).

5. William B. Hunter, "The Provenance of the *Christian Doctrine*," *SEL* 32 (1992), 132.

6. Hunter, "Forum: Milton's *Christian Doctrine*," *SEL* 32 (1992), 166.

7. Hunter, "Provenance," 132.

8. *Ibid.* C. S. Lewis was the first to insist that Milton's epic "was accepted as orthodox by many generations of acute readers well grounded in theology." See *A Preface to Paradise Lost* (Oxford, 1942), p. 82.

9. Hunter, "Provenance," 132.

10. I list evidence drawn from Michael E. Bauman, "Heresy in Paradise and the Ghost of Readers Past," *College Language Association Journal* 30 (1986), 59–68. He relies primarily on John T. Shawcross, ed., *Milton: The Critical Heritage* (New York, 1970), and records only those instances that "may easily be discovered by any interested student of Milton" (p. 66). For a fuller discussion of early readers' reactions to the heretical potential of Milton's epic, see Joseph Wittreich's essay, chapter 12 of this volume.

11. Maurice Wiles, *Archetypal Heresy* (Oxford, 1996), p. 63.

12. William B. Hunter, C. A. Patrides, J. H. Adamson, *Bright Essence* (Salt Lake City, 1971), p. 10; Gordon Campbell, "The Son of God in *de doctrina Christiana* and *Paradise Lost*," *Modern Language Review* 75 (1980), 507–14; Michael E. Bauman, *Milton's Arianism* (Frankfurt, 1987), pp. 238–42.

13. John Marshall, *John Locke: Resistance, Religion, and Responsibility* (Cambridge, 1994), p. 389.

14. William B. Hunter, "The Provenance of the *Christian Doctrine*: Addenda from the Bishop of Salisbury," *SEL* 33 (1993), 195.

15. Wiles, *Archetypal Heresy*, p. 70.

16. Hugh Trevor-Roper, "Toleration and Religion after 1688," in Ole Peter Grell, Jonathan I. Israel, and Nicholas Tyacke, eds., *From Persecution to Toleration* (Oxford, 1991), p. 402.

17. Marshall, *Locke*, p. 329.

18. Wiles, *Archetypal Heresy*, p. 4.

19. Balachandara Rajan, *Milton and the Seventeenth Century Reader* (1947, 1962; rpt. London, 1966), pp. 23–31. It was C. S. Lewis, *A Preface to Paradise Lost*, p. 91, who described Milton's theology as whimsical, and Patrides, n. 3 above, who thought it inept.

20. Jonathan I. Israel, "William III and Toleration," *From Persecution to Toleration*, p. 153. See also Trevor-Roper, "Toleration and Religion," pp. 391, 400–2.

21. Wiles, *Archetypal Heresy*, p. 4.

22. My analysis follows Bauman, *Milton's Arianism*. See also Wiles, *Archetypal Heresy*, pp. 5–17.

23. Hunter, "Provenance," 132–33. This chapter's discussion of subordinationism repeats arguments from *Milton Unbound*, pp. 41–47.

24. *A Milton Encyclopedia*, ed. William B. Hunter, et al., 9 vols. (Lewisburg, PA, 1978–83), vol. VIII, pp. 14, 90.
25. Dennis Danielson, *Milton's Good God* (Cambridge, 1982), p. 54.
26. C. A. Patrides, *Milton and the Christian Tradition* (Oxford, 1966), p. 16.
27. Bauman, *Milton's Arianism*, pp. 203–318.
28. William Empson, *Milton's God*, rev. edn. (London, 1965), p. 278. My thanks to Stephen Dobranski, who brought this reference to my attention.
29. *Paradise Lost* 3.383–86. All citations of Milton's poetry are taken from *The Poetical Works of John Milton*, ed. Helen Darbishire, 2 vols. (Oxford, 1952).
30. John Fry is quoted by H. J. McLachlan, *Socinianism in Seventeenth-Century England* (Oxford, 1951), p. 241.
31. Against Hunter, Barbara K. Lewalski observes that though for Milton the Son shares in divine substance, this does not fundamentally distinguish him from the rest of creation. See *Milton's Brief Epic* (London, 1966), pp. 138–46.
32. Frank E. Manuel, *The Religion of Isaac Newton* (Oxford, 1974), p. 60, cites this passage from the *Yahuda Manuscript*, 15.5, fol. 98ᵛ.
33. See Hunter's "Milton's Arianism Reconsidered," in *Bright Essence*, pp. 38–41. Hunter's claims are critiqued by Bauman, *Milton's Arianism*, pp. 126–32.
34. Newton, *Yahuda Manuscript*, 15.7, fol. 108ᵛ; cited by Manuel, *Religion of Isaac Newton*, p. 69. G. L. Prestige, *God in Patristic Thought* (London, 1952), p. 128.
35. Hunter, "Milton's Arianism Reconsidered," p. 43.
36. Bauman, *Milton's Arianism*, p. 133.
37. Manuel, *Religion of Isaac Newton*, pp. 42–43.
38. *Ibid.*, p. 60.
39. Thomas Fuller, *The Church History of Britain*, vol. X, section iv, as cited by McLachlan, *Socinianism*, p. 33.
40. *Ibid.* See also McLachlan, *The Religious Opinions of Milton, Locke and Newton* (Manchester, 1941), pp. 103–04.
41. Richard S. Westfall, *Never at Rest* (Cambridge, 1980), p. 650; Manuel, *Religion of Isaac Newton*, p. 7.
42. Westfall, *Never at Rest*, p. 332.
43. Hunter, "Provenance," 132.
44. Manuel, *Religion of Isaac Newton*, p. 10.
45. Westfall, *Never at Rest*, p. 315.
46. William Lamont, *Richard Baxter and the Millennium* (London, 1979), p. 13, observes that Baxter's position hearkens back to that of John Foxe, *Acts and Monuments*, 8 vols. (rpt., New York, 1965), who portrayed Elizabeth as following Constantine's example (vol. I, pp. xvi–xxiv, 4–5, 248–50, 285).
47. Robert Baillie, in *A Dissuasive from the Errors of the Time* (London, 1645), expressed the common Presbyterian opinion that the notion of a literal reign of Christ was a heretical misreading of mystical and allegorical apocalyptic scriptures (pp. 80–85, 224–27). For the opposed, Independent position, see, for example, the sermon *A Glimpse of Sion's Glory* (published in London, 1641) usually attributed to Thomas Goodwin, in *The Works of Thomas Goodwin*, ed. Thomas Smith, 12 vols. (Edinburgh, 1861–66), vol. XII, p. 66. Hugh Peters preached on the same,

implicitly anti-monarchical theme before Parliament in April of 1645, *Gods Doings and Mans Duty* (London, 1646), pp. 9–25. John Cooke, Charles's prosecutor in 1649, wrote to similar effect and explicitly counter to the Presbyterian position in *Reintegration Amoris* (London, 1647), pp. 80–84. Or refer to various works of John Goodwin, including *Theomachia* (London, 1644), p. 48, *Innocency and Truth* (London, 1646), p. 10, and, with particular relevance to the Independents' disagreement with the Presbyterians, *The Obstructours of Justice* (London, 1649), p. 85.

48. Ironically, in the same passage, Milton, who in 1641 was certainly an orthodox trinitarian, also berates Constantine for Arian inclinations.

49. Wiles, *Archetypal Heresy*, pp. 1–6.

CHAPTER 5

"Elect above the rest": theology as self-representation in Milton

Stephen M. Fallon

In May of 1619, the Synod of Dort, defending orthodox Calvinist teaching on predestination and election, warned against "curiously scrutinizing the deep and mysterious things of God."[1] That same year, perhaps the same month or day, the ten-year-old John Milton sat for a portrait, his closely-cropped hair a visible sign, his widow would tell John Aubrey years later, of the influence of his Puritan teacher, perhaps the Calvinist Thomas Young.[2] Whatever the principles instilled by Young, Milton would become the kind of curious scrutinizer rebuked by the Synod, and he would come to echo the Arminian or Remonstrant doctrines of universal and sufficient grace that the Synod condemned. Impatient with mystery,[3] he would not balk at skeptically probing divine justice; instead he would reject the Calvinist claim that divine justice is inscrutable and unquestionable.[4] God's actions are subject to rational scrutiny and approval, because they conform to accessible standards of reason. Freed from its equivocating context, Milton would subscribe to the aphorism he authors upon Satan, "Not just, not God."[5] Though Calvinists denounced as sinfully presumptuous attempts to subject God's justice to rational evaluation, Milton was confident that, aided by the Spirit, he could draw out this leviathan with the hook of his reason.

Readers from his time to ours have agreed that Milton attempts to recast the biblical story on rational lines; on his success, though, at least in *Paradise Lost*, the jury is still out. Andrew Marvell recognized the implications of Milton's great argument, worried that Milton would "ruin ... / The sacred Truths," but concluded by endorsing his friend and colleague's claim of prophetic status.[6] Alexander Pope, whose concern is more exclusively literary than Marvell's, famously reproaches Milton for having his epic God argue like a "school divine."[7] More recently, the success of Milton's rational exploration of divine justice in *Paradise Lost* has been claimed explicitly by Dennis Burden and implicitly by Dennis Danielson.[8] But even that most ardent of admirers of Milton's rationalist redaction of scriptural myth, Philip Gallagher, wonders uneasily if Milton's lust for order has flattened some salutary mysteries in the Bible.[9]

Given Milton's eagerness to rationalize the myth and the doctrines of fall and salvation, it is all the more surprising that there remains in *Paradise Lost* one crucial passage that resists this rationalizing urge. When the Father describes the economy of salvation in Book 3, an apparent residue of Calvinist teaching on election disturbs the otherwise Arminian and libertarian doctrine of the mature Milton, resulting in a tension between claims for different and incompatible forms of distinction. In this chapter I will reverse a common strategy and use *Paradise Lost* as a gloss upon *de doctrina Christiana*.[10] The unresolved tension in the Father's speech helps bring to light similar tension in *de doctrina Christiana*. Not surprisingly, given the demands of the genre, the conflicting forces left unresolved in *Paradise Lost* are resolved in the treatise. But the mere presence of the conflicting forces in the treatise betrays the degree to which the *de doctrina Christiana*, despite the appearance of impersonality required by its genre, shares with Milton's other works a project of self-justification. Through epic and treatise run fault lines in Milton's self-conception and self-representation.

In this chapter I employ the terms "Calvinist" and "Arminian" to label opposed beliefs on soteriology in general and predestination in particular: the Calvinist asserts the unconditional predestination of elect individuals, who receive irresistible grace, and reprobate individuals, to whom this grace is denied; the Arminian asserts conditional predestination to election and reprobation, contingent upon an individual's choice to accept or reject universal and resistible grace.[11] That is to say, I am not using the term "Arminian" as defined by Nicholas Tyacke in his *Anti-Calvinists*, according to which Milton must be counted in some ways not merely not Arminian but positively anti-Arminian.[12] Unlike Tyacke's "English Arminians," for example, Milton denied that sacraments conferred grace (to say nothing of his opposition to the High Church "Arminian" politics and ceremonialism of William Laud). It should be noted, however, that this and other "English Arminian" positions are not found in Arminius himself.[13] Arminius and Milton, working in and from a Calvinist context, share much with Calvin, but both reject Calvin's understanding of predestination. Milton's Arminianism is continental; analogues for his thought can be found in Arminius himself, in Simon Episcopius, and in Stephanus Curcellæus. Given the lively debate sparked by Tyacke's book, I might have dropped the term "Arminian" for this essay, but the alternatives – "anti-predestinarian," "opposed to Calvin on predestination," "libertarian" –

are cumbersome or ambiguous or both. Moreover, in using the label "Arminian" to designate Milton's acceptance of Arminius' anti-Calvinist doctrines of conditional election, unlimited atonement, and resistible grace, I am following the lead not only of Maurice Kelley, Don M. Wolfe, and Arthur Barker, but also of seventeenth-century polemical writers, including Milton himself, who uses the term in this way in the 1644 *Doctrine and Discipline of Divorce* (*CP* II: 293).[14]

In Book 3, Pope's "school divine" reads a lecture on the economy of salvation:

> Some I have chosen of peculiar grace
> Elect above the rest; so is my will:
> The rest shall hear me call, and oft be warn'd
> Thir sinful state, and to appease betimes
> Th' incensed Deity, while offer'd grace
> Invites; for I will clear thir senses dark,
> What may suffice, and soft'n stony hearts
> To pray, repent, and bring obedience due.
> To Prayer, repentance, and obedience due,
> Though but endeavor'd with sincere intent,
> Mine ear shall not be slow, mine eye not shut.
> And I will place within them as a guide
> My Umpire *Conscience*, whom if they will hear,
> Light after light well us'd they shall attain,
> And to the end persisting, safe arrive.
> This my long sufferance and my day of grace
> They who neglect and scorn, shall never taste;
> But hard be hard'n'd, blind be blinded more,
> That they may stumble on, and deeper fall.
> *(Paradise Lost* 3.183–201)

The division of souls here is trifold: those elect by special grace, those who with the aid of general grace accept God's call to salvation, and those who reject this general grace and who are thus damned. Each of the relevant theological contexts, on the other hand, disposes souls into two categories. Calvinists divide persons into the elect and the reprobate. In terms of the passage itself, the Calvinist elect are those "chosen of peculiar grace," and the reprobate are those who, though hearing God's call, "neglect and scorn" it; there are none who respond properly to the call without being specially elect.[15] The Arminian twofold distinction, again in the terms of the passage, falls *within* the category of the "rest" who "hear [God] call"; in the Arminian view, there are none chosen for salvation by special grace.

Milton seems for the moment to equivocate. In the first four lines of the passage, Milton sounds a Calvinist note. The elect are set off against the "sinful" rest. But as the speech unfolds that "rest" turn out not to be the reprobate, but the elect (who choose to accept grace) and the reprobate (who choose not to).

The opening and body of the passage compete for control of lines 185–86 ("The rest shall hear me call, and oft be warn'd / Thir sinful state"). As in the familiar drawing of the cube, the lines change character depending on whether they are viewed from the perspective of the preceding two lines or the succeeding fifteen. The apparently Calvinist perspective of lines 183–86 is contextualized and corrected by the straight Arminianism of lines 185–202.[16] It is wrong to read the opening of this speech as evidence of Milton's unreconstructed Calvinism, but not simply wrong. If the evocation of a Calvinist-style elect in the opening lines is tightly circumscribed by the Arminian discourse that follows, at the same time it encodes the author's characteristic self-understanding as elect prophet, a self-understanding purchased at the expense of his otherwise consistent theology of salvation. The Father draws an either/or distinction between "some" (line 183) and "the rest" (line 185), but in the theology of salvation as articulated by Arminius and in Milton's *de doctrina Christiana* the handful of those "elect above the rest" are subject to the same conditions of salvation applicable in the Father's speech to "the rest." The first category is re-assimilated into the second in the treatise but not in the poem.

The problem with God's speech is that the Calvinist and Arminian perspectives coexist no more peacefully here than they did at the Synod of Dort. The conflicting imperatives of Milton's theology and their place in Milton's self-construction are thrown into relief by a comparison of *de doctrina Christiana* and *Paradise Lost*. The comparison reveals the manner in which the treatise repeatedly approaches and then explicitly neutralizes or domesticates the quasi-Calvinist position of 3.183–84 ("Some I have chosen of peculiar grace / Elect above the rest"). It is a commonplace to point out the perils of treating the poem as if it were a treatise; it is no safer to treat the treatise as a poem. Juxtaposition of the Father's speech and the several related passages in *de doctrina Christiana* demonstrates how the demands of treatise do not allow Milton the kind of equivocation that marks *Paradise Lost*.

It is not surprising, given the unresolvable tensions of the Father's speech, that the two best guides to the successful embodiment in *Paradise Lost* of the theology of the *de doctrina Christiana*, Maurice Kelley and Danielson, are uncharacteristically inadequate here. Kelley quotes lines 183–84, without elaboration, as an item in a list of otherwise univocally Arminian passages from the treatise and *Paradise Lost* 3.173–202.[17] Danielson demonstrates that Kelley's reading of these lines as Arminian is untenable.[18] He suggests instead that "Milton is attempting a sort of compromise solution ... Perhaps Milton ... posits some kind of 'super-elect' (*PL* 3.183–4), and then a generality who receive sufficient grace (3.189), some of these availing themselves of it (3.195–7), some neglecting and scorning the offer (3.198 ff.) ... Milton's 'elect above the rest' can reasonably be seen as a category with which he complements an otherwise generally Arminian position."[19] Scholars like the middle ground, but by having recourse to the terms "compromise" and, even more, "complement," Danielson risks obscuring or minimizing the great divide on predestination and election that separated orthodox Calvinism and its repudiated stepchild Arminianism.[20] The incoherence of compromise between them is illustrated by the fact that Milton, working under the imperatives of discursive prose, rationalizes the contradiction left standing in the speech not by finding a middle ground between Calvin and Arminius but by qualifying the suggestion of a super-elect so drastically that it becomes a fully Arminian position.[21] The conflicting imperatives that dwell so incongruously and uneasily together in the Father's speech come into conflict at several moments in the treatise before being resolved as they never are in the poem. The speech opens a window on Milton's incompatible desires to be both among a special super-elect, marked out by a kind of birthright from among the general run of souls, and among those who are elect by virtue of their free choices; in a word, he wishes to be elect by both birthright and merit.[22] The speech begins and ends in a discursive moment that recurs but that is repeatedly mediated and rationalized in the treatise. Intimations of a super-elect are admitted and then overturned in a recurring drama evoked but not completed in the poem.

The argument of this chapter implies my skepticism concerning William Hunter's recent attempts to question the attribution of *de doctrina Christiana* to Milton; the case for Milton's authorship mounted in response to Hunter strikes me as insurmountable.[23] More recently, Paul Sellin has attempted to breathe new life into Hunter's proposal with an argument that the conceptions of predestination in *de doctrina Christiana* and *Paradise Lost* are incompatible with each other and with Arminius's writings.[24] As I do, Sellin points to a tension between the handling of predestination in the treatise and the Father's identification in the epic of a group "elect above the rest"; unlike me, he concludes that the texts were not written by the same author, and moreover that neither text is Arminian. As I shall demonstrate, the tension between the texts falls far short of contradiction, and the anomalous moment in the epic itself has an analogue in Arminius. Sellin's argument is flawed in several essential respects. While pointing to minor differences in detail and terminology, Sellin fails to demonstrate any significant disagreement among treatise, epic, and Arminius on the doctrinal matters most at issue among Reformed theologians in the late sixteenth and early seventeenth centuries: whether grace is universal or particular, whether grace is resistible or irresistible, whether the predestination of individuals is or is not based on foreseen merit, and, as entailed by the preceding, whether human beings have free will.[25] He argues that *de doctrina Christiana* is supralapsarian – and thus closer to Calvin than to Arminius – on the basis of the treatise's indication that the decree of predestination took place "before the foundations of the world were laid." This argument ignores the fact that this biblical formula is common to all discussions of predestination in the period, whether supra- or infralapsarian and whether absolute or conditional, and it fails to distinguish between chronological priority – meaningless with reference to an eternal creator – and logical priority, on which the distinction between Arminian and Calvinist depends.[26]

While Hunter and Sellin have been unsuccessful in casting significant doubt on Milton's authorship of *de doctrina Christiana*, the self-referentiality of the treatise, uncharacteristic of a normally abstract and impersonal genre but highly characteristic of Milton, constitutes strong if circumstantial evidence of Milton's authorship. Milton is moved to write when the shoe wrings his own foot: the antiprelatical tracts reflect bitterness over being "Church-outed by the Prelats"; the *Doctrine and Discipline of Divorce* owes something to the early failure of his first marriage; *Areopagitica* follows the negative response to the unlicensed publication of that divorce tract. Barker argued that Milton's "real concern is not with men in general but with good men."[27] Milton called for liberty, although concerned about the potential for license, because he would not tolerate restrictions placed upon good men, who know better what is virtuous than any earthly government and do not need external coercion to act on their knowledge. I would like to press Barker's point and suggest that Milton's real concern is not with men in general but with men like Milton, and that the set is sufficiently small that it is almost at times as if Milton is writing for himself. This is true of his theological as well as his political discourse.

In the anatomy of the self-regarding and social virtues in the second book of *de doctrina Christiana* Milton follows John Wolleb's *Compendium theologiae christianae* (1642) so closely that his additions are revealing. Milton, for example, approaches paraphrase of Wolleb in his discussion of "contentment," "frugality," and "industry," but he adds "lautitia," which Charles R. Sumner translates as "liberality" and John Carey as "elegance," or "the discriminating enjoyment of food, clothing and all the civilized refinements of life" (*CP* VI: 732; *CW* XVII: 233). This virtue sits strangely among modesty, decency, contentment, industry, frugality, humility, and high-mindedness, but it does reflect Milton's niceness of taste and his hostility to asceticism. Milton echoes Wolleb on "urbanity," but he adds an extra-ethical dimension to Wolleb's definition. For Wolleb, "urbanity" is "the virtue by which conversation is carried on with good humor and good taste, suited to the circumstances, as required by manners and ethics."[28] Milton writes, "URBANITY entails not only elegance and wit (of a decent kind) in conversation, *but also the ability to discourse and to reply in an acute and apposite way*" (*CP* VI: 769–70; my emphasis). This is the Milton who impressed the academies of Florence, the Milton who would himself be a "true poem" (*CP* I: 890). We hear the Miltonic voice as well in the discussion of modesty. From Wolleb Milton takes his definition, "abstinence from obscene words and suggestive behavior," but he adds his idiosyncratic flourish, "and, in fact, from anything which fails to conform with the strictest standards of personal or sexual conduct" (*CP* VI: 727).[29]

Perhaps the most revealing self-referential addition to Wolleb occurs in the discussion of the lawfulness of usury. Milton follows Wolleb point for point, citation for citation, but then goes on to make two additions in the concluding discussion. Wolleb writes,

That interest is not condemned absolutely and in itself is obvious because (1) if it were wicked under all circumstances, God would not have permitted loans to be made at interest to the foreigner (Deut. 23:20); (2) if land, house, horse, and other goods may be let out at interest, so also can money. God did not want profit to be received from interest in the land of Canaan for reasons connected with the ceremonial law, just as he did not allow land there to be sold in perpetuity (Lev. 25:23). (II.xii.2; p. 249)

Usuram per se ac simpliciter improbandam non esse, patet: I. Quia si simpliciter turpis esset non concessisset Deus, ut extraneo in usuram daretur, Deut. 23:20. *II. Quia si fundus, demus, equus & similia ad fructum elocari possunt, tum & pecunia. Regionis Cananae fructus deus usuris subjici noluit, sacremoniali significatione: quemadmodum nec agros ejus, lege mancipii vendi voluit,* Levit. 25:23. (pp. 272–73)

The scrivener's son, whose leisure was purchased by the interest earned from his father's loans (and who met his first wife while collecting on one of those loans), elaborates:

Usury, then, is no more reprehensible in itself than any other kind of lawful commerce. The proof of this is, in the first place, that if it were blameworthy in itself God would not have let the Israelites take interest from foreigners, Deut xxiii.20, *especially as he elsewhere instructs them to do no injury to foreigners but rather to assist them in all kindness, particularly those in need.* Secondly, if we may make a profit out of cattle, land, houses and the like, why should we not out of money? *When money is borrowed, as it often is, not to relieve hardship but simply for the purpose of gain, it tends to be more profitable to the borrower than to the lender.* It is true that God did not wish the Israelites to devote the produce of their land to usury, but this was for purely ceremonial reasons, as was his desire that they should not sell their land permanently, Lev. xxv.23. (*CP* VI: 776–77; my emphases)

Usuram itaque per se ac simpliciter non magis improbandam esse quam cætera quævis commercii civilis genera, ipsa ratio demonstrat: 1. quia si simpliciter reprehendenda esset, non permisisset Deus ut Israelitæ ab extraneo fœnus acciperent, Deut xxiii.20. *præsertim cum alibi præcipiat ne extraneo iniuriam facerent, sed omni potius humanitate, egenti præsertim, subvenirent: 2. si iumenti, fundi, tecti et similium fructus esse potest, cur non pecuniæ? quæ cum non inopia sublevandæ, sed lucri faciendi causa sæpe mutuo accipiatur, accipienti mutuo quam danti fructuosior esse solet. Terræ quidem Israeliticæ fructum Deus usuris addictum esse noluit, cæremoniali quadam significatione, quemadmodum et agros mancipio noluit vendi,* Lev. xxv. 23. (*CW* XVII: 338–40)

Wolleb's discussion implies that usury, carrying associations of predatoriness, is generally suspect; if not commendable, it is not always wicked, and in some manifestations it can be defended on scriptural grounds. In Milton's reworking usury is stripped of associations with wickedness; it is simply one more acceptable business strategy. Moreover, in Milton's additions, the defense is transmuted into commendation; far from being a predator, the usurer acts benevolently toward those in need and may even place himself at a disadvantage in order to help the borrower. In Milton's reworking of Wolleb we witness the manner in which Milton allowed his self-conception and the project of self-justification to play a role in the formation of his theology.

The incoherence of the Father's speech in Book 3 derives from the kind of intrusive self-regard that marks the discussion of usury in *de doctrina Christiana.* The opening lines, with their momentary suggestion of a Calvinist elect anomalous in the context of the developing Arminian argument, tell us more about Milton's self-conception, and about his need to be outstanding, than about his theology. The hesitation between models betrays his desire to be elect by both birthright and merit. Similar intrusions occur and are contained in *de doctrina Christiana,* in which we witness a dialectic of attraction to and repudiation of the idea of a Calvinist elect.

Danielson, as I noted earlier, suggests that Milton proposes in the Father's speech a compromise position; he offers the following passage from Richard Baxter as an analogue:

The Act of *faith* sometimes followeth this [divine] Impulse through its *invincible force*; And sometime it followeth it through its *sufficient force* . . . And sometimes it followeth it *not at all* . . . And if the question be, Why *sufficient Grace* which is *Effectual ad Posse* is not *effectual ad agere?* It is because (being but *sufficient,*) mans *Indisposition* and *wilful neglect* or *opposition,* maketh him an *unfit Receiver.*[30]

Noting Milton's discussion in *de doctrina Christiana* I.iv of the election of individuals as instruments of God (*CP* VI: 172), Danielson suggests that Milton's "categories are not the same as Baxter's, but similar." He concludes that if the two difficult lines in the Father's speech do not mark a "relapse into orthodox Calvinism," they nevertheless "should probably not be squeezed into a tightly Arminian mold."[31] This is an astute conclusion as regards *Paradise Lost* by way of a less astute reading of *de doctrina Christiana*. In the treatise, gestures in the direction of Baxter's first category are quickly reined in and "squeezed into a tightly Arminian mold." On the crucial question of saving faith Milton's categories in *de doctrina Christiana* are decidedly different from Baxter's; no divine impulse comes with invincible force as far as Milton is concerned.

At three points *de doctrina Christiana* explores individual election. In I.iv, Milton distinguishes the general predestination to salvation of all who freely choose to believe from "the election by which he chooses an individual for some employment . . . whence they are sometimes called elect who are superior to the rest for any reason (*unde electi nonnunquam dicuntur quicunque cæteris re aliqua præstant*)" (*CP* VI: 172; *CW* XIV: 98). He also distinguishes his anti-Calvinist general predestination from national election such as "that by which God chose the whole nation of Israel as his own people." Some few individuals stand out among others, just as Israel stands out among nations, as specially chosen by God. Are these individuals given special (or Baxter's "invincible") grace? Is there, in other words, an opening for a Calvinist-style elect? If so, Milton quickly closes the opening, arguing from the history of the Israelites that neither individual nor national election supports the doctrine of irresistible grace, as Calvinists contend.[32] Milton maneuvers the analogy in the opposite direction: just as the Israelites at times refused God's grace, so individuals chosen for special employment can turn against God.

Even the faithful apostles are not given irresistible grace: "Peter is not predestined or elected as Peter, or John as John, but each only insofar as he believes and persists in his belief" (*CP* VI: 176). Peter appears again as Milton elaborates the implications of this firmly Arminian conviction for his understanding of the election of individuals for service:

Who was more certainly elect than Peter? Yet we find a condition imposed, John xiii. 8: *if I do not wash you, you bear no part with me*. What then? Peter willingly complied and bore a part with Christ: had he not complied, he would have borne no part. For Judas bore no part, although it is said not only that he was elected, which may refer to his apostleship, but also that he was given to Christ by the Father. (*CP* VI: 179)

The condition imposed upon those chosen for individual employment is the same as that imposed upon all; those who by free choice believe and persist in belief will be saved (and by virtue of that choice will be included in God's general and conditional decree of predestination and participate in the merit of Christ's saving act).[33]

    The problem with an argument that a Calvinist-leaning conception of a "super-elect" complements or poses a compromise within a generally Arminian framework – universal sufficient grace and general and conditional election of those who freely choose to believe – is that the Calvinist position is specifically and repeatedly repudiated in the treatise. From Milton's point of view, any separation of salvation from free human choice to accept sufficient but not invincible grace would throw grave doubt on God's justice and undermine Milton's theodicy. He argues that "by separating election from faith," i.e., by supposing that God elects any individuals to salvation without foreknowledge of their free acceptance of grace in choosing to believe, "we become involved in perplexing and, indeed, in repulsive and unreasonable doctrines (*durioribus doctrinis, immo odiosis et ratione carentibus, implicemur*)" (*CP* VI: 180; *CW* XIV: 118).[34]

    In this first discussion in *de doctrina Christiana* of the election of individuals, we begin with something that parallels the Father's lines in *Paradise Lost*, "Some I have chosen of peculiar grace / Elect above the rest." But very quickly in the treatise the apparent Calvinism is reined in, and thus prevented from unsettling the otherwise Arminian argument.

    Milton returns to the question of specially chosen individuals in the seventeenth chapter of the first book, "Of Renovation and also of Vocation."[35] After discussing general vocation or calling, Milton turns to special calling:

Special vocation means that God, whenever he chooses, invites certain selected individuals, either from the so-called elect or from the reprobate, more clearly and more insistently than is normal. (*CP* VI: 455)

Vocatio specialis est qua Deus hos quam illos, sive electos quos vocant sive reprobos, clarius ac sæpius, quandocunque vult invitat. (*CW* XV: 348–50)

Once again it seems that Milton approaches a Calvinist super-elect; his first example is Abraham, the hero of faith. It is not clear at first what Milton means when he says that individuals are chosen "either from the so-called elect [*electos quos vocant*] or from the reprobate."[36] It cannot mean, of course, from among those predestined to salvation or damnation regardless of their choosing whether or not to believe. But does it mean that they are chosen without regard to virtue or other meritorious suitability?

Surprisingly, the biblical passages with which Milton illustrates his conception of special vocation are not of much help in answering this question. They say little or nothing about individuals; instead, they point to God's call to groups who either accept or reject his call to belief or obedience. Indeed, two of the four New Testament passages illustrating the selection of individuals by special vocation, Romans 8:28–30 and 2 Timothy 1:9 (*CP* VI: 456), are employed earlier to illustrate arguments on general (i.e., Arminian) predestination (*CP* VI: 181 and 173). The passages illustrating the special vocation of individuals among the reprobate have in common the theme of the rejection of God's call by those to whom grace is offered; it is the groups receiving the call, not the individual carrying the call, who are reprobate.[37] By special vocation, then, Milton seems to mean little more than any message concerning salvation delivered by God directly or through intermediaries. When he speaks of individuals selected from the reprobate, he seems to mean recalcitrant groups chosen to receive special embassies from God's spokespersons.[38]

The discussion of the change wrought (or not wrought) by the divine call follows on the discussion of special vocation, with no hint that we have been returned to the category of general vocation. Milton explains that the proper response to the call is a hearing or listening, and concludes, "What can this mean but that God gives us the power to act freely, which we have not been able to do since the fall unless called and restored? We cannot be given the gift of will unless we are also given freedom of action, because that is what free will means" (*CP* VI: 457). The category of special vocation, which seemed to promise high spiritual status to a few chosen spokespersons or heroes of faith, more or less dissolves in front of our eyes in chapter seventeen. Does it apply to the Abrahams of the world, or to the innumerable who are called? Does it involve some special grace that seals one's status among the elect? Whatever hints that we are being led toward a super-elect are quickly undone, until the category seems to leave us with little more than the general call through which all are given the opportunity to believe.

Any putative category of the super-elect is further undermined by

Milton's anti-Calvinist discussion of perseverance. Whereas Calvinists insist on the perseverance of the saints, or the impossibility of the apostasy of the elect faithful,[39] Milton understands the continued faithfulness of the saints as conditional. While Calvinists suggest that the saints may stumble and sin but not fall permanently from grace, Milton argues that "NO POWER OR GUILE OF WORLD OR DEVIL MAKES THEM [the saints] ENTIRELY FALL AWAY, SO LONG AS THEY DO NOT PROVE WANTING IN THEMSELVES, AND SO LONG AS THEY CLING TO FAITH AND CHARITY WITH ALL THEIR MIGHT" (*CP* VI: 505). Aware that the conditional clauses will run afoul of Calvinist consensus, Milton defends his opinion as following "the overall tendency of Scripture," which affirms the freedom of individuals to accept or reject grace and which makes clear that "God's seed remains" in the faithful "only so long as he does not himself extinguish it, for even the spirit can be extinguished" (*CP* VI: 506, 513). In *de doctrina Christiana*, the assurance of perseverance in faith for the elect (which for Calvin and his followers comes before the beginning of time) comes presumably only with the glorification of saints with the Last Judgment, although even here Milton resists stipulating this assurance.

In the chapter on predestination as well as in the chapter on vocation, Milton exhibits his characteristic concern for the reasonableness of the plan of salvation and the justice of God's disposition of human beings, a concern articulated by the Father in *Paradise Lost*:

> I made him just and right,
> Sufficient to have stood, though free to fall.
> Such I created *all* th'Ethereal Powers
> And Spirits, *both them who stood and them who fail'd*;
> Freely they stood who stood, and fell who fell.
> Not free, what proof could they have giv'n sincere
> Of true allegiance, constant Faith or Love,
> Where only what they needs must do, appear'd,
> Not what they would? what praise could they receive?
> What pleasure I from such obedience paid,
> When Will and Reason (Reason also is choice)
> Useless and vain, of freedom both despoil'd,
> Made passive both, had serv'd necessity,
> Not mee.   (3.98–111; my emphasis)

Certain individuals may be chosen for special ministries, but Milton repeatedly insists that these individuals are subject to the universal condition for election, the free choice to remain faithful and obedient. The quasi-Calvinist category of those "elect above the rest" articulated by the

Father shortly after the speech just quoted is not underwritten by the discussions of election and vocation in *de doctrina Christiana*.

Milton returns to the question of God's selection of individuals yet once more in his discussion of "extraordinary ministers" (I.xxix, "Of the Visible Church"). This discussion is far briefer than that in the chapter on vocation, as if Milton is resisting the elaboration of this category of special election, and hence its inevitable dissolution by the Arminian solvents of the treatise. Milton writes that "EXTRAORDINARY MINISTERS are sent and inspired by God to set up or to reform the church by both preaching *and by writing*. To this class the prophets, apostles, evangelists and others of that kind belong" (*CP* VI: 570; my emphasis). Milton (in the Latin) gives twenty-five words to his discussion of extraordinary ministers (followed by six illustrative biblical verses); William Ames devotes to the same topic several pages of *The Marrow of Theology* (Book I, ch. 33). Milton's own definition follows Ames's closely, but despite its brevity, Milton makes a point of adding that the extraordinary minister works "by . . . preaching *and by writing.*" The author who had added, self-referentially, elegance to his discussion of virtues, along with a defense of usury, the practice by which his own studious leisure was purchased, now adds the medium by which one "Church-outed by the Prelats" carried on his own work in reforming the church "of power beside the office of a pulpit" (*CP* I: 823, 816). The discussion of ordinary ministry that follows immediately is, significantly, in large part an attack on the exclusive franchise of the ordained clergy.[40]

In the chapter on vocation, as we saw a moment ago, the discussion of special vocation follows that on general vocation; in the course of this discussion the category of special vocation is domesticated and re-assimilated into what we would normally consider general vocation. In the chapter on ministry, the order is reversed and the discussion of the special or "extraordinary" category is foreshortened. The result, whether by design or not, is to spare the category of extraordinary minister the kind of Arminian leveling that takes place elsewhere in the text. In its brevity, the discussion acts as a marker of Milton's desire for a special status for such selected heralds as himself. He can remain the heroic figure who has virtuously achieved salvation by choosing faith and obedience, and he can also for the moment think of himself as standing on a special spiritual plateau, inaccessible to the undifferentiated mass of the faithful.

Milton's Arminian economy of salvation parallels his republican distrust of hereditary aristocracy. He favored demonstrated merit over inherited blood as the proper determinant of an individual's position in social and political hierarchies. But however radical Milton's politics may have been, he was no democrat. In *The Ready and Easy Way*, for example, he expresses distrust of the mob and imagines elections (without universal suffrage) leading by degrees to the most refined individuals.[41] A similar movement and counter-movement mark his theology of salvation. *De doctrina Christiana* most often posits a kind of egalitarianism in the divine plan. There is no designation of a spiritual elite before birth, and even those chosen for special ministry by God are subject to the same conditions for eventual election, what Milton will call in *Paradise Lost* the "free / Acceptance of large Grace" (12.304–05). The treatise does, however, allow for different degrees of grace. God

undoubtedly bestows grace on all, and if not equally upon each, at least sufficient to enable everyone to attain knowledge of the truth and salvation. I say not equally upon each, because he has not distributed grace equally, even among the reprobate, as they are called ... For like anyone else, where his own possessions are concerned, God claims for himself the right of making decrees about them as he thinks fit, without being obliged to give a reason for his decree, though he could give a very good one if he wished. (*CP* VI: 192)

In endorsing God's arbitrariness in dealing with "his own possessions," Milton echoes Calvinist defenses of predestination. But if Milton tempers here the egalitarianism of his conception of the providential plan, he insists with Arminius that sufficient, if not equal, grace is universal: "So God does not consider everyone worthy of equal grace, and *the cause of this is his supreme will*. But he considers all worthy of sufficient grace, and *the cause is his justice*" (*CP* VI: 193, my emphases).[42] The result is that, despite a reassertion of universal, sufficient grace, Milton leaves an opening for a spiritual aristocracy.[43]

This discussion follows one in which Milton wrestles with a verse that apparently undermines his argument, Acts 13:48: "*when the Gentiles heard this they were glad and glorified the word of the Lord; and as many as were ordained to eternal life, believed*" (*CP* VI: 184). First Milton points to ambiguity surrounding the term translated "ordained" (*tetagmenoi*); some interpreters, "more acute" in Milton's view, "consider it equivalent to 'well or moderately disposed or affected,' that is, of a composed, attentive, upright and not disorderly mind" (*CP* VI: 185).[44] Read thus, the verse suggests not a divine decree of predestination but a disposition Milton often sought in his readers: openness, attentiveness, impartiality.[45]

From where would these dispositions come, differentiating those more and less well disposed and affected? Perhaps from variable, inborn shares of the traces of the divine image:

Some traces of the divine image remain in man, and when they combine in an individual he becomes more suitable, and as it were, more properly disposed for the kingdom of God than another. Since we are not mere puppets [*neque enim stipites plane sumus*], some cause at least should be sought in human nature itself why some men embrace and others reject this divine grace. One thing may be established at the outset . . . some are worse than others. This may be observed every day, in the nature, disposition, and habits of those who are most estranged from God's grace. (*CP* VI: 185–6; *CW* XIV: 128)

Given Milton's general argument concerning the centrality of the free acceptance of grace in election, it would be essential for faith to be freely chosen rather than made inevitable by a divinely given predisposition, for the same reason that any predisposition to sin would compromise the freedom of Adam and Eve in, and hence the theodicy of, *Paradise Lost*. But in this passage Milton flirts with just such inborn predispositions. As inheritors of the original sin we are inheritors of some reduced "traces of the divine image," which presumably would come to us at birth. Interestingly, Milton here uses the metaphor of the puppet he had used in *Areopagitica*, but it points now in the opposite direction. In the earlier work Milton wrote that "when God gave him [Adam] reason, he gave him freedom to choose, for reason is but choosing; he had bin else a meer artificial *Adam*, such an *Adam* as he is in the motions" (*CP* II: 527). Without freedom, Milton suggests, Adam would be a marionette pulled by the strings of divine will. In the passage in *de doctrina Christiana*, Milton is seeking a cause for why some respond to grace while others don't, playing with the theodicial fire of sufficient causation for human choices. The logic apparently is that we bring something to God's calling, that we are not merely interchangeable blocks of wood. With the language of "nature," though, Milton is in danger of falling back into the "error" of particular predestination.[46]

Milton has worked himself into a position in which election is tied to what might be an inborn virtue, or at least a healthy allotment of the "traces of the divine image." Anticipating Calvinist citation of verses (Deuteronomy 9:5 and Luke 10:13) indicating that God does not choose according to our merited righteousness, Milton suggests that these verses do not pertain to election to eternal life, but to earthly favors. The more difficult verse is Romans 9:16, "*it does not depend on him that wills or on him that runs but on God who is merciful*" (*CP* VI: 187). Roused from an interlude in which he has toyed with quasi-Calvinist predispositions to sin or obedience, Milton reasserts his libertarian, Arminian argument:

But I reply, I am not talking about anyone willing or running, but about someone being less unwilling, less backward, less opposed, and I grant that God is still merciful, and is, at the same time, supremely wise and just. On the other hand, those that say *it does not depend on him that wills or on him that runs*, do presuppose a man willing and running, only they deny him any praise or merit. However, when God determined to restore mankind, he also decided unquestionably (and what could be more just?) to restore some part at least of man's lost freedom of will. So he gave a greater power of willing or running (that is, of believing) to those whom he saw willing or running already by virtue of the fact that their wills had been freed either before or at the actual time of their call. These, probably [*verisimile*], represent here the "ordained." (*CP* VI: 187; *CW* XIV: 134)

There is drama in the equipoise of "*verisimile*"; the verse from Romans is difficult to assimilate to Milton's argument, and the strain appears in the "probably." But there may be some ambivalence at the domestication of the verse to the Arminian argument, connected to Milton's recurrent yearning for a status "elect above the rest," as in his claim in the *Reason of Church-Government* to be among God's "selected heralds" (*CP* I: 802) and in his comparison of himself to Jeremiah, Isaiah, and the evangelist John in the same text and to Ezekiel in the *Doctrine and Discipline of Divorce* (*CP* I: 803, 820–21; II: 222–23).[47]

Milton's ambivalence finds expression in a dialectic that I have been tracing in *de doctrina Christiana*. After setting up a clearly and unequivocally Arminian framework, according to which God shares sufficient grace with all and does not exempt even his chosen instruments from the common test of salvation (free acceptance of grace leading to faith and obedience), Milton on several occasions hints at a special status for the few. When he does so, however, this special status is quickly re-assimilated into the general condition of humankind. The dialectic opens windows alternately on two deeply ingrained but incompatible self-representations on Milton's part, both tied to his palpable desire to have his merit recognized. Milton is unwilling or unable to accept that faith might be an unmerited gift of God, not merely because of the imputation on God's justice (on what grounds could God withhold from some what he gives to others?) but also because of the imputation on human, and therefore Milton's merit (what is the value of saving faith if it is not acquired at least in part by one's own effort and merit?). Milton will not see himself as a "meer artificial Milton," a puppet of divine providence. In his hostile review of Arminianism of 1643, the Calvinist John Owen, who would be Cromwell's aide and eventually Chancellor of Oxford University, suggests that attacks on Calvinist predestination arise from a delusion that one can merit praise and from a desire to be outstanding; Arminians attempt "to vindicate unto themselves a power, and independent abillitie of doing good, of making themselves to differ from all others, of attaining everlasting happinesse, without going one steppe from without themselves."[48] Owen describes here a temptation to which Milton seems to have been particularly prone.

There is a price to pay for claiming the merit of free will, not only in terms of the scorn of Calvinists, but also in terms of self-conception and representation. To give up the category of the Calvinist elect is to give up one avenue of conceiving oneself as separate from and above the generality of people. No longer is one born into a spiritual aristocracy; instead one is submerged in, to borrow a phrase from the *Doctrine and Discipline of Divorce*, the "common lump of men" (*CP* II: 253). Arminius himself acknowledges that the Calvinist view offers the elect individual the promise of special distinction: "You will say that, if he [the elect individual] has apprehended the offered grace by the aid of peculiar grace, it is, then, evident that God has manifested greater love towards him than towards another to whom he has applied only common grace, and has denied peculiar grace. I admit it."[49] Having made this acknowledgment, Arminius continues with a surmise – to the best of my knowledge unique in his writings – in which he hints at the kind of hybrid that Milton toys with in the Father's speech:

I admit it, and perhaps the theory [Arminius's own theory of general and resistible grace], which you oppose, will not deny it. But it will assert that *peculiar grace* is to be so explained as to be consistent with free-will, and that *common grace* is to be so described, that a man may be held worthy of condemnation by its rejection, and that God may be shown to be free from injustice.

It is not surprising that Arminius does not elaborate on this idea here or elsewhere, for the idea itself of a peculiar saving grace sits awkwardly in the context of his otherwise consistent insistence on the justice of the universality of saving grace. His nod toward a Calvinist conception of saving grace, even though redefined as resistible, is momentary and anomalous. We view for a brief moment the dueling of imperatives that apparently moved Milton in his composition of the Father's speech. Milton can have either the self-satisfaction of the self-made spiritual man or the self-satisfaction of the one chosen by God in a manner different from that by which others are chosen, but he cannot have both self-satisfactions at once. I have been suggesting that Milton's Arminian position satisfies his concern for theodicy even as it partially satisfies his need to have his merit acknowledged, and that the Calvinist eruptions, re-assimilated in *de doctrina Christiana* but not in *Paradise Lost*, point to a need for recognition that the Arminian economy cannot satisfy. The Milton who implausibly adds elegance and conversational wit to Christian virtues will not think of himself as just another interchangeable puppet or block of wood.

What, in the end, can we make of the tensions in the Father's speech in Book 3? Not, I have argued, that Milton as theologian (or as theological poet) is undecided between Calvin and Arminius. And not even that he is trying to find a compromise or hybrid form, to become the Tycho Brahe of the motions of faith. Instead, *de doctrina Christiana* helps us to see the dialectic that gives rise to the anomaly of placing in an Arminian setting the apparently Calvinist lines "Some I have chosen of peculiar grace / Elect above the rest." This incompletely assimilated gesture responds to the requirements of Milton's self-construction as a heroic and select servant of God, i.e., to Milton's own need to be outstanding in as many ways as possible, or in more ways than are possible at once. At the same time the pair of lines helps us to recognize the forces behind the dialectic in the treatise, forces that the treatise, because of its imperative of rational consistency, must domesticate.

NOTES

Work on this chapter was aided by a 1995–6 National Endowment for the Humanities Fellowship. Versions were presented at the Fifth International Milton Symposium in Bangor, Wales, and at the Newberry Milton Seminar in Chicago; the chapter benefited from questions and comments on both occasions. For advice and encouragement, I would like to thank, along with the editors of this volume, Ted Cachey, Nancy Fallon, Michael Lieb, Janel Mueller, Hong Won Suh, and Henry Weinfield. I owe a considerable debt to my research assistant, Jeffrey Speaks.

1. "Of the Doctrine of Divine Predestination," art. 12, quoted from *The Articles of the Synod of Dort*, trans. Thomas Scott, D.D. (Philadelphia, 1841). Further quotations from the *Articles* will be taken from this edition.
2. William Riley Parker, *Milton: a Biography*, 2 vols. (Oxford, 1968), vol. I, p. 8, vol. II, pp. 701–02. For Elizabeth Milton's comment, see *Aubrey's Brief Lives*, ed. Oliver Lawson Dick (1949; rpt. Ann Arbor, 1957), p. 200.
3. Witness his rejection of the Trinity in *de doctrina Christiana* (three is three and one is one). There are mysteries in *Paradise Lost*; why, e.g., would one occupying Satan's position conceive sin? But the mysteries cluster around events and characters before creation, as Milton, as much as one writing a universal epic can, remains true to the position of *de doctrina Christiana* (I.vii): "Anyone who asks what God did before the creation of the world is a fool; and anyone who answers him is not much wiser," CP VI: 299. Quotations from the Latin original and Charles R. Sumner's translation of *de doctrina Christiana* are taken from volumes XIV–XVII of *CW*.
4. John Stachniewski suggests that Milton's project of "justifying" God is a reaction

against Calvinist insistence, in response to attacks on the doctrine of predestination, that "God should not be brought before the bar of human justice" (*The Persecutory Imagination: English Puritanism and the Literature of Religious Despair* [Oxford, 1991], p. 333).

5. *Paradise Lost* 9.701, quoted from *John Milton: Complete Poems and Major Prose*, ed. Merritt Y. Hughes (New York, 1957), p. 394. Further quotations from Milton's poetry will be taken from this edition.

6. "On Paradise Lost," lines 7–8, 43–44. Quoted from Hughes, ed., *Milton: Complete Poems*.

7. Alexander Pope, *Imitations of Horace*, "Epistle to Augustus," lines 99–102.

8. Dennis Burden, *The Logical Epic: A Study of the Argument of Paradise Lost* (Cambridge, MA, 1967); Dennis Danielson, *Milton's Good God: A Study in Literary Theodicy* (Cambridge, 1982).

9. Philip Gallagher, *Milton, the Bible, and Misogyny* (Columbia, MO, 1990), p. 48.

10. My phrasing here invokes Maurice Kelley's *This Great Argument: A Study of Milton's De Doctrina Christiana as a Gloss upon Paradise Lost* (Princeton, 1941).

11. For Calvin on predestination, see the *Institutes of the Christian Religion* (1559), III.xxi–xxiv; for Arminius, see his "Declaration of Sentiments," in the *Writings of James Arminius*, trans. James Nichols and W. R. Bagnall, 3 vols. (Grand Rapids, 1956), vol. I, pp. 198–275; for Arminius's pointed opposition to Calvinist predestination, with the charge that it makes God the author of sin, see *Writings*, vol. I, p. 228, vol. III, pp. 44, 363.)

12. *Anti-Calvinists: The Rise of English Arminianism c.1590–1640* (Oxford, 1987). Tyacke's definition of the term "Arminian" is useful to historians in large part because it is localized. For a pointed critique of Tyacke, see Julian Davies, *The Caroline Captivity of the Church* (Oxford, 1992), pp. 87ff.; Davies's skepticism about the possibility of separating Arminian from Calvinist views of predestination (pp. 92–93) seems overstated. For a concise and lucid overview with bibliography of the controversy over English Arminianism occasioned by Tyacke, see the editor's "Introduction" to *The Early Stuart Church, 1603–42*, ed. Kenneth Fincham (Stanford, 1993).

13. Tyacke (*Anti-Calvinists*, p. 176) provides evidence of the belief among English Arminians that the sacraments confer grace. Calvin is clear that they do not (*Institutes* IV.xiv.14–17). Agreeing that sacraments function as signs instead of repositories of magical efficacy, Arminius remarks of baptism that "it is unwisely asserted that, through it, grace is conferred . . . For grace cannot be immediately conferred by water" (*Writings*, vol. II, pp. 160–61). For Milton's agreement with Calvin and Arminius that the sacraments are signs or seals that cannot confer grace, see *CP* VI: 556.

14. Kelley, *This Great Argument*, pp. 14–20; Don Wolfe, *Milton in the Puritan Revolution* (New York and London, 1941), p. 64; Arthur Barker, *Milton and the Puritan Dilemma 1641–1660* (Toronto, 1942), pp. 184, 308. While Peter White, like Julian Davies, argues that Arminianism and Calvinism are not easily or clearly separable, and that it is more accurate to plot theologians along a "spectrum" rather than thrust them to two poles (*Predestination, Policy and Polemic: Conflict and*

Consensus in the English Church from the Reformation to the Civil War [Cambridge, 1992], p. xiii), it remains true that in seventeenth-century polemic belief in universal and resistible saving grace is labeled as Arminian (or Remonstrant) in opposition to "orthodox" Calvinism. See, for example, Robert Baillie, *Ladensivm Autokatakrisis, The Canterbvrians Self-Conviction* (London, 1641) and John Owen's *A Display of Arminianisme* (London, 1643). Milton's admired Hugo Grotius gives voice to the polarity of these terms, even as he calls for mutual toleration, in *Ordinum Hollandiae ac Westfrisiae pietas* (1613), ed. Edwin Rabbie (Leiden, 1995).

15. For a poetic expression of Calvinist binarism, see Michael Wigglesworth's *The Day of Doom* (the first of several American editions appeared in 1662, and the first [pirated] London edition in 1666), especially stanzas 40–47, 144–63. The distance between Wigglesworth and Milton is measured by the distance between Milton's Arminian formula, the "free / *Acceptance* of large Grace" (*Paradise Lost* 12.304–05; my emphasis) and Wigglesworth's Calvinist insistence on *God's* freedom in dispensing grace: "Else should my Grace cease to be Grace; / For it should not be free, / If to release whom I should please, / I have no libertee" (stanza 177), in *The Poems of Michael Wigglesworth*, ed. Ronald A. Bosco (Lanham, MD, 1989), p. 55; see also stanzas 163 and 179. I would like to thank John Shawcross for bringing this poem to my attention.

16. The concluding lines, on God's hardening of sinners, may strike the modern reader as Calvinist, but it should be noted that Arminius endorses the idea that God hardens those who have freely chosen to reject sufficient grace. See, e.g., *Review of Perkins*, in *Writings*, vol. III, pp. 329–30.

17. Kelley, *This Great Argument*, p. 17.

18. Danielson, *Milton's Good God*, pp. 82–83; Danielson cites not *This Great Argument* but Kelley's "The Theological Drama of *Paradise Lost*, III, 173–202," *PMLA* 52 (1937), 75–9.

19. Danielson, *Milton's Good God*, p. 83.

20. In my view John Shawcross does obscure the divide between Calvinist and Arminian conceptions of predestination in his *John Milton: The Self and the World* (Lexington, KY, 1993), pp. 138–40. Shawcross writes that "some Calvinists seem to have believed in a strict doctrine of election and thus of absolute grace, others in varying ways and degrees held that . . . election included both those elect from the beginning of time and those who gained salvation through obedience and faith" (p. 138). The latter position, compatible with Arminius's, is anathema to Calvin and is expressly repudiated by the Synod of Dort. While Shawcross is correct that Arminius "staunchly argued his Calvinist orthodoxy" (p. 139), one should note that Arminius attacks Calvin's version of supralapsarianism for "mak[ing] God the author of sin [*Deum peccati auctorem facis*]" (*Writings*, vol. III, p. 363; *Opera Theologia*, 2nd edn. [Frankfurt, 1631], p. 536; see also *Writings*, vol. I, p. 228, vol. III, p. 44).

21. Milton's prose is not free of contradictions, but the genre of theological treatise requires an attempt to sort out themes and arguments that could be left ambiguous in poetry.

22. Strictly speaking, Arminius agrees with Calvin that the merit of election is God's rather than ours, but Calvinists charged Arminians with claiming for themselves the glory and merit of God in their insistence on human freedom to accept or reject saving grace.

23. For references to the controversy over the provenance of *de doctrina Christiana*, see the introduction to this volume, n. 9. In addition to the criticisms of Hunter's respondents, one might mention such weaknesses as Hunter's offering as evidence differences between treatise and epic on divorce ("The Provenance of the *Christian Doctrine*: Addenda from the Bishop of Salisbury," *SEL* 33 [1993], 191–207), where his speculative reading of the epic moves away from the sense of the divorce tracts, which themselves foreshadow the discussion of divorce in the treatise.

24. Paul Sellin, "John Milton's *Paradise Lost* and *De Doctrina Christiana* on Predestination," *Milton Studies* 34 (1996), 45–60.

25. There *are* differences of detail between the treatise and Arminius. Unlike Arminius, e.g., the treatise excludes reprobation from the decree of predestination (*CP* VI:190), but this difference may not amount to much. The treatise prefers to say that God does not reprobate, but the effect for the individual is identical. Those who choose not to accept universally offered and sufficient saving grace are reprobate. For a passage in Arminius in which the difference from the treatise is minimal, see "A Discussion of the Subject of Predestination between James Arminius and Francis Junius," in *Writings*, vol. III, pp. 22ff.

26. Sellin makes much of the treatise's placing of predestination "'*ante iacta mundi fundamenta*' – that is, 'before the foundation of the world were laid'" (pp. 50–51; quoting *CW* XIV: 90), but Arminius agrees that predestination is a decree that "God resolved within himself *from all eternity* [*apud se ab æterno statuit*]" (Arminius, "Public Disputations" XV, in *Writings*, vol. I, p. 565, my emphasis; *Opera Theologia*, p. 227; see also his "Letter to Hippolytus a Collibus," where predestination is defined as "an eternal and gracious decree of God in Christ [*illam esse decretum Dei æternum & gratiosum in Christo*]" [*Writings*, vol. II, p. 470; *Opera*, p. 771] and his *Review of Perkins*, in *Writings*, vol. III, p. 333). The phrase in *de doctrina Christiana* so important for Sellin, "*ante iacta mundi fundamenta*," is a quotation from Ephesians 1:4 (see *CW* XIV:100), a verse that Arminius himself, along with virtually every writer on predestination, quotes in the same connection: "We attribute Eternity to this decree . . . For . . . 'He hath chosen us in Christ before the foundation of the world [*antequam iacerentur fundamenta mundi*].' (Eph. i,4)" (*Writings*, vol. I, p. 566, *Opera*, p. 227). If an assertion that the decree of predestination is eternal makes one a supralapsarian, then Arminius himself is a supralapsarian, and the term loses all distinguishing meaning. The order of causal priority in Arminius (the act of predestination follows upon the existence in God's mind of man as created and upon God's foreseeing of the fall) fits snugly with both the order in *de doctrina Christiana* and, given the requirements of linear narrative, the order in *Paradise Lost* (*Review of Perkins*, in *Writings*, vol. III, p. 299). To call the position of *de doctrina Christiana* "supralapsarian" is deeply misleading, for the term normally describes the belief, found

in Calvin but repudiated in Arminius, in *de doctrina Christiana*, and in *Paradise Lost*, that God decreed (i.e., ordained as part of the divine plan) the fall of the human race. This misunderstanding of theological context unfortunately characterizes Sellin's article at several crucial points, as I hope to elaborate elsewhere.

27. *Milton and the Puritan Dilemma*, p. 313.

28. *Compendium* II.xiii, in *Reformed Dogmatics: J. Wollebius, G. Voetius, F. Turretin*, trans. John W. Beardslee III (New York, 1965), p. 255. Further references to Wolleb in translation will be taken from this edition and cited by section and page number in the text.

29. In this passage as in many others, Milton quotes rather than paraphrases. Compare Wolleb's "*Verecundia est temperantia a verborum obscoenitate, & gestuum lascivia*" (*Compendium theologiae christianae* II.xi.2 [Cambridge, 1642], p. 261) with Milton's "*Verecundia est temperantia a verborum obscœnitate et gestuum lascivia; ab iis denique omnibus quæ ratione sexus aut personæ probatissimis moribus minus conveniunt*" (*CW* XVII: 220). Like Wolleb, Milton cites Hebrews 12:28 to illustrate his point.

30. Danielson, *Milton's Good Good*, p. 83, quoting Baxter's *Catholick Theology*; the bracketed word is Danielson's. For reasons to be cautious in using Baxter as analogue for Milton, see John Rumrich, *Milton Unbound: Controversy and Reinterpretation* (Cambridge, 1996), pp. 30–32.

31. Danielson, *Milton's Good God*, p. 83.

32. See Calvin, *Institutes* III.xxi.5–7.

33. For further discussion of the conditional nature of general predestination in Milton, see *de doctrina Christiana* I.xxv (*CP* VI:506).

34. The Synod of Dort, in its condemnation of Arminian doctrine, in turn specifically repudiates as an imputation on God's omnipotence any claim that predestination to election is conditional on God's foreknowledge of freely chosen belief (*Articles of the Synod of Dort*, "Of the Doctrine of Divine Predestination," pp. 261, 271, 274–78). For Calvin's denial of the possibility that predestination is based on the foreknown merit of chosen faith, see *Institutes* III.xxii.1–2, 9.

35. For Milton on vocation, see John Spencer Hill, *John Milton: Poet, Priest and Prophet: A Study of Divine Vocation in Milton's Poetry and Prose* (London, 1979).

36. Milton must qualify the "elect" as "the so-called elect" or "those whom they call elect" because an individual's elect status is not logically prior to vocation but dependent on one's proper response and continued faithfulness to the call.

37. Isaiah 28:13; Ezekiel 2:4–5 and 3:12; Matthew 10:18, 11:21, 22:8–10, and 23:37; Luke 7:30; and Acts 7:51 and 13:46.

38. For Calvin's very different discussion of special calling, see *Institutes* III.xxiv.8.

39. See, for example, Calvin, *Institutes* III.xxiv, 6–11; Wolleb, 1.32, in Beardslee, pp. 174ff.; François Turretin, *Institutio theologiae elencticae*, Locus IV, Q.12, in Beardslee, pp. 383ff.; *Articles of the Synod of Dort*, "Concerning the Perseverance of the Saints," pp. 314ff.

40. For an alternative but not incompatible view, see William Kerrigan's argument that with the corruption of the institutional church and with the resort of

the Spirit to individuals rather than to an ecclesiastical body described in
Paradise Lost 12.524–40, "the ordinary ministers defined in the *De doctrina christiana* lose their function, which is predicated on a true church externally established in a just society" (*The Prophetic Milton* [Charlottesville, VA, 1974], p. 179).

41. Not surprisingly, Milton's opinion of the common people grew more pessimistic as they failed to rally around the Good Old Cause. He is more consistent in his high valuation of his own class, the middle class. In *Eikonoklastes*
(1649), Milton alternates between castigating the common people for their
susceptibility to monarchic show and praising them as the Talus who drove
out the bishops (*CP* III:344, 391, 601). In *A Defence of the English People* (1651)
Milton argues that "More often far more of the commoners surpass the lords
in character and intellect" (*CP* IV:470); these commoners are the gentry and
middle class, as becomes clear in the reference a page later to "the middle
class, which produces the greatest number of men of good sense and knowledge of affairs."

42. For Calvin and his orthodox followers, there is no distinction between God's
supreme will and his justice, so that predestination to salvation or reprobation, without reference to foreknowledge of the individual's free choices, is
just *because* it arises from God's will.

43. Milton gestures again toward a spiritual aristocracy in his astonishing discussion of implicit faith. In *Areopagitica* he had dismissed contemptuously those
who let others perform for them the labor of interpreting scripture, charging
them with laziness and Romanizing idolatry (*CP* II:544). But in *de doctrina
Christiana* he finds a role for implicit faith: "Implicit faith, which blindly
accepts and so believes, is not real faith at all. Unless, that is, it is only a temporary state, as in novices and new converts who believe even before they enter
upon a course of instruction . . . It is the case, also, with those who are *dull of
understanding and practically unteachable*, but who believe, nevertheless, according
to their light and attempt to live by faith, and who are thus acceptable to God"
(*CP* VI:472; emphasis mine). The first sentence follows Wolleb closely
(*Compendium* I.xxix.9, in Beardslee, p. 163), but Milton adds what follows. The
apparent sense of the final sentence is that God will be merciful to the slow-
witted, and that he will set the gate lower, so that even a Catholicizing implicit
faith will be sufficient. It is not like Milton to be moved solely by tender-heart-
edness and indulgence toward those with fewer gifts than himself. One might
reasonably surmise that the "dull of understanding" is a large group indeed,
and that Milton's indulgence toward this group is one more way of setting the
few apart from the many.

44. In his annotation, Maurice Kelley suggests that the "more acute" interpreters
are Remonstrant or Arminian theologians.

45. On Milton's invocation of "ingenuous" readers and its Reformed context, see
Dayton Haskin, *Milton's Burden of Interpretation* (Philadelphia, 1994), pp. 242–45.

46. Milton earlier, in *The Doctrine and Discipline of Divorce*, had written of inborn
predispositions or temperaments in a way that uncharacteristically suggested
determinism (*CP* II:235–37, 249, 253, 260, 272, 328, 342, 345, 346, 355).

47. For a brief survey of Milton's self-representation as a select spokesperson, see my "Intention and Its Limits in *Paradise Lost*: The Case of Bellerophon," in Diana Trevino Benet and Michael Lieb, eds., *Literary Milton: Text, Pretext, Context* (Pittsburgh, 1994), pp. 164–69.

48. John Owen, *A Display of Arminianisme* (London, 1643), ch. 6, p. 50. The subtitle tells the same story: "Being a Discovery of the old Pelagian *Idol Free-will*, with the new Goddesse *Contingency*, advancing themselves, into the Throne of the God of heaven to the prejudice of his *Grace, Providence,* and *Supreme Dominion* over the children of men."

49. *Review of Perkins*, in *Writings*, vol. III, pp. 481–82.

CHAPTER 6

Milton's kisses

William Kerrigan

This chapter discusses a motif in *Paradise Lost* that appears first in the context of Eden eroticism, then migrates into the story of the fall of man. The motif bears in a general way on Milton's unorthodox cosmological speculations, particularly on the one Stephen Fallon calls "animate materialism."[1]

During the twentieth century, the first wave of interest in the heretical aspects of Milton's religious cosmos was prompted by Denis Saurat's *Milton, Man and Thinker* (1925). Maurice Kelley's *This Great Argument: A Study of Milton's De Doctrina Christiana as a Gloss upon Paradise Lost* (1941) is largely an argument with the excesses of Saurat, whom Kelley saw as adding to Milton's heresies some even more peculiar ideas of his own about the creation of the world and the nature of the Godhead. For Kelley, as later for the authorial trinity of *Bright Essence: Studies in Milton's Theology* (1971), Milton's suggestion that the Son of God had a beginning, and so was not coeternal with the Father, constituted much the most disturbing of his heresies.[2] One of the greatest Christian poets had tampered with the center of Christian devotion; this was the heresy to be gotten right, to be placed with utmost care in the history of ideas. Compared to his christology, Milton's conception of matter scarcely counted as heretical.

Saurat, nonetheless, had jumbled everything together, producing base mixtures. Combining Milton's generated Son of God with a literalizing interest in metaphors attached to the creation of the world, including the notion of a matter somehow instinct with God, Saurat had produced a vision of Milton's cosmos sure to frighten and appall his admirers – a kabalistic God of emanations who has some manner of sexual congress with his own alienated divinity, the upshot being the creation of the universe. I choose almost at random from Saurat's work one example of the sort of passage Kelley hoped to eradicate from Milton studies: "This divine origin of the substance of which all beings are made has the same consequence in psychology and ethics for Milton and for the *Zohar*. The physical instincts of the body are good and legitimate, and, especially, that of sex is good and legitimate; both the poet and kabalists find it in God himself."³

It was perhaps because Saurat had indulged an untoward curiosity over God's sexuality that Kelley took a narrow line on the vitalism of *Paradise Lost*. Glossing Raphael's speech on "one first matter," Kelley accurately maintained that the "whole of being is one huge chain or ladder ascending by gradations from the inanimate to God."⁴ Yes indeed, but what difference does animate materialism make in *Paradise Lost*? For Kelley it simply explained why an angel eats dinner – *really* eats dinner, not "the common gloss / Of Theologians" (5.435–36) – with Adam and Eve: "It is owing to this identity of essence that food can be assimilated by spirits such as Raphael." At this point Kelley directed his reader to a passage in Saurat where monism is discussed solely in alimentary terms. Even in the citation of Saurat, boundaries had to be carefully drawn.

But a crucial truth was left behind in Saurat's unclean mixtures. It is not just that angels really eat. Heaven-directed metabolism is only half of monism's consequences. For as Adam learns at the end of Raphael's visit, angels also really make love. Love "is the scale / By which to heav'nly Love thou may'st ascend, / Not sunk in carnal pleasure, for which cause / Among the Beasts no Mate for thee was found" (8.592–95). Just as carnal matter can be gradually elevated to spirit, so carnal pleasure can be gradually refined into heavenly love. John Rumrich, arguing that Milton's spiritual materialism fuses Aristotelian substance with biblical glory, distinguishes between metabolism and married love as paths to divinity: "Appropriately enough, then, while nutrition provides the dominant natural metaphor in *Paradise Lost* for the intellectual incorporation of variety into a unified whole, marriage offers the best volitional metaphor."⁵

Both of these paths open to unfallen man belong to a still larger configuration of metaphors in *Paradise Lost*. If I were asked to name the single most stunning phrase in the 1645 *Poems*, my choice would be the "Blind mouths!" of *Lycidas*. Here the young Milton was dallying almost mystically with his future excellence. "Blind" and "mouth": these two most Miltonic words lead us from the apocalyptic invective of *Lycidas* to the blind bard's sublime mythopoeic universe in *Paradise Lost*. There is no work of art in our language, perhaps not in any language, that creates a more ample mythology of the mouth – the Satanic mouth that first whispers rebellion in the ear of Beelzebub, the mouth of the serpent entered by Satan and inspired with speech, the mouth of the Muse who brings the poem nightly to Milton's ear, the mouth of the poet-singer, the mouths that take both spiritual matter and forbidden fruit into the human body. We discover the detail I intend to study on the path of married love, where mouths converse sweetly, sing prayers giving voice to the created world, and sometimes touch each other.

LYRIC KISSING

You must remember this, but maybe you don't. It crisscrosses life and art, yet goes almost unnoticed by critics of Renaissance literature. Perhaps its neglect stems from the fact that it seems on first glance to have little to do with sovereignty or subversion, things critics of the Renaissance do notice, though by the end of this chapter I will be addressing exactly these subjects. But power is not the first or second thing you would think of in the vicinity of it, unless you think about power in the vicinity of anything. It does not matter much to science or epistemology. I should hasten to add, lest I lose your interest entirely, that it does pertain to some of the questions being posed just now in literary studies. It pertains to gender, and one could not get very far on the subject of desire without taking it into account, though few modern probers of desire have done so, which forces me to conclude that they have not gotten very far. It has a great deal to do with one of yesterday's hot binaries, presence and absence, since it is among the ways we say hello and goodbye, framing presence and absence, in Western culture.

Yet very little has been written about this. The title character of Kierkegaard's *Diary of a Seducer* considers writing a book to be entitled *Contribution to the Theory of Kissing*, "dedicated to all tender lovers." "It is quite remarkable," he goes on to note, "that no such work on this subject exists ... Could this lack in literature be due to the fact that philosophers do not consider such matters, or that they do not understand them?"[6] I too am intrigued by its near invisibility in contemporary literary prose, since this is one of the dominant topics of artistic representation, especially in the Renaissance, and most especially in the seventeenth-century English lyric. Kierkegaard is dead right about modern philosophers, but this may be a case of dissociation of sensibility. Thomas Stanley, author of *The History of Philosophy* (1656), the first such history in our language, was also a love poet fascinated by kissing. Something so ubiquitous, so deeply interwoven in our yearnings and our consolations, could only have become invisible to modern intellectuals semi-deliberately, because it has been written off as one of life's and art's minor niceties, beneath serious notice, and the fact that it preoccupied the courtly lyricists of the seventeenth century is no doubt filed away under Further Evidence of Their Grasshopper Escapism.

But the old lyricists were right. There are large stores of poetry in this way we have of welcoming and departing, of renewing the dearness of others and touching again the sources of our innocence. Kisses can also express, with surprising thoroughness, every last shred of our treachery and desperation. Kissing's a little thing, but one whose tracks extend across the full tonality of our existence. A kiss means, can mean, everything. It can be written with an X, like Christ and the unknown. Judas and Dr. Faustus did it, Corinna and Christ and Cleopatra did it, monks and nuns, whores and rakes, did it, Clark and Vivien, Fred and Ginger, did it, you and I and everyone, even Kings in Siam, do it. But in Milton's century it was done in verse.

The male poets of the seventeenth century felt compelled, as those in no other century have, to write down in verse the diplomatic history, real or imaginary, of male sexual desire, and in this huge mailbag of poetic love we have received thousands of lyric kisses. The movies of our own day provide an obvious historical analogue. One film historian recalls "Among the peep-show epics of 1896 . . . one showing May Irwin and John C. Rice in the prolonged kiss episode from their stage success, 'The Widow Jones.'"[7] From the luminous embraces of the silent film, during which the very silence of the medium is felt as representational, and no longer a subtraction from life, to the high-tech romances of Spielberg, the kiss has occupied a central position in cinematic iconography. At the moment of the embrace stars, directors, and films may compete with each other, but in doing so they resist the tendency of all movie kisses to fall together into a single oblivion that belongs specifically to the medium, and is an emblem of our abandonment to it – in the dark, and eyes closed, as it were, to everything but our lover, the screen.[8] One of my favorites, to dally a moment with movie kisses, occurs in *That Hamilton Woman*.

It is the eve of the nineteenth century, and Vivien Leigh's Lady Hamilton is entertaining Laurence Olivier's Lord Nelson at a gala ball in Naples. They walk out on a moonlit terrace. They kiss. Cut to shots of Nelson's fleet in the harbor, forebodings of the Napoleonic Wars to come. We then rejoin the lovers, who are, somewhat remarkably, still enjoying the same kiss. They part at last, and Nelson says, with breathtaking literality, "My dear, I have kissed you through two centuries." At the moment between centuries, we now realize, in the middle of this kiss, in its oblivion, we were looking at Nelson's ships. War and love, war and peace, together forge the continuity of historical time.

This seems to me a Renaissance kiss, and more particularly, as I will try to show, a Miltonic kiss. We recognize it first, however, as a Shakespearean kiss, and if time allowed an extended discussion of Shakespeare would be instructive here. Kissing, Freud remarked, "is permitted in theatrical performances as a softened hint at the sexual act."[9] Shakespeare clearly regarded it as one of the most dramatic things an actor could do on a stage, right up there with sword-fighting and suicide. Othello's death has all three, in fact, as the narrative of smiting the malignant Turk ends with the narrator smiting himself ("O bloody period!"), which in turn yields to a kiss: "No way but this, / Killing myself, to die upon a kiss" (5.2.359–60).[10] Serious values are reckoned in kisses on Shakespeare's stage. Cleopatra's are the priciest in Renaissance literature: "Give me a kiss," says the loser of Actium, "Even this repays me" (3.9.70–71). Cleopatra's death speech threatens to spin on without end, until, revealing that his kiss is as much to her as hers was to him, she applies the asp so that Iras will not receive "that kiss / Which is my heaven to have" (5.2.301–02). These Shakespearean kisses, troping grandly on death, desire, and conquest, are not easily outdone. But the Jacobean dramatists did their best, indulging their famous penchant for oddly cheerful horror. So I remember in passing the lethal skull kissed in *The Revenger's Tragedy* and the reworking of Othello's terminal kiss in *'Tis Pity She's a Whore*.

But the lyric post office of the seventeenth century is the context closest to Milton. Elizabethan poets pointed the way. When Corinna came to Ovid on that memorable noon, no kisses were mentioned; but Marlowe, translating *Amores* 1.5 for the Renaissance, interpolated several of them, a telling one at the end: "Judge you the rest; being tired, she bade me kiss. / Jove send me more such afternoons as this."[11] The suggestion here that kissing, because it can be done when we are "tired," stands apart from intercourse, and might be compared to intercourse, will have a considerable future in the lyrics of the next century.[12] But the most influential Elizabethan precedents are, I would think, *Amoretti* sonnet 64, "Comming to kisse her lyps," where the woman at this intimate distance becomes for Spenser a garden of fragrances, and the four kiss sonnets in *Astrophil and Stella* (79–82). With their prolonged play on "sweetness," and their emphasis on the youthfulness of kissing (sonnet 79, line 8: "Nest of young joyes, schoolmaster of delight"), Sidney's poems remind us that kissing, as the lineal descendant of the first signifier of love, born at the sweetness of the breast, remains in our adult experience the most innocent of all those practices we are inclined to think of as "sexual acts."

But the very association of kissing and childhood, as Sidney presents it, makes the kiss a means to an end. It is "Poore hope's first wealth, ostage of promist weale, / Breakfast of *Love*," a preliminary stage, a promise or opening deposit or breakfast, in a narrative directed toward the dinner feast of consummation – first base, as the guys in my high school used to call it.[13] The kiss as prelude belongs to Petrarchism as a genre, since its lover-poet writes in secrecy and frustration to woo an unforthcoming lady. A kiss is a perfect sign, because it is the substance, of this condition. It can be done in seclusion. Since it does not leave a trace, it cannot bind ("No man can print a kiss," as Greville observed).[14] It falls short of fully requited passion. It tantalizes, producing frustration even as it fulfills.

If intercourse is lust in action, the Petrarchan kiss is icy fire in action. Thus in Sonnet 81 Astrophil declares that Stella coldly disapproves of his kiss poems, since her reputation should be built on "higher seated fame." He cannot, however, stop himself, so that Stella will have to seal his mouth with a kiss to prevent him from speaking of her kiss – a nifty conceit in which the silence of the kiss, stilling the speaking voice, is said to be unrepresentable in the spoken literary text, when in fact the silence of the writing has, before our very eyes, placed a kiss inside the text. That kisses are implored in Petrarchan verse because they are what the poet feels he might get, and not what he finally wants, we learn from the following poem, where Astrophil has been admitted to the garden of Stella's body, and, whatever this may mean, has eaten a cherry, at which offense was taken. "I will but kisse," the poet vows, making do, as the genre requires, with something less than fulfillment. "I never more will bite."[15]

Characteristically, the kiss in seventeenth-century lyrics has been decontextualized, and is no longer prelude to a bite, but an act distinct from consummation, an end in itself precisely in its difference from consummation. Ben Jonson negotiated this transition, extricating kisses from the narrative of fulfillment inherent in Petrarchan desire. Translating Pseudo-Petronius, he endorsed a sentiment also found in Shakespeare's "The expense of spirit" and Donne's "Farewell to Love" – the melancholy conviction that there is an ineradicable flaw or deficiency in the design of male sexuality. "Doing a filthy pleasure is, and short, / And done, we straight repent us of the sport": the immediate legacy of male orgasm is shame, depletion, sorrow, and a sharp debasement in the value of the woman. The exile of being cut off from rapture inevitably follows its brief possession. Shakespeare despairs of a cure, since no man knows how to shun the heaven that leads him to this hell. Donne, with his usual extremity, vows to swear off women altogether.

The seriousness of the problem can be measured by the enthusiasm with which Cavalier poets embraced the advice of Pseudo-Petronius, for unlike Shakespeare and Donne, Jonson recommended an alternative inside the

province of physical love. There was a way to be sexual without being solitary, poor, nasty, brutish, and short:

> Let us together closely lie, and kiss,
> There is no labour, nor no shame in this;
> This hath pleased, doth please, and long will please; never
> Can this decay, but is beginning ever.[16]

Kissing is consummation's supplement, differing from orgasm in its capacity for a limitless increase of pleasure, and deferring orgasm by virtue of
that increase. "Pleased, doth please, and long will please": this is the three-
part before/during/after grid that Shakespeare rigorously imposes on
intercourse in Sonnet 129, but with kisses, the market is always up, always
gaining, without the aftermath of depression.[17]

In an essay on Jonson's poetry of praise Stanley Fish has brilliantly identified its self-proclaimed structure as an ideal economy. The praiser,
because he recognizes the virtue of the praiseworthy, participates in that
virtue; to praise another, therefore, is to praise oneself; and though praise
be given and self-given, it is understood that virtue does not *need* such
recognition, being its own praise. "The dynamics of this exchange," Fish
writes, "trace out what every society has vainly sought, an economy that
generates its own expansion and is infinitely self-replenishing, an economy
in which *everyone gains*."[18] Love poetry's version of this happy superfluity is a
booming economy of kisses, in which there is no "spending" or depletion,
but only unlimited renewal of capital, "beginning ever." Catullus had
counted up the kisses in "Vivamus, mea Lesbia" – 3,300 in all. Walter
Ralegh, in "Serena bee not coy," envisions wanton kisses that will outnum-
ber the days Ulysses spent in travel, or the stars in the sky:

> If this store
> Will not suffice, wee'le number o'er
> The same againe, untill we finde,
> No number left to call to minde
> And shew our plenty. They are poore
> That can count all they have and more.[19]

When Jonson redoes Catullus, he too glimpses infinity; Thomas Randolph's
kisses will exceed "the Atoms in the sun"; Alexander Brome, translating
Catullus, ups the ante from the classical 3,000-plus to an early modern
"millions of kisses." The Renaissance imagination, as Ernst Cassirer and
others have noted, warmed to the idea of infinity: as in space, as in atoms
and planets, so in erotic time, so in kisses.[20]

Some of Jonson's best-known songs center on kissing. "Or leave a kiss but in the cup,/And I'll not look for wine": given his large affection for wine, Celia's must indeed have been an estimable kiss. His major exploration of the subject is the lyric sequence *The Celebration of Charis*, where Jonson teaches a young woman the "long" kiss:

> Join lip to lip, and try:
> Each sucks out other's breath.
> And whilst our tongues perplexèd lie,
> Let who will think us dead, or wish our death.[21]

Jonson had this poem by heart, and recited it for William Drummond. Lyric poetry has once again retrieved something from what early Heidegger liked to call "the hiddenness of the obvious." Unlike intercourse, the orifices joined in kissing have no gender difference. Both have lips, both have tongues, and both are, so to speak, *both*. Kissing is here an equation.

Jonson's delicious kisses reverberate throughout the seventeenth century. The poem we scholars would hope to find, a kiss lyric about kiss lyrics combining the encyclopaedic strain in the Renaissance literary imagination with its devotion to rhetorical classification, was written by Edward Herbert, the Puttenham of osculation:

> Kissing
> Come hither, womankind and all their worth,
> Give me thy kisses as I call them forth.
> Give me a billing kiss, that of the dove,
>   A kiss of love;
> The melting kiss, a kiss that doth consume
>   To a perfume;
> The extract kiss, of every sweet a part,
>   A kiss of art;
> The kiss which ever stirs some new delight,
>   A kiss of might;
> The twaching smacking kiss, and when you cease,
>   A kiss of peace;
> The music kiss, crotchet-and-quaver time;
>   The kiss of rhyme;
> The kiss of eloquence, which doth belong
>   Unto the tongue;
> The kiss of all the sciences in one,
>   The kiss alone.
> So, 'tis enough.[22]

The catalogue has its puzzles. What exactly is a "kiss of might"? Perhaps a kiss of "might be," awakening intimations of the unknown future to come?

Jonson's favorite is unmistakable; he taught the "kiss of eloquence." Maybe the cutest is the "kiss of peace" – the brief buzzer at the end, signing off. Herbert, in a studied anti-Catullan gesture, has had enough. The endless renewability of the kiss might also cloy, which affords us a glance ahead to Milton's Eve.

Up to a point, the most loyal of the Sons of Ben followed after him in lyric kissing. But in Robert Herrick the economy of kisses becomes strangely and intriguingly disturbed. On the one hand, he completes what Jonson started in isolating kissing from the drama of consummation. Aside from a two-line epigram, "Kissing," and the uncharacteristic "Up tailes all," where Herrick would "Begin with a kisse" and proceed to consummation, the only orgasm evoked in his work appears in "How Lillies came white" – suggestively, this is a maternal ejaculation, a happy splash of the "creme of light" pinched out by Cupid from his mother's breast and fallen down on the lillies like an epigram on a page. Herrick expressly rejects the Jonsonian "kiss of eloquence," which he rechristens the "slimy" or "loathsome" kiss:

> Kisses Loathsome
> I abhor the slimy kiss
> (Which to me most loathsome is).
> Those lips please me which are placed
> Close, but not too strictly laced,
> Yielding I would have them, yet
> Not a wimbling tongue admit.
> What should poking-sticks make there,
> When the ruff is set elsewhere?[23]

An annotator tells us that Herrick alludes to the stays placed in a "ruff" or ruffled collar.[24] "Poking-sticks," tongues, belong in a "ruff . . . set elsewhere." We have stumbled upon a classic psychoanalytic plot: deny one of life's formidable masters, such as genital sexuality, and it will reappear symbolically in the very terms set forth to deny it. I believe the poem alludes to cunnilingus, which Herrick also evokes with considerable shame in "The Shoe-tying" and "The Vine."

EPIC KISSING

Enter Milton. Is there to be a kiss in *Paradise Lost*? Of course there is: its author is hands down the most ambitious poet of the century. Jonson had advised perplexed tongues; Herrick had unperplexed them; Edward Herbert had catalogued the kinds; every two-bit Cavalier had written of them, or in solicitation of them. The young Milton had indicated his flair for poetic kissing in a single dense couplet of his lyric "On Time": "Then long Eternity shall greet our bliss / With an individual kiss."[25] Milton's "individual" is often glossed as "undivided," "unending"; this kiss truly is, in Jonson's phrase, "beginning ever." But at the middle of the seventeenth century the word "individual" was gradually acquiring its modern sense of distinct selfhood, and in this respect Milton's undivided, ever-beginning kiss also aims at, and recognizes, individuality, the bliss of each distinct Christian soul.

Certainly there would be a kiss in *Paradise Lost*. To be sure, it was part of Milton's mythology about himself that his muse had no commerce with the sons of Belial, flown with wine, insolence, and kisses. Yet as he wrote Book 4 of *Paradise Lost*, he must have realized, with a certain private pleasure, that no fit reader would ever believe him. There would be a kiss. But what sort of kiss would it be? Milton was ready to play verse post office, and was in a mood to win. What was left, though? What sort of kiss would animate the greatest poem of the English Renaissance?

I think of Milton in Book 4 of *Paradise Lost* as a great film director. Satan has arrived. The camera has discovered Adam and Eve. It is time to shoot the kiss. In *Vertigo* Hitchcock had put James Stewart and Kim Novak on a revolving platform, and circled them with his camera turning in the opposite direction: vertiginous! He had filmed Grace Kelly and Cary Grant kissing as the fireworks shot off in *To Catch a Thief*. Spielberg had kept his lovers apart throughout *Indiana Jones and the Temple of Doom* because each was too proud to approach the other, then, in his final frames, neatly resolved the impasse by having Indiana, while standing his ground *and at the same time* expressing desire, wrap his trademark whip around her waist, and yank her to him for a kiss, topping it off with a shower from an elephant's trunk, that nose, or hose, or snake, or whip, or something else also in love with the heroine. Again, what was there left to do? How, moreover, would Adam and Eve, our great-grandparents, kiss? What would a kiss be so close to our creator, and so in tune with his designs?

Predictably, Milton once again rose to the occasion. Remembering the mythology of seasonal renewal in Vergil's *Georgics*, he found a "clean" schema for his kiss that had never, to my knowledge, been invoked in the conceit-happy love lyrics of the English Renaissance. Having introduced the human "Two" (4.288), "the loveliest pair / That ever since in love's imbraces met" (4.321–22), Milton proceeds to treat them as a grammarian would, and conjugates them. They walk together, eat together, talk together, then at last embrace:

> hee in delight
> Both of her Beauty and submissive Charms
> Smil'd with superior Love, as *Jupiter*
> On *Juno* smiles, when he impregns the Clouds
> That shed *May* Flowers; and press'd her Matron lip
> With kisses pure: (4.497–502)

Thomas Newton recognized that the simile had been stitched in between smiling and kissing: "the construction is *Adam smil'd with superior love, and press'd her matron lip*, the simile being understood as included in a parenthesis."[26] The parenthesis is also a conduit. Since *matron* signifies "A married woman considered as having expert knowledge in matters of childbirth, pregnancy, etc." (*OED* 2nd edn.), the schema of the simile is realized or brought to fruition in Eve's matronly reception of Adam's mouth, accepting his imprint as the paper does the press. His lips deliver the promise of his smile. The simile will intrude into the actual plot of the epic when we learn in Book 11 that Eve has in prefiguration of her maternal future "bred up with tender hand," and named, a bed of flowers (273–79). Milton's kiss, the kiss of Edenic sublimity, is the one and only example in the seventeenth-century lyric post office of Airmail Special Delivery Federal Express Super-Deluxe Same-Day Registered and Insured Mail-O-Gram: *the kiss that impregnates.*

This is on several accounts, I think you will agree, a most Miltonic kiss.[27] Redressing the decontextualization of his century, Milton restores the kiss to a narrative of consummation, which is where the day of Book 4 will end for Adam and Eve. Kissing, his simile implies, is subordinate to intercourse. But more importantly – and this is Milton's signature within the tradition of poetic love – intercourse itself is subordinate to impregnation, and both to marriage. From the viewpoint of *Paradise Lost*, the love tradition in its entirety is judged to have been an exercise in imaginative decontextualization, inasmuch as it treated love, by and large, outside the sphere of marriage. Milton celebrates "wedded Love" (4.750), "the Rites / Mysterious of connubial Love" (4.742–43) that take place in the bower of a "Nuptial Bed" (4.710). It is clearly part of the artistic agenda of the epic to charge the vocabulary of matrimony with great libidinal force, joining the luxuries of the lyric tradition to the spiritual dignity of marriage for the sake of creating a love poetry that advances beyond the first night of the epithalamion. Thus, in this most Miltonic kiss, a paternal lip impresses itself on a matron lip.

It has become fashionable to speak of Milton as the champion of a guilty secret named patriarchy, but few critics seem to realize how aggressively,

how libidinally, Milton sponsors old-style procreation. Sexual desire in
Paradise Lost is root and branch the creation of the family, the proliferation
of the human image, the image and likeness of God: Milton's is a breeder's
lust, the ambition that makes fathers fathers and mothers mothers. We
would expect no less in Eden, where sexuality and marriage have been
enjoined by divine commandment as fruitfulness and multiplication. That
we should be reminded of impregnation as we view this kiss is also of a
piece with the poet's sense of time. As always in Milton, the end is in the
origin; for example, the equivalent of an impregnating kiss in poetic form
might be the end of *Paradise Regained*, where everything is over, and yet
everything is now to begin. Milton's appreciation for the proleptic energy
coiled into beginnings can be observed, not only in his way with poetic
form, but in the metaphors of his self-dramatized authorship. The voice of
his invocations prepares itself to receive inspiration from the Spirit that

> from the first
> Wast present, and with mighty wings outspread
> Dove-like satst brooding on the vast Abyss
> And mad'st it pregnant: (1.19–21)

And so the omnific Word of the Old Testament Jupiter impregnated the
Juno of the vast abyss. In the beginning, as in Milton's representation of his
artistic strength, as in the kisses of Eden, the oral is the seminal.[28]

Psychoanalysts speak of "ego boundaries" and their "dissolution."
When teaching this material, I remind students of kissing, a fairly common
event in which we really do experience some melting of ego boundaries
and a sense of merger with another person. In Milton's kiss, this psychological or spiritual merger points toward the actual physical amalgamation of
the kissers in a child. Certain children, the father of psychoanalysis wrote,
suppose "that a baby is got by a kiss – a theory which obviously betrays the
predominance of the erotogenic zone of the mouth. In my experience,"
Freud went on, "this theory is exclusively feminine."[29] We have found
some confirmation for Freud's dangerous adverb "exclusively" in the
many non-impregnating kisses penned by male poets in the seventeenth
century. Then along comes Milton. The ideology of his Edenic kisses is
patriarchal, but their unconscious source is womanly, which is no doubt
why Milton alone in his century, a peculiar male poet whose strength
resides in equating his blindness with the womb of an internal woman,
could unearth the fantasy of an impregnating kiss.[30]

Adam and Eve are wholly entranced with each other. But the oral is the
seminal, and the poem looks ahead. Because his showpiece kisses enfold

impregnation, Milton's Edenic embraces reach toward us in lines of affiliation. The idea of this pair conceiving offspring is the idea of history coming our way.[31] We exist by virtue of hazards and contingencies. Grandpa had to go to Cleveland to get vaccinated, where he chanced to meet Grandma. But these are reimaginable contingencies: one might still exist if they had met another way. Readers open to affiliation with Milton's myth must be reminded, as Adam and Eve kiss, that the unreimaginable necessity in the human story that ends for the time being with us, together, now, is a long series of impregnations, as the Bible suggests in its inventories of begettings. The impregnating lust of the Edenic kiss engenders, or looks forward to engendering, the family of man, and the generation of this community among his readers enables Milton to resolve in our hearts, theological abstraction aside, the great vexations of the fall, death, evil's triumph, an apparently passive and unjustifiable God. When first introduced, Adam and Eve are better than we are, more lovely and more indulged. But the smiles and kisses glance ahead. The final passage of *Paradise Lost*, where we feel the bonds of the human family most profoundly, is the wisest thing Milton ever wrote about the problem of God's justification that preoccupied him almost from the beginning of his literary career. In this sense, too, the "kisses pure" represent Milton's poetic power – the silent or non-expository half, the better and manifesting half, of his great argument. Satan himself realizes that he beholds "The happier Eden" (4.507).

So the context woven about kissing in *Paradise Lost* could not be broader or more serious. Yet these "kisses pure" do after a fashion become decontextualized. Eve departs from the afternoon symposium because she prefers the matronly game of sweet reluctant amorous delay:[32]

> Her Husband the Relater she preferr'd
> Before the Angel, and of him to ask
> Chose rather; hee, she knew, would intermix
> Grateful digressions, and solve high dispute
> With conjugal Caresses, from his Lip
> Not Words alone pleas'd her.   (8.52–57)

Eve anticipates an intermixing of elevated subjects and kisses. Her mind produces a perfect image of carnal pleasure being refined in the direction of heavenly love: kisses aspire toward heaven in Eve's imagination; sexual pleasure so conceived is an aspect of animate materialism.

But what of the idea that kisses "solve high dispute"? Are kisses wise? To my mind it is not *altogether* condescending of Milton to have Eve think that conjugal caresses solve high dispute. They do, as all wedded lovers know, and in this poem they do: the epic's labor of justification ends with a couple walking hand in hand, looking for a new bower in which to kiss, conceive, parent, and rest. Kissing teaches that the "high disputes" about the design of the heavens in Book 8 really do not matter, as Raphael maintains and Adam concedes. Moreover, does not the "higher Argument" (9.42) of this entire poem almost come down to a kiss, to almost precisely that – the meaning and value of a kiss?

Cleopatra's may be the richest kisses in Renaissance literature, but Eve's are the most momentous. For she herself is destined to single them out, isolating the happier Eden from the rest of Eden. In Book 9 Eve feels distracted and diverted by the behavior we have witnessed at their first appearance, the inefficient looking and smiling (9.222); though she does not mention kisses, we know whereto those smiles tend. Conjugal caresses no longer solve high dispute, but occasion it, and the result is to give the devil his wish, "Eve separate" (9.422). Perhaps she feels anxious over undone work: in that case, the Catullan excellence of easy renewability has become kissing's defect, and the economy of caresses threatens to disturb the economy of garden maintenance (which will divide, after the fall, into male work and female domesticity). Perhaps, as is suggested by Eve's insistence on the justice, in principle, of being alone, the closeness of Adam in their imparadising arms engulfs and obliterates her. Perhaps it is a requirement of Milton's moral vision that real temptation occur in solitude, since the constraint of external observation makes it impossible to tell someone who is good because they do not wish to be seen from someone who constrains herself because she truly chooses the good. At any rate, Eve absents herself. Technically, it is no sin. But the question of what she can do by herself has supplanted the question of what they can do together, and this turning away rhymes ominously with her initial flight from Adam, and still more ominously with Satan's revulsion at the "Sight hateful" (4.505) of their embrace.

Strictly speaking, there are no more kisses in *Paradise Lost*. Yet as the snake approaches Eve, he "lick'd the ground whereon she trod" (9.526). This servitude of the mouth is one measure of her forthcoming lapse. As love dilates into sovereignty, the kiss also falls down. Conjugal caresses from the lip are traded for the groveling, prostrate kisses owed to tyrants. The Greek *proskynesis* (originally, "kissing towards") names the human and historical version of the snake's prostration before the divinity of Empress Eve; Alexander the Great tried without success to introduce this oriental practice into his court.[33] Thinking of Christian variations on such rituals of subjection, Donne wrote contemptuously of the descent of the kiss in Renaissance courts:

> Civilitie we see refin'd: the kiss
> Which at the face began, transplanted is,
> Since to the hand, since to th'imperial knee,
> Now at the Papal foot delights to be.[34]

One step further in this refinement and the deferential kiss, unable to close with any part of the august personage, can only touch the dirt she walks on. This, remembering one of Edward Herbert's designations, is a "kiss of might" indeed! Licking the ground is Satan's perverse and hypocritical deployment of the "Knee-tribute . . . prostration vile" (5.782) he would not pay to the Son in Heaven. It might also be Satan's mocking allusion to the devotion he used to render the Father: "who more than thou," Gabriel recalls, "Once fawn'd, and cring'd, and servilely ador'd / Heav'n's awful Monarch" (4.958–60)? At the fall in *Paradise Lost*, being loved – looked upon, smiled upon, kissed – passes into the pseudo-religious isolation of imperial vanity.

Milton adumbrates this movement from mutuality to aloneness to imaginative sovereignty in Book 4. For unlike Jonson's gender-effacing kisses in *The Celebration of Charis*, Milton's are unmistakably and systematically encoded with gender differences. Adam prints, Eve's matron lip receives. Adam inseminates, Eve conceives. Adam's "superior Love" bends down to Eve's "submissive Charms." Some readers of the epic labor mightily to preserve their belief that *Paradise Lost* represents a perfect Edenic innocence broken by the sin of Book 9. Fallen intonations lurk in the words that describe this innocence, but readers must cancel them with acts of moral reinvention. There is a good wantonness, a good errancy. The presence of submission in Edenic love constitutes the major test for this style of reading Milton's epic.

It is the snake in the happier Eden. No doubt, as some critics insist, Eve consents freely to her submission. Of course she does not consent to the necessity of this consent, but that would be tantamount to consenting to her creation, and nobody in Milton, as we learn from his portrait of Satan, comes into the world as their own idea. Inferiority, however, is an unruly idea. By inserting dominance and submission into the very seam or correspondence of his kiss, Milton releases an etiological speculation that leaps from these gender differences to the tyrannies of fallen politics. Satan and womankind have common ground. They both know submission, and submission cannot exist in such creatures without the desire to rule. What else does Milton show us when "superior" closes with "submissive"? The budding philosopher of kissing in Kierkegaard's *Either/Or* maintains that "a kiss comes nearer the ideal when a man kisses a girl than when a girl kisses a man. When in the course of years there has come about an indifference in this relation, then the kiss has lost its significance."[35] Its significance, to attempt a relatively unabrasive translation, is that men (usually, often, sometimes at least) want to express sexual desire and enjoy the feeling that women answer it, or better perhaps, surrender to it. Down the line from kissing to foreplay to intercourse there will be many occasions to ring changes on the master game of initiation and surrender. With regard to the fundamental assumption here, it really doesn't matter if the woman kisses the man. It wouldn't matter in *Paradise Lost* if a superior smiling Eve were to kiss a submissively charming Adam; as Adam himself confesses to Raphael, he often feels inferior to Eve. The point to keep in mind is that desire, as Milton and Kierkegaard and many others have represented it, is enmeshed in the polarity of dominance and submission.[36] The epic looks ahead. Cain is the first baby in Milton's proleptic kisses, and he brings with him what Claudius in *Hamlet* terms "the primal eldest curse" (3.3.37) of fratricide and familial division. Even as the unfallen couple embrace, the fleets are in the harbor. War – between woman and man, brother and brother, subject and tyrant, nation and nation – inhabits the middle, the political middle, of Milton's kisses.

This is a severe teacher. Do dominance and submission go all the way to the ground in human beings? As helpless infants we are thrust into the care of apparent gods. We are born under governments. We learn from teachers, and some of us go on to teach. We are employed. We worship. Freud emphasized the masters of the ego; Lacan wrote the master/slave dialectic into the genesis of the ego. Is there no kiss without a political middle? If not, are we prepared to give up the mathematics-inspired fantasy of perfect equality, concede that such an ideal, while it has inestimable value as a national political fiction, simply does not grip our personal lives, acknowledge the polarity that cleaves our desire, and try to imagine good superiorities, good submissions? These are hard questions, and Milton chose to introduce them to us on an unlikely, but on second thought brilliantly apt, occasion. Kissing can seem an oblivion. We close our eyes, our high disputes dissolve. Seventeenth-century poets in the Cavalier tradition surrendered to this oblivion, often distinguishing it from the fretful satisfactions of intercourse. Milton, even as he submits to their topos, will not let us forget intercourse, conception, family, worship, hierarchy, history, all.

The Petrarchan kisses of a Sidney are rich with desire, ambition, and frustration. Jonson's influential kisses have ardor, grace, and wit, as if they were the essence of lyric aspiration. Shakespeare's kisses measure the hyperbolic emotions of his large-spirited characters. But the "kisses pure" of John Milton, animate materialist, are the profoundest in our language, for they alone bear nature's power to create new human beings.

Other kisses delight. Milton's, after delighting us, lead us into age-old but ongoing arguments.

NOTES

1. Stephen Fallon, *Milton among the Philosophers: Poetry and Materialism in Seventeenth-Century England* (Ithaca, 1991), pp. 79–110.
2. The three authors of *Bright Essence* (Salt Lake City, 1971) are William B. Hunter, C. A. Patrides, and J. H. Adamson. Doing all a scholar can to inoculate Milton against Saurat-like constructions, Hunter no longer believes that Milton wrote *de doctrina*; see "The Provenance of *The Christian Doctrine*," *SEL* 32 (1992), 129–42.
3. Denis Saurat, *Milton, Man and Thinker* (New York, 1925), p. 294.
4. Maurice Kelley, *This Great Argument: A Study of Milton's De Doctrina Christiana as a Gloss upon Paradise Lost* (1941; rpt. Gloucester, MA, 1962), p. 126.
5. John Rumrich, *Matter of Glory: A New Preface to Paradise Lost* (Pittsburgh, 1987), p. 107.
6. Søren Kierkegaard, *Either/Or*, trans. D. F. Swenson and L. M. Swenson, 2 vols. (Princeton, 1971), vol. I, p. 411.
7. A still from this Edison Kinetograph, "The Kiss," may be found facing page 262 of Terry Ramsaye's *A Million and One Nights: A History of the Motion Picture Through 1925* (New York, 1964).
8. *Kisses*, ed. Lena Tabori (Secaucus, NJ, 1991), is a handsome book about movie kisses that prints the dialogue surrounding them.
9. *Introductory Lectures on Psycho-Analysis*, in James Strachey, ed., *The Standard Edition of the Complete Psychological Works of Sigmund Freud*, 24 vols. (London, 1953–64), vol. XVI, p. 322.
10. Othello's death remembers Romeo's "Thus with a kiss I die" (5.3.120).
11. *The Works of Christopher Marlowe*, ed. C. F. Tucker Brooke (Oxford, 1910), p. 565.
12. I discuss the comparison of kissing to intercourse in "Kiss Fancies in Robert Herrick," *George Herbert Journal* 14 (1990–91), 160–66.
13. *Astrophil and Stella*, sonnet 79, lines 12–13, in *The Poems of Sir Philip Sidney*, ed. W. A. Ringler (Oxford, 1962), p. 206.
14. *Caelica* XII ("I with whose colours Myra dress'd her head") in *The Selected Poems of Fulke Greville*, ed. Thom Gunn (Chicago, 1968), p. 59.
15. This is perhaps a deliberate reversal of Johannes Secundus's *Basia*, where the beloved bites the poet's tongue. A translation of this brief sequence of kiss lyrics, a key precedent for the English examples discussed in this essay, may be found in Fred R. Nichols, *An Anthology of Neo-Latin Poetry* (New Haven, 1979).

16. "Fragmentum Petronius Arbiter," in *Ben Jonson: The Complete Poems*, ed. George Parfitt (New Haven, 1975), p. 251.
17. Donne notes in "Sapho to Philaenis" that lesbian love, all kissing and touching, leaves no sign of finality, unlike "the tillage of a harsh rough man." For a closer analogue to Jonson's Pseudo-Petronius, see Campion's "Turne back, you wanton flyer," where the extended session of kissing (in high school, "making out") is figured as perfect agriculture: you give, you get, you sow, you reap. *Works*, ed. Percival Vivian (Oxford, 1966), pp. 9–10.
18. "Authors-Readers: Jonson's Community of the Same," *Representations* 7 (1984), 50.
19. *The Poems of Sir Walter Ralegh*, ed. Agnes Latham (Cambridge, MA, 1951), p. 20. Suggestively, the concluding proverb of this poem reappears at the end of Suckling's "Against Fruition I." See also Shakespeare, *Antony and Cleopatra* 1.1.15: "There's beggary in the love that can be reckoned."
20. Catullan examples are all drawn from Gordon Braden, "*Vivamus, mea Lesbia* in the English Renaissance," *ELR* 9 (1979), 199–224. The classical source for the infinite kissing of the Renaissance is Martial's competition with Catullus in *Epigrammata* 6.34. For a sacred parody of Catullan kisses, see Crashaw's "Prayer. An Ode" in *The Complete Poetry of Richard Crashaw*, ed. George Walton Williams (Garden City, NY, 1970), p. 144.
21. *Ben Jonson*, p. 132. For an extended discussion of *Charis*, see my "Kiss Fancies in Herrick," 161–64.
22. *Minor Poets of the Seventeenth Century*, ed. R. G. Howarth (London, 1966), p. 22. It seems clear that Herbert is imitating the "Tenth Kiss" of Johannes Secundus's *Basia*.
23. *The Poetical Works of Robert Herrick*, ed. L. C. Martin (Oxford, 1956), p. 282.
24. Thomas Clayton, ed., *Cavalier Poets* (Oxford, 1978), p. 144.
25. Here and elsewhere Milton's poetry is cited from *Complete Poems and Major Prose*, ed. Merritt Y. Hughes (New York, 1957).
26. Thomas Newton, ed., *Paradise Lost*, 2 vols. (London, 1749), vol. I, p. 267.
27. The mythological fancy here is that clouds are pregnant air, or, recalling from "L'Allegro" the genealogy of Mirth, "debonair." It would appear that Milton had been trying, Ixion-like, to produce this image in his early verse. "The Passion," that fragment above his years, breaks off with the false surmise that the poet's loud sorrows have "got a race of mourners on a pregnant cloud." The inspired springtime poet of Elegy 5 wanders, in his liquid rapture, through and in *vagas nubes*. The Petrarchan sigh of Sonnet 5 is an "ardent vapor," raining tears at night. On the barren mountains of the mirthful landscape "laboring clouds do often rest" ("L'Allegro," line 74). Finally, in the kiss of *Paradise Lost*, Milton delivers the metaphor in its full elated glory.
28. Thus Donne in his sermon on Psalms 212 ("Kiss the son, lest he be angry"): "In the Old Testament, at first, God kissed man, and so breathed the breath of life, and made him a man." Sermon 15 in *The Sermons of John Donne*, ed. George Potter and Evelyn Simpson, 10 vols. (Berkeley, 1952–63), vol. III, p. 320.
29. Freud, *Three Essays on Sexuality*, in the Standard Edition, vol. IX, p. 223.

30. I expand on this point in *The Sacred Complex: On the Psychogenesis of Paradise Lost* (Cambridge, MA, 1983), pp. 42, 44, 48–50, 72, 181, 184–86, 188–89; "The Irrational Coherence of *Samson Agonistes*," *Milton Studies* 22 (1987), 217–32; and "Gender and Confusion in Milton and Everyone Else," *Hellas* 2 (1991), 195–220. On the female side of Milton, see also James Grantham Turner, *One Flesh: Paradisal Marriage and Sexual Relations in the Age of Milton* (Oxford, 1987), pp. 306–07, and Michael Lieb, *Milton and the Culture of Violence* (Ithaca, 1994), pp. 84–86, 92–94, 97–99.

31. It might spoil the kiss altogether to dwell on the fact that their first-born will be Cain. But there is an element of tragedy, of violence foretold, in the simile, as I will suggest by the end of the chapter.

32. On the meaning of delay in the epic, see William Kerrigan and Gordon Braden, "Milton's Coy Eve: *Paradise Lost* and Renaissance Love Poetry," *ELH* 53 (1986), 27–51.

33. See J. R. Hamilton, *Plutarch, Alexander: A Commentary* (Oxford, 1969), pp. 150–53; Pierre Jonquet, *Alexander the Great and the Hellenistic World*, trans. M. R. Dobie (Chicago, 1975), pp. 75–76. In *Persian Wars*, trans. Francis R. B. Godolphin (New York, 1942), Herodotus remarks of the Persians: "When they meet each other in the streets, you may know if the persons meeting are of equal rank by the following token; if they are, instead of speaking, they kiss each other on the lips. In the case where one is a little inferior to the other, the kiss is given on the cheek; where the difference of rank is great, the inferior prostrates himself upon the ground" (p. 75). Herbert alludes to *proskynesis* in his ironic question about the fate of gravesite statuary: "What shall point out them, / When they shall bow, and kneel, and fall down flat / To kisse those heaps, which now they have in trust?" ("Church Monuments" in *The Works of George Herbert*, ed. F. E. Hutchinson [Oxford, 1941].) Appropriately enough, Milton has used one of the many etiological slots in his narrative to make Satan the originator of *proskynesis*. God's punishment for the snake is confinement to the dust, precisely the "prostration vile" Satan thought debasing in heaven.

34. "Loves Progress," lines 81–84, in John Donne, *The Elegies and the Songs and Sonnets*, ed. Helen Gardner (Oxford, 1966), pp. 16–19. In the sermon cited in note 27, Donne writes of the political kiss in biblical times: "This kisse was also in use, as *Symbolum subjectionis*, A recognition of sovereignty or power" (*Sermons*, vol. III, p. 321). In his preface to *Of the Laws of Ecclesiastical Polity*, Hooker remarks: "In the Apostles' times that was harmless, which being now revived would be scandalous; as their *oscula sancta*." *The Works of Mr. Richard Hooker*, ed. John Keble, 4 vols. (Oxford, 1836), vol. I, p. 198.

35. Kierkegaard, *Either/Or*, vol. I, p. 411.

36. On this point, see Turner, *One Flesh*, pp. 285–87.

PART III

Heresy and Community

CHAPTER 7

Licensing Milton's heresy

Stephen B. Dobranski

The only completely consistent people are the dead.

Aldous Huxley[1]

In *Areopagitica*, Milton singles out "books of controversie in Religion" as among the most dangerous because they spread an "infection" "most and soonest catching to the learned, from whom to the common people what ever is hereticall or dissolute may quickly be convey'd" (*CP* II: 519, 520). Milton's larger point is that Parliament's inability to extirpate such books – "likeliest to taint both life and doctrine" (*CP* II: 520) – demonstrates the futility of trying to enforce pre-publication licensing. He could not have anticipated that five years later as Secretary for Foreign Languages he would himself hold the post of licenser and be involved in the suppression of a "book of controversie in Religion," the heretical *Racovian Catechism*, whose antitrinitarianism was the focus of religious controversy during the late seventeenth century.

Biographers have taken pains to explain away such inconsistencies and reconcile Milton's argument against licensing in *Areopagitica* with his censorial duties as secretary under the Commonwealth. David Masson assures us that he can provide "an easy explanation, which will save Milton's consistency": he emphasizes Milton's "more honourable" responsibilities and downplays his licensing of a government newsbook, *Mercurius Politicus*, as merely a "friendly superintendence."[2] William Riley Parker is equally "confident that Milton's activities as licenser of a newsletter were altogether perfunctory," and Christopher Hill infers from Milton's apparent refusal to suppress *The Racovian Catechism* that the author's "service to the republic . . . seems to have been selective."[3]

This chapter challenges standard interpretations of Milton's activities as a censor in light of the tolerationist stance articulated in *Areopagitica* and questions the assumption of authorial autonomy that underpins attempts to resolve his inconsistency. While working for the government, Milton may have allowed his heretical religious opinions to influence some

139

of his decisions. But in emphasizing this possibility, critics have mistakenly posited a coherent set of beliefs for Milton and underestimated the influence of his historical circumstances. Instead, to understand Milton's work as licenser, and indeed any of his literary acts, we need to take into account the impact of the changing communities in which he was involved, especially the collaborative practice of textual production. Both heresy and authorship are community phenomena: heresy, as we have seen in the introduction, evolves naturally out of orthodoxy through a rational process; this chapter examines how authorship, too, is a complex, dynamic, cooperative process.

<h2>MILTON'S LICENSING</h2>

Any understanding that we can attain about Milton's licensing duties will of necessity be limited and uncertain, for a re-examination of surviving documentary records suggests how little we know about what Milton accomplished as licenser – and how our desire for his constancy has skewed our interpretations. We do not know whether Milton ever objected to specific passages in *Mercurius Politicus*, and if he refused to license the publication of other books during his tenure as secretary, those records also do not survive. The Stationers' *Register* and the Council's Order Books record what the government asked of Milton and what, in some cases, he performed, but we can only guess as to whether he accepted his duties earnestly, half-heartedly, or not at all. If biographers have taken liberties with the facts of Milton's secretaryship, the fault lies in their deductive methodology, by which they take for granted that Milton acted consistently and righteously and then interpret the documental evidence to fit their assumptions.

If we work inductively instead, the surviving records suggest that Milton worked more as a censor than a translator during the first years of his secretaryship. For over ten months, between March 17, 1650/51 and January 22, 1651/52, the name "Master Milton" is entered regularly as the licenser of *Mercurius Politicus* in the Stationers' *Register*. We also know that Milton licensed more than this newsbook: on December 16, 1649 an entry appears in the Stationers' *Register* "under the hand of Master Milton" for the *Historie entiere et veritable du Proces de Charles Stuart Roy d'Anglitere &c.* On October 6, 1651 another entry "under the hand of Master Milton" registers the most recent copy of John Rushworth and Samuel Pecke's newsbook, *The Perfect Diurnall*. According to the Council's Order Books, Milton prepared only seven letters and wrote two translations during his first year as a government employee; he found himself, for the most part, policing the papers of authors, printers, and booksellers – what Masson refers to as a "squalid, but perhaps necessary, business."[4] Although Milton was not acting as a censor in this regard, these responsibilities suggest his complicity in the government's attempts to silence its opponents by preventing seditious publications and seizing incriminating evidence.

On April 20, 1649, for example, the Council of State ordered that "the letters brought in by Mr. Watkins to be examined by Mr. Frost or Mr. Milton, to see if they contain anything concerning the exportation of prohibited goods" (1649: 100). In a similar entry on May 30, the government required "Mr. Milton to examine the papers found upon [John] Lee" (1649: 165), and on June 11, the Council ordered Milton and the Sergeant-at-Arms Edward Dendy to inspect "the papers of Mr. Small" and confiscate any that dealt with public matters (1649: 179).[5]

Similarly, as a government representative to the Stationers' Company, Milton frequently negotiated with printers and booksellers, and would have known of the Council's efforts to supervise and exploit the printing trade; indeed, acting on the government's behalf, he was complicit in at least some of these policies. When, for example, on January 8, 1649/50 the Council wished to have published a book "containing examinations of the bloody massacre in Ireland," it ordered "Mr. Milton to confer with some printers or stationers about the speedy printing of this book, and give an account of what he has done therein" (1649: 474).[6] Both the enactment of a new licensing law in 1649 and the Council's surviving orders and warrants concerning the book trade suggest that the government had made supervising the press a priority shortly after Milton's appointment. Perhaps his experience of having published sixteen books and his long acquaintance with various printers and booksellers influenced the Council in assigning Milton these responsibilities. Not long after Milton accepted his appointment his life-long friend Matthew Simmons became a printer for the Council of State. We may also detect Milton's influence in the Council's employment of the printer Thomas Newcomb, who in 1648 had married Ruth Raworth (the printer of Milton's 1645 *Poems*) and who worked with Milton on seven of his prose tracts between 1650 and 1660.

Certainly, the most well-known instance of Milton's official involvement with members of the book trade concerns *The Racovian Catechism*. On January 27, 1651/52, the Council of State issued a warrant for the arrest of the printer William Dugard and the seizure of a heretical, Socinian manifesto in his possession, *Catechesis Ecclesiarum quae in Regno Poloniae*, also commonly known as *The Racovian Catechism* (1652: 550).[7] The tract espoused a

religion based on strict and strenuous biblicism, but which also emphasized human reason for understanding scripture.[8] It advocated the separation of Church and State while vehemently denying the trinity – rejecting
both the preexistence and divinity of Christ – and objecting to the theory
that Christ's crucifixion atoned for human sin.

Milton's writings, in particular *de doctrina Christiana* and *Paradise Lost*,
suggest that he may have sympathized with the Socinians' antitrinitarian
theology. In *de doctrina*, Milton cites "the plain and exhaustive doctrine of
the one God" (*CP* VI: 214) and in his epic, he refers to the "Only begotten
Son" not as one in being with God, but as the "first" of all God's "Creation"
(3.80; 383).[9] Critics have suggested that in principle, too, Milton supported
heretical sects like the Socinians, for in *Of True Religion*, published a year
before he died, Milton advocated the toleration of all Protestant schisms,
specifically "Anabaptists, Arians, Arminians, & Socinians" (*CP* VIII: 421,
437).

According to a manuscript report by the Dutch ambassador Leo de
Aitzema, Milton may have even licensed *The Racovian Catechism*. Aitzema
made the following observations on February 24, 1651/52, shortly after his
arrival in England:

There was recently printed here the Socinian *Racovian Catechism*. This was frowned
upon by the Parliament; the printer says that Mr. Milton had licensed it; Milton,
when asked, said Yes, and that he had published a tract on that subject, that men
should refrain from forbidding books; that in approving of that book he had done
no more than what his opinion was.[10]

Scholars have accordingly concluded that Milton remained true to his
antitrinitarian theology and tolerationalist principles, and must not have
taken seriously his duties as licenser: in approving a heretical pamphlet, he
was openly disregarding the government's interests in favor of his own
beliefs.

Acceptance of Aitzema's claim that Milton licensed *The Racovian
Catechism*, however, poses some logistical problems. Among the govern-
ment's surviving papers, Milton's name appears only once in connection
with the tract. On April 2, 1652, Gilbert Millington spoke before
Parliament on behalf of a committee appointed by the House to examine
the catechism: Millington reported that the committee had heard Dugard's
"Considerations humbly presented" and his "humble Petition."[11] The
committee had also questioned Henry Walley, Clerk of the Stationers'
Company; Francis Gouldman, an editor and lexicographer; and John
Milton, Secretary for Foreign Languages.

The committee had examined, too, "a Note under the Hand of Mr. *John Milton*, of the 10th of *August* 1650," which could represent Milton's official license of the catechism. But according to the Stationers' *Register*, the book had been entered on November 13, 1651, fifteen months after Milton's note.[12] If Milton's note did contain his formal approval as licenser, the book's owner would not likely have waited more than a year to have the text registered. The longest delay between licensing and registration that I have so far discovered from this period is only five months.[13] Whatever its nature, Milton's note must have played a minor role in the government's proceedings: Millington's committee did not see fit to include a copy of the note among the official resolutions that it presented to the House, nor did the committee mention it or Milton in these resolutions. Instead, the committee concentrated on the other three men, resolving that only "the several Examinations, and Re-examinations, of Mr. *Walley*, Mr. *Dugard*, and Mr. *Goldman* [*sic*], be . . . offered to the House."[14]

Milton thus seems to have suffered no consequences for his involvement in the matter. Acting on the committee's findings, Parliament declared *The Racovian Catechism* "blasphemous, erroneous, and scandalous" and ordered the sheriffs of London and Middlesex to seize all the printed copies of the book to be burnt publicly in London and Westminster. Dugard, who had been arrested in 1649 for printing the first edition of *Eikon Basilike* as well as Salmasius's *Defensio Regia*, was formally found guilty along with Gouldman "of Printing and Publishing this blasphemous and scandalous Book." Milton, however, continued to work as Secretary for Foreign Languages.

Moreover, although Milton's name does disappear in the Stationers' *Register* as licenser of the *Mercurius Politicus* on January 29, 1651/52, we cannot assume that the Council relieved him of his licensing duties because of *The Racovian Catechism*. Milton may have stopped licensing *Politicus* after he went blind or because he was preoccupied with writing his defense tracts. Perhaps Milton became so immersed in supervising the newsbook that he began acting more as a co-author than a censor. Most likely, because John Rushworth's name disappears a few days later on February 2, from the licensing of another government newsbook, *The Perfect Diurnall*, Milton and he continued licensing their respective weeklies, but the practice of recording the licensers' names temporarily ceased.

In order to preserve a consistent authorial identity for Milton, we may hypothesize that as secretary he was willing to license political works that threatened the Commonwealth, but as a defender of Christian liberty and holder of unorthodox opinions, could not bring himself to suppress a heretical religious pamphlet like the catechism. This explanation, however, imposes an artificial distinction between seventeenth-century political and religious writings. Although the Printing Act passed in September 1649 focused primarily on political publications, the Commonwealth government tended to label as "heretical" or "blasphemous" any opinion or action that might undermine its interests or authority.[15] As B. Reay notes, the royalist party "stood for stability and the preservation of hierarchy in both church and state," and, at the opposite end of the political spectrum, the Levellers also believed that religious and political liberty could not be separated.[16] According to one contemporary writer, Socinians in particular posed a political threat: they were "not to be suffered in any *State*, for they will not shew any obedience or respect to Magistrates; they say they have no power to punish hainous offenders in time of peace, nor have they power to defend themselves or the people by the Sword, in time of Warres."[17]

The incident of *The Racovian Catechism* raises the intriguing possibility that Milton commented on other books in other handwritten notes that no one recorded elsewhere: if the Council had not arrested Dugard for printing the catechism, we would not know of Milton's involvement – whatever it may have been. I am not arguing that Milton did *not* approve the Racovian tract, but with so little evidence corroborating Aitzema's report, we ought to hesitate before using the episode to judge Milton's activities as licenser. J. Milton French, who reproduces the report in *The Life Records of John Milton*, notes that he has not seen the original manuscript held in the Dutch Archives in The Hague and admits that its authenticity "is not certain."[18]

In light of entries in the Stationers' *Register* and the Council's Order Books, we know that Milton participated in the government's regulation of the book trade to a greater extent than critics commonly recognize. Did Milton, a government licenser and searcher who had represented the Council in its dealings with the Stationers' Company, suddenly tell the government that it "should refrain from forbidding books"? If we want to believe that he acted in accordance with his argument in *Areopagitica* and approved the catechism, then we need to acknowledge that he was contradicting his more recent duties as employee of the Commonwealth. He was also contradicting the implication of *Areopagitica*'s logic, that "books of controversie in Religion" were especially dangerous and thus ought to be censored. If, on the other hand, we accept that Milton actively assisted the government in regulating the book trade, then we need to admit, despite biographers' claims to the contrary, that Milton's behavior in 1649 seems to have been "un-Areopagitic."[19]

THE CASE FOR INCONSISTENCY

The possibility that Milton licensed *The Racovian Catechism* has appealed to critics precisely because it enables us to reconcile *Areopagitica*'s argument against pre-publication censorship with Milton's duties as secretary under the Commonwealth. Biographers tend to frame discussions of Milton's licensing with this question: how could such an eloquent critic of censorship come to work as a government censor? If Milton approved a tract that the government later deemed "blasphemous, erroneous, and scandalous," we can console ourselves with the fact that he at least remained an uncompromising freethinker. While working for the government, in other words, Milton subverted policies with which he disagreed.

We need to remember that *Areopagitica* did not advocate complete freedom of expression. Milton accepted that if a book "prov'd a Monster . . . it was justly burnt, or sunk into the Sea" (*CP* II: 505). He also took for granted that some writings ought to be suppressed: Catholic books, "open superstition," and any text "which is impious or evil absolutely either against faith or maners" (*CP* II: 565). But even with these qualifications, *Areopagitica* had roundly criticized pre-publication censorship. Describing the exhaustion and dissatisfaction of the first Parliamentarian licensers, Milton predicted "that no man of worth, none that is not a plain unthrift of his own hours is ever likely to succeed them." According to Milton, "we may easily foresee what kind of licensers we are to expect hereafter, either ignorant, imperious, and remisse, or basely pecuniary" (*CP* II: 530). If a licenser tried to execute his duties fairly, Milton argued, pre-publication censorship would still hinder the discovery of truth: a licenser's "very office, and his commission enjoyns him to let passe nothing but what is vulgarly receiv'd already" (*CP* II: 534).[20]

In a recent essay on *Areopagitica* and Milton's licensing, Abbe Blum interprets this apparent contradiction as evidence that Milton advocated "an ideal of authorial independence" while paradoxically depending on "the idea of prescriptive authority."[21] The usefulness of Blum's reading lies in part in her observation that readers expect Milton to have behaved consistently. We want to believe that the poet remained true to his personal principles and acted in accordance with *Areopagitica*'s democratic impulses. Critics who treat *Areopagitica* as a manifesto of individual liberty have concluded that Milton must not have taken seriously his duties as licenser, and critics who emphasize *Areopagitica* as a conditional argument against censorship have deduced that Milton as secretary acted within its parameters. The assumption of an autonomous author underpins both readings: in interpreting Milton's choices, scholars have turned, not to his changing historical situation, but to Milton himself.

The Milton I am describing is heretical for defying our perception of him as independent thinker and deviating from our traditional understanding of what it means to be an author. Modern criticism's strategy for defining the author requires the resolution of inconsistencies: the notion of the author, as Michel Foucault has observed, "constitutes a principle of unity in writing" and "serves to neutralize the contradictions that are found in a series of texts."[22] According to this theory, Milton was not behaving like an author from 1644–49, having first written against pre-publication censorship and then agreeing to help the government enforce its licensing policy. Even Milton's argument against censorship in *Areopagitica* is unauthorial because, as we have seen, it lacks conceptual coherence. More than one reader on finishing the tract has concluded that Milton objected to censorship but favored censoring anyone who disagreed with him.[23]

We need not resolve these contradictions, however, to understand Milton's actions and writings. On the contrary, we can use these inconsistencies to see beyond the theoretical construction of "the author" and glimpse the real person, John Milton, operating within his specific historical situation. The relationship between *Areopagitica* and Milton's responsibilities as licenser exceeds the self-contained, religio-political philosophy that critics have ascribed to him; the pamphlet and the secretaryship are connected, not by the choices of a single author, but by the complex circumstances of their production. Human beings, as Montaigne reminds us, "are all patchwork, and so shapeless and diverse in composition that each bit, each moment, plays its own game. And there is as much difference between us and ourselves as between us and others." He advises that the "surest thing . . . would be to trace our actions to the neighboring circumstances."[24]

The category of "the author" represents a theoretical, still point that critics have conveniently created out of a writer's circumstances, out of the collaborative processes of book-writing and book-making – much like the eye that forms amidst the swirling activity of a hurricane.[25] To believe that Milton, or any writer, remained constant in all things is to hold him up to a standard of behavior that no one can realize. To expect Milton to have behaved predictably, especially while secretary under the Commonwealth, is to underestimate how such a politically tumultuous period must have affected his choices.

Even before Milton's tenure as secretary, an abundance of religious books was circulating in London. Writing during the 1630s, Robert Burton had complained that "There be so many books in that kind, so many commentaries, treatises, pamphlets, expositions, sermons, that whole teams of oxen cannot draw them."[26] With the assembling of the Long Parliament in 1640 the number of publications skyrocketed; part of this increase can be attributed to works once considered unpublishable that suddenly began to appear in print. The elimination of the Courts of Star Chamber and High Commission in July 1641, along with Parliament's preoccupation with what it termed "present distractions," left printers virtually free to print what and how they wished.[27] According to D. F. McKenzie's provisional estimate, 867 items appeared in 1640; in the following three years, 1,850, 2,968, and 1,495 items were published, respectively.[28]

It is within this context that we need to read *Areopagitica* and Milton's specific warning about "books of controversie in Religion." On the one hand, he is acknowledging in 1644 that the book trade would benefit from limited governmental regulation as a safeguard from inaccurate reprints in small, cheaply made editions and as a protection for printers against the unlawful publishing of their copies.[29] On the other hand, his endorsement of post-publication licensing may represent a response to the trade's chaotic freedom and the increased availability of texts that he considered "impious or evil absolutely." In *The Humble Remonstrance* (April, 1643), with which Milton was likely familiar, Stationers had complained that the government's neglect of the printing trade would result in an abundance of "errors and heresies," as in Poland and the Netherlands "where the poyson of *Socinus* and *Arminius* spreads unregarded."[30]

The collapse of ecclesiastical control over the book trade in 1641 allowed heretical opinions like Socinianism to be published more widely – although it mostly increased anxiety about the spread of such so-called anti-Christian ideas. During the first part of the seventeenth century, Socinianism had gained popularity in England, arriving from Poland via Holland and, as Hill explains, gradually merging with the "indigenous radical tradition."[31] In 1643, the year before *Areopagitica*'s warning that the "infection" caused by heretical works was "most and soonest catching to the learned," a scholar had been expelled from Oxford for his antitrinitarian translations. Francis Cheynell in *The Rise, Growth, and Danger of Socinianisme* (Wing C3815), published the same year, complains about the "Art and care" that was "used to propagate the Arminian errours in England" (F2r). He notes, for example, that the Archbishop of Canterbury "did pretend to crush this cockatrice of *Socinianisme*," but fears "his Canon was ordained for concealing, rather than suppressing" this heresy (F1r).

Citing "a great complaint of late that men are turned Atheists" (G4r), Cheynell blames Socinians who, he claims, "proceed in a destructive way; now destroy all Religion" (H2r) and "labour to pick up Christianity by the roots, and overthrow the very foundation of Religion" (D4v).

Although Cromwell and the Commonwealth government seem to have been more tolerant of Socinianism, Cromwell in principle believed that religious toleration should not be "stretched so farr as to countenance them who deny the divinity of our Saviour, or to bolster any blasphemous opinions contrary to the fundamentall verities of religion."[32] The Heresy Ordinance of 1648 and Blasphemy Act of 1650 accordingly included sentences of imprisonment, death, and banishment for anyone who endorsed various heretical opinions; the Ordinance of 1648 specifically concentrated on antitrinitarianism.[33] Yet, these acts were enforced selectively and, it seems, their complicated stipulations never carried out systematically.[34] In the case of the Socinian author and leader, John Biddle, for example, Cromwell intervened to mitigate his punishment, despite numerous complaints about Biddle's disputations and pamphleteering.[35]

Even if Milton did approve *The Racovian Catechism* he was thus not opposing the Commonwealth government's *de facto* policy of toleration. As an employee of the government, he was already working (to borrow Milton's expression from the antiprelatical controversy) "not as mine own person, but as a member incorporate into that truth wherof I was perswaded" (*CP* I: 871). Perhaps Milton's announcement to Parliament that he approved *The Racovian Catechism*, as reported by Aitzema, was a conscious attempt by the poet/secretary to create the perception of himself as an independent freethinker. It is also pleasing to speculate whether the incident of *The Racovian Catechism* served as a catalyst for some of Milton's still inchoate heretical opinions – just as "the acute and distinct *Arminius*" had been "perverted" when called upon to refute a heretical "namelesse discours" (*CP* II: 519–20).

In an attempt to buttress the argument for Milton's consistency, biographers have sometimes emphasized the resemblance between *Areopagitica* and the Printing Act of 1649. Parker, for example, has suggested that this act – passed six months after Milton's appointment as secretary – reduced the scope of the government's licensing system in accordance with Milton's earlier argument. Milton may have nominally served as licenser, in other words, but he still objected to pre-publication censorship and would have helped to draft the new, more lenient legislation.

The new law, however, actually represented an attempt to toughen the previous ordinances. Parker, following Masson's lead, claims that under

Milton's guidance the government "technically abandoned licensing of books," but according to my count, the total number of books entered in the Stationers' *Register* rose dramatically after the new law's passage.[36] By establishing the Council of State as the final authority in the regulation of printing, the act tried to stiffen the government's policy: it granted Cromwell, as Cyprian Blagden notes, the "administrative bite" that Archbishop Laud had once provided.[37]

Also, the government's policy for regulating the book trade contradicts the assumption of an autonomous author that informs arguments for Milton's consistency. Among its specific conditions, the Act of 1649 distributed responsibility for a printed text among authors, printers, and licensers. It not only required that every "Book, Pamphlet, sheet or sheets of News or Occurrences whatsoever" be licensed, and that the "Author's name ... or at least the Licensers names where Licenses are required" appear on the title-page, but it also specified that printers enter into a bond of £300, which they would forfeit if they produced unlawful documents.[38] Parliament explicitly acknowledged the collaborative process of textual production: it ordered that only licensed books "shall henceforth be printed, bound, stitched or put to sale" and "no person whatsoever shall compose, write, print, publish, sell or utter, or cause to be made, written, printed or uttered, any Book or Pamphlet, Treatise, sheet or sheets of News whatsoever, unless Licensed."

The new act's stipulation that "the Printers or Authors name bee entered that they may bee forth coming if required" does indeed echo Milton in *Areopagitica*. But, contrary to Parker's claim, the idea is neither an original nor major point in that pamphlet. When in *Areopagitica* Milton accepts "that no book be Printed, unlesse the Printers and the Authors name, or at least the Printers be register'd," he paraphrases the Ordinance of 1642, what he calls "that Order publisht next before this" (*CP* II: 569).[39]

Any influence that Milton may have exerted on the Printing Act of 1649 does not suggest, therefore, an abiding objection to pre-publication licensing, but instead implies that he, too, believed a book's various creators ought to be held accountable for their work. Whereas Foucault has claimed that texts were historically "assigned real authors ... only when the author became subject to punishment and to the extent that his discourse was considered transgressive," seventeenth-century licensing laws suggest that a book had more than one "real author."[40] All the people who helped to compose and publish a text – including licensers – could be punished for their respective contributions. According to the Ordinance of September 30, 1647, for example, the author, printer, and bookseller were legally accountable for an unlicensed book: the law stipulated that the author would be fined 40s. or be imprisoned for 40 days; the printer, 20s. or 20 days; the bookseller, 10s. or 10 days. Hawkers or mercuries of illegal books would be "whipt as a Common Rogue" and have their wares confiscated.[41]

Returning to the government's proceedings concerning *The Racovian Catechism*, we recall that the official resolutions focused on "the several Examinations, and Re-examinations, of Mr. *Walley*, Mr. *Dugard*, and Mr. *Goldman*." By formally finding guilty the printer Dugard and the editor/lexicographer Gouldman, Parliament was punishing these two men as the tract's "authors." The government was recognizing that authorship required the cooperation of various people and that books were not the product of an isolated individual operating autonomously.

COLLABORATION AND SELF-PROMOTION

Milton's inconsistency exposes the fallacy of authorial autonomy by showing that historical circumstances influence authors' choices. His specific decision to serve as licenser, on the other hand, points up the collaborative nature of the book trade. The "essential fact" is that literary works, as Jerome McGann has observed, "are not produced without arrangements of some sort" and must be "trained" through a "series of interventions" into their final shape.[42]

While working for the Commonwealth, Milton mostly collaborated with the Council of State and had to conform with the wishes of its forty-one members. When, for example, they asked him to prepare an official, Latin version of a paper that the Council had begun drafting in English, Milton could determine the document's style, preferring, as Leo Miller notes, "what he considered purist classical Latin" or his own "original neo-classical neo-Latin." Milton's colleagues, however, reserved the right to edit his work, often inserting new terminology in the final, official versions.[43] One can imagine these same men doctoring the final versions of the original pamphlets that Milton produced for the government. According to Milton's nephew Edward Phillips, Milton as secretary had to write not "his own Sense, but what was dictated to him by his Superiors," and Milton himself draws attention in his prose tracts to his status as a government agent.[44] He explains in *Eikonoklastes* that "I take it on me as a work assign'd rather, then by me chos'n or affected" (*CP*III: 339), and claims that he wrote *Pro Populo Anglicano Defensio Secunda* "Because I was so ordered . . . publicly by those whose authority ought to have weight with me; otherwise, I would hardly have put my hand to the task" (*CP* IV: 767). Even in his earlier pamphlets, Milton suggests that he had to be persuaded to write them. He frames *Of Reformation* (1641) and *Of Education* (1645) as responses to his friends' requests, and in *Areopagitica* (1644) he claims that he has been "loaded" with "entreaties and perswasions" to speak to Parliament about removing pre-publication licensing (*CP* II: 539).

But as an employee of the Commonwealth, Milton became formally and more thoroughly engaged in a cooperative process. While secretary, he shared responsibility with the Council of State for the pamphlets that he wrote, and as licenser had to accept partial responsibility for the books that he approved. When the Council ordered Milton to oversee the weekly publication of the *Mercurius Politicus*, he worked with the writer Marchamont Needham so as to ensure that the tract did not contain anything injurious to the Council, army, or Parliament.[45] Although a government-sponsored newsbook posed little threat politically, the two men seem to have developed, in the context of their prescribed duties, a mutually beneficial alliance of opportunity and interest.

Many of the lead editorials in *Mercurius Politicus* are based, as J. Milton French has demonstrated, on excerpts from Needham's *The Case of the Common-Wealth of England* (1650; Wing N376) and another book attributed to him, *The Excellencie of a Free-State* (1656; Wing N388).[46] For the issues published between September 19, 1650 through August 5, 1652, French has identified the pages from which most of the editorials originate. Although these discoveries limit Milton's involvement with the *Politicus*, many of these editorials contain extensive emendations: whole paragraphs are added or reorganized, phrases edited, and other sections omitted entirely; some editorials paraphrase only a few lines from Needham's other works. The editorials that appeared in *Politicus* account for less than thirty-five of the ninety-four pages in *The Case of the Common-Wealth*. Among those passages from *Common-Wealth* not reproduced in the newsbook are Needham's entire first chapter in Part I, "That Governments have their Revolutions and fatall Periods" (B1r-B3r) as well as his entire fourth chapter in Part II, "Concerning the Levellers" (K3r-L4r). Some of these omissions could represent Milton's intervention on the government's behalf: the Council, for example, would surely not want to have recognized the prospect of its own "fatal period." That twenty-eight editorials appear to be wholly original to *Mercurius Politicus* leaves plenty of opportunity for Milton to have contributed ideas to the tract; twenty-three of these were published during Milton's known tenure as licenser.

We should not assume that any or all of the changes to the newsbook represent Milton's influence: many of the views in the newsbook are political commonplaces that could have been written by Milton, Needham, or anyone else who supported the Commonwealth. Except for the period during which Milton's name appears in the Stationers' *Register*, we also cannot pinpoint when Milton served as licenser of the newsbook – perhaps as early as September 19, 1650 and/or as late as August 12, 1652. But the fact remains that the material published in Needham's books and the material published in *Mercurius Politicus* fall far short of a one-to-one correspondence. Who better to edit the text for the Council of State than the man under whose hand the book was weekly licensed? French concludes that the *Politicus* and other newsbooks were "vulgar little ... petty things not worth a serious thought."[47] He is suggesting, it seems, that a Great Author such as Milton – the autonomous poet who remained consistent in all things – would not have deigned to participate in the government's propaganda, and he interprets the surviving evidence accordingly. But such deductive reasoning, as in the case of *The Racovian Catechism*, ignores the collaborative process of authorship and prevents us from understanding Milton's possible choices within their specific historical environment.

Yet, if French and other critics have wrongly emphasized Milton's autonomy in discussing his licensing duties, the blame lies at least in part with Milton. Throughout his career, Milton forged an authorial persona in print, as if inviting readers to organize his poems and pamphlets according to his sense of them. He offers provocative, autobiographical digressions in *The Reason of Church-Government* (1642), *An Apology against a Pamphlet* (1642), and *Defensio Secunda* (1654), and he continues to construct a narrative of his poetic progress in other works such as the *Poems* (1645; 1673) and *Pro Populo Anglicano Defensio* (1651). In *Defensio Secunda*, for example, Milton includes an annotated bibliography that begins to interpret his accomplishments for us: he qualifies his intentions in *The Tenure of Kings and Magistrates* and drawing up his writings into neat categories, defines his purpose in works like *Areopagitica* and his divorce pamphlets (*CP* IV: 624–27).

When discussing Milton's licensing, we should note that the *Mercurius Politicus* also helped to construct Milton's persona as an independent author: beginning in January 1650/51 through January 1651/52, it described favorably the continental reception of his *Pro Populo Anglicano Defensio*.[48] A "very victorious Reply to *Salmasius* is now in motion in the Presse," teases the first advertisement in a report from Leyden, and toward the end of the year *Politicus* continues to chronicle the conflict: "Miltons

Reply lies as a raw indigested gobbet upon his [Salmasius's] stomack." Hardly providing an objective account, the *Politicus* recasts potentially damaging news about Milton's book being burnt in Toulouse and Paris ("for fear of making State-heretiques") into a victory for its author: "the Court, in burning the Book, will make it a Martyr, whose ashes will be scattered far and wide, and the Cause and Book be more inquisitively desired."[49]

Just as Milton had used the antiprelatical controversy to meditate on his literary aspirations, as licenser he once again found that his public responsibilities and personal interests dovetailed. Like the biographical comments in the *Poems* that present the texts in terms of their author, the reports in *Politicus* use Milton's identity as an organizing principle: they cast a political conflict in easily understandable, human terms – Milton versus Salmasius, a David versus a Goliath.[50]

Serving as licenser, Milton could bolster his personal reputation while simultaneously advancing the Commonwealth's. On the one hand, Milton was cooperating with Council members, amanuenses, secretaries, printers, booksellers, ambassadors, journalists, and informants. On the other hand, his efforts within this network were directed toward short-circuiting the larger collaborative practices of the London book trade. Milton thus benefited from a social process of production, but he did so while working for a government that hindered the free trade of ideas.

Both Milton and the Commonwealth government depended on this paradoxical conjunction of cooperation and censorship in creating themselves. Through the efforts of its several agents – including Milton – the Council of State struggled to stifle dissension while promoting a favorable image of the Commonwealth. The government not only confiscated the papers of suspicious authors and stationers, but tracts like *Eikonoklastes*, *Articles of Peace*, and Milton's first two defenses also represent an integral part of its efforts to gain respect and combat dissenting opinions. While pursuing the suppression of heretical and seditious books and pamphlets, the Council turned to its secretaries to defeat rhetorically any arguments that its licensers and searchers had failed to extirpate.

Whereas the Council constructed itself as a righteous and just form of government, Milton in helping to suppress his detractors constructed himself as a righteous and independent author. When ideas that Milton endorsed were attacked in the press, Milton as secretary now had the authority to suppress the attackers – men like William Prynne, whom the Council apprehended on June 25, 1650 "for seditiously writing and practising against the commonwealth," and another of Milton's detractors,

Clement Walker, whose books and papers the Council ordered Milton to search following Walker's arrest on October 24, 1649.[51]

Our expectations of Milton's consistency are thus predicated on a theory of autonomy that Milton helped to fabricate – not by acting independently, but, paradoxically, by cooperating with Needham, the Council of State, and other government agents. Even the placement of his autobiographical digressions ought to strike us as curious: in 1654 Milton writes about himself in the middle of a public, international document, commissioned by the republic for political reasons.[52] The obvious authorial perspective that Milton's texts conjure emerges through a collaboration, both in the act of writing and in the books' material creation. If there is consistency in his work as licenser, it is this tension between cooperation and self-promotion – not his advocacy of a free press nor even his commitment to heretical religious ideas.

Milton was, of course, no Marchamont Needham, whose zigzagging, political allegiances exemplify the extremes of authorial inconsistency: he first sympathized with the Presbyterians, then with the Royalists, then with the Independents, and late in life he wrote on behalf of Charles II. Nor did Milton ever make an about-face of the magnitude of writers like Donne or Dryden. Yet, we ought not to take for granted or exaggerate Milton's constancy. In using his antitrinitarianism to gloss his government licensing duties, we may oversimplify how and when he came to accept such heretical opinions. During the early 1640s, Milton still seems to have believed in the trinity: arguing that not everyone who suffers for religion is a martyr, he specifically cites Arians and Pelagians, whom, he says, "we take ... for no true friends of *Christ*" (*CP* I: 533–4). As late as 1649 – two years before the entrance of *The Racovian Catechism* in the Stationers' *Register* – he was still referring publicly to the "*infections* of Arian and Pelagian *Heresies*" (*CP* III: 507; my emphasis). The challenge facing scholars when reading Milton's works is to account accurately for such necessary and normal rethinkings, revisions, and gradual realizations.

Milton's licensing reminds us of the license we too often take in treating him as a category of one within English literary history. To posit an autonomous author in reading Milton's poems and pamphlets robs us of their rich complexity; to assume that he remained constant in all things prevents us from understanding the inconsistencies in his life and from appreciating the man, John Milton, participating in a process of collaborative authorship and adapting to his changing historical situation.

NOTES

1. Aldous Huxley, "Wordsworth in the Tropics," *Do What You Will* (London, 1929), p. 125.
2. David Masson, *The Life of John Milton*, 7 vols. (1877–96; rpt. New York, 1946), vol. III, p. 434; vol. IV, p. 326.
3. William Riley Parker, *Milton: A Biography*, 2 vols. (Oxford, 1968), p. 394; Christopher Hill, *Milton and the English Revolution* (London, 1977), p. 184.
4. Masson, *Life*, vol. IV, p. 155. All references to the proceedings of the Council of State are taken from the *Calendar of State Papers, Domestic Series*, ed. Mary Anne Everett Green, 13 vols. (London, 1874–86). For the reader's convenience, I cite specific volumes of Green's edition according to their year, followed by the page number.
5. We find further evidence of Milton's surveillance work in the Council's State Papers on June 23, 1649, October 24, 1649, November 21, 1649, February 2, 1650, May 6, 1650, May 15, 1650, August 14, 1650, and July 9, 1653. Milton's duties in this regard apparently decreased as his secretaryship proceeded.
6. Similar entries occur in the Council's Order Books on December 23, 1650, March 5, 1650/51, and July 20, 1652.
7. *Catechesis Ecclesiarum quae in Regno Poloniae* (London, 1649; Wing C1465): see Thomason Collection, British Museum, E. 1391.
8. See H. John McLachlan, *Socinianism in Seventeenth-Century England* (London, 1951), pp. 9–17.
9. Citations of Milton's poetry are taken from *Complete Poems and Major Prose*, ed. Merritt Y. Hughes (New York, 1957).
10. J. Milton French, ed., *The Life Records of John Milton*, 5 vols. (New Brunswick, 1949–58), vol. III, p. 206. According to Aitzema's (gregorian) calendar, he recorded these remarks on March 5, 1652.
11. This and all subsequent references to the Parliament's proceedings are taken from vol. VII, *The Journals of the House of Commons* (August 15, 1651 to March 16, 1659), pp. 86, 113–14.
12. We do not know whether the entry for *The Racovian Catechism* named a specific licenser, for the Council had it canceled two days after issuing the warrant for Dugard's arrest. A note in the margin of the Stationers' *Register* reads, "This Racovian Catech is Crost out by the consent & desire of Master Dugard 29° Jan. 1651[/52]."
13. The delay occurs with a book by Peter White entitled *A Memorable Seafight* (Wing W1799A): the book appears in the Stationers' *Register* on August 9, 1649; it was licensed five months earlier on March 6.
14. The House had granted the committee for examinations the "Power to send for Persons, Papers, Witnesses." Milton may have qualified as a member of this last category, for the only other entry recorded in the Stationers' *Register* on November 13, 1651 (the date of the catechism's registration) was a copy of *Mercurius Politicus*, licensed by Milton.
15. See "An Act against Unlicensed and Scandalous Books and Pamphlets, and for better regulating of Printing," *Acts and Ordinances of the Interregnum, 1642–1660*, ed. C. H. Firth and R. S. Rait, 3 vols. (London, 1911), vol. II, pp. 245–54.

16. B. Reay, "Radicalism and religion in the English Revolution: an introduction," in J. F. McGregor and B. Reay, eds., *Radical Religion in the English Revolution* (Oxford, 1984), pp. 1–21; D. M. Wolfe, ed., *Leveller Manifestoes of the Puritan Revolution* (New York, 1944).

17. Francis Cheynell, *The Rise, Growth, and Danger of Socinianisme* (London, 1643; Wing C3815), sig. F1r.

18. French, *Life Records*, vol. III, p. 206.

19. Masson, *Life*, vol. IV, p. 93.

20. Milton again attacks licensing in *Colasterion* and advises Cromwell against prepublication censorship in *Pro Populo Anglicano Defensio Secunda*. See *CP* II: 727–8; IV: 679.

21. Abbe Blum, "The Author's Authority: *Areopagitica* and the Labour of Licensing," in Mary Nyquist and Margaret W. Ferguson, eds., *Re-membering Milton* (New York, 1988), pp. 74–96.

22. Michel Foucault, "What is an Author?", *Language, Counter-Memory, Practice*, trans. Donald F. Bouchard and Sherry Simon (Ithaca, 1977), pp. 113–38.

23. Stanley Fish makes this argument in "There's No Such Thing as Free Speech, and It's a Good Thing, Too," *There's No Such Thing as Free Speech* (New York, 1994), pp. 102–19.

24. Michel de Montaigne, "On the Inconsistency of Our Actions," *The Complete Essays of Montaigne*, ed. Donald M. Frame (Stanford, 1965), pp. 239–44; these quotations are taken from pp. 244, 241.

25. Milton himself helped to create the myth of the autonomous author in *Areopagitica*'s oft-cited description of a book as "the pretious life-blood of a master spirit" (*CP* II: 493). For a fuller discussion of Milton's collaborative authorship and its expression in *Areopagitica*, see Dobranski, "Letter and Spirit in Milton's *Areopagitica*," *Milton Studies* 32 (1995), 131–52.

26. Robert Burton, *The Anatomy of Melancholy*, 4th edn. (London, 1632; STC 4162). See Masson, *Life*, vol. I, p. 548.

27. "An Ordinance for the Regulating of Printing [June 14, 1643]," Firth, *Acts and Ordinances*, vol. I, p. 184.

28. McKenzie emphasizes that the figures for British book production remain "very provisional" for the years 1475–1640 and "even more tentative" for the years 1641–84. See Appendix B of his "The Economies of Print, 1550–1750: Scales of Production and Conditions of Constraint," *Produzione e Commercio della Carta e del Libro secc. XIII–XVIII*. Istituto Internazionale di Storia Economica, "F. Dantini" Prato, Serie II – Atti delle "Settimane di Studi" e altri Convegni 23 (Prato, 1992), pp. 389–425.

29. See Nigel Smith, "*Areopagitica*: Voicing Contexts, 1643–5," in David Loewenstein and James Grantham Turner, eds., *Politics, Poetics, and Hermeneutics in Milton's Prose* (Cambridge, 1990), pp. 103–22; and Dobranski, "Letter and Spirit," 131–52.

30. *To the High Court of Parliament: the Humble Remonstrance of the Company of Stationers* (London, 1643), sig. A1v, in the Thomason Collection, E. 247(23).

31. Hill, *Milton and the English Revolution*, p. 288.

32. See W. K. Jordan, *The Development of Religious Toleration in England* (Gloucester, MA, 1965), pp. 203–8; *Mercurius Politicus*, September 22, 1655.

33. See Firth, *Acts and Ordinances*, vol. I, pp. 1133–36; vol. II, pp. 409–12. As David Loewenstein reminds us, Milton in *A Treatise of Civil Power* (1659) approvingly described the 1650 Blasphemy Act as "prudent and well deliberated." See Loewenstein's chapter in this collection, "Treason against God and state: blasphemy in Milton's culture and *Paradise Lost*."

34. Reay, "Radicalism and religion," p. 11.

35. See Jordan, *Religious Toleration*, pp. 204–07; Masson, *Life*, vol. V, pp. 64–66.

36. Parker, *Biography*, p. 394; see Masson, *Life*, vol. IV, p. 118.

37. Cyprian Blagden, *The Stationers' Company, A History, 1403–1959* (London, 1960), pp. 146–47. Summarizing the new law as basically the "same old regulations . . . with the same old prohibitions and punishments," Blagden does find noteworthy three less stringent conditions: a press was allowed to operate at York, another was allowed to continue printing religious matter at Finsbury, and no limit was set on the number of master printers.

38. Firth, *Acts and Ordinances*, vol. II, pp. 247, 249.

39. *Ibid.*, p. 247. See "An Order made by the Honourable House of Commons" in the Thomason Collection, E. 207(2).

40. Foucault, "What is an Author?", p. 124.

41. "An Ordinance against unlicensed or scandalous Pamphlets, and and [*sic*] for the better Regulating of Printing," Firth, *Acts and Ordinances*, vol. I, pp. 1021–23.

42. Jerome McGann, *Critique of Modern Textual Criticism* (Chicago, 1983), pp. 48, 51.

43. Leo Miller, *John Milton's Writings in the Anglo-Dutch Negotiations, 1651–1654* (Pittsburgh, 1992), p. 6.

44. Edward Phillips, ed., *Letters of State, written by Mr. John Milton* (London, 1694; Wing M2126), sig. A3r.

45. For a discussion of Milton's relations with Needham, see Blair Worden, "Milton and Marchamont Needham," in David Armitage, Armand Himy, and Quentin Skinner, eds., *Milton and Republicanism* (Cambridge, 1995), pp. 156–80.

46. J. Milton French, "Milton, Needham, and *Mercurius Politicus*," *Studies in Philology* 33.2 (April 1936), 236–52.

47. *Ibid.*, 246.

48. The references to Milton's battle with Salmasius occur in *Mercurius Politicus*, January 16, 1650/51, February 13, 1650/51, February 27, 1650/51, March 27, 1651, April 10, 1651, May 1, 1651, June 26, 1651, July 3, 1651, July 10, 1651, September 4, 1651, December 25, 1651, and January 8, 1651/52. Later, advertisements for Milton's books occur in issues published on June 1, 1654, November 18, 1658, February 10, 1659, September 1, 1659, October 13, 1659, and March 1, 1660.

49. These quotations are taken from *Mercurius Politicus*, January 16, 1650/51; December 25, 1651, and July 3, 1651, respectively.

50. See, for example, *Mercurius Politicus*, February 13, 1650/51.

51. See the *Calendar of State Papers, Domestic Series*, 1650: 550 and 1649: 550.

Anticipating a royalist resurgence with the advent of war with Scotland, the Council sought to disable its detractors. On June 25, it thus issued a warrant for the arrest of Prynne and ordered Milton to study the facts of the earlier uprisings in Essex and Kent so that "the Council may judge what is fit to be considered" (1650: 213, 214). Milton's own feud with Prynne began in 1644 with the latter's representation of Milton's *Doctrine and Discipline of Divorce* as an argument for *"divorce at pleasure."* See Prynne, *Twelve Considerable Serious Questions touching Church Government* (London, 1644; Wing P4116), p. 7. In like manner, Walker had criticized Milton at length in *Anarchia Anglicana: or, The History of Independency, the Second Part* (London, 1649; Wing W316): see Thomason Collection, E. 1052. Walker refers to Milton's argument in *The Tenure of Kings and Magistrates* (1649) as "the froth of wit and fancy, not the Dictates of true and solid Reason" (Cc4v) and attacks the author as a "Libertine that thinketh his Wife a Manacle, and his very Garters to be Shackles and Fetters to him: one that (after the Independent fashion) will be tied by no obligation to God or man)" (Cc4r).

52. For an insightful analysis of the license that Milton takes as autobiographer, see A. E. Barker, *Milton and the Puritan Dilemma* (Toronto, 1942), pp. xvi–xx, and Christopher Grose, *Milton and the Sense of Tradition* (New Haven, 1988), especially pp. 10–39.

CHAPTER 8

Milton and the rationale of insulting

John K. Hale

Most writers on Milton's political prose sidestep its voluminous insults. Some Milton scholars deplore them because they are not only numerous but cover the entire range of mudslinging. Worse still, they suspect he enjoyed it. Others simply ignore the insulting, as unworthy of the poet or of their own attention. Historians, though very interested these days in Milton's radical politics or heretical dogmatics, nonetheless speed past the insults as subordinate to the deeds and agents of those lively years, 1642–60. Here, therefore, I call attention to his gems of vituperation, because they show us a side of Milton that we tend to ignore.[1] In his insults, their humor and their offensiveness alike, he is making deliberate stylistic choices and revealing his character as a rhetor. Applying to his occasions of insulting the resources of his reading and his vivid imagination, he shows himself *hairetikos* in the primary sense: the Greek word first meant "able to choose."

Particularly in the Latin of the *First Defence* (1651) Milton chooses to present a humanist self to European readers. In an authentically classical manner, he persuades not only through his argument but also by giving pleasure, the peculiar pleasure that pertains to adept insult and its mingling of delight and instruction. This is not to imply that only then, in 1651, did he vituperate in public. He uncovers a lively vein of abusive satire in the university prolusions and his antiprelatical tracts. He unleashes choice Anglo-Saxon phrases, often involving derogatory animal imagery, in *Colasterion* and other English polemics of the 1640s. Insults also figure in memorable episodes of *Paradise Lost* and *Samson Agonistes*. Still, as the introduction to this volume makes clear, 1651 is near the paradigmatic moment of Milton's career as a political agent. He speaks now for England, not himself. And he speaks in Latin, the language of international discourse and humanist tradition, opening up a more learned, richer, wittier seam of insulting. Milton's insults, furthermore, are well described as what the Greeks called *parrhasia*, meaning simultaneously "loose talk" and "free speech." Milton uses Latin to insult in a Greek spirit; his insults use, mime, and advocate choice. Even here we find consistency with his Arminian theology and tolerationist views.

Yet we tend to ignore Milton's insults, and an almost equal neglect prevails toward the kind of utterance – speech-act or sub-genre – to which insults belong. They seem to lie beneath the notice of literary studies. First, then, I investigate the most apposite of contexts: the history of insults together with some theories of it. Then I bring these wider concerns to bear on Milton in the *First Defence*, so as to conduct a relevant critique of his insults.[2] I shall further explore the rationale of insulting, in terms of a social therapy having psychoanalytical affinities, to argue that insulting remains a reliable measure of societal health and candor.

TRADITIONS OF INSULTING

To the best of our knowledge, insults are a universal human activity. That is obviously so when they afford merely a verbal channel of aggression – a way to fight. Yet they also seem to be culturally universal – something to be enjoyed, played with, ritualized, tolerated, and even depended on as a source of societal self-regulation.

Most cultures accept insulting and even approve of it within specified contexts. At the rites of Demeter at Eleusis the procession stopped on its way to Demeter's shrine, and on a certain bridge (*gephura*) exchanged insults at some length. The resultant metonymic coinage, *gephurizo*, became a common term for abuse.[3] As Demeter's name and cult recur in these contexts, there may be a link between abuse and fertility rituals. Elsewhere in the ancient world, Roman writers drew on a tradition of "Fescennine" verses, ribald wedding-songs, resembling the verses sung by soldiers at triumphs. Both, of course, entail ritual context and a clear place within that. One of the ancient etymologies linked Fescennine to "fascinum," witchcraft.[4] Abuse, then, might avert evil. It might be apotropaic, an inoculative or sympathetic magic.

In biblical Israel insulting may not have been ritualized or conducted as a game, but many a passage of denunciation shows that insulting was alive and eloquent there also. In the oldest portion of the Bible, Judges, Jotham likens kings to trees – olive, fig, vine – and Abimelech is a vicious "bramble" (9:14). Elsewhere, denunciative force seems an accepted part of a prophet's eloquence, and hence a recognized power within jeremiad, a genre which had its recognition and vogue in the Renaissance. At its most extreme, biblical insulting becomes cursing. At 2 Samuel 16:5 when King David came to Bahurim, Shimei, "a man of the family of the house of

Saul" (so harboring a grudge against David as Saul's replacement) "came forth, and cursed [David] still as he came" (King James version): "Come out, come out, thou bloody man, and thou man of Belial" (verse 7). Abishai asks David, "Why should this dead dog curse my lord the king?" (verse 9). Cursing arises from deadly serious intent, whereas insulting is more peaceable, an aggression-channeling and harm-averting obverse of cursing. The evil is imagined but diffused by the pleasures of expression and audience response. Insulting is, or at least may be, a verbal war-game: cursing *is* war.

Robert C. Elliott discerns three main purposes of abuse rituals.[5] First, to find a winner, who may be, offensively, the wittiest insulter or, defensively, the most tolerant recipient. Second, to secure a society's judgment in a quarrel which has arisen – insults as a trial by combat between the contestants. And third, to achieve a cathartic release of "that perilous stuff that weighs about the heart." In every case, the society benefits, by entertainment and/or by release and thus dispersal of ill feeling through the licensed and ultimately holy medium of expression. In every case, the contestants gain something also; if not victory, at least calm of mind. But these advantages may come at some cost: in some instances the losing contestant may lose face, even go into exile.

The relevance of *all* this to Milton's challenge to Salmasius appears from a description of the Eskimo "drum match" or "song duel".[6] "The two enemies face each other before the assembled tribe" (publish books in Latin for continental readership) "who look on the affair as a festive occasion and are delighted with the lampoons, the obscene scurrilities, the mockery and jibing and flouting which the two contestants hurl at each other" (accurate description of the subject matter of the First Defence, and of contemporary humanists' response to it), "each accompanying himself on the drum" (the art of humanist erudition may be the analogous term, adding rhythmic pleasure to the slanging).[7]

The speech-act of insult thus appears in widely varying times and places, including Milton's own. It might be urged against my argument that by viewing insults as so universal, I dehistoricize Milton. Milton himself, operating from humanist premises, would not have understood the objection. A similarly learned, humanistic poet, Ben Jonson begins his *Alchemist* with the immortal and culturally widespread insult, "I fart at thee." The gloss in one edition cites the idiom of Aristophanes, "*sou kataperdomai*," literally, "I fart you downwards." Jonson scarcely needed Aristophanes to prompt this insult. Jonson did not need classical precedent, yet it could have figured in his choice. For the humanist, the power and joy of insulting,

as of everything which a poet could express with force, lay in saying universal and everyday things with a finesse derived straight from antiquity.

Keith Thomas has illustrated how in early modern England, under such
pressures as the Reformation and the rise of a middle class, laughter was
changing; even possibly declining.[8] Protestantism, particularly, moved
away from the laughter of mockery as a weapon in its ideological struggle –
despite its splendid showing in the time of Martin Marprelate. Only, no
one seems to have told Milton. In fact, the tendency is partial only. The two
English universities retained a licensed fool through at least the Tudor
period, the "Terrae filius" at Oxford and the "Prevaricator" at Cambridge –
for use upon occasion. Milton's base comparisons in his undergraduate
writings have many parallels in the quips of these fools and in his dealings
with Salmasius.

While insult is virtually universal, therefore, particular forms in the
early modern period might have influenced Milton, whether directly or
environmentally. They include flyting, defamation actions, philippics,
licensed fooling, and the London drama. Flytings were stand-up abuse
contests, often between the sexes. From time immemorial they entertained
in the traditions of folk festival or festive comedy.[9] Thence they contributed to drama on the popular stages, for example in *Much Ado about
Nothing*. The stand-up contests between Beatrice and Benedick proved so
entertaining that the play was being renamed "Benedick and Beatrice" by
1613.[10] The exchanges of abusive epithets between Falstaff and the Prince
were perhaps even more popular.[11] Defamation suits in the bawdy courts
exhibited the talents of women in this kind, as feminist historians have discovered (following F. G. Emmison's pioneering work on the Essex bawdy
courts). Here, one topos in particular catches the eye of the Miltonist,
namely that of the masculine woman and the correlative effeminate male.
Endless insults were exchanged by women in the courts about women who
"wore the breeches," and, conversely, husbands received penalties for sub-
mitting to petticoat government. Two works were devoted to this phenomenon in 1620: *Hic Mulier: or, the Man-Woman*, whose title applies a masculine
modifier to the feminine noun, and, in response, *Haec Vir: Or the Womanish
Man*, with feminine modifier and masculine noun. In the *First Defence*,
Milton poured related scorn on his allegedly henpecked opponent, femin-
izing his name by punning on "Salmacis", the androgynous nymph.[12] Two
other kinds of speech-act that contain insults or have affinities to them are
jeremiad and philippic. Jeremiad was modeled on the lamentations of
Jeremiah over Jerusalem.[13] From its main aim of recalling backsliders it
reached upwards to testifying before God and downwards to denigrating

the opposition. Milton typifies the genre in *Ready and Easy Way*. Philippic lies closer to the spirit of Milton's *Defences*. They attack Salmasius in order to defend the English republic, just as Cicero's philippics attacked Mark Antony to defend the Roman republic. Cicero, we shall see, is a key player in the *First Defence*, insults and all.

TRADITIONS OF INSULTING: THEORETICAL

The ancient world bequeathed to humanism more than a huge and varied practice of insulting and more than an eloquence in that direction for emulation: it left a body of theory, issuing in practical instruction. Humanists were all brought up on both, because their education was imbued with rhetoric and declamation (and most usefully, too, in their expected career-paths as lawyers or politicians or preachers). What, then, did ancient theory say about insulting? And did Milton use it overtly in his polemics?

Aristotle explained insult by reference to poetry (*Poetics*, ch. 4).[14] Just as some poets represented (*emimounto*) fine deeds in lofty verse, others represented the actions of fools like Margites (the original dumb hero), "at first by making up abuse-verses," then later in the related meter, iambics: they "iambified" one another – *iambizon allelous*, 1448[b]32. The best-known of such iambic abusers was Archilochus. But he was only one of many; as one commentator notes, Aristotle's remark "implies abusive exchanges of a ritual nature such as we know to have been common in many societies."[15] In his *Rhetoric*, Aristotle systematizes the strategic rationale behind such abuse. Rhetoric is "that faculty by which we understand what will serve our turn, concerning any subject to win belief in the hearer" (1.2). Demonstrative oratory praises or dispraises (1.9); and though Aristotle says most about praise, the ideas hold in antithesis for dispraise. Praise of one person implicitly recommends that others do the like, so dispraise implicitly dissuades. Insults figure within dispraise. Effective insult deters unworthy action through scathing insight and ridicule.[16] From the Aristotelian perspective, a key part of Milton's defense of the English Commonwealth is to attack its critics at their weak points and so deter imitators.

While Aristotle indicates the strategic rationale, Quintilian illuminates the ethos of Milton's attacks. For Quintilian, only the morally good man can rise to the best oratory. He seeks, himself, to define and educate the "*vir bonus dicendi peritus*"; the good man, who is (also, secondly) expert in speaking. We know that Milton had Quintilian in mind while writing the *Defence* because he uses this key epithet. Sneering at Salmasius's pretension to it, Milton aspires to Quintilian's rectitude, not least in the solemnly

Ciceronian peroration added in 1658.[17] Despite his emphasis on rectitude, Quintilian – far from deploring insult on the lips of his "good man" – devotes much time to instructing him how to do it well. We must heed the methods and spirit that Quintilian advocated. They, more than any modern distaste for rhetoric or abuse, provide the criteria of any judgment upon Milton's efforts. They will guide us to Milton's desired impact, together with the actual impact upon his audience of humanists, themselves reared on Quintilian.

The section called "Altercatio" (VI.4 in Quintilian's *Institutio Oratoria*) identifies *inventio* as the chief skill required. This power of invention comes from wit, in its old sense of *ingenium* or natural powers; more exactly, from an "*ingenium velox et mobile*," a genius that is rapid and mobile (VI.4.1). It does not come best from anger in the speaker, but from moderation and patience (VI.4.10), because its objective is not simply to refute the opponent but to ensure his disparagement, diminution, and ridicule. What the disputant needs to show is *urbanitas*: sophistication and good taste, through wit.

So our questions can be refined: how does Milton set about showing *urbanitas* in his insults of Salmasius? And how effective as he?

A third strand of ancient theory on insulting pervades the classical tradition and its Renaissance practitioners. It is found in Plato, Aristophanes, Horace, and Erasmus. The Greek word for it was *spoudogeloion*, the "laughing-serious." Horace spoke of "*ridentem dicere verum*" ("telling the truth in a jest"). Plato (*Laws* 816E) says "without the comic it is impossible to understand the serious." Aristophanes "made this mixture of the gay and the grave the essence of his plays."[18] And so it is he who gives the most moving explanation of *eros* in the most drunken and comical speech in Plato's *Symposium*.

Milton was well aware of this received idea too. In *Smectymnuus*, he translates the tag from Horace: "*ridentem dicere verum/ Quid vetat?*" becomes "laughing to teach the truth/ What hinders?"[19] Milton devotes two pages there to the efficacy of laughter in teaching, citing the Old Testament, Cicero, and Seneca. Insults provoke laughter to scorn what is also refuted in earnest. The two tones meet; necessarily so at transitions, but sometimes they run on in harness.

MILTON VERSUS SALMASIUS IN THE *FIRST DEFENCE*

The pleasures of insulting begin on the title-page of "Joannis Miltoni/ Angli/Pro Populo Anglicano Defensio/Contra/Claudii *Anonymi, Aliàs*

Salmasii/Defensionem Regiam" – "John Milton an Englishman His Defence of the people of England against *Claudius Anonymous, alias Salmasius* his defence of the King" (pages 2–3, my emphases). Milton thus exposes his opponent and ridicules his coyness. Next, he mocks Salmasius' titular claim to defend Charles I "to Charles the Second": why, says Milton, plead the father's cause to the son? – surely you can't lose (pages 12–13).

Worse is to come, for Salmasius had boasted that his *Defence of the King* (*Defensio Regia*, 1649) was written "*Sumptibus regiis*," at the King's expense. Why, asks Milton, if the King was such a good king, do you need pay? Salmasius looks yet more mercenary when Milton gives derogatory details of the transaction: 100 Jacobuses were brought you by a royal chaplain, and you were seen to reach out greedy hands; supposedly to embrace the chaplain but actually to embrace the pay-packet (*"novimus qui te avaras manus porrigentem vidit, in speciem quidem ut Sacellanum Regis missum cum munere, re vera ut ipsum munus amplecterere"*) (p. 14). This resembles a shot from a film, where one party to an embrace is caught by the camera registering some low passion over the embraced one's shoulder, behind the seemly courtesy. Milton is working toward dramatization, presenting Salmasius as a character (the greedy Parasite) out of Roman comedy.

Milton was well aware of the process; the next reference to Roman comedy is explicit:

> Sed eccum ipsum, crepant fores, prodit histrio in proscenium.
> Date operam, et cum silentio animadvertite,
> Ut pernoscatis quid sibi Eunuchus velit.
> Nam quicquid est, praeter solitum cothurnatus incedit.   (p. 14)

("But here comes the man himself; the door creaks; enter the actor. 'In silence now and with attention wait, / That ye may learn what th'Eunuch has to prate.' For whatever's the matter with him, he struts on with heroics more than usually stilted.") Though wordy at the close, Samuel Lee Wolff's translation captures Milton's dramatizing verve. Salmasius is becoming Terence's Eunuch, the eponymous busybody of that favorite play. Milton will later develop the allusion to suggest that Salmasius is a eunuch in nature as well as in this name.

Also in the opening pages, Milton accuses Salmasius of unclassical Latinity, a sin of the utmost iniquity for a humanist: "persona" as "person" or "body" (p. 16). He makes amusing play with Salmasius's name, punning on its resemblance to Ovid's "Salmacis," the nymph who ended up metamorphosed into a blend of hermaphrodite and Siamese twin (p. 20).[20]

Milton does not court subtlety or finesse in these early thrusts, since he needs the audience, all of it, to laugh with him at the target. Roman humor was not of the subtlest anyway. Yet he knows what he is doing, since the theme of an Ovidian metamorphosis is apt, suggesting in a glancing *moralitas* that the eminent humanist has just exchanged fame for notoriety. He had undertaken to write for money on a topic which, as a Frenchman, he cannot know about.

The depth of that ignorance must await the seriatim rebuttals that constitute the serious bulk of the work. In the meantime, Milton attacks his opponent on the strongest – humanist – grounds, with a more erudite and dexterous wit. Salmasius had dubbed the Commonwealth leaders ignoble upstarts, ("*manii*," paupers of obscure descent, p. 32). Milton quotes back at him a passage of Horace:

> Valet ima summis
> Mutare, et insignem attenuat Deus
> Obscura promens.

("God can make highest and lowest things exchange places: he deposes the eminent and exalts things humble": my translation). Not only is Horace, to the humanist, inevitably a fount of wisdom. Horace repeats what Holy Scripture ("*libri sacri*") teaches, namely, the Magnificat ("He hath put down the mighty from their seats, and exalted them of low degree").[21] This, surely, is unanswerable by any Christian humanist, and Milton does the job with Horatian brevity.

These early instances suffice to show how Milton fights Salmasius with accepted humanist weapons, whether crudely or learnedly, robustly or dexterously, leaning most on image in the form of cartoon or dramatic allusion. What impact is it having on the European, Latin-reading audience? Responses are on record, and the approval of the non-partisan as well as the like-minded is significant.[22] It implies an interested, appreciative audience for insults, indeed, a humanist taste for such. Milton relies on a similar mix of argument with invective in the whole *First Defence*. I shall select examples from throughout the *Defence*, to cultivate the same appreciative voice in myself and the contemporary Miltonist.

The castigating of the opponent and the taking of the high moral ground are equal parts of the opening sentence (the *exordium*, of what is finally conceived of as on *oratio*). Then principle dominates: kings are not above law (pp. 2–8). Principle and insult mingle thereafter, in differing proportions. So it is not the case that insulting is relief, let alone light relief. Insulting is a proper, decorous part of the exordium. Because an inept speaker betokens a weak cause, the orator can attack the latter by moving between the two.

Insult works best, nonetheless, when it both pleases and teaches. The sense that it lands on target enhances the pleasure. Take exposure which is simultaneously witty. Milton uses that method to cap his devastating rejoinder to aristocratic arrogance, in which he links Horace with the Bible (p. 32). Better that our leaders be "*Manii*," "sons of the soil," because they at least have a soil and work hard there: *you* are a "landless homeless worthless straw-stuffed scarecrow-knight, selling smoke to stave off starvation in someone else's land where you are their slave" ("*sine terra et lare fumos vendendo quod tu facis, homo nihili et stramineus eques, in aliena terra dominorum nutu*") (pages 32–34). Wolff's rendering in the Columbia edition is more rhythmic and Aristophanic than the Latin, so analysis is needed to show that Milton's strength lies in the images which are the thought and in their sequencing. Salmasius has no land, no house or hearth. He stays alive by selling smoke: someone who will sell you smoke will sell you anything (with a side-glance at smoke-screening). From smoke to nothing ("*nihili*") is a progression, from virtual to total lack of substance. A "straw knight" tightens the noose, for if a straw man means a man of straw (linking landlessness with being a dummy) to be *knight* of straw is a contradiction: in England at least to be a "knight" entails being landed. But not this knight, who lives outside his own country and does what his masters tell him ("*dominorum nutu*," obedient to the "nod" of "slaveowners"). The sequence of the imaging is a witty train of thought in itself, one which increasingly exposes the opponent. It discredits not merely the immediate remark about nobility, but the complacent or self-serving aristocratic presupposition.

Beyond these immediate perceptions, however, consider the many affinities we are placed to recognize between the tradition of insulting and the above imagery. Milton composes an abusive exchange, following the opponent's attack. It is apotropaic, to avert evil from England in crisis. It is a licensed release of animus. It turns politics toward festivity by making the audience laugh. It is ludic to the speaker also, having a good imaginative work-out. It is a gladiatorial contest in image-making (political allegiance being naturally expressed by image). It is penetrative, an agent of change, to the uncommitted humanists of Europe. It is verbal war to the participants, but they know it is entertainment to the audience. It is seeking, by ridicule, to remove a pest.

Milton's wit plays nimbly whenever he moves out of argumentation into personal attack. He plays, for example, with sound and sense, and with their relationship to each other. Onomatopoeia enters the cartoon: Salmasius is a "*balatroni mercenario et peregrino, perfugarum dictata exscribenti*" (p. 430). (You are a "venal outlandish buffoon, transcribing what is dictated to you by a bunch of English runaways": my translation). This unflattering picture is mainly reiterating that the opponent is writing to order, the orders of the exiled royalists. But the imagery makes him into a clown, and that clown-ishness is being made more convincing by sound, not only by the exciting pile-up of adjectives leading into the cartoon image of the servile clerk, but by the rhythm of the repeated "r"-sounds. Milton was known for his fierce pronunciation of the letter R, says Aubrey, "like all those of a satirical temper."[23] The seven words have eight such examples of the letter known to Elizabethans as the "growling letter." The Latin is letting the growling letter off the leash. And if humanist readers still read aloud, they would hear the satirical growling as well as receive its mental equivalent.

Whether they read aloud is disputed, but in the case of Latin, and a Latin which is rhetoric, I cannot help thinking their rhetorical education would ensure they kept their ears in action. It would immeasurably enhance their pleasure in the performance aspect, and go far to explain how they read it to the end. They were – literally – kept listening. (Milton keeps up his clausulae on this same principle of orality.) I conclude that the sound of his insults did more for his argument than we can recover except in principle. And more for his *urbanitas*, combining here Horatian humor with Juvenalian ferocity.

A simpler onomatopoeia is the cataloguing vituperation: "Plinian exercise-writer, verbosest of blatherskites" (*blateronum verbosissimus*) (p. 366). *Blateronum* is inherently mimetic, but it is Milton who makes the next word sound out its meaning, tripling the sibilant by the superlative, to suggest an orator frothing at the mouth through exertion, all *composure* gone, so devoid of *urbanitas*. Like any good satirist, like Dryden in *MacFlecknoe*, Milton avoids the imitative fallacy by "creating" the object of his satire into a free-standing cartoon image that has life, despite, not because of, the original. The life is Milton's imagination's.

Puns are another example of his Latin's orality and mobility. Puns are mainly surprise, when two separate things fuse because of contingent sound. Surprise creates delight, and the possibility of more conceptual humor (wit, in the old sense again). Puns are especially devastating when they bring together name and nature. Cicero had done this in accusing Verres, the rapacious ex-governor of Sicily: he was a "*verres*," an uncastrated male pig, in name as in nature. Milton does the same with Salmasius, as noticed, metamorphosing him into the nymph – nympho-maniac, rather – "Salmacis." But more could be done with the opponent's title, the "Sieur de St. Loup" or "knight of Saint Wolf." He exploits the obvious associations of "wolf," such as hungry, violent, cruel, rabid. But his energy of invention – his *urbanitas* – takes the image past cliché. The Lord of St. Wolf can philosophize from his "wolf-den," *lupanari*, but *lupanar* doubles as the regular word for a brothel (p. 286). This "brothel" is dubbed his "lyceum" or "*lycée*," both deriving from the Greek word for "wolf," *lukos*. Etymologizing puns beget some bewildering metamorphoses at such times in the discourse, yet they do cohere, and probe nature through name. A greedy nature has turned the life of the mind into pimping.

I am not claiming that every such insult is equally wondrous. (I withhold the analysis of what may be less effective to a later section.) But this one, at any rate, exemplifies *urbanitas*. So do others, if we accept that insults may function as a verbal aggression which is licensed by the occasion and needs of controversy. Take the noisy jingle "*rabbinicaris ... rauces*" ("you quote excessively from the rabbis, you roar yourself hoarse": p. 366, my translation). He coins the first verb, and alliteration makes the two words a hendiadys: you shout yourself hoarse with half-understood lore. Or he twits Salmasius as that contradiction in terms, a Frenchman who prefers to live outside France: "*te Gallum et errabundum*" (p. 62): hearing the pun crossing "Gallus" with "gallus" ("Gaul" and "cockerel") we would get "an erratic *coq*." Certainly elsewhere Milton makes extravagant play with the same pun. Salmasius had unwisely supported the principle of monarchy by saying that the domestic cock, *Gallus gallinaceus*, lords it over males and females in the farmyard. Milton refutes this by saying, "You may be Gallus but you are henpecked; still, you do make a lot of noise from your dunghill, and for that matter the huge books you write give you a huge dunghill to crow from" (p. 280, my summary). Still not subtle, but agreeably quick-moving, throwing dung lustily without becoming stuck to it.

MODERATION AND EXCESS WITHIN INSULTING

Chicken-jokes may be fine, but seven sentences of such jokes seems a lot. Does Milton infringe the moderation which was held by Quintilian to be part of *urbanitas*? He felt some misgiving: "Perhaps ... by rather too often answering also his silliness and threadbare quibbles as if they were arguments, I may seem to have given them an importance that they nothing deserved" (p. 550). The remark actually concerns his argument and its structure, which followed that of Salmasius but more concisely. Still it shows the fear that by covering everything he may have got things out of proportion.

It is not solely a question of length. When Milton calls Salmasius a "seller of flat wine," he may mean that his arguments about English law are ignorant and old-hat, but the image is now too short to be clear (p. 528). Soon afterwards he calls Salmasius a "frenetic bag-snatching Frenchman" ("*cerebrosus iste et crumenipeta*": p. 530, my translation). The alliterated polysyllables achieve energy, but no clarity; heat without light is not *urbanitas*.

These examples matter, more than might first appear, because they come in the run-up to Milton's allusion to Quintilian himself. His very next insult is to call Salmasius, sarcastically, "you good man, skilled in speaking" ("*vir bone, dicendi perite*": p. 530, my rendering, as Wolff misses the allusion). These words are so well known that they bring into view the standards that should be guiding the whole exchange. Doing so, they may expose dung on Milton's own hands.

Against these doubts, we should in general remember that fluency, or *copia*, was esteemed both anciently and in Milton's world. The rush of insults here is just like the flow of undergraduate wit in Milton's *Prolusions*, or for that matter the exhaustive character-demolitions of Cicero, his model. It is clearly not enough to trust a detached modern's view that all of them go on too long. We are too disengaged: the parallel is a political debate, or a television confrontation on some hot topic – any arena where the audience cannot have too much of gladiatorial word-stand-off.

So how far does Milton's insulting fulfill all the parts of *urbanitas* as Quintilian described it? Quickness and mobility of imagination, he does indeed show: he abounds in wit of words and image. Sophistication, too, yes. Good taste? In terms of humanist expectation and scope, yes: his taste is wide and correct and cultivated, also imply aimed. But patience? and moderation?

As the *Defence* draws to a close, every chapter of his opponent's having been dealt with by laborious seriatim rebuttal, Quintilian may help us detect signs of strain, weariness, impatience, immoderation:

By whom, though, were you asked [to write the Defensio Regia]? By your wife [whom you're afraid of]...? Or were you asked by the younger Charles and that profligate crew of vagabond courtiers, like a second Balaam solicited by King Balak, to deign to restore by curses and ill writing a king's desperate cause that was lost by ill fighting? [*male pugnando / maledicendo*}
... [But the difference then is that] he was a clever man sitting upon a talkative little ass: you are a very talkative ass yourself, sat upon by a woman; and being overgrown with the healed heads of the bishops that heretofore you had wounded, you seem to present a sort of miniature portrait of the beast in Revelation. (p. 548)

The homology, Balak/Charles II and Balaam/Salmasius, certainly comes
as a surprise, and is vivid. Careful balance continues, of "ill writing" with
"ill fighting" (similar jingle in the Latin). We sense there is more to come,
since who could introduce Balaam without his ass? So Milton switches the
point of attack: Salmasius is *not* Balaam after all; he is the ass. And the one
riding the ass is not so much Balaam (in the vehicle of the simile), as
Salmasius's wife (in the tenor). The confusion, upon reflection and a fair
hearing, is calculated – taking the form of many good jokes. Milton has
more, too. Asses ridden by women connotes female domination and possibly sex, which brings Milton to his *coup de théâtre*: the hag-ridden Salmasius
resembles the biblical Beast ridden by the Whore of Babylon – with the
hydra heads of the beast changed to restored heads of prelates. That the
comparisons begin so balanced and deliberate helps the sense of acceler-
ation and hectic shape-changing at the close.

A cognate apparent lapse comes in the next quip, a lengthy comparing
of Salmasius to Judas. Milton makes Salmasius out to be a traitor; previously he was a venal foreigner, which might seem to disqualify him for the
role of the traitor. But I now think the contradiction would pass unnoticed
by a reader who had been drawn along by the rest so far. Whether or not
Milton does find Salmasius to be both venal and treacherous, the whirl of
the counter-insulting imagery and allusion is what the reader is bound to
be following (as the end of the book visibly approaches).

To turn the doubt round: why should Milton show patience, if he was
dealing with a pest by the approved method? In context, the two ostensibly
labored and contradictory image-sequences just cited represent a climax
of the insulting. It is the climax of "laughing to teach the truth." As such, it
receives a mighty closing period (eighty-eight words, all on the subject of
Judas, pp. 548–50), followed by a resounding spondaic clausula – "*supplicii
sedes praemittas.*" Rising steadily in register from a laughing to a condemning onslaught by image, Milton launches his noble, Ciceronian peroration.

Milton is taking insult as far as he can before he abandons it; he stops
playing the man rather than the ball, to address the fellow citizens on
whose behalf he is speaking ("*Pro Populo Anglicano*"). He praises them, and
admonishes them: God had done great things through you, do not now
waste them by dissension. The final period is a lengthy, thunderous warning. It betrays drastic misgiving. Not only insults, but even reasoning, *may*
not be enough.

The record shows that Milton need not have worried. The *First
Defence* entertained the bystanders, and discredited Salmasius. It helped to
make Milton on the continent of Europe the second best-known English

revolutionary. He pleased Protestants there, for sure, as well as enemies of Salmasius. But he impressed ambassadors and even princes.[24] Some sense of recognizing the facts shines through the 1658 postscript, written for the third edition and the umpteenth printing within seven years. It contains no insults, no admonition, only contentment at having borne witness for his country in a crisis – with extended allusion to Cicero, who as consul thwarted the conspiracy of Catilina.

So should we conclude that Milton did, in the main, heed Quintilian and succeed thereby? Or that his satirical temper united with the crisis to lead him beyond Quintilian? It is significant that he quotes or adapts Martial, and strives to sound like the denunciatory Juvenal – neither of them exactly embodiments of patience or moderation. Nothing succeeds like *excess*. He uses whatever form of pleasing comes handy, not only to leaven the austerities of the arguments from law and nature and religion, but to communicate them both gaily and seriously – in accordance with the ancients' approval of *spoudogeloion*.

Milton's insults illustrate some curious perennial things human nature, and our social nature, some of which have a bearing on the continuance of free speech and an open society. One powerful reason for insult is anxiety. Anxiety is a kind of imagination, since both think outwards from the literal to aggrandize and trans-shape their object. Both can then reduce it, by pigeonholing it. But paradoxically, the more this is done, the less any one image may stick: the object may escape the ridiculous, taming categorization. Salmasius did not, but his cause did. And the anonymous *Eikon Basilike*, pure sentimental image, went on harming the Commonwealth cause.

Similarly, insulting by imagery remains as apotropaic as it was on that bridge at the Eleusinian rites. To cut the enemy down to size, or blow that enemy up so big that he bursts, is to reduce the force of an evil where it does most damage, in the mind. Only, for how long? Will it return the next day – when holiday returns to workaday? There is no one answer. Sometimes the butt is finished once thus exposed. This in turn may be achieved by the truth of the reductive image. Instead, it may be done by its wit. (No one took Korchnoi's accusations of black magic against Karpov seriously once some wag called them "Korchnoi's Complaint.") Insults are certainly diverting. They are worth a try in any polemic or adversarial relationship, though they may backfire.

In any case, social health depends on their continuance. To have an authority which stopped all insulting would be to lose more than, collectively, we lose by toleration. Presumably this is why things can be said in parliaments which would be actionable elsewhere. We do not love the people who are best at put-downs (unless we are bullies in our secret hearts). We can let them play on their windbags because we are not obliged to love them, nor to vote for them next time. Meanwhile, pests may neutralize one another, and the bystanders can enjoy.

Whatever may be the best contribution of insulting to a modern open society, it clearly contributed to the health and continuance of traditional closed ones, that more face-to-face "world we have lost." It functioned like the Saturnalia, like feasts of misrule, like any seasonal rite during which the world goes upside down: it defined the limits of normal order in speech by a licensed exceeding of them. As learned as he is when insulting, Milton shows as well a traditional festive knockabout spirit. Since learning is a pleasure to the humanist anyway, he has mixed the pleasurable decorously throughout with the useful.

For the twentieth-century reader of Milton's practice it may not be simple to experience at firsthand this "pleasurable" – if only because translations spoil the flair and especially the speed of the Latin. Yet unless we do experience the pleasure, we will not grasp how and why Milton's defense had such success with its readership. I have tried to show that he won readers over by making them laugh. Milton's insulting is a form of Longinus's "sublime." It persuades not by argument, but by laughter from the aroused imagination, yet another instance of eloquence sweeping away resistance.[25]

To put that in terms of *hairesis*, choosing, Milton is choosing the appropriate registers from a vast humanist repertoire, to combine them fitly for the great occasion of 1651. He chooses a supple Ciceronian staple for facts and issues. He chooses a syncretic high style to praise what he finds noble and advocates. He chooses a rabelaisian *parrhasia* to derogate the ignoble, Salmasius and what he stands for. This rises in its own way, back to Cicero, the Cicero of philippic, that sublimity of the combative.[26] The flexible decorum, found in the whole and in its parts, makes the *Defence* natural, powerful, and effective to contemporaries. Just as in principle reason is but choosing, so in his 1651 practice of insulting Milton's *hairesis* is reasonable. The insulting is in its own way a *hairesis*, an active search for truth, perhaps truth of feeling. As a part of Milton's rhetoric it is crucial to his choice of argumentation. Indeed, at this distance from the issues and crises themselves, might it even draw most applause from ourselves, becoming our own heretical preference?

NOTES

1. The issue is addressed by David Loewenstein, "Milton and the Poetics of Defense," in David Loewenstein and James Grantham Turner, eds., *Politics, Poetics, and Hermeneutics in Milton's Prose* (Cambridge, 1990), pp. 171–92. Loewenstein quotes C. A. Patrides for the disapproval of "intemperate language" (p. 191, n. 18). William Riley Parker, *Milton: A Biography*, 2 vols. (Oxford, 1968), pp. 372–3, 383, is one biographer who speeds past the insults. Loewenstein, too, neglects them in a way; he considers the politics, poetic rationale, and theory of Milton's mudslinging, not the mud itself. My own approach is more inductive.

2. The Latin text of the *First Defence* used throughout is from vol. VII of *CW*, *Joannis Miltoni Angli Pro Populo Anglicano Defensio*, ed. Clinton W. Keyes; page numbers are cited parenthetically within the text. The translations used are Samuel Lee Wolff's from this edition except where I prefer my own.

3. In addition, W. B. Stanford on *Frogs* lines 374–76 refers to exchanges of jeers and ritual abuse at various other Athenian festivals. All "were perhaps a general apotropaic rite in popular processions." See Aristophanes, *Frogs*, ed. Stanford (London, 1958), pp. 107–08.

4. See *The Oxford Classical Dictionary*, ed. N. G. L. Hammond and H. H. Scullard, 2nd edn. (Oxford, 1970), s.v. "Fescennini (Versus)."

5. Robert C. Elliott, *The Power of Satire: Magic, Ritual, Art* (Princeton, 1960), especially the first two chapters.

6. See *ibid.*, pp. 70–73.

7. Examples of insulting within high culture would come from Homer, Archilochus, Aristophanes, Catullus, Petronius, Martial, Rabelais, and Shakespeare. Milton knew all of these authors well, and particularly emulated Catullus and Martial.

8. Keith Thomas, "The Place of Laughter in Tudor and Stuart England," *TLS* (January 21, 1977), 77–81.

9. C. L. Barber, *Shakespeare's Festive Comedy. A Study of Dramatic Form and Its Relation to Social Custom* (Princeton, 1959), continued in François Laroque, *Shakespeare's Festive World. Elizabethan Seasonal Entertainment and the Professional Stage*, trans. Janet Lloyd (Cambridge, 1991).

10. *Shakespeare. An Illustrated Stage History*, ed. Jonathan Bate and Russell Jackson (Oxford, 1996), p. 31.

11. See *Henry IV Part I* 1.2 and 2.4.

12. Details in Laura Gowing, "Gender and the Language of Insult in Early Modern London," *History Workshop Journal* 35 (1993), 1–21. See also F. G. Emmison, *Elizabethan Life. Morals and the Church Courts* (Chelmsford, 1973).

13. See Laura Lunger Knoppers, "Milton's *The Readie and Easie Way* and the English Jeremiad," in Loewenstein and Turner, *Politics, Poetics, and Hermeneutics*, pp. 213–26.

14. Aristotle, *Poetics*, ch. 4, 1448^{b}25–34, cited from the commentary by D. W. Lucas (Oxford, 1968), p. 7.

15. Lucas, commentary to Aristotle, *Poetics*, pp. 76–77.
16. All citations from the *Rhetoric* in this paragraph are taken from *Aristotle's Poetics and Rhetoric (with other Essays in Classical Criticism)*, ed. T. A. Moxon, rev. edn. (London, 1953), see pp. 92 and 95 on *Rhetoric* I.9. I use Hobbes's Digest from this edition because, among other reasons, it shows us what seemed salient for a mid-seventeenth-century humanist and intellectual.
17. Milton refers to Quintilian's theme-phrase at p. 530. The 1658 peroration is pp. 554–58.
18. Stanford, p. 108 on *Frogs* line 389. Also Gilbert Highet, *The Classical Tradition: Greek and Roman Influences on Western Literature* (Oxford, 1949), p. 305: "*spoudogeloion* equals *ridentem dicere verum* – joking in earnest."
19. Horace, *Satires*, I.i.24–26 and *CP* I: 904.
20. The insulting comparison is developed, by means of quotations from Ovid, into a mock warning to readers that this "Salmacis" may emasculate men's minds.
21. Horace, *Odes* I.34; Luke 1:52 (King James Version).
22. The reception of the *First Defence* led to numerous reprintings. There is partisanship or malice in many, yet not all, of the recorded plaudits: see Parker, *Biography*, pp. 387–89, 985–88.
23. See *Aubrey's Brief Lives*, ed. Oliver Lawson Dick (1949; rpt. London, 1962), pp. 273–74.
24. Details are given in Parker, *Biography*, pp. 387–89.
25. In *On the Sublime* Longinus does in fact instance a joke as sublimity in his affective sense: "the field he had was smaller than a letter" (section 38). See *Classical Literary Criticism*, trans. T. S. Dorsch (Harmondsworth, 1965), p. 150.
26. These matters are discussed further in John K. Hale, *Milton's Languages. The Impact of Multilingualism on Style* (Cambridge, 1997), ch. 5.

CHAPTER 9

Treason against God and state: blasphemy in Milton's culture and "Paradise Lost"

David Loewenstein

During the upheavals of the English Revolution, the offense of blasphemy was closely linked with heresy and seemed horrifying to godly Puritans who feared religious division and radical sectarianism. Considered the most execrable kind of behavior and verbal offense, blasphemy became an intensely politicized issue, illustrating the intersection of religion and politics and their relation to threatening forms of linguistic and symbolic expression. In 1648 the Presbyterian Parliament issued a fierce Ordinance aimed at "the preventing of the growth and spreading of Heresie and Blasphemie" (including antitrinitarianism); and then in 1650 the Purged Parliament issued a strict Blasphemy Act which, perhaps surprisingly, the theologically radicalized Milton himself would recall in *A Treatise of Civil Power in Ecclesiastical Causes* (1659) as "that prudent and well deliberated act."[1] In the language of that Act, first issued to restrain the flamboyant behavior and writings of the Ranters, "Blasphemous and Execrable Opinions" threatened to subvert established authority and were considered "derogatory to the honor of God, and destructive to humane Society."[2] Thus the notorious Ranter Abiezer Coppe, having shocked godly Puritans with his eccentric visionary writings proclaiming that sin and transgression were finished, observed that he had been prosecuted and imprisoned "for suspition of Blasphemie and Treason against the State."[3]

The famous episode of the charismatic Quaker leader James Nayler, who "acted the part of Christ at *Bristol*,"[4] likewise illustrates how intensely controversial the offense could become for Milton's contemporaries and how it could indeed acquire the most urgent political ramifications – as a subversive deprecation of both God and state. Having symbolically ridden into Bristol on an ass in October 1656 with enthusiastic supporters accompanying him, as though blasphemously parodying Christ's entry into Jerusalem, Nayler was savagely punished by Parliament after having been accused of assuming the gestures, words, names, and attributes of Christ.

Pilloried, whipped, and bored through the tongue (which might utter blasphemies), he was also branded on the forehead with the letter "B" to signify his "horrid blasphemy" and imprisoned so that he might be "restrained from the Society of all People."[5] The blasphemer's extravagant symbolic and theatrical behavior and his claim that he was set up as a sign of the inward Christ's coming had led to a political/religious crisis fueling protracted debates in Parliament and testing the Cromwellian regime's commitment to freedom for godly consciences.[6] To orthodox godly members, who wondered whether the stern Mosaic injunctions of Leviticus against blasphemy applied in this instance, the Quaker's blasphemous behavior and declarations symbolized the religious and social subversion threatening both magistracy and ministry: "let us all stop our ears, and stone him – for he is guilty of horrid blasphemy," cried out one member.[7] Such fervent Old Testament language often characterized the theological debates over what many godly Parliamentarians considered appalling blasphemy.

During the religious and political crises of the 1640s and 1650s, the accusation of blasphemy was among the sharpest used to vilify religious and polemical opponents, especially those perceived to practice aberrant religious or political behavior.[8] Milton himself had been accused by the enraged Confuter of not only frequenting bordellos and play-houses – as if that weren't bad enough – but, as Milton gallingly complained in *An Apology for Smectymnuus*, "of blaspheming God and the King." "Horrid blasphemy!" the Confuter had lashed out at Milton and added, "You that love Christ, and know this miscreant wretch, stone him to death, lest yourselves smart for his impunity," a charge evoking the punishment for blasphemy in Leviticus 24: 16, the same biblical punishment evoked in the Interregnum debates over Nayler and one that Luther and Calvin had justified for blasphemers.[9] Later, on the eve of the Restoration, Roger L'Estrange, still horrified by Milton's powerful dismantling of the image of the martyred king, attempted to smear his republican opponent by linking his irreverent language and transgressive writing with the verbal crime of blasphemy: "not content to see that Sacred Head divided from the *Body*; your piercing Malice enters into the private Agonies of his struggling *Soul*; with a Blasphemous Insolence, invading the Prerogative of God himself."[10] The heretical Digger Gerrard Winstanley, who had followed the impulse of the Spirit to prophesy and write, likewise found himself stung by the disturbing accusation soon after Parliament's Ordinance was issued: "I my selfe [am] branded by some of your mouthes, as guilty of horrid *blasphemy*," he complained, referring to the established ministry whose "Pulpit wrings against Errors" propagated by those who deny "God and Christ, and the Scriptures, and the Gospel, and prayer, and all Ordinances."[11] The epithet "blasphemy" expressed the ultimate abhorrence of mainstream Puritans (or royalist pamphleteers, in the case of L'Estrange) for the verbal danger and disturbing symbolic conduct of heterodox groups and antinomians who were perceived as repudiating clerical authorities, orthodox beliefs, divine ordinances, moral restraints, and the existing social order itself.

Blasphemy seemed particularly frightening because it was expressed in potent verbal and symbolic ways – through a rapid proliferation of heretical tracts, through factious preaching and verbal assaults aimed at clerical and political authorities, and through shocking symbolic actions (as the case of the Quaker James Nayler illustrates). Heresiographers and orthodox Puritans associated blasphemy with dangerous equivocal speaking that threatened mainstream Protestant beliefs and authorities. Disturbed by the antinomian doctrines and language of the Quakers, who rejected the ministry, insisted upon the Christ within, and used reviling words, Richard Baxter complained that "The very person of Jesus Christ many of them blaspheme, and speak ... equivocally when they mention his name and nature," showing "that indeed they are not Christians."[12] During this age, the transgression of blasphemy, in its alarming verbal and symbolic manifestations, seemed in one sense like Satan's equivocal, blasphemous statements against the Godhead in *Paradise Lost*: it was in danger of becoming a "discourse without control" (5.803) and could inflame the most heated responses.[13] Horrified by blasphemous writings pouring forth from the presses, and the social and religious disorder they could incite, Presbyterians warned the Lord Protector Cromwell that the Beast of Revelation, who opens his mouth in blasphemy against God, was now manifesting his terrible powers throughout England: "How can the Friends of Christ chuse but endeavour the stopping of this mouth of Blasphemies."[14]

Nevertheless, the accusation of blasphemy was by no means the exclusive weapon of alarmed orthodox Puritans lashing out at the heretical writings, symbolic actions, preaching, and verbal threats of ultra-radical groups or subversive antinomians. As I will try to show later in this chapter, Milton evokes the terrifying and transgressive sin in *Paradise Lost*, but there he transforms mainstream Puritan responses so that the keen warnings about blasphemous actions and utterances, delivered by characters who tend to follow their conscience, do not reinforce religious orthodoxy. Milton's was a culture anxious about the dangerous offense of blasphemy;

yet despite Parliament's legislation, the definition of blasphemous behavior and language remained subjective and unstable, and could vary according to the ideological perspective of the particular writer or authority.

In the middle of *Civil Power*, his bold tract rejecting the authority of any church, civil magistrate, or outward power to intervene in matters of conscience and religious belief, Milton directly addresses the controversial issue of blasphemy. He attempts to distinguish blasphemy from "conscience in religion," not only by citing the authority of scripture but by citing, with apparent admiration, the 1650 Blasphemy Act:

> But some are ready to cry out, what shall then be don to blasphemie? Them I would first exhort not thus to terrifie and pose the people with a Greek word: but to teach them better what it is; being a most usual and common word in that language to signifie any slander, any malitious or evil speaking, whether against God or man or any thing to good belonging: blasphemie or evil speaking against God malitiously, is far from conscience in religion; according to that of *Marc 9. 39. there is none who doth a powerfull work in my name, and can likely speak evil of me.* If this suffice not, I referre them to that prudent and well deliberated act *August 9.* 1650; where the Parlament defines blasphemie against God, as far as it is a crime belonging to civil judicature . . . in plane English more warily, more judiciously, more orthodoxally then twice thir number of divines have don in many a prolix volume. (*CP* VII: 246–7).[15]

As Milton must have known, the Act was originally intended by the Purged Parliament as a political measure to suppress the extravagant behavior and writings of Ranter prophets and other sectarians exhibiting extreme religious enthusiasm and rejecting Protestant orthodoxy. Less than two years before *Civil Power*, it had been cited as authoritative legislation in the conservative godly provisions of "The Humble Petition and Advice": presented to Cromwell, this constitution aimed to prevent those guilty of blasphemy from serving in Parliament.[16] Furthermore, while Milton never mentions the Nayler episode in his late pre-Restoration writings, he must also have known that the Quaker leader, who seemed to follow the leadings of the Spirit, had been harshly punished by the state and humiliated for blasphemy. As we shall see, some of the Parliamentarians Milton had recently praised in the *Defensio Secunda* (1654) were themselves directly engaged in adjudicating that celebrated case of blasphemous behavior and symbolism; the horrid blasphemer Nayler, whose troublesome episode had not been forgotten by 1659, was still imprisoned when Milton published his tract defending the guidance of the Spirit's inward persuasive motions and insisting that "it is not lawfull for any power on earth to compell in matters of Religion" (*CP* VII: 238).[17] So how could the unorthodox

Milton, who objected to placing any yoke on the Holy Spirit within, recall
the Blasphemy Act with approval? Did he recall its punishment for blasphemy – six months in prison for the first offense and banishment from the
Commonwealth for the second? Is this a contradictory moment when he
aligns himself with the mainstream godly who considered blasphemous
those separatists who repudiated the moral law, rejected the Trinity,
impersonated Christ, or worshipped the Christ within?[18] After all, we
might note that he himself had once defied the authority of the Rump by
licensing the infamous *Racovian Catechism*, a Socianian manifesto flagrantly
denying the trinity: that book was condemned by Parliament as "blasphemous and scandalous."[19]

   In a political text that otherwise seems imprudently to oppose civil or
ecclesiastical powers interfering in matters of spiritual inward persuasion,
Milton's polemical assertion might be construed as an attempt to concili-
ate the conservative Parliament of Richard Cromwell who had himself
been convinced that Nayler "ought to die" for his blasphemy.[20] Nevertheless, it is hard not to sense the incongruity of Milton's polemical gesture
in a work whose theological and anticlerical arguments are often close to
the radical spiritualism of the Quakers whose combination of social and
religious heterodoxy proved to be troublesome throughout 1659 – though
Milton, probably in order not to compromise his authority as a writer,
never refers directly to them or their doctrines.[21] Even if he may not have
recalled the strictness of the Blasphemy Act, he must surely have understood that it enforced a Puritan code of morality, a human law, in the words
of the republican poet George Wither, "To keep *Blasphemous Libertines* in
aw; / And to correct their *Manners*, who transgress / Against the *Rules* of
Moral Righteousness."[22] Though Milton goes on to note that those authorities that adjudicate blasphemy may not be "unnerring always or infallible"
(*CP* VII: 247), his positive reference to the Act remains a vexed and,
arguably, a contradictory moment in his radical religious writing: he
scorns the orthodox divines and pays tribute to the Rump's judicious piece
of legislation, while evading the uncomfortable implications of a symbolic
act used to curb "Blasphemous and Execrable Opinions" during the
Interregnum – including those of leading Quaker prophets prompted by
the Spirit and illuminated by the "inner light" (both Nayler and Fox had
suffered under the Act of 1650 which superseded the 1648 Ordinance).[23]

   The Spirit, after all, might well take on more than one form, as less conservative Parliamentarians perceived when confronted by the dramatic
blasphemy of Nayler. Thus William Sydenham observed that the doctrine of
the light within, which led to behavior many of his colleagues considered

horrid blasphemy, was not easily distinguishable from the Puritan notion that truth could be found in the Holy Spirit within. As this Parliamentarian, whom Milton had praised in his *Defensio Secunda*, acutely remarked, "that which sticks most with me, is the nearness of this opinion to that which is a most glorious truth, that the spirit is personally in us"; and he added, "the opinions [the Quakers] hold, do border so near a glorious truth, that I cannot pass my judgment that [this behavior] is blasphemy."[24] Another figure Milton had singled out for praise in the *Defensio Secunda* likewise registered his doubts about Nayler's blasphemy: John Lambert, under whom the extravagant Quaker served in the Dunbar campaign, observed that the alleged blasphemer, while he appeared "puffed up" "by pride or otherwise," "was a man of a very unblameable life and conversation, a member of a very sweet society of an independent church."[25] Furthermore, Henry Lawrence, the "virtuous Father" of Milton's sonnet ("Lawrence of virtuous Father virtuous Son") and the Baptist Lord President of the Council debating the case, questioned whether Nayler's behavior should be called blasphemy at all, arguing that if Parliament were to "hang every man that says, *Christ is in you*," then they would indeed "hang a good many."[26] So why didn't Milton himself perceive the inconsistency of eloquently defending the Spirit's inward persuasive motions, while paying tribute to an Act used to repress alarming antinomians who exalted the indwelling light of Christ above any human law?[27] We may acknowledge the polemical strategy behind Milton's approval of the "prudent" Blasphemy Act, but we may also notice the inconsistency of invoking its authority in a work that seeks to persuade readers that civil and ecclesiastical councils, when it comes to judging matters of conscience, are fallible indeed.[28]

Another way of regarding Milton's positive citation is that it may serve as a gauge as to how far he was genuinely willing to go in tolerating more outlandish expressions of antinomian behavior and blasphemy. His praise of the Act suggests that, however heterodox his religious beliefs had become by 1659, he never would completely align himself with the most extreme symbolic behavior of contemporary antinomians and sectarians – that in some sense he remained aloof from them. Though they shared "a glorious truth" with Milton and moderate Parliamentarians whom he admired, they could not go altogether unchecked or without all restraint.[29] Even the Quaker Margaret Fell linked the verbal excesses of the Ranters to the terrifying Beast of Revelation 13 (as the poet of *Paradise Lost* would link Satan's), claiming that they give their "power unto the Beast; and … speakest great things, and blasphemies."[30] The issue of blasphemy going unchecked is indeed an urgent concern in *Paradise Lost*, as we shall see next:

but there Milton has revised the religious politics of blasphemy so that the deprecation of God and his creation remains a disturbing abomination, though one disengaged from radical spiritualism. There too Milton would place greater emphasis on the discerning responses of the faithful saint and his individual conscience to the dangers of horrid blasphemy.

Indeed, judging by the intensity with which *Paradise Lost* dramatizes the offense, Milton remains anxious about horrid blasphemy that involves a flagrant assault on the sacred and holy – including high-handedly reviling the name, powers, majesty, and honor of God and his begotten Messiah.[31] As Milton dramatizes the origins of blasphemy, he prompts his fit godly readers to consider afresh both the character and dangers of an offense so often regarded in his age as an alarming manifestation of the subversive and transgressive sectarian spirit. By dramatizing the sin, he would implicitly challenge the orthodox politics of blasphemous behavior and language. A subject where verbal, symbolic, religious, and political issues converge, blasphemy has been neglected by scholars working on Milton's poem and its mid-seventeenth-century milieu. Yet at least one seventeenth-century reader, John Beale, in an unpublished letter to John Evelyn, was disturbed by the devilish blasphemies in *Paradise Lost*: "he [Milton] mistakes the name of Poetry, to put such long & horrible Blasphemyes in the Mouth of Satan, as no man that feares God can endure to Read . . . or without a poysonous Impression."[32] In order to examine the offense of blasphemy in the poem, I will highlight several tense moments – the debate in Heaven in Book 3 and Satan's fueling of rebellion in Book 5 – where its dangers are powerfully dramatized and redefined by the heterodox Puritan poet.

The drama of the debate between God and his "only begotten Son" (3.80, 384) is itself heightened by evoking the terrifying sin of blasphemy whose implications are informed not only by biblical contexts but by the context of the offense as it was perceived in Milton's age of religious upheaval. Moreover, it may well be significant that the visionary poet brings up the highly provocative offense in a section of his sacred poem where, having invoked the light to shine "inward," he dramatizes his heterodox theology, including his antitrinitarianism – regularly linked with Quakers and blasphemy during the Interregnum and Restoration. Thus the year after *Paradise Lost* was published, the polemical William Penn, one of the most cultured Quaker writers, was committed to the Tower of London for publishing "a blasphemous treatise" attacking the Presbyterian doctrine of the trinity for lacking scriptural authority, an argument the heretical Milton concurred with.[33] In the antitrinitarian cosmos of *Paradise Lost*, blasphemy, while a disturbing offense against God and his creation, turns out, then, to have little to do with a radical religious doctrine or conscience. Rather, the sin is meant to unsettle the poem's readers who confront its Antichristian implications for Satan's unchecked power and malicious purposes. The Bible, Milton observes in *Areopagitica*, "oftimes relates blasphemy not nicely" (*CP* II: 517): and so, one might add, does *Paradise Lost* at a number of dramatic moments, including this one. The Son introduces the offense at the conclusion of his first speech to the Father in which, through a series of challenging questions highlighting the dialectic discourse of Milton's unorthodox Heaven, he stresses the deep malice and revenge fueling Satan's mission:

> shall the Adversary thus obtain
> His end, and frustrate thine, shall he fulfil
> His malice, and thy goodness bring to naught,
> Or proud return though to his heavier doom,
> Yet with revenge accomplish't and to Hell
> Draw after him the whole Race of mankind,
> By him corrupted? or wilt thou thyself
> Abolish thy Creation, and unmake,
> For him, what for thy glory thou hast made?
> So should thy goodness and thy greatness both
> Be question'd and blasphem'd without defense.   (3.156–66)

In boldly responding to the Father, the Son has indeed dared to follow his individual conscience and warn God that Satan's revengeful plan to frustrate his end, should it be realized, would be the greatest of all blasphemies. The Son's provocative rhetorical questions, escalating in emotional pressure as he elaborates the potential consequences and effects of Satan's malice, culminate in the last two lines of his speech, where he presents the disturbing possibility that such blasphemy might indeed go unchecked as God's "goodness" and "greatness both" would "Be question'd and blasphem'd without defense." By evoking the horrid sin of blasphemy in the Son's first dramatic address, Milton immediately heightens the tension of the debate in Heaven.[34] The Son's reference to Satan's "malice," when he wonders whether God's adversary shall "fulfil / His malice, and thy goodness bring to naught," is by no means limited to verbal abuse as a transgression of the sacred – in other words, blaspheming the name of God – though it recalls the association of blasphemy in *Civil Power* with "malitious or evil speaking . . . against God or man or any thing to good belonging."[35] The Son's reference to blasphemy places Satan's wilfully malicious designs in apocalyptic context, aligning his power with the crime of the Beast of Revelation 13 itself, a point especially pertinent to the confrontation between Satan and Abdiel discussed below: upon his heads, that beast has "the name of blasphemy" (Rev. 13:1). Moreover, bent "on desperate revenge" (3.85) and adamantly refusing to "repent" "though in pain" (1.96, 125) – unlike the stubborn and deeply anguished Adam who repents in Book 10 – the arch-blasphemer of *Paradise Lost* resembles the anguished followers of the Beast who "blasphemed the God of heaven because of their pains and their sores, and repented not of their deeds" (Rev. 16:11; see *CP* VI: 699). Like Satan, these hardened followers blaspheming God, "repented not to give [God] glory," as Revelation 16:9 notes.[36] This was a scriptural passage which the radical spiritualist George Fox, in a tract commenting on blasphemy, proud blasphemers, and the Book of Revelation, linked directly to the Beast in its "unrepented state": "blaspheming of the name of the God of heaven," Fox observed about hardened blasphemers, "you have not yet repented to give glory to God," and the Quaker visionary prophesied that the fierceness of God's wrath would punish those high-minded ungodly "who are in the uncontroverted state unrepented" and "blaspheme the God of Heaven."[37] The Son's bold questions wondering whether such an unrepentant "Adversary" shall "obtain / His end, and frustrate" God's (3.156–57) powerfully evoke as well the challenging inquiry of the psalmist for whom it is altogether unthinkable that the name of God might be left in disrepute and blasphemed without defense: "O God, how long shall the adversary reproach? shall the enemy blaspheme thy name for ever?" (Ps. 74:10). "Arise, O God," the psalmist provocatively urges the Lord – much like Milton's Son – and "plead thine own cause" (Ps. 74:22).

Milton the controversialist was at moments anxious himself about blasphemy as a political and religious crime with dangerous Antichristian implications. Thus, to take one example, the blasphemous Beast of Revelation, possessing the power and authority of the Dragon, became a particularly potent symbol of popish treason, idolatry, superstition, and verbal profanation for the zealous Protestant engaged in defending, in providential terms, the Republic's aggressive campaign against the Irish Catholics: in his *Observations Upon the Articles of Peace* (May 1649), Milton links the symbolic monster and the obdurate papist Irish Rebels of the 1640s, who exemplify "Popery, plung'd into Idolatrous and Ceremoniall Superstition, the very death of all true Religion; figur'd to us by the Scripture it selfe in the shape of that Beast, *full of the names of Blasphemy*" (*CP* III: 316; see Rev. 17:3).[38] By evoking the Beast of Revelation, as he castigates the Irish and the Presbyterians who assist them and as he justifies Cromwell's republican campaign, Milton shows that in his polemical writing he could indeed exploit contemporary fears about Antichristian blasphemy as a horrifying crime with apocalyptic resonance. The connection between blasphemy and the Beast of Revelation remains one, as we have begun to see, with suggestive implications for *Paradise Lost* and the Antichristian powers of its hardened arch-blasphemers. As Milton well knew from his own years as a polemicist, blasphemy was indeed at times a horrific offense: as a threat perceived in apocalyptic terms, it urgently needed to be checked.[39] But in dramatizing the Antichristian danger of the sin in his great spiritual poem, he would also reconceive and implicitly challenge the more orthodox politics of blasphemous behavior and language.

In the rebellion in Heaven, the political, religious, and verbal dimensions of blasphemy converge as Satan attempts to repudiate the authority of God and the recently exalted Son. Indeed, Satan's blasphemy, as he imitates God and assumes his attributes, acquires a symbolic and theatrical dimension as well. The transgressive Quaker leader Nayler, we may recall, was accused of blasphemy by mainstream Puritan authorities for exalting himself so that he made himself equal with Christ and God: he makes "himself God himself" so that "Our God is here supplanted," proclaimed one horrified MP; he impersonates "the names, attributes, titles, power, and honour of Christ: he assume[s] them all," proclaimed another. In "making [himself] equal with God or Christ," nothing less than "treason" and "blasphemy," he had "suffer[ed] adoration as God and Christ" and had even assumed the title "The Only begotten Son of God."[40] Blasphemy and theatricalism thus converged in the Nayler case, alarming orthodox Puritans. Yet quite unlike Milton's Satan, the blasphemous Quaker was not actually setting himself up to be Christ or God, but to be a sign of the inward Christ, though this distinction was misconstrued by orthodox authorities who regarded his imitation as "a horrid piece of pageantry and impostery."[41] The arch-blasphemer of *Paradise Lost*, however, does indeed attempt to make himself equal with God just before speaking his blasphemous arguments in public (provoking Abdiel's fierce rebuke): thus Raphael describes him as "Affecting all equality with God, / In imitation of that Mount whereon / *Messiah* was declar'd in sight of Heav'n" (5.763–65; cf. 725–26). Parliament's Blasphemy Act itself had condemned all who "in Honor, Excellency, Majesty and Power" "proceed to affirm and maintain" themselves "to be equal, and the same with the true God."[42] Moreover, the exalted Satan not only assumes the gestures and attributes of God; he immediately assumes the words of God as well: when, "High on a Hill" (5.757), he addresses his legions in terms of "Thrones, Dominations,

Princedoms, Virtues, Powers" (5.772), he assumes the exact words God had spoken when he, on the "holy Hill" (5.604), addressed the angels and proclaimed the anointing of his only begotten Son (see 5.601).

But in *Paradise Lost* the blasphemous Lucifer, it turns out, is no antinomian whose threatening theatrical and verbal imitation of God horrifies orthodox Puritan authorities reigning in Heaven. Rather, this proud blasphemer more closely resembles, at least in one sense, orthodox Protestants who invoked the authority of synods or convocations to determine matters of faith. It is Satan, after all, who proclaims, when confronted by Abdiel the second time, that he and his legions "in Synod met / Their Deities to assert, who while they feel / Vigor Divine within them, can allow / Omnipotence to none" (6.156–59). The term "Synod," used by Satan to characterize his assembly (cf. 2.391, 10.661) which has just rejected and scorned Abdiel, was a particularly resonant one in Milton's age of religious controversy: it evoked an assembly of the Church of England and, more specifically, a council of Presbyterian ministers.[43] Milton had used the ecclesiastical term with derision in his polemical prose where he associates synods with the fraudulent contrivings of ecclesiastical councils: "let it bee produc'd what good hath bin don by Synods from the first times of Reformation," he remarks, noting that they are "liable to the greatest fraud and packing" so that they offer "no solution ... of evil, but an increase rather" (*CP* III: 535; cf. 492). And in *Civil Power* he would argue, contrary to the Presbyterian Assembly of Divines, that "no synod, no session of men" could determine controversies of faith or cases of religious conscience (*CP* VII: 248; cf. 243).[44] *Paradise Lost* thus complicates and revises the orthodox Puritan politics and language of blasphemy. The proud blasphemer invokes the authority of a synod, an orthodox ecclesiastical assembly, while his challenger, the saint accusing him of horrid blasphemy, turns out to be a fiery Puritan dissenter ("I alone / Seem'd in thy World erroneous to dissent / From all" [6.145–47]) in an antitrinitarian Heaven where all the saints freely serve and possess "the same free Will and Power to stand" (4.66) or fall. Milton, indeed, has dramatized the inflammatory issue of blasphemy in such a way as to highlight the response of the faithful saint who follows his own individual conscience.[45] Having lived through a turbulent age when religious assemblies and political councils tended to abhor and chastise aberrant behavior, Milton has, quite strikingly, made the individual saint in his poem – and not the fallible convocation – the righteous enemy and arbiter of horrid blasphemy.

In dramatizing the origins of blasphemy as a heinous crime, Milton's theologically heretical epic reveals to its godly readers that the highly controversial offense, while a threat to the social order of Heaven, in fact has little to do with "conscience in religion." As a crime in *Paradise Lost*, "Blaspheming God, or the Holiness or Righteousness of God," to use the words of the Blasphemy Act again,[46] is not associated with the flamboyant behavior, antinomian doctrines, or verbal abuses practiced by the unorthodox faithful – as it so often was during the upheavals of the Civil War and Interregnum. Rejecting the new laws of Heaven, while affecting equality with God and imitating the Son, the charismatic arch-blasphemer of Milton's poem reveals that he is no radical spiritualist prompted by the spontaneous inward motions of the Spirit (unlike Nayler or Milton's Samson with his "rousing motions"); rather, in his meditated revenge he is moved by the envy, rage, malice, and all-consuming hatred he expresses towards Milton's Son of God who "by right of merit Reigns" (6.43; cf. 3.309) in this unorthodox Heaven. Indeed, malice, wrath, envy, as well as corrupt or evil speaking against God – especially in conjunction – were construed in Milton's culture as signs of blasphemous behavior. Thus Walter Strickland, another moderate Parliamentarian praised in Milton's *Second Defence*, denied that the antinomian Nayler was guilty of blasphemy because not only had he not cursed or reviled "the Creator," as some MPs noticed, but he had "showed no malice to Christ, or envy" and had "no evil spirit or malice in him against God."[47] And that of course is precisely what Satan, with his blasphemous mouth, does show toward God as well as the newly anointed Messiah whom he claims has eclipsed him and his legions of angels: "fraught / With envy against the Son of God," his subversive actions and "Ambiguous words," agents of corruption which "taint integrity," are fueled by his "Deep malice" (5.661–62, 703–04, 666).

Blasphemy is the first crime Lucifer is accused of in Heaven: "O argument blasphemous, false and proud!" Abdiel fires back at him, "Words which no ear ever to hear in Heav'n / Expected, least of all from thee, ingrate" (5.809–11). Abdiel's sharp accusation, his very first utterance, is an immediate response to Satan's provocative and abusive speech in Heaven which rejects the "high Decree" (5.717) of the Father and distorts the issue of political freedom and service among God's angels:

> Who can in reason then or right assume
> Monarchy over such as live by right
> His equals, if in power and splendor less,
> In freedom equal? or can introduce
> Law and Edict on us, who without Law
> Err not?   (5.794–99)

As I have argued elsewhere, Satan as equivocal politician often speaks with "a double contradictory sense" – proclaiming to his legions the authority of their "magnific Titles" (like a royalist apologist; 5.773), while seeming a "Patron of liberty" (4.958) urging, like a revolutionary, his compatriots to cast off their yoke.[48] Satan's "impious obloquy" – his abusive language reviling the king of kings and condemning his "just Decree" – is itself a horrid blasphemy, an equivocal discourse capable of fueling rebellion (5.813–14). Indeed, Satan's subversive verbal discourse – his "evil speaking against God maliciously" aimed at quitting "the yoke / Of God's *Messiah*" and the "indulgent Laws" of Heaven (5.882–83) – violates a basic scriptural injunction, that of Exodus 22:28. The origin of the crime of blasphemy in the Bible and Western Christendom, this scriptural passage is a charge conjoining religious and political crimes (including sedition and treason), one Milton cited and quoted in *de doctrina Christiana*: "Thou shall not revile [God], nor curse the ruler of thy people" (*CP* VI: 234, 799). It is Satan's crime of horrid blasphemy, as much as any of his "Acts of hateful strife" (6.264), which defines what it means to be called "alienate from God" (5.877).

In the colloquy in Heaven, the Son had dared to warn God that his "goodness and [his] greatness both" / might "Be . . . blasphem'd without defense" (3.165–66): here, when the goodness and greatness of God have indeed been blasphemed, the solitary angel provides that defense – "by experience taught," Abdiel counters Satan's abusive words, "we know how good / And of our good, and of our dignity / How provident he is, how far from thought / To make us less, bent rather to exalt / Our happy state under one Head more near / United" (5.826–31). Abdiel, moreover, responds with particular severity because he recognizes that a verbal expression of unrestrained blasphemy could easily induce others from "Heav'n's Host," a third of whom have been "allur'd" by ambiguous words, to blaspheme and violate God's ordinances: "Cease then this impious rage," he concludes his initial fiery speech blasting Satan's transgressive words, "And tempt not these; but hast'n to appease / Th' incensed Father, and th' incensed Son" (5.709–10, 845–47). The fear that a dangerous blasphemer, through potent verbal expression or symbolic actions, could easily seduce others to blaspheme was often expressed by defensive godly Puritans during the Civil War and Interregnum years, as I began to show earlier. Nayler had "not only committed blasphemy himself," protested one MP, "but he [had] caused many others to commit blasphemy."[49] In *Paradise Lost* the tense confrontation between Abdiel and the arch-blasphemer and his "Apostates" who "despise / God and *Messiah*" (6.717–18) thus imaginatively recreates, though in less orthodox terms, the godly's detestation of blasphemy and its power to spread quickly. Orthodox Puritans in particular felt the urgent need to warn against the contagious power of blasphemous discourse and behavior: "we cannot show too great a detestation of it," responded one horrified member to Nayler's blasphemy, while the fear of blasphemy going unchecked prompted another to urge his colleagues to "put on courage; and let not the enemies of God have . . . liberty to blaspheme his name."[50] This "great seducer of the people," orthodox authorities feared, was evidence that "pernicious" blasphemers were themselves "spreading, infectious, and contagious."[51] Even Cromwell thought that "many" had "apostatized" and justified themselves "under the notion of Liberty": he worried about "prodigious blasphemies" plaguing the nation, including "contempt of God and Christ, denying of him, contempt of him and his ordinances and of the Scriptures."[52] In *Paradise Lost*, the "Apostate" who abjures his faith, seems a patron of liberty, and inflames others to blaspheme is indeed "Contemptuous" of God and the Son; and contemptuous too of all that has been created by the Father's Word as he resolves "With all his Legions to dislodge, and leave / Unworshipt, unobey'd the Throne supreme" (5.670–71).

Nevertheless *Paradise Lost*, while vividly recreating the fear of blasphemy in Milton's age, does not conform to the more orthodox Puritan detestation of this horrid crime and its power to proliferate quickly. In this daring sacred poem where the godly are not orthodox Puritan saints, it is a lone dissenter, after all, who remains "unseduc'd" by the tempter's blasphemy and in "a flame of zeal severe" (5.899, 807) shows his great detestation of the sin, much as the unmoved Son of God of *Paradise Regained*, following only his conscience and the Spirit within, abhors "blasphemous" talk aimed at getting him to serve and worship Satan as Lord (4.170–92). In *Paradise Lost* it is the zealous dissenter who also defines the apostate angel's perverse blasphemy as an infectious crime "spread" by "contagion" (5.880) among the ungodly who do not fence their ears against its discourse. Despite Abdiel's dissenting presence, Satan's sophistry and contemptuous claim that he and his legions are "self-begot, self-rais'd" (5.860) and therefore do not owe their being to a prior creator who "form'd the Pow'rs of Heav'n" (824), wins immediate approval from his audience of innumerable faithless angels. Their response confirms the potency of blasphemous discourse to captivate listeners and ensnare their consciences: "as the sound of waters deep," Raphael's narrative tells us, "Hoarse murmur echo'd to his words applause / Through the infinite Host" (5.872–74).[53]

Satan's blasphemous discourse is therefore an instance of a powerful, potentially uncontrolled verbal assault on the most sacred values. It is a form of abuse involving seditious words associated with, as Milton put it in *An Apology*, "the rancor of an evill tongue" and the "seducing malice" (*CP* I: 869, 875) capable, as Michael tells Satan, of instilling "malice into thousands, once upright / And faithful" (6.270–71). Employing "the terror" of his "potent tongue" (6.134–35) to defy God and Messiah, the verbal powers of the arch-blasphemer resemble those of the Beast of Revelation who would make war with the saints (Rev. 13:7), not to mention those of Spenser's Blatant Beast with his unrestrained blasphemous tongue at the end of the *Faerie Queene* (6.12.32–40). Possessing, much like Satan, "his own dominion and throne and mighty power," as Milton noted of the scriptural Beast in the *First Defence* (*CP* IV: 384), "there was [also] given unto him," in the words of Revelation, "a mouth speaking great ... blasphemies," so that "he opened his mouth in blasphemy against God, to blaspheme his name, and his tabernacle, and them that dwell in heaven" (Rev. 13:2, 5–6).[54] The verbal crime in *Paradise Lost*, with its apocalyptic resonance, underscores, moreover, the vulnerability of a radical Puritan poet anxious about having fallen on "evil tongues" (7.26) of blaspheming cavaliers. The phrase "evil tongues" aligns the sacred poet not only with the fearless Abdiel but with "the Holy One of Heav'n" who is subjected, in the midst of the wars of Truth fought in Milton's Heaven, to the "tongue blasphemous" of that "furious King" Moloch (6.359–60, 357). In his antimonarchical prose, where he had cited approvingly Christopher Goodman on kings who "become blasphemers of God" (*CP* III: 250), Milton associated blasphemy and the profanation of the holy with the evil tongues of dissolute cavaliers "flown with insolence and wine" (*Paradise Lost* 1.502). Countering the claim that the martyred king's chiefest arms against his persecutors had been "Prayers and Teares," Milton caustically answered in *Eikonoklastes* that there were "thousands of blaspheming Cavaliers about [the King], whose mouthes let fly Oaths and Curses by the voley; were those the Praiers? and those Carouses drunk to the confusion of all things good or holy, did those minister the Teares?" (*CP* III: 452).[55]

The highly charged accusation of blasphemy, so often used by orthodox authorities in Milton's age to malign sectarians and religious radicals for their perceived subversive behavior, heterodox writings, equivocal speaking, and verbal assaults challenging the authority of scripture, God, ministry, and magistracy is thus now directed against the "seducing malice" and equivocal discourse of Satan and his blaspheming followers. We have already seen how Old Testament language and punishments were invoked in the fierce debates about blasphemy and had been used to condemn that greatest of blasphemers, Nayler. The scriptural story of the rebellious Korah, Dathan, and Abiram from Numbers 16 alluded to at the end of Abdiel's first dramatic encounter with Satan and his blasphemous discourse likewise evokes the dreaded crime of blasphemy and the wrathful divine punishment it may provoke: "Yet not for thy advice or threats I fly / These wicked Tents devoted, lest the wrath / Impendent, raging into sudden flame / Distinguish not" (5.889–92), responds the loyal seraph to his blasphemous adversary with his murmuring and faithless legions. Here Milton's lines recall the warning of Moses to the congregation of Israelites following the blasphemous Korah, Dathan, and Abiram: "Depart, I pray you, from the tents of these wicked men, and touch nothing of theirs, lest ye be consumed in all their sins" (Num. 16:26). The earth opened her mouth to swallow up Korah and his assembly of blasphemers (Num. 16:32) much as Tartarus "opens wide / His fiery *Chaos* to receive" (6.54–55) those who have reviled Milton's God and Messiah – though that does not occur until after their blasphemous words and actions have brought Heaven to a state of "horrid confusion" (6.668).

During the Interregnum orthodox Puritans, alarmed by the growing sectarian threat, evoked this scriptural story to condemn frightening antinomians whose behavior and language seemed blasphemous. Thus Richard Baxter compared the reviling language of blasphemous Quakers toward magistrates to the language of Korah and his rebellious followers, while the author of *Nayler's Blasphemies Discovered* evoked the biblical story specifically to attack Nayler's horrid blasphemies and to convey the sinfulness and dangers of an antinomian and his followers scorning and reviling the godly ministry: "Did not your spirit speak in *Corah, Dathan, Abiram*, and their adherents? and did not they raile against their Ministers?" he demanded.[56] How Milton himself would have handled this biblical story about blasphemous rebellion in a full-scale tragedy, since he listed it among his possible plans (see *CP* VIII: 555), is a matter we can only speculate about. But in *Paradise Lost* the potent biblical allusion operates much differently than it does in orthodox Puritan writings castigating the horrid blasphemies of radical spiritualists and threatening antinomians. The grave spiritual danger and punishment Satan and his "Spirits apostate" (7.610) face is not the result of railing against an orthodox ministry or clerical authority but rather the consequence of blasphemously scorning the unorthodox Godhead and the newly anointed Messiah whose authority, justified by merit and worthiness more than anything else, the restless adversary deeply disdains and reviles. And so the one angel who follows his conscience and warns Satan's multitudes of God's impending wrath evokes biblical charges against blaspheming the sacred name of God, while his fierce confrontations reconceive the politics of blasphemy that had become sharply intensified during the Civil War and Commonwealth years.

Thus by dramatizing one of the most fearful religious offenses of Milton's age, *Paradise Lost* reengages freshly the implications of blasphemy as a transgressive crime that was widely perceived as an intolerable verbal and symbolic assault on religious orthodoxy and considered treason against magistracy as well as ministry. In its own less topical way, the poem illustrates, as vividly as any Puritan polemic or the heated Nayler debates, the unsettling power, contagious effects, and divisive consequences of blasphemous behavior and utterances. But in the heterodox spiritual world of his great poem, where Milton resourcefully transforms the religious politics of blasphemy, the poet shows his fit readers the urgency of discerning, to recall *Civil Power*, between a radical "conscience in religion" and "blasphemie or evil speaking against God maliciously." And he does so in an imaginative work where the arbiter of horrid blasphemy is neither a Parliament nor an ecclesiastical council but the individual conscience of a single saint and a heterodox Son of God.

NOTES

1. *CP* VII: 246. For the 1648 Ordinance and the 1650 Act, see *Acts and Ordinances of the Interregnum, 1642–1660*, ed. C. H. Firth and R. S. Rait, 3 vols. (London, 1911), vol. I, pp. 1133–36; vol. II, pp. 409–12. The Blasphemy Ordinance carried the death penalty if the accused party failed to recant.
2. For blasphemy as a threat to both church and state, see also the *Diary of Thomas Burton*, ed. John T. Rutt, 4 vols. (London, 1828), which records a member of Parliament asserting in 1656 that the principles of blasphemous sectarians "strike both at ministry and magistracy" (vol. I, p. 25); one MP debating James Nayler's blasphemy, discussed below, echoed the Blasphemy Act when he asserted that "this man's principles and practices are destructive to human society" (vol. I, p. 124). See also *A List of some of the Grand Blasphemers and Blasphemies* (London, 1654) for a list of blasphemers imprisoned in the early 1650s.
3. See Coppe's letter to Salmon and Wyke in *A Collection of Ranter Writings from the 17th Century*, ed. Nigel Smith (London, 1981), p. 117. On heresies as blasphemous in doctrine and dangerous to the state, see also Ephraim Pagitt, *Heresiography, Or a Description of the Heretickes and Sectaries Sprang up in these latter times*, 5th edn. (London, 1654), sig. B2v.
4. The phrase suggesting Nayler's theatricalism comes from Richard Baxter's *Reliquae Baxterianae*, ed. Matthew Sylvester (London, 1696), p. 77.

5. *Journals of the House of Commons*, vol. VII, pp. 468–69. For a sampling of contemporary accounts of Nayler as blasphemer, see *Diary of Thomas Burton*, vol. I; *Cobbett's Complete Collection of State Trials and Proceedings for High Treason and Other Crimes and Misdemeanors*, comp. Thomas Bayley Howell, 34 vols. (London, 1809–28), vol. V, pp. 801–42, which also contains John Deacon's *The Grand Imposter Examined* (1656); Thomas Collier, *A Looking-Glasse for the Quakers* (London, 1657); Anon., *A True Narrative of the Examination, Tryall, and Sufferings of James Nayler* ([London,] 1657); William Grigge, *The Quakers Jesus* (London, 1658); *Mercurius Politicus*, December 11–18, 1656, in Joad Raymond, ed., *Making the News: An Anthology of the Newsbooks of Revolutionary England, 1641–1660* (New York, 1993), pp. 410–13.

6. On Nayler as a sign to convince the nation of Christ's coming, see *Diary of Thomas Burton*, vol. I, p. 48. On issues of religious liberty and its limits, see Blair Worden, "Toleration and the Cromwellian Protectorate," in W. J. Sheils, ed., *Persecution and Toleration* (Oxford, 1984), pp. 199–231. See also now Leo Damrosch, *The Sorrows of Quaker Jesus: James Nayler and the Puritan Crackdown on the Free Spirit* (Cambridge, MA, 1996), an excellent study that appeared after my chapter was completed.

7. *Diary of Thomas Burton*, vol. I, p. 75. For references to Leviticus in the Nayler blasphemy debates, see vol. I, pp. 25, 55, 87, 112, 113, 121, 128–29, 134. The proposal to issue the death penalty for Nayler, however, was defeated by ninety-six votes to eighty-two: *Journals of the House of Commons*, vol. VII, p. 468. On Nayler's blasphemy, see also T. A. Wilson and F. J. Merli, "Nayler's Case and the Dilemma of the Protectorate," *University of Birmingham Historical Journal* 10 (1965–66), 44–59; W. K. Jordan, *The Development of Religious Toleration in England*, 4 vols. (Cambridge, MA, 1932–40), vol. III, pp. 221–35; William C. Braithwaite, *The Beginnings of Quakerism*, 2nd edn. (Cambridge, 1955), pp. 241–68; Barry Reay, *The Quakers and the English Revolution* (London, 1985), pp. 53–55; Worden, "Toleration and the Cromwellian Protectorate," pp. 222–25.

8. The practice of describing opponents as blasphemers has, however, been carefully traced back to the Reformation: see the discussion of Luther and Calvin in Leonard W. Levy, *Treason Against God: A History of the Offense of Blasphemy* (New York, 1981), ch. 5. Levy's study remains a helpful account of the offense beginning with ancient Jewish thought; the subject has otherwise been relatively neglected by historians. See, however, G. D. Nokes, *A History of the Crime of Blasphemy* (London, 1928), a study of the crime in England.

9. *A Modest Confutation of A Slanderous and Scurrilous Libell, Animadversions upon the Remonstrants Defense against Smectymnuus* (London, 1642), "To the Reader"; cf. pp. 2, 22. For *An Apology*, see *CP* I: 893–95 (where Milton mocks the Confuter's Mosaic suggestion for punishing blasphemy: "I beseech ye friends, ere the brick-bats flye"). For Reformation writers, see Luther's "An Exposition of the Eighty-Second Psalm" (1530), trans. C. M. Jacobs, in *The Works of Martin Luther* (Philadelphia, 1931), vol. IV, pp. 310–11, and Calvin, *Commentaries on the Last Four Books of Moses*, trans. Charles W. Bingham (Grand Rapids, 1950), vol. II, pp. 431–32, vol. IV, p. 94. See also Levy, *Treason Against God*, pp. 128–32.

10. *No Blinde Guides* (London, 1660), p. 2; the tract, a response to Milton's "seditious pamphlet" attacking the royalist preacher Matthew Griffith, was published in April 1660. L'Estrange then went on to assert that Milton's "Bold Design" was suited to his "*Irreverence* of *Language*." See also James Heath's reference to *Eikonoklastes* as "an impudent and blasphemous Libel": *A Brief Chronicle Of the Late Intestine Warr* (1663), p. 435, in William Riley Parker, *Milton's Contemporary Reputation* (Columbus, 1940), p. 109.

11. *Truth Lifting up Its Head above Scandals* (1649), in *The Works of Gerrard Winstanley*, ed. George H. Sabine (Ithaca, 1941), p. 101.

12. *One Sheet against the Quakers* (London, 1657), pp. 3–4. See also Pagitt, *Heresiography*, p. 145. On the responses of the orthodox godly to sectarianism during the Interregnum, see Ann Hughes, "The Frustrations of the Godly," in John Morrill, ed., *Revolution and Restoration: England in the 1650s* (London, 1992), pp. 70–90.

13. All references to Milton's poetry are taken from *John Milton: Complete Poems and Major Prose*, ed. Merritt Y. Hughes (Indianapolis, 1957).

14. *A Second Beacon Fired. Humbly Presented to the Lord Protector and the Parliament* (London, 1654), p. 9; referring to Rev. 13:6. Likewise distressed about the voluminous number of printed texts spreading blasphemous doctrines and affronting the old order, Daniel Featley complained that "the Presses sweat and groane under their load of blasphemies," citing as examples recent heretical works by Roger Williams, Richard Overton, and of course Milton himself: *The Dippers dipt* (London, 1651), "The Epistle Dedicatory."

15. Unlike many of his contemporaries Milton wished to distinguish blasphemy, in the sense of "evil speaking against God malitiously," from heresy: "Those who, in all sincerity, and with no desire to stir up controversy, teach or discuss some doctrine concerning the deity which they have quite apparently, as they see it, learned from Holy Scriptures, are in no sense guilty of the sin of blasphemy." The zealous defender of radical Christian liberty likewise remained concerned about the inflammatory accusation of blasphemy easily abused by authors who "denounce out of hand as blasphemy [*protinus blasphemiam esse clamitent*] pretty well any opinion about God or religious matters which [does] not tally with their own" (*de doctrina Christiana, CP* VI: 700). For the Latin, see *CW* XVII: 158.

16. See *The Constitutional Documents of the Puritan Revolution, 1625–1660*, ed. Samuel R. Gardiner (Oxford, 1906; rpt. 1979), pp. 450–51; cf. pp. 448, 455: no one guilty of the offenses mentioned in the Act was allowed to serve. The Humble Petition and Advice was a less tolerant constitution than the Instrument of Government which it replaced: Worden, "Toleration and the Cromwellian Protectorate," p. 227. See also the citation of the Blasphemy Act in the 1654 ordinance for ejecting scandalous ministers: *The Stuart Constitution*, ed. J. P. Kenyon (Cambridge, 1986), p. 315.

17. Nayler was released from prison by the reinstated Rump in September 1659; on people's memory of his episode, see Reay, *Quakers and the English Revolution*, pp. 84, 93.

18. Cf. Winstanley who complains of those "professors" who "call this blasphemie, to say Christ is in you" (*The Works*, p. 476).

19. For details, see *Journals of the House of Commons*, vol. VII, pp. 113–14, and William Riley Parker, *Milton: A Biography*, 2 vols. (Oxford, 1968), vol. I, pp. 394–95, vol. II, p. 994, n.152.

20. On Richard Cromwell's conservative leanings, including his sympathy toward the Presbyterians, see Michael R. Watts, *The Dissenters: From the Reformation to the French Revolution* (Oxford, 1978), p. 212. On his response to Nayler, see *Diary of Thomas Burton*, vol. I, p. 126, and Reay, *Quakers and the English Revolution*, p. 24.

21. On the fear of sectaries and the hostility toward Quakers in 1659 and the period leading up to the Restoration, see Reay, *The Quakers and the English Revolution*, ch. 5.

22. George Wither, *The British Appeals, with Gods Mercifull Replies, On the Behalfe of the Common-wealth of England* (London, 1651), p. 26.

23. For Fox punished under the Blasphemy Act, see *The Journal of George Fox*, ed. John L. Nickalls (London, 1975), p. 52; for other charges of blasphemy: see pp. 133–35, 159, 359. See also Christopher Hill, Barry Reay, and William Lamont, *The World of the Muggletonians* (London, 1983), p. 23, for the imprisonment of John Reeve and Lodowick Muggleton for six months under the provisions of the Blasphemy Act. For other victims of the Blasphemy Act, see J. F. McGregor, "Seekers and Ranters," in J. F. McGregor and B. Reay, eds., *Radical Religion in the English Revolution* (Oxford, 1984), pp. 132–34.

24. *Diary of Thomas Burton*, vol. I, pp. 69, 86; cf. p. 99. See also Worden, "Toleration and the Cromwellian Protectorate," pp. 207–08. See *CP* IV: 675–78 for the Parliamentarians highly praised in the *Defensio Secunda*, including several not mentioned in my paragraph (John Desborough, Walter Strickland, Sir Gilbert Pickering): all were voices for leniency in these impassioned debates over Nayler's blasphemy. Cromwell's response to the Nayler case was more muted: see Derek Hirst, *Authority and Conflict: England, 1603–1658* (London, 1986), p. 344.

25. *Diary of Thomas Burton*, vol. I, p. 33.

26. *Ibid.*, pp. 62–63, where the Lord President Lawrence confesses that "it is hard to define what is blasphemy." Even Cromwell, who had no sympathy for the excesses of James Nayler, was worried about Parliament's religious intolerance going too far: as he asked a meeting of leading Army officers on February 27, 1656/57, might not "the Case of Nayler . . . happen to be your own case"? See *The Writings and Speeches of Oliver Cromwell*, ed. Wilbur C. Abbott, 4 vols. (Cambridge, MA, 1937–47), vol. IV, p. 417.

27. See *Civil Power*, which stresses that "we ought to follow" the "Spirit within us . . . rather then any law of man" (*CP* VII: 242).

28. The issue of the fallibility of magistrates and assemblies of divines regarding matters of conscience runs throughout *Civil Power*: see e.g. *CP* VII: 243, 244, 246, 247, 252. The last part of the final sentence containing his discussion of the Blasphemy Act could also be read as a rhetorical qualification of Parliament's

authority on the same grounds: "although in all likelihood they whose whole studie and profession these things are should be most intelligent and authentic therin, as they are for the most part, yet neither they nor these unnerring always or infallible" (VII: 247).

29. One of course recalls his statement in *Areopagitica* where he notes that one of "only two sorts of writings" magistrates in Greece took notice of was "blasphemous" writings (*CP* II: 494).

30. Fell, *A Testimonie of the Touch-Stone* (London, 1656), p. 24. Even the radical spiritualist and communist Winstanley was alarmed at the extravagant practices of the blasphemous Ranters: see *Works*, pp. 366, 399–403, 482, 519, and the postscript to *England's Spirit Unfoulded*, ed. G. E. Aylmer in *Past & Present* 40 (July 1968), 14–15.

31. See *de doctrina Christiana*, which emphasizes just before discussing blasphemy as a kind of evil-speaking, that "we are taught to mention God's name in a holy and religious way" (*CP* VI: 698).

32. Letter from John Beale to John Evelyn in the Evelyn collection (British Library), dated March 9, 1680/81; MS Letters 145. See also MS Letters 108 (dated December 24, 1670) where Beale notes that Milton "hath great faults in his *Paradyse Lost* in his plea for our Original right, & in the long *blasphemies* of Devils; For which he hath no Authority, & they beget a bad, and afflict a good Spirit." I am grateful to Nicholas Von Maltzhan for calling my attention to Beale's unpublished letters.

33. On Quakers, including Nayler, denying the doctrine of the trinity, see Jonathan Clapham, *A Full Discovery and Confutation of the wicked and damnable Doctrines of the Quakers* (London, 1656), pp. 16, 74. On Penn's antitrinitarianism, see his *Sandy Foundation Shaken* (London, 1668); cf. *de doctrina Christiana, CP* VI: 420. On Penn's blasphemy, see *The Diary of John Evelyn*, ed. E. S. De Beer (London, 1959), p. 527. There would later be, in 1698, a new act against antitrinitarian blasphemy.

34. For a full account of the debate's dramatic elements, see Michael Lieb, "Milton's `Dramatick Constitution': The Celestial Dialogue in *Paradise Lost*, Book III," *Milton Studies* 23 (1987), 215–40.

35. On Milton not limiting the offense of blasphemy to evil speaking against God, see *de doctrina Christiana, CP* VI: 699.

36. See also the Geneva Bible gloss on this passage: "The wicked were hardhearted & stubbern when God punished them" (*The Geneva Bible: A facsimile of the 1560 edition* [Madison, WI, 1969]). Cf. the "hard'n'd" rebel angels during the war in Heaven: *Paradise Lost* 6.789ff.

37. *A Declaration of The Ground of Error & Errors, Blasphemy, Blasphemers, and Blasphemies* (London, 1657), pp. 11–19, esp. 16–17. See also *Newes Coming up out of the North Sounding towards the South* (London, 1654), pp. 6, 13, 34–36.

38. Cf. the Geneva Bible commentary on the reference in Rev. 17:3 to the Beast "full of names of blasphemie": it is "Ful of idolatrie, superstition and contempt of the true God."

39. Milton accused both Salmasius and Alexander More of blasphemy, as well as malice and calumny – all of which are associated with the great blasphemer of

Paradise Lost (see e.g. *Pro Se Defensio, CP* IV: 724, 735, and cf. Satan's "calumnious Art" [*Paradise Lost* 5.770] and Satan as "the calumniator" in *de doctrina Christiana, CP* VI: 350). On Salmasius's blasphemous mouth and the Beast of Revelation, see *CP* IV: 367; for More see also *CP* IV: 598–600. For Milton's association of the English Presbyterian divines with Antichristian blasphemy, see the Digression to the *History of Britain* (*CP* V: 449). Furthermore, Milton considered nothing more "blasphemous against our Saviour" than the Antichristian utterances of worldly hirelings whom he linked with the blaspheming Beast and the Whore of Revelation 13:1 and 17:3 (*CP* VII: 318, 306, 308, 320).

40. *Diary of Thomas Burton*, vol. I, pp. 27, 67–68, 55, 60–61; see also vol. I, pp. 24, 35, 50, 56, 59, 67, 129. On Nayler called "begotten Son," see also Howell, *State Trials*, vol. V, p. 809. Cf. [Francis Higginson], *A Brief Relation of the Irreligion of the Northern Quakers* (London, 1653), on the "horrid Blasphemies of the Quakers against God and his Christ" (p. 2).

41. *Diary of Thomas Burton*, vol. I, p. 72; cf. vol. I, p. 76; on the misinterpretation of the significance of Nayler's symbolic behavior, see also the useful account in Ivan Roots, *The Great Rebellion, 1642–1660* (London, 1966), pp. 205–09.

42. *Acts and Ordinances*, vol. II, p. 410.

43. See the *OED* s.v. "Synod" 1b, and *The Reason of Church-Government, CP* I: 789. The word is discussed by Thomas N. Corns, *Milton's Language* (London, 1990), p. 107.

44. For the *Westminster Confession of Faith* and the authority of synods, see *CP* VII: 248, n. 26. Cf. John Saltmarsh on the fallibility of synods: *The Smoke in the Temple* (London, 1646), "Spiritual Principles drawn forth," p. 68; and Richard Overton in *A Remonstrance of Many Thousand Citizens* (1646), in *Leveller Manifestoes of the Puritan Revolution*, ed. Don M. Wolfe (New York, 1944), p. 121.

45. For Milton's concern that "the standard of judgment" should be "individual conscience itself," see *de doctrina Christiana, CP* VI: 623.

46. *Acts and Ordinances*, vol. II, p. 410.

47. *Diary of Thomas Burton*, vol. I, p. 56. See pp. 99, 122–23, 129 where other MPs stressed that Nayler had not cursed God. However, one MP did argue that "in his passion . . . [Nayler] committed that cursing" (p. 124). In his commentary on blasphemy and blasphemers, George Fox echoed the Epistle of Paul to the Colossians when he urged believers in the Light during the Interregnum "to put away Malice, Wrath, Blasphemy, [and] filthy communication out of their mouths" (see Col. 3:8): *A Declaration of the Ground of Error & Errors*, p. 14.

48. See "'An Ambiguous Monster': Representing Rebellion in Milton's Polemics and *Paradise Lost*," *Huntington Library Quarterly* 55 (1992), 295–315; the phrase "a double contradictory sense" comes from *The Tenure of Kings and Magistrates*, where Milton accuses the Presbyterian divines of equivocal behavior: *CP* III: 195.

49. *Diary of Thomas Burton*, vol. I, p. 51; cf. p. 70 where another MP notes that "the spreading of [blasphemy] in England and Ireland . . . appears . . . to proceed from some encouragement it hath." On Nayler bewitching his followers to

commit "strange Absurdities" and utter "many horrible Blasphemies," see
Mercurius Politics, December 11–18, 1656, in *Making the News*, p. 412.

50. *Diary of Thomas Burton*, vol. I, pp. 27, 51.

51. *Ibid.*, pp. 79, 124; *Journals of the House of Commons*, vol. VII, p. 465. On the fear
that England would be reputed "the great nursery of blasphemies and heresies" see *Diary of Thomas Burton*, vol. I, p. 86. For the fear of blasphemy spreading "by Preaching, Teaching, Printing, or Writing," see the 1648 Ordinance in
Acts and Ordinances, vol. II, p. 1133.

52. *Writings and Speeches of Oliver Cromwell*, vol. III, pp. 226–68, 436. See also
Marchamont Needham's remark on "the spreading abroad most blasphe-
mous opinions" in *A True State of the Case of the Commonwealth* (1654), cited in
Worden, "Toleration and the Cromwellian Protectorate," p. 217.

53. Cf. this response to that of the fallen angels to Mammon's rhetoric: *Paradise
Lost* 2.284–92.

54. The reference to the Beast whose vile tongue speaks "great things and
blasphemies" is in fact one that Milton quotes, referring to the Vulgate text, in
his discussion of blasphemy in *de doctrina Christiana* (*CP* VI: 699).

55. In *Samson Agonistes* Milton associates the crime with "the idolatrous" Philistines
"amidst their wine" blaspheming God during the great pomp of their
Dagonalia (lines 440–43), reminding us as well of the association between
blasphemy and idolatry that had origins in the Hebrew Bible (see e.g. Ezekiel
20:24, 27).

56. John Deacon, *Nayler's Blasphemies Discovered* (London, 1657), p. 59. For Baxter,
see *One Sheet*, p. 5: "They will not only deny civil honour to the Magistrate, but
revile him if he displease them. Their language is like the rebellious followers
of *Corah, Numb.* 16.3. *Ye take too much upon you – Wherefore lift ye up your selves above
the Congregation of the Lord?*"

CHAPTER 10

The politics of performance in the inner theater: "Samson Agonistes" as closet drama

Elizabeth Sauer

This chapter examines *Samson Agonistes* in terms of the genre of the *closet drama*, a printed play designed to be read rather than staged, which had also served during the late Renaissance and Civil War years in England as a vehicle for political criticism.[1] In his lengthy *Memoirs* of Milton, Francis Peck observed that *Samson Agonistes* was written "*exactly on the same plan*" as George Buchanan's *Baptistes sive Calumnia*, a connection supported by his references to *Dagonalia* and *Baptistes*, two of Milton's proposed tragedies in the Trinity College Manuscript. Peck, moreover, attributed to Milton a seventeenth-century translation of *Baptistes sive Calumnia*, which he interpreted as a topical political allegory.[2] Like this translation, entitled *Tyrannicall-Government Anatomized*, *Samson Agonistes* negotiates between conflicting traditions as it interweaves biblical and contemporary English history. Furthermore, while its lofty style and classical sources place the text out of reach of the vulgar, *Samson Agonistes* nevertheless speaks to an anti-establishment culture through its visionary politics, its redefinition of authority and heroic performance, and through the contesting interpretations it presents and encourages.

Though regarded as a type of Christ in the exegetical literature of the period, as Thomas Taylor's *Christ Revealed* reminds us,[3] the tragic figure of Samson was for the disillusioned revolutionary a necessary successor to the inimitable character of Christ in *Paradise Regained*. In the seventeenth century, Samson was frequently invoked (in name and meaning): the "over-mastred" Charles I is portrayed as Samson in Eleanor Douglas's *Samsons Legacie*; Milton creates a prophetic vision of the "noble and puissant Nation rousing herself like a strong man after sleep" in *Areopagitica* (*CP* II: 558); and the imprisoned John Lilburne characterizes his fight for freedom in *The Resolved mans Resolution* as a "*Sampson* like" struggle.[4] In *Samson Agonistes*, Milton adds to the controversy surrounding the identity of Samson as a fallen, tragic hero by casting him as a performer in the "carnivalesque" setting of the Philistine theater. Then by including various responses to the act of (self-)destruction, which is described rather than staged in the poem, Milton complicates Samson's motives and role-playing. He thereby invites a re-examination of the relationship between performance – both theatrical and political – and the act of interpretation by the critical, heretical readers of the text and of its received tradition.[5]

By virtue of the interpretive act in which they engage, the readers of Renaissance and early modern closet dramas develop a relationship of *communitas*, defined in contemporary terms as "a bond uniting ... people over and above any formal social bonds." This social antistructure is produced in a state of liminality, "a condition outside or on the peripheries of everyday life."[6] In this chapter, I identify the interpretive community with the *communitas*, which is created out of the dynamic relationship between readers and texts, texts and contexts. In developing his theories on the interpretive community, M. M. Bakhtin foregrounds the critic's dialogic role and the concrete social and historical milieu in which the readers or critics are situated. Bakhtin's model differs radically from that of Stanley Fish, who offers a model of inter-communal relations as devoid of conflict. For Fish, the essentially authoritarian interpretive community imposes meaning on ahistorical textual determinacy.[7]

Fish's model has proven to be highly influential, certainly among literary critics but also among historians. Roger Chartier, for example, identifies the construction of "communities of readers as 'interpretative communities' (Stanley Fish's expression)" as one of the avenues available to those who wish to understand the nature of reading practices as historians.[8] However, Fish does not in fact adequately problematize the relationship between reader and text, precisely because he dehistoricizes it and posits an authoritarian reading community. In a 1988 essay, Fish applied his theories about reading communities to an analysis of *Areopagitica*, a text that at once injects books with "life-blood" (*CP* II: 493) and simultaneously and vehemently attributes to the readership absolute authority to determine the meaning of those books. According to Fish, this apparent contradiction is one that the treatise cannot sustain: "the argument against licensing ... is really an argument that renders books beside the point: books are no more going to save you than they are going to corrupt you; by denying their potency in one direction, Milton necessarily denies their potency in the other and undercuts the extravagant claims he himself makes."[9] Thomas Corns reminds us in a chapter on "Milton as Heretic and Poet" in *Uncloistered Virtue* that Fish's reading fails to consider the polemical context of the treatise, in which Milton, arguing against censorship, insists that the publication of "bad books" (*CP* II: 512) poses no threat to the state. The defense and consequent empowerment of the reader in *Areopagitica* thus serve Milton's larger political objectives.[10]

To understand the unorthodox nature of the community that Milton establishes in and through his writings, we must first recall *Areopagitica's* description of the building of God's house: "Yet these are the men cry'd out against schismaticks and sectaries; as if, while the Temple of the Lord was building, some cutting, some squaring the marble, others hewing the cedars, there should be a sort of irrationall men who could not consider there must be many schisms and many dissections made in the quarry and in the timber, ere the house of God can be built" (*CP* II: 555). God's work is carried out by sectarians and heretics, and in *Areopagitica*, by those who oppose Parliament's censorship practices, which restrict the dissemination of knowledge and thus inhibit the formation of the collective. Milton's religious commitment is channeled through a "religious commitment to political process," which in turn is expressed through his interest in collectivity and effective communities. These concerns, as Joan S. Bennett also reminds us, are repeatedly embodied in his poetry.[11] Milton's literary texts, then, perform cultural and political work by conditioning the creation of an invisible public[12] involved in resisting conformity and oppressive authoritarian establishments. An investigation of ways in which literature participates in the construction of the *communitas* by promoting critical inquiry and inviting the reader to assemble the "scattered body of Truth" proves especially rewarding in a study of *Samson Agonistes* as a closet drama, a genre amenable to the expression of heretical impulses.

CLOSETED PERFORMANCES

The first section of this chapter provides a brief overview of the history of the Renaissance and seventeenth-century closet drama as a moral alternative to the staged play and as a genre produced when theatricality is displaced by the writing, printing, and the reading of plays as acts of political engagement and resistance. In explaining Milton's decision to write a "Dramatic Poem" unintended for the stage, David Masson declares that the poet would have been repulsed by the Restoration stage despite his association with William Davenant, Robert Howard, and John Dryden, and that the successors of Thomas Killigrew and Davenant would not have wanted such a drama staged. Masson speculates, furthermore, that the authorities would perhaps not have allowed this kind of representation; as a result "Milton had published the tragedy merely as a poem to be read."[13] Milton's reliance on the conventions of the closet drama for his final performance is of literary and political significance; thus I take issue with John T. Shawcross's claim that genre "has nothing to do with the author's 'philosophy' or 'political persuasion' or 'critical stance' or such matter." Indeed I would argue, in agreement with Thomas Healy, that genre is a more powerful agent of expression than critics often assume: genre "can enable the author to be more than just a force of social and cultural agency which originates the text. Exploitation of generic conventions enables the structures which allow a re-figuring of accepted representations."[14]

As a dramatic work of the Restoration which denies performability, *Samson Agonistes* repudiates the "infamy" of the Restoration theater and theater audiences,[15] thus defining itself against an antagonistic community – an incarnation of the "Image-doting rabble," which had earlier been seduced by *Eikon Basilike* and Charles's performance on the scaffold (*Eikonoklastes, CP* III: 601). As a closet drama indebted to the classical tragedy, *Samson Agonistes* creates an elite readership, whose engagement with the text becomes an "internalized, read-only, version" of the collective experience that the theaters in the ancient republics had once provided.[16] And as an extension both of Renaissance anti-persecution drama and of the radical, anti-establishment culture that informed Milton's visionary politics, *Samson Agonistes*, I will argue, imagines a heterogeneous, agonistic community of readers.

Early English tragedies, including *Gorboduc* and *The Spanish Tragedy*, focused on sensationalism, revenge, and death and were characterized by their intricate plots and extravagant rhetorical styles. Under the patronage of Sidney's sister, the Countess of Pembroke, playwrights of the Sidney circle refined the conventions of the Senecan models in developing the Sidnean closet dramas. English translations of Robert Garnier's neo-Senecan tragedies provided the basis for the overtly political, anti-tyrannical texts produced by members of the Sidney circle, including Fulke Greville, Samuel Daniel, William Alexander, Samuel Brandon, and Elizabeth Cary. The classicizing dramas of the late Renaissance examine theories of monarchy, tyranny, and rebellion by treating the evils of absolutism, the corruption of kings and royal favorites, and the nature and duties of kingship. Generic features include the trappings of Italianate Senecanism; the primacy of speech and narrative over action; long rhetorical monologues and philosophical and moral discourses; the casting of women as heroes and villains; and the inclusion of a nuntius and of a chorus that speaks from a limited rather than an authoritative position. The closet drama, moreover, provides an effective medium for staging the conflicts of a social rebel. The reader's task is to assess the heroic nature of this controversial figure while recognizing that the text ultimately resists any conclusive judgments about the protagonist.

Though the Scottish writer George Buchanan was not formally connected to the Sidney circle, reference to an English translation of one his biblical tragedies, *Baptistes sive Calumnia*, allows us to link Buchanan's drama, Sidnean closet drama, and *Samson Agonistes*.[17] Peter Hume Brown, Buchanan's biographer, regards *Baptistes*, which was written between 1541 and 1544 and first published in England in 1577, as a "poetical draft" of his famous tract *De Jure Regni apud Scotos* for which he became regarded as a political revolutionary.[18] *Baptistes sive Calumnia* was interpreted variously as a warning against Henry VIII's marriage to Ann Boleyn, an expression of Buchanan's disgust at Henry's execution of Sir Thomas More, and as an admonition to James I about the evils of tyranny, specifically, his attachments to the Scottish Catholic nobility.[19] In his exhaustive study of the tragedy's anonymous seventeenth-century translation that he attributed to Milton, Peck claimed that the revolutionary, who was inhibited by political censorship, acted on William Prynne's advice to "print his said work, not as a play, but as an *history* or *dialogue*" and to retitle the text in order to expose the king, court, and clergy as much as possible (p. 288).[20] Indeed the original tragedy was intended for performance by Buchanan's pupils, including Montaigne. Still it was regarded as a closet drama by Stephen Gosson, who claimed that the moralizing and didactic effect of Buchanan's *Baptistes* depended upon its being read and not performed. In *Playes Confuted in Five Actions*, Gosson locates *Baptistes* in the tradition of *Christ Suffering*, with which Milton would later associate *Samson Agonistes*.[21]

While performing political work by displaying the evils of tyranny, closet dramas also avoided the problems and abuses of stage productions, which plagued antitheatricalists, including Stephen Gosson, Philip Stubbes, John Rainolds, William Perkins, and William Prynne. According to these critics, playwrights and actors transfixed and corrupted spectators. Rainolds, the Oxford theologian and controversialist, warns against the affective power of the stage in *The overthrow of stage-plays*: "can wise men be perswaded that there is no wantonnesse in the players partes, when experience sheweth ... that *men are made adulterers and enemies of all chastitie by comming to such playes?*"[22] Performance, moreover, put the players themselves in moral danger. Invoking the Deuteronomic prohibition against the male adoption of female apparel, Rainolds declares that in playing the woman's part, the actor becomes "dishonested and defiled, because he transgresseth the boundes of modestie and comelinesse, and weareth that which

Gods lawe forbiddeth him to weare" (p. 16). In the act of repeated imitation, then, the actor is metamorphosed into the character he impersonates.

If performances emasculated actors and rendered spectators captive, the off-stage activity of play-reading could prove both redemptive and liberating. During the closing of the theaters in the seventeenth century, prefaces defending play-reading were added to plays and collections published in the *"silence of the Stage."* Closet dramas were produced largely by royalists, who, by reclaiming the performative through print, created their own hermeneutic circles. Printed by the *"guiltles presse,"*[23] the closet dramas expose the hidden thoughts and motives of the playwrights, while also displaying to the reader the behind-the-scenes activities not shown to theater audiences; in his address to the reader in the 1647 Beaumont and Fletcher volume, Humphrey Moseley declares the victory of textuality over theatricality: "When these *Comedies* and *Tragedies* were presented on the Stage, the *Actours* omitted some *Scenes* and Passages (with the *Authour's* consent) as occasion led them . . . . But now you have both All that was *Acted*, and all that was not; even the perfect full Originalls without the least mutilation."[24] As suggested in the Preface to *The Queene, or the Excellency of Her Sex* – written after a raid on an illegal performance at Red Bull – the press in "acting" to produce the play offers to readers and playwrights, furthermore, a form of political immunity: *"no ladies swoune / At the read coates intrusion: none are strip't; / No Hystrimastix has the copy whip't"* (A3r).[25]

Predictably, the Restoration period witnessed a dramatic decline in the number of closet dramas with the reopening of the theaters.[26] Court culture dominated theater culture once the Stuarts again gained control of the public theater of English history. But politicians and playwrights alike were conscious of the role of the people in determining the success of performances in the theater and on the political stage. Having taken center stage in the early Stuart masques, the king in the Restoration theater, though still occupying a position of authority, sat with the other spectators. It was after all the people who had welcomed him back to the theater and restored him to a prominent place on the national stage.[27]

"SOME GREAT ACT, OR OF MY DAYS THE LAST"

To problematize *Samson Agonistes* is to oppose the strong tendency in Milton studies to resist textual indeterminacy and difference, on which Leah Marcus and John Rumrich have most recently remarked.[28] My reading of the poem is intended partly to challenge the effort at claiming Milton for a (neo-)Christian tradition, which has been reinforced by interpretations of Samson's spiritual regeneration, interpretations that have "achieved the status of orthodoxy" in Milton studies.[29] A later part of this chapter offers an interventionist reading of the poem as a heretical text, which concludes with different accounts of Samson's act of (self-)destruction, thus setting the stage for a controversial critical history. The last act presents an especially contested site of reading for both the onstage and off-stage readers by describing a play-within-the-play in which, I will demonstrate, the roles of the actors, spectators, and readers break down. In his final encounter with the Philistines, Samson is brought into their world and assigned a part on their stage, a performance in which he becomes at once an object of derision as well as a dissembler and a champion.

Peck's defense of his attribution of *Tyrannicall-Government Anatomized* to Milton includes a discussion of the similarities between the structures and particularly the final scenes of Buchanan's and Milton's tragedies. Observing that *Samson Agonistes* was composed *"exactly on the same plan"* as *Baptistes*, Peck concludes that

the plan of this tragedy appeared so just to Mr. MILTON, that, when he came to write his SAMSON AGONISTES, he formed that poem entirely upon the same model with this. That is, with a *Chorus* (after the manner of the antients) & a *nuntius* brought in to relate the death of SAMSON; just as we find a *chorus* & a *nuntius* introduced here, to relate the death of JOHN. (p. 278)

The reporting of Samson's death by the Messenger in the *exodos* of the poem is a convention of classical tragedy, which had downplayed spectacle. Aristotle regarded spectacle as "the least integral of all to the poet's art"; "even without seeing a performance, anyone who hears the events which occur will experience terror and pity as a result of the outcome."[30] In the Renaissance, the messenger was regarded as an appropriate device for conveying horrific or imaginary events. Reported actions are included in tragedies by the greatest Greek playwrights, Aeschylus, Sophocles, and Euripides, whom Milton identifies as "the three Tragic poets unequall'd yet by any."[31] Milton's indebtedness to classical and neoclassical dramatic prescriptions in composing *Samson Agonistes* is not, however, the only satisfactory explanation for the narration of the catastrophe by the Messenger. The reporting of Samson's final act and the reliability of the Messenger need to be examined in light of Milton's interest in studying and problematizing closeted performances and the motives of controversial figures and in terms of his efforts at encouraging critical reading and active engagement with open-ended texts.

Though presenting the eye-witness testimony of Samson's destruction

of the Temple of Dagon, the Messenger's retrospective account is compromised by the reporter's own limited vantage point and by his uncertainty
about the significance of the narrated events. What propelled the impassioned Messenger in the direction of Manoa in the first place is unclear;
he cites three explanations: "providence or instinct of nature . . . / Or reason
though disturb'd, and scarce consulted" (lines 1545–46). Moreover, the
Messenger, at some distance from the spectacle, relies on reports of
Samson's deeds; the exhausted performer sought permission to lean on
the temple's main supports, the Messenger explains, adding "For so from
such as nearer stood we heard" (line 1631). The qualification, which
momentarily directs attention away from Samson's actions, reminds us
that the scene is reconstructed from a narrated account. At the same time,
it renders Samson's motives even more elusive for the audience who must
rely on hearsay.

In his account of the tragedy, the Messenger foregrounds the language
of theatrical performance and staging. The account of the "horrid spectacle" (line 1542) requires "No Preface" (line 1554), the impatient Manoa
decides. The Messenger's script sets the stage inside "a spacious Theater"
(line 1605). Milton constructs this classical amphitheater from the house
in Judges 16:26–27, and transforms the scene into one of comedy and carnival. The Philistines' observance of hierarchical distinctions in this parodic, unruly scene, in which "thir hearts [are fill'd] with mirth, high cheer,
and wine" (line 1613), proves especially ironic when only the "vulgar"
among the Philistines escape once the temple is destroyed (line 1659).
Nicholas Jose attributes a contemporary significance to the spectacle when
he identifies the theater with Christopher Wren's Sheldonian Theater,
which was constructed from 1664 to 1669 and was designed to represent
the glories of the Augustan Roman empire.[32] In this theater, Samson is
forced to take center stage amidst the clamor and confusion of Philistine
festivities (lines 1616–22) by which Milton too was enveloped. Samson's
sports constitute the first act which is followed by an intermission (line
1629). Cast as a jester, fool, or "a Clowne in a Play"[33] on this stage, Samson
manages, nevertheless, to rewrite his enemies' script in the second act, to
steal the show, and bring the house down.

The turn in the action is signaled by Samson's utterances that break
through the Messenger's account. In this, his final speech, Samson appro-
priates the language of performance and theatrics.[34] His act of defiance,
thus, invites comparison with Milton's creation of a stylistics of indirection
and with his strategy of deploying the language of theatricality to produce
the closet drama in the Restoration:[35]

Hitherto, Lords, what your commands impos'd
I have perform'd, as reason was, obeying,
Not without wonder or delight beheld.
Now of my own accord such other trial
I mean to show you of my strength, yet greater;
As with amaze shall strike all who behold.   (lines 1640–45)

In *Samson Agonistes*, the tension between playing an assigned part and intentionally assuming a role is heightened in this final scene. Samson's performance, which initially provoked the wonder and delight of the stage-managers and viewers, is converted into a show of strength that amazes and strikes (down) all spectators in the theater. *Samson Agonistes* is thus appropriately characterized as "an antitheatrical text about the theatricality of an iconoclastic act."[36]

In his final performance, rather than refusing to play the fool (line 1338), Samson deliberately assumes this role, having been called at the same time to play a much more significant "part" in providential history (line 1217): Samson was cast as "the Athlete of God and failed. Now he is the Fool of God and succeeds."[37] While Samson performs his part, the Philistines ironically become drawn into the spectacle they stage. The scene is at once tragic and parodic, breaking down the distinctions between spectators and performers as the different characters participate in the carnival act.[38] Two transferences of power occur in the play-within-the-play: the "Lords, Ladies, Captains, Counsellors, [and] Priests, / Thir choice nobility and flower" (lines 1653–54), who come from every Philistine city to solemnize the feast, ironically wreak havoc upon themselves (line 1684), while Samson, cast as the Philistines' "drudge . . . thir fool or jester" (line 1338), redeems this role by emerging from his experience of defeat to destroy his enemies, though at the expense of his life.

The theatricalized setting mirrors a world turned upside down. Comedy and parody, which add elements of indeterminacy and incivility to the scene, are apparent in the elaborate descriptions of Dalila's theatrics, Harapha's braggart character, and the accounts of the idolatrous Philistines' bacchic frenzies. The comic and parodic elements include as well the descriptions of Samson's sporting before and with the Philistines and of Samson's performance of the jester's part, which destabilizes the autonomous construction of selfhood, destroying "the naive wholeness of one's notions about the self that lies at the heart of the . . . tragic image of man" (Bakhtin, *Problems*, p. 120). Such features, moreover, unsettle the definition of the tragedy as "the gravest, moralest, and most profitable of all other Poems" (*Samson Agonistes*, p. 549, lines 1–2), which Milton applies in

defending the poem against the "infamy" to which it is subject in his day
(p. 550, line 2). They also expose the "otherness" of the dignified and grave
text: "the essential carnival element" in the organization of drama "does
not merely concern the secondary, clownish motives ... The logic of
crownings and uncrownings, in direct or indirect form, organizes the
serious elements also" (Bakhtin, *Rabelais*, p. 275).[39]

The adaption in *Samson Agonistes* of classical prescriptions and generic
conventions for the tragedy includes Milton's development of the double
issue of the poem's action. Aristotle wrote that "a fine plot-structure
[must] be single and not double (as some assert), and involve a change from
prosperity to affliction (rather than the reverse) caused not by wickedness
but by a great fallibility on the part of the sort of agent stipulated" (*Poetics*,
ch. 13; p. 44–45). The double issue of the plot in *Samson Agonistes* emphasizes distributive and not retributive justice, thus tempering rather than
purging the passions.[40] Rewards and punishments are meted to characters
according to their deserts: Samson dies nobly while the Philistine lords
"thir own ruin on themselves ... invite" (line 1684). This catastrophe narrated by the Messenger is in turn separated from the denouement, which is
divided into two distinct sections, bringing about a double catharsis – that
of the tragic hero and of the Chorus or the onstage audience who activates
the readers' responses. In *Samson Agonistes*, Milton devotes nearly twice as
many lines to the Chorus's reactions in the denouement than to the
Messenger's description of the catastrophe (Radzinowicz, "Distinctive,"
p. 252) in order to deemphasize spectacle and performance and instead to
highlight the interior drama while encouraging active interpretation of
the reported events. Far from being suppressed, the question of agency is
scrutinized in various ways when the significance of Samson's theatrical/
antitheatrical final act is assessed by the reading community in and outside
of the text.

The account of Samson's performance needs to be situated in terms of
the larger debate about Samson's suicide,[41] which Milton first politicizes,
contemporizes, and leaves unresolved in *The First Defence*: the antiheroic
Samson, who was "prompted by God or his own valor," "thought it not
impious but pious to kill those masters who were tyrants over his country,
even though most of her citizens did not balk at slavery" (*CP* IV: 402).
Samson Agonistes invites an examination of the motives for Samson's actions
by presenting different interpretations of Samson's death, and Milton
thereby takes us "on a roller coaster of possible truths" (Dobranski,
"Samson and the Omissa," 161). The inclusion of conflicting viewpoints
that prevent closure is characteristic of the closet drama, and may provide

a partial explanation for Fish's astute observation that *Samson Agonistes* departs from Milton's sources and analogues by lacking interpretive direction ("Spectacle," 567). Still in light of Milton's literary, theological, and political fascination with the story of Samson, we must view the reporting of his tragic hero's violent act as something more than just a dramatic convention or an attempt to highlight the indeterminacy of the Judges account, a complication of interests that makes its way into the exegetical literature and the received tradition. The various readings of Samson's final act in the poem problematize the question of agency for the critical reader whose role is once again foregrounded.

The poem develops the tension between contradictory reports of Samson acting willfully (line 1643) and of being "tangl'd in the fold / Of dire necessity" (line 1665–66). Manoa first raises the issue of "Self-violence" (line 1584) in his inquiry about the events leading to the deaths of the Philistines and Samson. Though the Messenger declares that Samson committed the slaughter with his own hands, he responds to Manoa by identifying the cause "At once both to destroy and be destroy'd" (line 1587) as "Inevitable" (line 1586). Thereafter, however, the Messenger offers a more complex reading of the scene when he attempts to recreate the interior drama: Samson stood "with head a while inclin'd / And eyes fast fixt," "as one who pray'd, / Or some great matter in his mind revolv'd" (lines 1636–38). Samson's own speech recalled by the Messenger heightens the ambiguity: "Now of my own accord such other trial / I mean to show you of my strength, yet greater; / As with amaze shall strike all who behold" (1643–45).[42] This veiled threat to the Philistine Lords displaces the prayer in the Judges story in which he pleads for vengeance (16:28), which had led theologians from St. Augustine on to declare that the act was divinely sanctioned.

While Samson's death is less controversial than Charles's martyrdom, it is more so than that of John in *Tyrannicall-Government Anatomized* or than Christ's acts of self-denial in *Paradise Regained*. The interpretive uncertainty surrounding the death is a function of the exegetical literature on the Judges account, as well as of the heightened ambiguity introduced in the poem by not only the Messenger but also the Danites whom Samson at first mistakes for his enemies (lines 110–14). Neither the Chorus nor Manoa sees the final act and thus essentially responds to it blindly. "In the absence of any witness or revelation that would lend them authority," Fish reminds us, the Danites' "words produce more problems than they resolve" ("Spectacle," 569). Addressing the charge of suicide, the Chorus attempts to dismiss it and clear Samson's name (lines 1664–66). The denouement is then suspended by the comments of the first and second Semichorus and

Manoa, who again respond to the second-hand account of the final performance by identifying it as a divine act of self-sacrifice. However, the references in their speeches to the Philistines' destruction and to Samson's
death, though heroic, along with the descriptions of Samson's body
"Soak't in his enemies' blood" and covered with "clotted gore" (lines 1726,
1728), anchor the scene less in triumph than tragedy.

The diverse, allusive responses of the onstage commentators on the
tragedy open the door to a range of interpretations. The transformation of
Samson's identity continues even after the character's death when the
second Semichorus compares the blind Samson's virtue to "an ev'ning
Dragon" (line 1693), "an Eagle" (line 1695), and a phoenix, "that self-
begott'n bird / In the *Arabian* woods embost" (lines 1699–700). The mythological phoenix acquires a political significance when it is used to represent
the Stuarts and the restored monarchists, as we find in Thomas Mayhew's
Upon the Joyfull and Welcome Return of His Sacred Majestie. However, in such
texts as *A Phoenix: or, the Solemn League and Covenant,* it is apparent that dissi-
dents too laid claim to the phoenix. The appearance of the *Phoenix* proved
to be symbolically and literally prophetic: when the royalist censor Roger
L'Estrange tracked down those responsible for the text, he discovered
Mirabilis Annus, or the Year of Prodigies and Wonders in which Charles II is ident-
ified, as his son was by seventeenth-century prophets like Eleanor
Douglas, with the idolatrous Belshazzar whose kingdom was fated to be
destroyed.[43] According to this book of revelation and its sequel *Mirabilis
Annus Secundus,* eclipses and other solar disturbances are common occur-
rences in a world turned upside down by the monarchy, a world *Samson
Agonistes* reflects from the moment Samson experiences "total Eclipse /
Without all hope of day!" (lines 81–82).[44]

The images of the masculine eagle and the feminine phoenix are displaced by the "secular bird of ages" (line 1707).[45] While the phoenix's body
dies, giving rise to the "fame" that endures (line 1706), the body of Samson
still needs to be disposed of, Manoa realizes. The cleansing of the body is
Manoa's first act of honoring his dead son (lines 1725–28), an act which
contrasts, on the one hand, with the ironic commemoration of Dalila by
"double-mouth'd" Fame (line 971) and, on the other, with the glorification
of Christ. By writing Samson's story after not before Christ's, Milton challenges the traditional identification of Samson as a type for Christ, which
he seemed at first to invite in citing *Christ Suffering* in the preface to *Samson
Agonistes.* Instead he portrays the Hebraic hero as self-legitimizing, self-
sacrificing, and at the same time, as the product of conflicting viewpoints
that make up the protean character and the poem.

***

The composition of *Samson Agonistes*, Milton's last "great act," develops, like Samson's performance, out of the experience of defeat as well as the poet's aversion to the Restoration theater and royalist politics. At the same time, however, Milton in writing the poem was simultaneously of the revolutionaries', the radicals', and of the royalists' parties without knowing it, or so the received tradition of *Samson Agonistes* suggests. The text provoked a wide variety of interpretations and reactions, from William Joyner's proroyalist play *The Roman Empress*, Andrew Marvell's association of Milton with the blind vengeful Samson, who "grop'd the Temple's Posts in spite," and Dryden's *Aureng-Zebe* in the Restoration period, to the later identification of Samson with William III, and to the historical, psychological, regenerationist, and political readings of our own day.[46] The poem conditions opportunities for resistance to the various literary and historical traditions – in which it nevertheless remains entrenched – while also providing similar opportunities for critical readers. The conclusion focuses on the catharsis of the readers, who are, according to the Chorus, left "calm of mind, all passion spent" (line 1758). Still the text resists closure, having redefined the nature of "performance" first through the complex representation of the main actor, Samson, and then through the transference of authority to the interpretive community and to the historical milieu and critical tradition in which the readers and the poem are cast.[47]

NOTES

1. According to Alfred Harbage, only a few closet dramas were produced in the Restoration years, and these consisted mainly of political dialogues and Latin plays (*Annals of English Drama 975–1700*, rev. by S. Schoenbaum, 2nd edn. [London, 1964], pp. 154ff.). *Samson Agonistes* belongs in neither category and thus merits special consideration as an antitheatrical and, as I argue, a politically charged text.

2. Francis Peck, *New Memoirs of the Life and Poetical Works of Mr. John Milton etc.*(London, 1740), p. 278. Also see *Tyrannicall-Government Anatomized: Or, A Discourse Concerning Evil-Councellors etc.* (London, 1642).

3. Thomas Taylor, *Christ Revealed: or the Old Testament explained etc.* (London, 1635), E6v. Martin Luther, Jean Calvin, Francis Quarles, Joseph Hall, Thomas Hayne, John Bunyan, among many others, also regarded Samson as a type of Christ.

4. Eleanor Douglas, *Samsons Legacie. Judges, the 16. Chap. etc.* (London, 1643). Also see *Samsons Fall, Presented to the House 1642* (London, 1642); and Sir Thomas Aston, *A Remonstrance, against Presbitery etc.* ([London], 1641), Kv. John Lilburne, *The Resolved mans Resolution, to maintain . . . his civill Liberties etc.* (London, 1647), Ar.

5. The second definition of "heretic" in the *OED* is "one who maintains opinions upon any subject at variance with those generally received or considered authoritative." The critical, heretic reader is one who resists orthodoxy in religion or government or one who promotes diversity of opinion. A text that encourages a range of (conflicting) interpretations creates heretical readers, and *Samson Agonistes* is such a text.

D. M. Rosenberg explains that Milton's intended readers "were analogous to the saving remnant who in his play were oppressed in Philistia but kept their faith in God" ("Milton, Dryden, and the Ideology of Genre," *Comparative Drama* 21 [1987], 3). Special thanks to Keith Hull for drawing my attention to both this article and his presentation "Was *Samson Agonistes* Really Never Intended for the Stage?" (Fifth International Milton Symposium, Bangor, Wales, 1995).

6. Victor Turner, *Dramas, Fields, and Metaphors: Symbolic Action in Human Society* (Ithaca, 1974), p. 45.

7. David Shepherd, "Bakhtin and the Reader," in Ken Hirschkop and David Shepherd, eds., *Bakhtin and Cultural Theory* (New York, 1989), pp. 96–97. Also see Stanley Fish, *Is There a Text in This Class?: The Authority of Interpretive Communities* (Cambridge, MA, 1980).

8. Roger Chartier, *The Order of Books* (Stanford, 1994), p. 23.

9. Fish, "Driving from the Letter: Truth and Indeterminacy in Milton's *Areopagitica*," in Mary Nyquist and Margaret W. Ferguson, eds., *Re-membering Milton* (New York, 1988), p. 238.

10. Thomas N. Corns, *Uncloistered Virtue: English Political Literature 1640–1660* (Oxford, 1992), p. 58.

11. Joan S. Bennett, *Reviving Liberty: Radical Christian Humanism in Milton's Great Poems* (Cambridge, MA, 1989), p. 5.

12. Leah S. Marcus, *Unediting the Renaissance: Shakespeare, Marlowe, Milton* (New York, 1996), pp. 211, 212–13.

13. David Masson, *The Life of John Milton*, 7 vols. (1877–96; rpt. New York, 1946), vol. VI, p. 666.

14. John T. Shawcross, "The Genres of *Paradise Regain'd* and *Samson Agonistes*: The Wisdom of Their Joint Publication," in Joseph Wittreich and Richard S. Ide, eds., *Composite Orders: The Genres of Milton's Last Poems* (Pittsburgh, 1983), p. 227. Thomas Healy, *New Latitudes: Theory and English Renaissance Literature* (London, 1992), p. 172.

15. On the controversy about the dating of the text, see Anthony Low, "Milton's *Samson* and the Stage, with Implications for Dating the Play," *Huntington Library Quarterly* 40 (1977), 313–24; and Blair Worden, "Milton, *Samson Agonistes*, and the Restoration," in Gerald MacLean, ed., *Culture and Society in the Stuart Restoration: Literature, Drama, History* (Cambridge, 1995), p. 111. On *Paradise Regained* and *Samson Agonistes* as a repudiation of Restoration drama, see Steven N. Zwicker, "Milton, Dryden, and the politics of Literary Controversy," in MacLean, *Culture and Society in the Stuart Restoration*, pp. 137–58.

16. Nigel Smith, *Literature and Revolution in England 1640–1660* (New Haven, 1994), p. 92.

17. On Buchanan's connection to the Sidney circle and on the response of its members to *Baptistes* and *De Jure Regni*, see James Emerson Phillips, "George Buchanan and the Sidney Circle," *Huntington Library Quarterly* 12 (1948–49), 23–55. See also Sandra Kerman's "George Buchanan and the Genre of *Samson Agonistes*," *Language and Style*, 19.1 (1986), 21–5; and Peggy Anne Samuels, "*Samson Agonistes* and Renaissance Drama," PhD dissertation, City University of New York (1993).

18. Peter Hume Brown, *George Buchanan: Humanist and Reformer* (Edinburgh, 1890), p. 124.

19. James M. Aitken, *The Trial of George Buchanan before the Lisbon Inquisition* (London, 1939), p. 25. On the sources for *Baptistes*, see Ian D. McFarlane, *Buchanan* (London, 1981), pp. 381–85 and *A Critical Edition of George Buchanan's Baptistes and of Its Anonymous Seventeenth-Century Translation Tyrannicall-Government Anatomized*, ed. Stephen Berkowitz (New York, 1992), pp. 105–59.

20. The attribution of the translation of *Baptistes* to Milton by Peck has been a subject of much critical inquiry; see Berkowitz, *Critical Edition*, pp. 343–46.

21. E5v; Arthur F. Kinney, *Markets of Bawdrie: The Dramatic Criticism of Stephen Gosson* (Salzburg, 1974), pp. 177–78. Milton's reason for mentioning *Christ Suffering* can be explained in light of his admiration of its Euripidean echoes as well as its revival in George Sandys's translation of Hugo Grotius's *Christus Patiens*, and in terms of his interest in the late Renaissance debate about whether the play was originally designed for performance or was composed to be read only, as Gosson maintained.

22. John Rainolds, *The overthrow of stage-plays by the way of controversy between D. Gager and D. Rainolds* (New York, 1972), p. 18. On this subject also see Jonas Barish's *The Antitheatrical Prejudice* (Berkeley, 1981).

23. [John Ford,] *The Queen, or the Excellency of Her Sex* (London, 1653), A3r.

24. Humphrey Moseley, "The Stationer to the Reader," *Comedies and Tragedies Written by Francis Beaumont and John Fletcher Gentlemen* in *The Works of Francis Beaumont and John Fletcher*, ed. Arnold Glover (Cambridge, 1905), p. xi.

25. Louis B. Wright demonstrates how the Civil War closet dramas conveyed political meanings ("The Reading of Plays during the Puritan Revolution," *The Huntington Library Bulletin* 6 [1934], 86ff). For more recent studies of the royalist closet dramas, see vol. 4 of *The Revels History of Drama in English*, ed. Lois Potter et al., 8 vols. (New York, 1975–83); and Lois Potter, *Secret Rites and Secret Writing: Royalist Literature, 1641–1660* (Cambridge, 1989).

26. See, for example, Sir Richard Baker's posthumously published, *Theatrum Redivivum: or the Theatre Vindicated* (London, 1662).

27. Nicholas Jose, *Ideas of the Restoration in English Literature, 1660–71* (Cambridge, MA, 1984), pp. 129–31.

28. See Leah Marcus's chapter on "John Milton's Voice" in *Unediting the Renaissance* and John Rumrich's *Milton Unbound: Controversy and Reinterpretation* (Cambridge, 1996), p. 2.

29. Stanley Fish, "Spectacle and Evidence in *Samson Agonistes*," *Critical Inquiry* 15.3 (1989), 557 n.2. See Rumrich's response to the " 'neo-Christian' bias of Milton

scholars" in "Uninventing Milton," *Modern Philology* 87.3 (1990), 249–65. Stephen B. Dobranski in "Samson and the Omissa," *SEL* 36 (1996), 149–69 points to the critical neglect of the "*Omissa*" printed at the end of the first edition of *Samson Agonistes* as an example of how modern editors have glossed over problems of textual variability and maintained the illusion of a unified authorial identity.

Unifying imperatives and what Fish calls the "regenerationist pieties" ("Spectacle," 580 n.18) are foregrounded in works by such critics as Anthony Low, Mary Ann Radzinowicz, Edward Tayler, and Don Cameron Allen. Also see Fish, "Question and Answer in *Samson Agonistes*," *Critical Quarterly* 11 (1969), 237–64; rpt. in *Comus and Samson Agonistes: A Casebook*, ed. Julian Lovelock (London, 1975). Such approaches have been subject to interrogation by a collective of divergent voices, which include Christopher Hill, Joseph Wittreich, Michael Wilding, Joan S. Bennett, Laura Lunger Knoppers, and even Fish himself in "Spectacle and Evidence." Also see Kenneth Burke, who had earlier commented on the complication of Samson's death in *A Grammar of Motives and A Rhetoric of Motives* (Cleveland, 1962), p. 529.

30. Aristotle, *Poetics*, trans. Stephen Halliwell (London, 1987), pp. 38, 45.

31. *Samson Agonistes*, in *John Milton: Complete Poems and Major Prose*, ed. Merritt Y. Hughes (New York, 1957), p. 550, lines 24–25.

32. Jose, "*Samson Agonistes*: the Play Turned Upside Down," *Essays in Criticism* 30 (1980), 139–40.

33. William Prynne, *Histrio-Mastix. The Players Scourge, or, Actors Tragaedie* (London, 1633), 558v.

34. See Laura Lunger Knoppers, *Historicizing Milton: Spectacle, Power, and Poetry in Restoration England* (Athens, GA, 1994), pp. 59–60. Paul Sellin explains that the agonistic action in *Samson Agonistes* should be interpreted as "dissembling," "assuming a mask," or "playing a part" ("Milton's Epithet Agonistes," *SEL* 4 [1964], 157).

35. For an overview of recent criticism on Milton's response to political censorship, see my *Barbarous Dissonance and Images of Voice in Milton's Epics* (Montreal, 1996), pp. 48–49.

36. David Loewenstein, *Milton and the Drama of History: Historical Vision, Iconoclasm, and the Literary Imagination* (Cambridge, 1990), p. 137.

37. Arnold Stein, *Heroic Knowledge: An Interpretation of Paradise Regained and Samson Agonistes* (Minneapolis, 1957), p. 196. On the spectrum of folly in *Samson Agonistes*, see Anna K. Nardo, " 'Sung and Proverb'd for a Fool': Samson as Fool and Trickster," *Mosaic* 22.1 (1989), 1–16. Blair Worden reminds us that the regicides who were subject to derision during the Restoration were frequently cast as fools ("Milton, *Samson Agonistes*, and the Restoration," pp. 123–24).

38. Mikhail Bakhtin, *Problems of Dostoevsky's Poetics*, ed. and trans. Caryl Emerson (Minneapolis, 1984), p. 122. On the "carnival," see Bakhtin's *Rabelais and His World*, trans. Helene Iswolsky (Cambridge, MA, 1968); Victor Turner, *The Anthropology of Performance* (New York, 1986), pp. 132–38. While not explicitly a scene of carnival in the contemporary sense, the theater spectacle in *Samson Agonistes* does create a space for the readjustment of barriers between social categories.

39. On carnivalization, see Bakhtin, *Problems*, pp. 100–49. On the link between *Carnaval* and *communitas*, see Turner, *Anthropology*, p. 132.
40. Mary Ann Radzinowicz, "The Distinctive Tragedy of *Samson Agonistes*," in Wittreich and Ide, *Composite Orders*, p. 251.
41. See Wittreich's discussion of the exegetical literature on Samson's death in *Interpreting Samson Agonistes* (Princeton, 1986), pp. 75–80, 321–8.
42. On the significance of the phrase "of my own accord," see *ibid.*, pp. 74–75, 112. Michael Lieb argued in response that the phrase belongs in a technical sense to the language of oath-swearing (" 'Our Living Dread': The God of *Samson Agonistes*" [Fifth International Milton Symposium, Bangor, Wales, 1995]).
43. *Mirabilis Annus*'s message is inverted in John Dryden's *Annus Mirabilis* in which the imperial city of London rises out of the engulfing fire "more august" or more Augustan (*Annus Mirabilis, John Dryden*, ed. Keith Walker [New York, 1987], line 1177).
44. *Upon the Joyfull and Welcome Return of His Sacred Majestie, Charls the Second, of England* (London, 1660), p. 12; *Mirabilis Annus, or the year of Prodigies and Wonders* ([London], 1661), A3v, Br-v; *Mirabilis Annus Secundus; or the Second Year of Prodigies* ([London], 1662). Imagery of eclipses in *Samson Agonistes* is significant, particularly because Milton invokes the meaning of the Hebrew name *Shimshon*, which is *shemesh*, "sun." Also see Sharon Achinstein's *Milton and the Revolutionary Reader* (Princeton, 1994), pp. 173–75, 210–12.
45. M. J. Doherty reads the passage as a critique of the heroic tradition, claiming that "Milton's inscription of the uniqueness of the sacred Phoenix in human, not angelic characters, produce[s] a profitable interpretive ambivalence" ("Beyond Androgyny: Sidney, Milton, and the Phoenix," in Margo Swiss and David A. Kent, eds., *Heirs of Fame: Milton and Writers of the English Renaissance* [Lewisburg, 1995], p. 48). Special thanks to Stella Revard for directing my attention to this book chapter and for sharing her insights on the significance of the phoenix for Milton.
46. Andrew Marvell, "On *Paradise Lost*," *Paradise Lost*, by John Milton, 2nd edn. (London, 1674), line 9; William Joyner, *The Roman Empress. A Tragedy* ([London], 1671); see Gerard Langbaine, *An Account of the English Dramatick Poets* (Oxford, 1691), pp. 308–09. *Memoirs of Thomas Hollis*, comp. Francis Blackburne, 2 vols. (London, 1780), vol. II, p. 624.
47. I am grateful to Sharon Achinstein, John Rumrich, and Stephen Dobranski from whose insights, criticisms, and editorial comments I benefited considerably, and to Marta Straznicky for our stimulating exchanges about the closet drama. I also acknowledge the generous support of the Social Sciences and Humanities Research Canada Council during the preparation of this essay.

PART IV

Readers of heresy

Asserting eternal providence: John Milton through the window of liberation theology

Joan S. Bennett

For the Christian the only safe way is the perilous one; living for the impossible hope, interlacing the prose of actuality with the rhythm of hope, calling defiance to Satan as he squats like a cormorant on the Tree of Life.[1]

INTRODUCTION

This chapter is written for Miltonists and students of Milton; at the same time, it invites consideration of a more general set of questions and problems by linking serious issues in Milton studies with serious issues facing Christian activists today. I offer a reading of Milton's poetry, primarily *Paradise Regained* and *Samson Agonistes*, through an imaginative window provided by the contemporary phenomenon of liberation theology.

Analogies, by definition, juxtapose phenomena that are alike in some ways and different in others. Linking Milton's life and works with the thought and actions of Christian activists over four centuries later calls forth questions about what we are doing when we draw analogies between phenomena from different points in history. Such a juxtaposition invites discussion of particular differences and of the very meaning of historical difference. I would like at the beginning to acknowledge the validity of these concerns but at the same time to set them to one side for the moment on the ground that the method I have chosen requires doing one thing at a time.

One advantage of the theoretical self-consciousness of our age has been academic writers' freedom to acknowledge and explore the ideological and practical contexts from within which we inevitably experience and explore our subjects.[2] A related opportunity is for scholars to widen their own experience by entering imaginatively the contexts of others. The present journey into liberation theology was prompted by questions of Milton's reaction to the defeat of the English revolutionary cause, questions that make their presence felt especially in readings of *Paradise Regained* and *Samson Agonistes*. Did the aging revolutionary renounce his former political activism? Is a new-found quietism the reason for his choice of original sin as the subject of his long-deferred epic? Why did he choose to write about Jesus' temptation in the wilderness instead of the passion? Why did he write about the Hebrew Judge Samson, and why in the genre of tragedy? Although I have written about these questions using more traditional scholarly methods, I am aware that many "first-world" academics and students today have trouble *imagining* someone with Milton's deep religiosity and profound humanism maintaining a revolutionary political commitment. To address the readerly capacity for "imagining," I offer a contemporary context in which Christian humanism means a radical commitment to social action.

My assumption is that if readers find the resulting view compelling, then an appropriate next step would be to examine the points of dissimilarity and to compare the competing force of other, different, contexts. Meanwhile, I am vulnerable to the criticism leveled against Christopher Hill by his revisionist challengers, that the approach is heavily "literary," emphasizing printed sources at the expense of other information relevant to the social history not only of the revolutionaries but also of those they opposed. No matter how much insight we gain by examining their multiple facets, however, the upheavals of the mid-seventeenth century did constitute a religious and political revolution, a campaign for liberation, "in the consciousness of those who lived through it and . . . transmitted [it] to their children and their children's children"[3] – indeed, to liberationists of our own world. As his critics gratefully acknowledge, Hill "has done more than anyone else to evoke the pain and striving and to recreate the mental world of the revolutionary decades."[4] I hope to render part of that mental and spiritual world accessible here as well.

Even if challenges to my analogy are saved for another time, however, there are two points relating to common perceptions of liberation theology as a movement that may need attention at the outset. One is the movement's relation to the Roman Catholic church, from which its most intellectually complex theoretical writers have emerged. Especially since I will be dealing with the works of Latin American writers, a reminder may be needed that the movement is world-wide, with many Protestant leaders. In charting a genealogy of modern individualism, intellectual history customarily contrasts the communitarian "tradition" of Catholicism with the individualistic "priesthood" of each Protestant believer, perhaps obscuring the fact that abandoning the authority of tradition to follow "the Bible only" was the corporate enterprise of a collective social movement, and very much so in seventeenth-century England. Liberation theologians today follow what they see as biblical authority, sometimes in conflict with civil and ecclesiastical authority. Protestant liberationists today do not see themselves as different from Catholic liberationists in this regard; both work collectively for social change; both are Christian humanists and bear comparison with seventeenth-century Christians who, because of and through their belief in their own Christian liberty, attempted to change the social structures of their world.

It could be objected that someone with the iconoclastic individualism of John Milton would never have accepted a "silencing" as did the Roman Catholic Leonardo Boff.[5] But if we substitute for the twentieth-century Bishop of Rome the Protector of the attempted Commonwealth, we may have a test for this aspect of Milton's commitment to the collective nature of the struggle. I find particularly interesting Milton's silence at the time of the Army's attack on the Levellers in 1649. It is most likely that he was asked at that time to write in defense of the government against the Levellers, yet he did not. From his remarks in the *Ready and Easy Way to Establish a Free Commonwealth* (1660), we can infer that in 1649 Milton may have wished to defend the Levellers' right to attempt to contribute to the construction of the Commonwealth but that he judged opposition to Cromwell at this point to be centrally destructive to the whole revolutionary effort. If so, would such a self-silencing be similar or dissimilar to Boff's?

The second point affecting a reader's willingness to enter imaginatively into the context I am offering concerns a common claim of churches and governments that liberation theologians are advocates of violence as a means of social change. It is important, in order to do justice to the analogy I shall be drawing, to recognize that liberation theology does not attempt to solve the disagreement between pacifists and just war theorists. The use of violence as a last resort in resistance is an unresolved issue for liberationists. The body of Christians living out a liberation praxis today includes both pacifists and nonpacifists; and while their two positions coexist with considerable tension, they coexist. Although liberationists do not share a common position on violent or non-violent resistance, they do hold in common a belief that the doctrine of Christian liberty entails social action, whether or not violence is ruled out as a means.

It is that religio-political commitment which I hope to render imaginatively present for the reader of this chapter. I have taken as an epigraph a quotation from the 1979 report of a study group commissioned by the Scottish Fellowship of Reconciliation, Christian activists seeking a new approach to issues of conflict and social justice. For this group, the "only [spiritually] safe way" is not that of the solitary contemplative; it is, as Milton's was, the "perilous" commitment to social action.

By publishing two editions of *The Ready and Easy Way to Establish a Free Commonwealth* in 1660 even as the Army was bringing the exiled monarchy back from France, John Milton risked not only his individual life but also his unfinished life's work of a poetry to which he believed he had a divine commission. In the same year, his regicide tracts—texts that had deconstructed the hegemonic use of a Christian ideology by political absolutists – were ordered publicly burned by the hangman of King Charles II. Enduring imprisonment and escaping execution, Milton went on to publish his great poems (1667 and 1671) and, at the first opportunity, another political tract (1673), his last work. Their own political and religious commitments led some of Milton's seventeenth- and early eighteenth-century readers regretfully to consider him a "vile mercenary" of rebellion who either wrote flawed poetry because of his politics or wrote great poetry in spite of his politics. Other readers happily considered him a "grand Whig" and took his poetry to undergird democratic liberalism.[6]

More recently, Milton has interested new theorists of Marxism whose purpose is not so much either to claim or to regret his aesthetic power but to classify it, as early-capitalist bourgeois, within a neo-Marxist taxonomy. While theorists working along these lines are not interested in literary close-reading,[7] some do regard seriously the politically committed religious context from which the poetry emerged[8] and the rigorous philosophical and political commitment that the poetry embodies.[9] A Marxist valuing both political commitment and literary reading is Christopher Hill, who observes that in 1644, writing his *Areopagitica*, Milton had seen England as a nation full of prophets. "Where," Hill asks, "are they now?"[10]

I would like to try the exercise of seeing such prophets now in Brazil, Argentina, and El Salvador; in South Africa and the Philippines; in Germany, Ireland, and even England – noticing that, like Milton's Londoners, they are "wholly taken up with the study of highest and most important matters to be reformed," developing a theology and praxis of liberation even as they are "besieg'd and blockt about" with "battell ... marching up" (*Areopagitica, CP*II: 556–57).[11] One of these voices, speaking from within the British tradition, has suggested the association: "This emergence of liberation theology, and of its European counterpart, political theology, may yet prove to be the most creative Christian political initiative since Puritanism in the seventeenth century."[12] Another, criticizing Rousseau's claim that "Christianity preaches only servitude and dependence," exclaims: "Had he never heard of John Knox, of Oliver Cromwell or of John Milton?"[13] This theologian views as a valid hope, even if not a historically defensible claim, the Leveller John Lilburne's assertion that "the most faithful servants of Christ in every country where they lived were ever the greatest enemies to tyranny and oppression"; and, in response to requests from Christian revolutionaries in both Latin America and Southeast Asia, he has examined seventeenth-century Puritan discussions of resistance that could serve as tools of thought "to assist Christians at the present day in their several countries to determine their relationship to the state."[14] These people are seeking in seventeenth-century Puritanism a context that gives clarity to their own liberation efforts.

In turn, I believe that it is worthwhile to examine liberation theology for the insight it can yield into Puritans' political religion and into the poetry of "their valiant and learned Champion" John Milton.[15] Political theology of any age needs to be understood in the context of its believers' praxis. Understanding the actual religio-political functioning of such doctrines as "original sin," "natural law," the *imitatio Christi*, the "kingdom of God," and discerning "the signs of the times" presents today's readers with a major challenge. For instance, the most ambitious neo-Marxist consideration of Milton, that of Christopher Kendrick, is handicapped by Kendrick's failure to differentiate "providence" from "predestination" and to relate either of these to the practice of "reading" the "signs of the times," "the providences."[16] "Predestination" was a doctrine concerning God's general plan for humankind; unlike Calvin, Milton and many other "Arminians of the Left" believed that all people are "predestined" for salvation even though many individuals exercise their God-given freedom to choose evil instead. "Providence," on the other hand, is not so much a doctrine as it is a name for the deity, like "Emmanuel" ("God-with-us"), a name that characterizes God's active relationship to humans in the course of history. In Milton's poetic conception, before the fall, Providence appeared to humans as a Person, but after the fall, that Person appeared more commonly in "providences" and "signs." Postlapsarian providential signs need to be "read" in the same way that the prelapsarian divine Person was listened to, reasoned with, and loved. Here is how Milton's archangel explains to the newly fallen Adam the providences of God:

> Yet doubt not but in Valley and in Plain
> God is as here, and will be found alike
> Present, and of his presence many a sign
> Still following thee, still compassing thee round
> With goodness and paternal Love, his Face
> Express, and of his steps the track Divine.   (*Paradise Lost* 11.349–54)

Liberation theology today – in spite of its sociological differences from radical Puritanism – may offer, then, a valuable window onto radical Christian experience. It articulates as fundamental tenets what, I shall assert, the revolutionary Christian humanist holders of these doctrines in the seventeenth century assumed: (1) that the Christian faith requires its adherents to work actively to achieve justice in the world: "World and church are not seen as two opposing blocs or powers but as two aspects of the one thing," holding that "the sacred is . . . the deepest meaning of the secular,"[17] and (2) that, as a young East German pastor expressed it in 1976, "correct theology does not precede correct action; it is not its precondition; on the contrary, it comes at a later stage as one reflects on one's praxis."[18] These two assumptions may be seen to underlie the angelic narrative with which Milton ends his *Paradise Lost*, in which God presents Adam with the phenomenon of history. "Reveal," God tells the archangel Michael, "what shall come in future days / As I shall thee enlighten, *intermix* / My Cov'nant in the woman's seed renew'd" (11. 113–16; emphasis added). Adam is taught to study history – "what shall come" – under the guidance of Providence – "my Cov'nant" – in order to fashion his theology in the context of human experience.

ORIGINAL SIN

What happens to original sin in the context of liberation theology? Milton's choice of the biblical story of original sin as the subject for what he had earlier intended as a nationalistic epic is generally held to result from the defeat of his political cause. However, many readers have assumed that this choice of subject indicates the poet's final belief that political activism is – given the fallen human condition – hopeless, if not wrong, and that to be sought instead is "the Spirit illuminating the solitary believer and fortifying him with 'inward consolations'."[19] Where this assumption is taken to include political quietism, it implies that Milton, while he had been caught up in the millenarian hopes of the 1640s, had ignored this doctrine's implications. It supposes that the doctrine of original sin has always stood as a reminder of the futility of idealistic collective human efforts to reform the structure of society.

Belief in original sin has not, however, always effectively underpinned authoritarian politics. It needs especially to be distinguished from today's ultimate pessimism, which, seeing itself as *fate*-ridden rather than *guilt*-ridden, is "unflanked by any affirmation about an original or natural order which has been violated."[20] Today, in fact, original sin "re-emerges in liberation theology as the analytical tool which highlights the tension between the human condition as it is and the vision of ultimate justice";[21] the doctrine of original sin underpins the commitment to bringing that justice into being. It is true that whenever the doctrine has been successfully employed by a Hobbesean purpose of absolutism, original sin has lost its serviceability as a tool of social analysis; but, as Milton's widow is said to have assured John Aubrey about "Mr. Hobbs" and her late husband, "their interests and tenets were diametrically opposite."[22]

For liberation theology today, original sin attests to "the perversion of all political action and structures by sin."[23] Milton too held that although there were only two people in the garden, their story is that of the "whole human race," and their sin will always have both social and individual dimensions: "For what sin can be named, which was not included in this one act?" (*de doctrina Christiana, CW* XV: 181–83).

Did such "meditation on original sin and the fall" by Milton and the Puritans in fact discourage belief in social activism? Did it bring about, as has been suggested by Fredric Jameson, a "displacement from politics to psychology and ethics"?[24] In liberation theology, "the sin of Adam ... is met not with fatalism, but with a call to justice and righteousness,"[25] and where Milton and his contemporaries looked to their contemporary social contract theory, liberation theorists have looked to their contemporary social theory of Marxism – not, in either case, for a philosophy to adopt, but for tools of social analysis to complement and help to activate ("to incarnate") the fundamentally sacred meaning of society. Both enact versions of radical Christian humanism.

Watching this process at work today should make it possible for us to see how Milton's choice of a subject for *Paradise Lost* was in his time and in his hands a politically revolutionary choice. He sought to give his readers an understanding of the creation and original sin because understanding creation and original sin could lead then, as it has now once again, to a commitment to the reformation of society. Milton wrote to "assert Eternal Providence, / And justify the ways of God to men" (*Paradise Lost* 1.24–25); and Milton's divinely commissioned angel taught Adam and Milton's readers that there is a steady link between the fall and the twice coming of the Son, however hard that link is to see while one lives within the flow of history. "It is the theodicy question, the dilemma of evil in a God-created world," according to liberation theology, which "provides the red thread of continuity ... from original sin to 'eschatology'." And the eschatological message of the kingdom, now as then, may be found "powering the chariot of revolutionary politics."[26]

PARADISE REGAINED: THE IMITATIO CHRISTI

The messianic message of the kingdom is Milton's subject in *Paradise Regained*. Since the eighteenth century, *Paradise Regained* (1671) has proven difficult for readers to recognize as an activist – or even political – work. Responding to early assumptions that the regaining of paradise should show the crucified and risen Christ "driving the Devil back again to Hell" (Thomas Newton, 1752),[27] and that "to attribute the redemption of mankind solely to Christ's triumph over the temptations in the wilderness is... untrue" (Henry Todd, 1801),[28] readers who inherit the Enlightenment separation of religion and politics (or the bourgeois displacement from politics to ethics) have largely inclined to consider Jesus in *Paradise Regained* "as an exemplar, whom Milton is urging his faithful, God-loving reader to emulate" in private daily life.[29] Indeed, a frequent assumption is that *Paradise Regained* offers its readers a direct model for quietism in the wake of a sobered recognition that collective political activism is doomed by inevitable human sinfulness to fail to achieve reform.

Recently, David Loewenstein has noted that the Christ of Milton's prose *Defence of the English People* (1651) is "no meek or submissive figure, but rather an active and unyielding liberator who boldly censures, accuses, reproves, and warns his adversaries."[30] Loewenstein believes that in the artistry of his political prose works, Milton saw himself as making "the aesthetic [do] essential political and cultural work" ("Milton and the Poetics of Defense," p. 186). Had Milton seen the danger and/or falsity of such a picture of Jesus by the time he published *Paradise Regained*? I have argued that the opposite is true, that in the poetry, as well as the prose, aesthetics does essential political work.[31] Milton's prose itself, published during the attempted building of the Commonwealth, shows us the link from the political tracts, with their revolutionary purpose, to this poem, published under renewed oppression. That we are given an activist Jesus in the *Defence* and a quiet Jesus in *Paradise Regained*, that Milton took as his poem's subject neither Jesus' social ministry nor his resurrection but his temptation, does not mean that he had changed his mind about Jesus' relation to politics. In the context of liberation theology, we can view another possibility.

In the aftermath of the events in Paris of May 1968, conservative theologians argued against revolution by saying that "Christ was the Suffering Servant who rejected the devil's temptation to pursue 'the road to triumph by means of force and violence'" and that the imitation of this Christ calls for quiet endurance from Christians. In response to this definition of the *imitatio Christi*, liberationists stress the need to recognize the historical uniqueness of Christ's role as savior of the world: Jesus' "suffering and death," they say, "constituted the sacrifice which overcame the separation of humankind and God and destroyed the power of Satan. This can be said of no other person. His role as the Suffering Servant . . . is the necessary corollary of his being the saviour . . . The sacrifice of Christ, according to the New Testament, is complete, once and for all. We Christians cannot repeat it."[32] They explain that human use of revolutionary power may be justified "in a perspective of *agape* as symbolized by the cross. Revolution, in the sense of planned overthrow and capture of the power structures of society, may be included in the active concern of love."[33]

"Christ himself," Milton explained in *Of Civil Power* (1659), "coming purposely to dye for us, would not be . . . defended" by his disciple's sword; and yet a Christian community "may defend itself against outward force" (*CP* VII: 257, 256). For Christ's bringing us into his kingdom – liberating us not from sin itself, but from bondage to our sins – has "made all the more possible" the political "struggle for freedom" (*CP* IV: 374). "At the cost of his own slavery," Milton explained in *A Defence*, Christ "put our political freedom on a firm foundation" (*CP* IV: 375).

The narratives to which revolutionary Christianity now turns under oppression are those about the kingdom, and they have their focus in the temptation of Christ in the wilderness. Jesus' temptations, liberationists point out, are about the true meaning of the kingdom and about power. The temptation story's "main and original concern," asserts the Salvadoran theologian Jon Sobrino, "is Christological. It is not a morality tale or a pious lesson . . . The idea is not that Jesus endured temptation simply to give us an example." The account of the temptations is given us in order to show us the dialectical "relationship between [Jesus'] fashioning of himself and his fashioning of the Kingdom"[34] and to show the political meaning of the commitment to an *imitatio Christi*. It is this dialectical relationship between self-fashioning and the shaping of the kingdom in their own time and place that his followers are called to imitate.

The drama that liberation Christology finds in the gospel accounts of the temptation may be seen as the drama of *Paradise Regained*. In Samuel Wesley's opinion (1697), *Paradise Regained* "draws out that in four Books which might have been well comprised in one."[35] What makes the poem so long, of course, is the concrete history included in the kingdom's temptation which Milton saw as essential to the story of Jesus' effort to "discern how to live a life of service that will authentically correspond with the concrete will of God." The drama of the temptation must be viewed "not in terms of a possible choice between God and Satan, but as a questioning search for the authentic reality of God" in history.[36]

The point is that, for the revolutionary Milton as well as for the Latin American liberationist, there is a very important sense in which "God's will is historical rather than eternal or universal" (Sobrino, *Christology at the Crossroads*, p. 129); the Christology of both affirms "a truly historical *logos*" (p. 83). Universal values exist in natural law, but to exist in human experience, in history, "they must be concretized in some way" (p. 85). The question at stake in the temptation, as Sobrino summarizes it, is: "What sort of power truly mediates God and hence brings his reign nearer?" (p. 98). The answer "is not based on inner intention (as the isolated scene in the desert might suggest at first) but in [Jesus'] clash with the historical forces of sin" (p. 99). Jesus' call is not to purify his own heart (already pure) – and his followers are not called to purify theirs before they may act (in Christ they are already forgiven). Rather, the call to liberation – expressed by the liberationists in terminology shared by the Puritans – is to discern "the signs of the times."

I would describe the liberationists as radical humanist antinomians.[37] They believe that although God's nature is reflected in a unified and universal natural law, humans have access to that law only as it is historicized. Consequently, it is never possible automatically to know, by sorting casuistically among a list of positive laws, what course of action should be taken in a particular situation. Given this understanding of morality, here is how Sobrino explains his guidelines for studying the development of Jesus' own faith and praxis, the real subject of the temptation story and the real meaning of Incarnation:

Every human action in history, insofar as it is positive, is guided by certain values accepted as basically good at the start: e.g., love, justice, brotherhood, trust in God, and so forth. But insofar as they unfold in a given situation, they must be concretized in some way ... the historical course of a person must entail the concretion of those values which triggered that course ... In the historical process we find a dialectical interplay between fashioning reality and fashioning oneself as an active subject. (p. 85)

In Jesus' case, as Sobrino describes it, there were two main stages of faith development, the same two stages that Milton shows his Jesus working out. First, Jesus appears as an orthodox Jew; the concrete embodiment of his faith is as a prophet proclaiming and making present the kingdom of God (pp. 90–92). Milton shows this part of Jesus' praxis in *Paradise Regained* through Jesus' memories of his belief in law and prophecy (1.205–25; 2.473–75) and, most extensively, through "the analysis and prophetic denunciation of a sinful situation"[38] which occur in his sustained discursive conflict with Satan.

> ... why should man seek glory? who of his own
> Hath nothing, and to whom nothing belongs
> But condemnation, ignominy, and shame? (3.134–36)

> As for those captive Tribes, themselves were they
> Who wrought their own captivity, fell off
> From God to worship Calves (3.414–16)

> That people victor once, now vile and base,
> Deservedly made vassal, who once just,
> Frugal, and mild, and temperate, conquer'd well,
> But govern ill the Nations under yoke. (4.132–35)[39]

The second stage of Jesus' faith occurred, Sobrino says, when he came to see his mediation of God's kingdom "in a novel way that he had never suspected before" (*Christology at the Crossroads*, p. 94). Though he had known that, like prophets before him, he would undoubtedly suffer hardship and danger, he had not seen that his primary calling would not be "to preach the Kingdom and perform deeds of power." Instead, it would be to "shoulder the very burden of sin" (p. 95). Jesus had to accept his own death "as the death of his cause" (p. 94) as well. Sobrino believes that the gospels' placement of the temptations at the start of Jesus' ministry is an "anachronism" though he concedes that the Synoptics needed to make clear, by the setting's connection with the baptism, how Jesus' temptation would "center around his relationship with the Father and ... service to the Kingdom" (p. 96). However, he says, the temptation passages are actually the fruit of theological reflection on the whole of Jesus' faith development.

The temptation story has the same import for Milton: as the "history of Jesus' faith" it offers the gospel message more fully than could a recounting of the facts of the passion and crucifixion because the faith that Jesus developed is what invests the cross and resurrection with their meaning. Thus, Milton shows Jesus working through, in advance, the stages of the praxis he will develop, reaching imaginatively beyond the defeat of his reformist cause to the surprising uniqueness of his self-sacrificial battle with sin. "What dost thou in this World?" a mocking and despairing Satan asks of Milton's Jesus (*Paradise Regained* 4. 372), clearing the space, in spite of himself, for Jesus' "novel way." "What if," Jesus is led to wonder, "I reject [a kingdom?]" (2. 457); "What if [God] hath decreed that I shall first / Be tried in ... things adverse" (3.188–89); "what if I withal / Expel a Devil" (4.128–29).

What are the implications for the reader of such an interpretation of the temptation story? Most importantly, they significantly complicate the *imitatio Christi*. "The following of Jesus does not come down to the mere imitation of Jesus," Sobrino explains. What, then, does Jesus' story show his followers? "We can say that Jesus showed us the absolute dimensions of a historical path but that he did not show us any path as being absolute in itself" (*Christology at the Crossroads*, p. 131). Such a statement is the root of antinomian Christianity. Jesus' concrete life decisions, including the final decision not to resist Caesar, are part of his own unique path. "We must accept the *historicity* of his concrete morality," and, in our turn, we must accept "the obligation to *historicize*" (p. 132) – to work out in our own circumstances our own *concrete* morality, which may well need to include decisions different from Jesus'. The "absolute dimensions" he embodied in his own morality are those of the divine love (p. 132). "We must be open [both] to love as effective action and love as suffering even unto death," Sobrino acknowledges, "but the relationship between the two can be very different [for his followers than they were for Jesus] because history presents us with the urgent tasks of rendering the kingdom of God present in at least partial form" (p. 132). Liberation theologians, as they discern the signs of our times, believe that the primary call now is for "effective action."[40] They pair study of the gospels with resolute, active resistance to oppression. Milton paired *Paradise Regained* with *Samson Agonistes*. Can Milton's tragedy be seen as art doing political and cultural work? as political activism?

SAMSON AGONISTES: DISCERNING THE SIGNS OF THE TIMES

"Oh how comely it is and how reviving / To the Spirits of just men long opprest! / When God into the hands of thir deliverer / Puts invincible might / To quell the mighty of the Earth, th'oppressor," the Chorus reflects in response to the captive Samson's renewed defiance toward Harapha, boastful soldier of the Philistine occupying forces (*Samson Agonistes*, lines 1268–72). "But patience is more oft the exercise / Of Saints," they worry, considering Samson's condition, "Either of these is in thy lot ... with might endu'd ... but sight bereav'd" (lines 1287–94). Christians must be open to both effective action and accepted suffering, Sobrino says; and these "two phases of love" may coexist simultaneously so that Christians must "continually seek effective power on behalf of human beings while being open to the realization that it may be snatched from them." This openness, Sobrino concludes, "is the most crucial and ticklish point in any Christian morality, the point where discernment becomes necessary" (*Christology at the Crossroads*, p. 136).

In recent decades, the argument has been advanced that discernment is what Milton's blind Samson lacks. He is seen as either making wrong choices or having no basis for choice-making. Under attack, after having held critical sway for about forty years, is a "regenerationist" reading of the poem, which infers from Samson's words and actions that in the course of the drama Samson undergoes a personal conversion, a regeneration in faith that leads him through repentance to self-awareness, acceptance of forgiveness, a new ability and providential occasion to serve God by destroying the entire Philistine ruling class. Two concerns impel the drama's newer questioners. One lies in the violence of the play's catastrophe: how could Milton the Christian and Milton the humanist, even given an ancient Hebraic setting, have meant to present this large-scale destruction of human life as heroic and God-willed?[41] In answer to this first question some have argued that Milton did not intend to portray Samson as heroic; that he intended rather, by contrasting *Samson Agonistes* with *Paradise Regained*, to provide a quietist critique of his own past political commitment, a condemnation of "royalist and revolutionary alike."[42] The second concern is raised by questioners whose world view is centered in philosophical indeterminacy;[43] these claim that Milton either consciously or unconsciously held conflicting values which surface in his pairing of contradictory poems, *Samson Agonistes* and *Paradise Regained*. Thomas Corns gives this reading:

In *Samson Agonistes* and *Paradise Regained*, despite the simultaneity of their issue, we find radically different perspectives on the nature of political action and by implication on the problems facing the godly in the Restoration. One, almost wholly pessimistic, looks for the simpler rewards of revolutionary justice or terrorist outrage; the other, transcendentally, assumes the major victory to be in heart and mind and that it has already been accomplished.[44]

Violence is a crucial concern of liberation theologians, for whom terrorism is never a possible course and for whom the rewards of revolutionary justice are never simple; and indeterminacy is a serious question for those committed to "discernment." Let us examine, first, the issue of violence: how do liberationists see its relation to Jesus' commitment to the "absolute dimensions" of love? The Argentinian theologian José Miguez Bonino sums up the framework for a consideration of violence by asserting that "love is the inner meaning of politics, just as politics is the outward form of love." This love is another name for the goodness, righteousness, justice of the kingdom, and "it is in the sphere of historical commitment, under the eschatological promise, that love finds it proper context."[45] It may not be hard to see how love for the oppressed leads to an attempt to liberate them from suffering, but can a project of liberation be seen as love for the oppressor? The Brazilian Paulo Freire explains: "As the oppressors dehumanize others and violate their rights, they themselves also become dehumanized. As the oppressed, fighting to be human, take away the oppressors' power to dominate and suppress, they restore to the oppressors the humanity they had lost in the exercise of oppression."[46] The prophetic analysis and denunciation of oppressors' wrongs, which Milton dramatizes in Samson's dialogues with his Philistine wife and with the enemy soldier Harapha (*Samson Agonistes*, lines 873–900 and 1139–223), allow us to hear the oppressed, both "fighting to be human" and struggling to "restore to the [here, Philistine] oppressors the humanity they had lost in the exercise of oppression."

Justice sought against an oppressor for the sake of fashioning the kingdom cannot, however, be vindictive or retributive according to liberation theology; and the words of Milton's Samson can be read as overcoming vindictiveness. Having judged both himself and Dalila, he forgives her, though at the "distance" (line 954) required to maintain his own firmness of purpose; his desire to fight Harapha is not finally to gain revenge but to establish by combat whose God is "the living God" (line 1140). When Providence shows him that this single combat will not be the way, he trusts that in whatever action or suffering will ensue, nothing will be "dishonorable, impure, unworthy / Our God, our Law, my Nation, or myself" (lines 1424–25). However imperfectly, Samson's is the justice of liberation.

Instead of retribution, Sobrino explains, the justice sought must be the "justice of 'the liberation of Israel'," in which "Yahweh is just, not because he gives all their due, but because he tries to re-create human beings and situations, to 'save' them" (*Christology at the Crossroads*, p. 119), to restore in them God's image given at creation. Some Christians will hold that the casting down of oppression by force must be left to God alone, that humans must not assume this role.[47] Liberationist have observed, on the other hand, that, overwhelmingly, God's action in history has been through human agents, and have therefore found themselves in agreement with a Puritan spokesman to Parliament in 1643: "if we have the honour to be God's instruments . . . we must go along with Providence."[48] However, this obligation of human agency – to serve actively even in the extreme situation where the oppressors' violence can be resisted only with violence – this responsibility raises for liberationists the awareness of a possible Christian tragedy.

Readers of *Samson Agonistes* have questioned how a Christian drama

could be tragic (is not Christianity ultimately a divine comedy?), and many, because they witness a personal renewal of faith in Samson, cannot finally see tragedy in this drama. Other readers see the world of *Samson Agonistes*, full of suffering, as genuinely tragic but not genuinely Christian; thus Martin Mueller believes that the Chorus is left at the catastrophe facing a universe shrouded in mystery, "which willing acceptance can mitigate but the terror of which it can never entirely remove."[49] More recently, readers with a biographical focus have seen not an ultimate existential philosophical awareness in the Chorus or Samson, but more simply, revolutionary terrorism, possibly even inscribing a vengeful "wish-fulfillment" in Milton himself.[50] Radical Christian humanism offers an angle of vision that includes together tragic suffering, personal sin, and divine redemption.

Liberationists see tragedy in the Christian liberation project, a tragedy of suffering and sin. The tragedy does not come, however, from a crisis of belief, from fear of a radical incoherence in the universe, or from a final yielding to the pressures of the repressed animal response to violence. Tragedy arises rather from the practice of force in love. To exercise force is to incur guilt.[51] Although there is love for the oppressor enacted in trying to stop oppression, there is also "a denial of love" if, in the process, an oppressor is injured or killed (Sobrino, *Christology at the Crossroads*, p. 158). God bears the cost of forgiving this guilt, having paid the price of redemption on the cross. "Christians who opt for force . . . engage in a tragic existence wherein they bear the burden of sin." Christian activists who opt for non-violence are in an equally tragic position; for the faithful, guilt is inescapable, because "to tolerate evil is to be as guilty as to react effectively against it" (p. 160). Tragedy comes for the liberationist not in a crisis of belief but in a praxis lived out under the condition of original sin. When force – either violent or non-violent – is used to combat oppression, then "guilt must be borne" (p. 161). When oppression is left effectively unopposed, then guilt must be borne. The Christian, like Jesus, must accept the burden of sin.

Does Milton show us a Samson who wrestles with such questions in a course of self-reformation as a faithful moral subject? Most agree that he does labor to discern the signs of his time. And many readers, looking in Samson for signs of personal conversion, have seen these specific interior processes taking place in the drama.[52] However, Stanley Fish makes the important point that Samson's spiritual path is not a direct line upwards toward "a single action so dazzling in its clarity and force that the moral structure of the universe comes clearly into view, and the relationship between God's will and events unfolding in history is fully known in a way

that can serve as a blueprint for future action."[53] Indeed, in the under-standing of radical Christian humanists, there can never be a "blueprint" for present or future action. Although God's incarnation manifested in *Paradise Regained* is, in one sense, "a single action so dazzling in its clarity and force that the moral structure of the universe" is known in an unde-niable way, Jesus provided no blueprint, as we have seen, but rather a model and mandate for a dialectical relationship between the self-fashioning of moral subjects and their shaping of God's kingdom in their time and place. Jesus left to God's people "the obligation to *historicize*" once he had shown, with dazzling clarity and force, "the absolute dimensions" of a historical path. God's people are left with the requirement to look for "the relation-ship between God's will and events unfolding" in their own histories, with the need, that is, for "discernment."[54]

When Samson leaves with the Philistine officer for the temple of Dagon, he appears not to know what is going to happen when he gets there – what others will do or what he himself will do. And from the moment that he leaves, Milton denies us and Samson's own people any further contact with him. How can we know, then, whether he is or is not regenerate? How can we think about our not knowing? "It is an oversimplification to say that one must first undergo a personal conversion and then go about the task of bringing about the kingdom," Sobrino points out (*Christology at the Crossroads*, p. 122). For the condition we seek to understand in watching Samson is the same we see in "the relational character of Jesus' own life"; human life "finds fulfillment insofar as its pole of reference, the kingdom of God, is brought to fulfillment" (p. 113). From the perspective of liberation the-ology, we would not expect to see Samson first fully purify himself and then act, because it is in the praxis (deed-and-reflection) that the self is regener-ated. The image of Samson "with both his arms on those two massy Pillars" and head down "as one who pray'd / Or some great matter in his mind revolv'd" presents an image of liberation praxis (*Samson Agonistes*, lines 1633–38).

Samson's story is unlike Jesus', but like Milton's readers', in that it must deal with the protagonists' very great personal burden of sin. But it can be seen to embody the message taught by liberationists today, that personal conversion "as such is not given once and for all. It is verified in the con-crete history of realizing the kingdom, and that history calls for ever new conversions."[55] Nevertheless, justice as a universal ideal – a reality of the eschatological kingdom – cannot be understood or rendered operational unless one approaches it through a concrete engagement with injustice. This is incarnational theology: "One must deliberately adopt some partial

stance in order to comprehend the totality" (Sobrino, *Christology at the Crossroads*, p. 124). Milton early taught "that the knowledge of good and evil, as two twins cleaving together, leaped forth into the world." Adam's descendants must know "good by evill" (*CP* II: 514). There is a moral corollary offered by Sobrino: "If we want to formulate the basic moral exigency in a phrase, we cannot say that it comes down to 'doing good and avoiding evil.' Rather, it comes down to 'doing good and fighting evil to wipe it out'" (*Christology at the Crossroads*, p. 125). Samson fights it and in this process ends his engagement with history.

Left to carry on are the Hebrew and the Philistine people, "the vulgar only" (*Samson Agonistes*, line 1659). Israel has freedom, "let but them / Find courage to lay hold on this occasion" (lines 1715–16). Readers who believe that *Samson Agonistes* implies Milton's renunciation of Christian activist politics know from reading biblical history beyond Judges 16 that in spite of the desolation of the hostile city (line 1561), the Hebrews' liberation did not last. Israelites would again fall short of the strenuous liberty. Many readers find Milton's Hebrew Chorus, who celebrate Samson's victory, to be men of limited insight. My own view is that the people's failure actively to support their leader's efforts at liberation is the reason for their stymied theology. Their limitation is one of praxis: their failure to act has resulted in failure to understand, which, in turn, has crippled effective action.[56]

THE PEOPLE'S CONSCIENTIZATION

Samson, their judge, for his part, however, has not provided a fully liberating leadership. Throughout his campaign, he had never boasted of his accomplishments or lorded over the people on whose behalf he fought, he had "us'd no ambition to commend [his] deeds" (*Samson Agonistes*, line 247). But he also had not called them to reflection, trusting rather that the "deeds themselves, though mute, spoke loud the doer" (line 249). Sure that Israel's governors and heads of tribes understood that it was God who offered deliverance through his successful revolutionary resistance, Samson attributes to fear and love of ease their failure to acknowledge the providential meaning of his victories by joining his fight.

The judgment of Samson on Israel is often read as Milton's judgment on the English who recalled Charles II from France:

> But what more oft in Nations grown corrupt,
> And by thir vices brought to servitude,
> Than to love Bondage more than Liberty,
> Bondage with ease than strenuous liberty. (lines 268–71)

236   JOAN S. BENNETT

The leaders of the people whom Milton's own political movement had sought to liberate had called themselves "a captain back for Egypt" (*CP* VII: 403). What Milton acknowledged at the Restoration had been feared by the reformers much earlier on. "The spirits of the people . . . are even vassalaged," Richard Overton wrote in *A Defiance* (1646), hoping against hope that the people would demonstrate support for the Levellers' *Agreement*, "the poor deceived people are . . . bestialized in their understanding . . . unman'd . . . as bruits they'll live and die for want of knowledge . . . of capacity to discern, whereof, and how far God by nature hath made them free."[57] Jesus himself deliberately chose as his followers and apostles "Plain Fishermen"; "no greater men them call," Milton insists (*Paradise Regained* 2.27). Nevertheless, Milton's Jesus, though he came to die for them, understands deeply that the people are "a herd confus'd": "They praise and they admire they know not what; / And know not whom, but as one leads the other" (3.49–53).

The term "the people" is held by liberation theologians today to include, but also to mean more than, social class. The people's collective reality, says Bonino, is "in the interaction between ethnic, cultural, and economic determinations." He draws upon the analysis of another Argentinean, Enrique Dussel, to acknowledge that "'People' is an ambivalent term: it has elements of the best and of the worst connotations." On the one hand, "the 'people' is a proprietary subject, a bearer in a process of liberation." On the other hand, "it is also an 'inert mass' that has introjected all the oppression and remains 'closed' to any transformation of its existence."[58] The republican Moses Wall urged Milton, with great sadness, on the eve of the Restoration to understand of those English now calling for Egypt that "whilst people are not free, but straitened in accommodations for life, their spirits will be dejected and servile."[59]

Remarking that, on the one hand, the revolutionary potential of the Christian faith was revealed in the trial and execution of Charles I, a British liberationist reflects that "on the other hand, the Commonwealth did not last. It proved unequal to the appallingly difficult task of creating a new focus of loyalty, a sense of identity, an alternative web of social relationships . . . A revolution transforms the political landscape overnight, but the people who rub their bleary eyes the next morning are the same people who were there the day before."[60] Liberationists today look for a solution to this fundamental problem of "the people" in a combination of "conscientization" and miracle. Milton shows Jesus considering both of these eventualities – "winning words" (*Paradise Regained* 1.222) and "some wond'rous call" (*Paradise Regained* 3.434) – and the gospels show Jesus effectively both using words and accepting miracles. Miracles Milton had, after the Restoration, to leave to God, but even in "evil days ... with dangers compast round" (*Paradise Lost* 7.25–27) he remained in control of his very powerful "moral voice."

"Conscientization," a rich and complex religio-political undertaking, is a form of Bible study, of listening to and telling over again, sometimes dramatizing, the Judeo-Christian stories, of breathing life into the dry bones of scripture, activating the "dangerous memory" they contain. In the contemporary "third world," as in seventeenth-century England, these narratives live in the cultural identity of the people. "The question now" for liberationists, Bonino acknowledges, "is whether the original explosive power of these symbols and myths – the 'dangerous memory' ... can be recovered and reactivated from within the life of the people."[61]

David Loewenstein has recently suggested that "Milton considered [*Samson Agonistes* ... an iconoclastic] weapon ... to alter the shape of history"; that through his dramatization of the "terrifying outcome of Samson's struggles" Milton himself was performing an act of verbal terrorism. According to this reading, Milton articulates deep "anxieties about national history, while demonstrating and valorizing God's power to intervene in that process." Milton is seen to have "conflicting or divided" responses to history, to have been unsure, at least subconsciously, whether the God who called England to reform was a God of freedom or of force.[62] With Loewenstein, I believe it is true that Milton's biblical story-making is performative discourse and that iconoclasm is a very important part of the work being done. But from a liberationist vantage point, iconoclasm need not in itself indicate internal division. The modern revolutionary identity more appropriately comparable to Milton than "terrorist" is perhaps, in a broad sense, "educator" – not psychological or cultural victim of irresolvable paradox, but practitioner of the dialectic of transformation.[63] We may think, for instance, of some aspects of the work of the basic Christian communities.

Basic Christian communities, which were appearing in Europe and North America as well as Latin America by the middle of the 1970s, range in size from 20 or 30 to over 200 members and in location from metropolis to jungle and share these characteristics: a largely lay leadership; informal, participatory collective worship; intense Bible study; and political activism.[64] Gustavo Gutierrez insists that both the theological undertaking and the base communities serve one end, the realization of liberty itself, of that time "when the oppressed themselves can freely raise their voices and express themselves directly and creatively in society and in the heart of the people of God, when they themselves account for the hope which they bear."[65]

Bonino relates a typical instance, recorded by the Brazilian priest Clodovis Boff, of Bible study as conscientization, the "transition in which, within a historical praxis, the people become aware of the hope and power behind the symbols and stories of their traditional faith and begin to shape a new ethos, a new way of dwelling in the world and in history":

In the Amazon jungles of Brazil a group reenacts the dramatic story of Naboth's vineyard. At the point where Ahab's police force apprehends Naboth, the audience suddenly intervenes spontaneously. It moves in and takes Naboth right out of the hands of the police. "That is not how the story runs in the Bible," comments Clodovis Boff, "but that is how the people lived it in the dramatization. It is the contemporary and creative way in which the people actually read and interpret the Word of God."[66]

Each occasion on which the Bible stories are re-experienced within a historical praxis offers awareness, hope, and power. Samson and his people, in the version of the story which Milton chose to tell, did not get their theology quite clear and were beginning only imperfectly to shape a new ethos. Yet they set forth all the dimensions of the struggle for liberation. Perhaps Milton hoped that his poetry would help people learn in their own contemporary and creative ways to interpret the liberating word of God, who "to *Israel* / Honor hath left, and freedom, let but them / Find courage to lay hold on" the occasion God would again offer (*Samson Agonistes*, lines 1714–16).

Stanley Fish assumes that what Milton's Hebrews, the Chorus and Manoa, most want "is that things once more be as they were" at the height of Samson's glory.[67] In a liberation context, however, this assumption yields an incomplete reading. What the Israelites *most* want – though not with enough courage to overcome their inaction – is freedom from the Philistine occupation, from the "daily fraud, contempt, abuse and wrong" (line 76); from "th' oppressor, / The brute and boist'rous force" of the army of the national security state "Hardy and industrious to support / Tyrannic power, but raging to pursue / The righteous" (lines 1272–76); from the blasphemy (line 442) and forced conversion to the worship of idols. In the end, their song of Samson's victory reveals their pent-up anger and humiliation. Its tone is too violent for many readers. But here we might consider the definition by Peter Matheson (himself a pacifist) of liberation as "love." The response to injustice, he says, "need not always be a reassured, emotion-free one . . . Unless we rage at injustice we are diminished in our humanity. Without a thought of aggression there is not true compassion." He argues for the inevitable, and not to be regretted, contingency of our position: "Who are we to play God, looking with an infinite fund of compassion at those who cheapen life and strip away the shreds of dignity? We have to take sides. To imagine that our spiritual vantage point puts us above the contending parties is either arrogance or self-delusion" (*Profile*, p. 150).[68] So Christians must discern the signs of their own times. "It is a tall order," Matheson concedes. "The merest hair-line separates firmness and obduracy, flexibility and weakness" (p. 151). Fish's deconstructionist reading of *Samson Agonistes*, in contrast, presents a view of contingency that focuses on interpretation; and where the liberationist sees "a tall order," the interpreter sees "a radical uncertainty." For the interpreter, God-as-God-really-is is inaccessible, because intellectually inconceivable; but for the liberationist, whose imperative is praxis, God-as-God-really-acts is accessible, in relationship, in "rousing motions." Fish finds that the freedom afforded to Samson by contingency, while "glorious and liberating" is "also terrifying."[69] Rather than terror, for the liberationist Matheson sees finally what he calls "a perverse confidence" and "a defiant gaiety." He says: "The immensity of the challenge is daunting. It is so clearly 'beyond us'. But if, as we believe, the way of the Cross has the future on its side, then even in our confused present we can be fired with a perverse confidence, a defiant gaiety" (*Profile*, p. 153). I suggest that we try hearing Milton's Samson, in his last act, speaking this gaiety in the *litotes* of radical Christian humanism:

> Hitherto, Lords, what your commands impos'd
> I have perform'd, as reason was, obeying,
> Not without wonder or delight beheld.
> Now of my own accord such other trial
> I mean to show you of my strength, yet greater;
> As with amaze shall strike all who behold.
>
> (*Samson Agonistes*, lines 1640–45)

He is calling defiance to Satan, who sits like a cormorant on the Tree of Life.

NOTES

1. Peter Matheson, *Profile of Love: Towards a Theology of the Just Peace* (Belfast, Dublin, Ottawa, 1979), p. 148.
2. I take as a partial precedent Stanley Fish's methodology in "Unger and Milton," *Doing What Comes Naturally: Change, Rhetoric and the Practice of Theory in Literary and Legal Studies* (Durham and London, 1989), pp. 399–588.
3. John Morrill, *The Nature of the English Revolution* (London and New York, 1993), p. 284.

4. *Ibid.*, p. 279.

5. See Harvey Cox, *The Silencing of Leonardo Boff: The Vatican and the Future of World Christianity* (Oak Park, IL, 1988).

6. See George F. Sensabaugh, "That Vile Mercenary Milton," *Pacific Coast Philology*, 3 (1968), 5–15, and *That Grand Whig, Milton* (Stanford, 1952).

7. Christopher Kendrick, *Milton: A Study in Ideology and Form* (London, 1986).

8. Fredric Jameson, "Religion and Ideology: A Political Reading of *Paradise Lost*," in Francis Barker et al., eds., *Literature, Politics and Theory: Papers from the Essex Conference, 1976–84* (London, 1986).

9. Andrew Milner, *John Milton and the English Revolution: A Study in the Sociology of Literature* (London, 1981).

10. Christopher Hill, *The Experience of Defeat: Milton and Some Contemporaries* (New York, 1984), p. 328.

11. Unless otherwise noted, quotations of Milton's poetry are from *Complete Poems and Major Prose*, ed. Merritt Y. Hughes (New York, 1957).

12. Matheson, *Profile*, p. 63.

13. J. G. Davies, *Christians, Politics and Violent Revolution* (New York, 1976), p. 44.

14. *Ibid.*, pp. 64–5.

15. John Lilburne, *As You Were* (1652), quoted in William Haller and Godfrey Davies, eds., *The Leveller Tracts, 1647–1653* (1944; rpt. Gloucester, MA, 1964), p. 32.

16. On Providence in the thought and experience of Milton and his contemporaries, see Joan S. Bennett, *Reviving Liberty: Radical Christian Humanism in Milton's Great Poems* (Cambridge, MA, 1989), especially ch. 3. The role of Marxist theory within Christian liberation theory is debated and dynamic. It is perhaps most fruitfully examined in the context of the Latin American praxis. A good text for this purpose is Clodovis Boff, *Feet-on-the-Ground Theology: A Brazilian Journey* (1984), trans. Phillip Berryman (New York, 1987), pp. 101–04; 113–14.

17. Matheson, *Profile*, p. 82.

18. *Ibid.*, p. 146.

19. John R. Knott, Jr., "'Suffering for Truth's Sake': Milton and Martyrdom," in David Loewenstein and James Grantham Turner, eds., *Politics, Poetics, and Hermeneutics in Milton's Prose* (Cambridge, 1990), pp. 153–70.

20. Matheson, *Profile*, p. 50.

21. *Ibid.*, p. 3.

22. John Aubrey, *Life of Milton*, rpt. in Hughes, eds., *Complete Poems and Major Prose*, p. 1023.

23. Matheson, *Profile*, p. 64.

24. The claim is Fredric Jameson's in "Religion and Ideology."

25. Matheson, *Profile*, p. 65.

26. *Ibid.*, p. 68.

27. Quoted in John Shawcross, *Paradise Regain'd: Worthy Not T'Have Remain'd So Long Unsung* (Pittsburgh, 1988), p. 134.

28. Quoted in *ibid.*, p. 133, n. 5.

29. Shawcross takes issue with this view, making a claim with which I agree: that

Milton is urging his reader not to take Jesus' own course of life as a model, but to take Jesus' faithful seeking after his own calling as an injunction for each person "to achieve an independence of worth, a spiritual inner being" of his or her own (*ibid.*, p. 82). Shawcross points out that the "political dimension" of the individual liberty thus achieved "lies in its need and employment in public service" (p. 126) and asserts "Jesus does *not* refute the possibility of an earthly nation under God" (p. 127). For a complementary discussion of this issue see Bennett, *Reviving Liberty*, ch. 6.

30. David Loewenstein, "Milton and the Poetics of Defense," in Loewenstein and Turner, eds., *Politics, Poetics, and Hermeneutics*, p. 178.

31. See Bennett, *Reviving Liberty.*

32. Davies, *Violent Revolution*, p. 152.

33. W. A. Beardsley quoted in *ibid.*, p. 158.

34. Jon Sobrino, *Christology at the Crossroads: A Latin American Approach*, trans. John Drury (Maryknoll, NY, 1978), pp. 87, 96.

35. Quoted in Shawcross, *Paradise Regain'd*, p. 132.

36. Sobrino, *Christology at the Crossroads*, p. 130.

37. For a discussion of seventeenth-century humanistic antinomianism, see Bennett, *Reviving Liberty*, pp. 97–118, especially pp. 109–11.

38. Sobrino, *Christology at the Crossroads*, p. 95.

39. See *Paradise Regained* 3.133–44; 3.414–32; 4.132–45; 4.309–64.

40. Even so, they are prepared for suffering. Sobrino himself lost his Archbishop and six fellow priests to assassins in the hire of the national security state. But theirs have not been quietist sufferings. Sobrino's own accounts can be found in *Archbishop Romero: Memories and Reflections* and *Companions of Jesus: The Jesuit Martyrs of El Salvador*, both Maryknoll, NY, 1990.

41. See especially Irene Samuel, *"Samson Agonistes* as Tragedy," in J. A. Wittreich, ed., *Calm of Mind: Tercentenary Essays on Paradise Regained and Samson Agonistes in Honor of John S. Diekhoff* (Cleveland, 1971), pp. 235–57, and Joseph A. Wittreich, *Interpreting Samson Agonistes* (Princeton, 1986).

42. Wittreich, *Interpreting*, p. 273.

43. See Stanley E. Fish, "Question and Answer in *Samson Agonistes,*" *Critical Quarterly* 2 (1969), 237–64, and "Spectacle and Evidence in *Samson Agonistes,*" *Critical Quarterly* 15 (1989), 555–86.

44. Thomas N. Corns, "'Some rousing motions': the Plurality of Miltonic Ideology," in Thomas Healy and Jonathan Sawday, eds., *Literature and the English Civil War* (Cambridge, 1990), p. 124. The two views partially overlap; both Fish and Wittreich look toward indeterminacy as a valuable perspective for at least problematizing a position that would otherwise seem to permit violence.

45. José Miguez Bonino, *Toward a Christian Political Ethics* (Philadelphia, 1983), p. 112.

46. Paulo Freire, *Pedagogy of the Oppressed*, trans. Myra Bergman Ramos (New York, 1970), p. 32.

47. Jacques Ellul, *Violence, Reflections from a Christian Perspective* (London, 1970), represents this position.

48. Davies, *Violent Revolution*, p. 160.

49. Martin Mueller, "*Pathos* and *Katharsis* in *Samson Agonistes*," *ELH*, 31 (1964), 168. Cf. William Riley Parker, *Milton's Debt to Greek Tragedy in* Samson Agonistes (New York, 1968).

50. David Loewenstein, *Milton and the Drama of History* (Cambridge, 1990), p. 145.

51. Some liberationists today, while they work actively in political resistance, whether legal or against the state, insist on revolutionary non-violence. The influential German writer Dorothee Solle wrestles with this issue; once a firm pacifist (though never a quietist), she came in the 1980s to question the moral viability of non-violent resistance where, as in Central America, the oppressor's violence is extreme. Whether readers of Milton come to his poem as pacifists or not, they must recognize that *Samson Agonistes* is portraying the extreme condition.

52. For a discussion of seventeenth-century humanist antinomian understanding of "discernment," see Bennett, *Reviving Liberty*, pp. 97–109.

53. Fish, "Spectacle and Evidence," p. 572.

54. George M. Muldrow traces the process in the terms of Puritan conversion literature in *Milton and the Drama of the Soul: A Study of the Theme of the Restoration of Man in Milton's Later Poetry* (The Hague, 1970). My own version is given in *Reviving Liberty*, ch. 5, "Liberty Under the Law: *Samson Agonistes*."

55. Sobrino, *Christology at the Crossroads*, p. 122.

56. Bennett, *Reviving Liberty*, pp. 119–39.

57. Quoted by Brian Manning, "The Levellers and Religion," in J. F. McGregor and B. Reay, eds., *Radical Religion in the English Revolution* (Oxford, 1984), p. 89.

58. Bonino, *Political Ethics*, p. 103.

59. Quoted in Hill, *Experience of Defeat*, p. 328.

60. Matheson, *Profile*, p. 41.

61. Bonino, *Political Ethics*, p. 105.

62. Loewenstein, *Drama of History*, pp. 143–50.

63. Sharon Achinstein, in *Milton and the Revolutionary Reader* (Princeton, 1994), responds to revisionist historians' failure to find an ideological coherency in, or consequence of, the English Revolution by seeking to demonstrate that the revolutionary writers' rhetorical practices "themselves constitute a form of ideology" that requires us, in turn, to imagine the modern political subject "not solely as a repository of rights, but as a reader: as a sum of polemical and rhetorical processes, not as a product" (p. 227). Her discrimination between "political rhetoric" and "propaganda" is, from a liberationist perspective, crucial. For another important characterization of Restoration nonconforming Christians' literary responses to the straitened conditions of their religious and political liberty, see N. H. Keeble, *The Literary Culture of Nonconformity in Later Seventeenth-Century England* (Athens, GA, 1987).

64. Harvey Cox, *Religion in the Secular City: Toward a Postmodern Theology* (New York, 1984), gives an overview of basic communities.

65. Gustavo Gutierrez, *A Theology of Liberation: History, Politics, and Salvation* (Maryknoll, NY, 1973).

66. Bonino, *Political Ethics*, pp. 105–06.
67. Fish, "Question and Answer," p. 556.
68. It should be noted that Matheson himself is committed to non-violent resistance although other members of his group in the extreme instance are not. All are agreed, however, that non-violence for its own sake is not love; only liberation is love (see *Profile*, pp. 152–53).
69. Fish, "Spectacle and Evidence," p. 579.

CHAPTER 12

Milton's transgressive maneuvers: receptions (then and now) and the sexual politics of Paradise Lost

Joseph Wittreich

he Ever was a Dissenter . . .

Jonathan Richardson

I'm increasingly uncertain, with Milton in particular, as to whether we have a way of talking about what it is that Milton is actually doing in *Paradise Lost*. I reject completely the orthodox accounts . . . Milton more even than Blake is an instance of someone who so persuasively redefines tradition, including Christianity itself, that he makes it entirely in his image . . . his orthodoxy is such a powerful transumption of Christian orthodoxy . . . that we can only speak of the Miltonic. To call him a Christian poet is . . . to beg the question in the extreme.

Harold Bloom[1]

There may be only one Milton, but in *Paradise Lost* there are at least two texts circulating at once: in the words of Richard Corum, one of "obedient submission" and another of "subversive mutiny."[2] This fact alone casts doubt upon the proposition that "students . . . would learn just as much about poetry from a professor who thought Milton was a sexist as they would from one who didn't,"[3] only because the initial thesis (that Milton is a sexist) requires that attention be given to the first of these texts, while the second thesis (that Milton was not a sexist) cannot be seriously addressed without engaging the inner workings of both texts – their dynamic tensions and complicated interactions. One lesson to learn from these two texts, read in conjunction, is that Milton's poem is an arena for conflict, a battleground for warring values, for contrary theologies, philosophies, and politics. Milton thus gives voice to inconsistencies and to contradictions within his culture that often he cannot transcend. Another lesson is that Milton's times, and especially his personal circumstances, prevent his transgressive maneuvers, his subversive gestures, his challenges to orthodoxy from being an open attack, instead ensuring that they will take the form of an ambush. But therein lies the risk, for those who go beneath the surface of a work of

244

art do so at their own peril; poets who display dazzling footwork and slick maneuvering, if meaning to ambush, may themselves be ambushed and, if once culture-heroes, may be transformed swiftly into culture-demons.

That is precisely what happened to Milton immediately after his death and at the end of his own century; it is what happened to Milton at the beginning of the twentieth century, when *Paradise Lost* was declared "a monument to dead ideas"[4] – a verdict that led almost immediately to declarations of Milton's pastness, of his irrelevance, by poets as diverse as Edwin Arlington Robinson and T. S. Eliot, and to calls for Milton's dislodgment by critics as eminent as Eliot and F. R. Leavis. And ambush is what is still happening to Milton in the current culture wars where he is presented, simply, as a representative of – and conduit for – the common culture; where, as Gertrude Himmelfarb might say, he stands for "traditional history . . . 'elite history' . . . high politics and great ideas."[5] Within the Milton establishment, a similar proposition is embraced by those who, worrying over "doctrinal inconsistency" and "contradictions of dogma" within the poet's writings, as well as the "theological mischief" attendant upon both, are bent upon reaffirming Milton's alliance with – and allegiance to – "mainstream Protestant thought of the seventeenth century."[6] If the reaffirmation requires the removal of *de doctrina Christiana* from Milton's canon, so be it.

Whether in the last decade of the twentieth century or in the first decade after Milton's death, whether from sites within the Milton establishment or outside it, the tendency has been for those who could not abide Milton's inconsistencies and contradictions, largely because they perceived the radical implications thereof, to resist Milton's transgressive maneuvers by repressing them. Sometimes even, this tendency has led to the formation of a radical Milton, the "polemical opposite"[7] of their own Milton, a formation these conservative critics would demolish as they proceed to create a Milton whose values and beliefs, if not fully in accord with those of our time, are nevertheless in compliance with those of Milton's own less enlightened era.

"Milton's poem," like others that have been "canonized" over the centuries, writes Barbara Lewalski, "can both abide of new questions generation after generation, and can also speak to some of our enduring concerns."[8] It is simultaneously conversant with – and critical of – cultural norms. A short view of literary history may yield the conclusion that Milton criticism is cumulative in character, every age impaneling a new group of critics to ask its own questions and, through its answers, to announce a new range of interpretive possibilities. On the other hand, a long view of the same history may suggest an alternative proposition: that we remain locked in place, at the end of every century since its publication fielding many of the same questions concerning where *Paradise Lost* stands in relation to patriarchy, misogyny, and what today we call feminism – questions which are at bottom about Milton's currency, durability, and relevance. Twentieth-century criticism begins with the same problems and in the same posture with which it will end. Thus we find Henry A. Beers, in his 1908 tercentenary lecture, brooding over "Milton's somewhat patronizing attitude toward women" wherein "there is something Mosaic – something almost Oriental" – an observation which leads him to conclude that "Milton does not belong with those broadly human, all tolerant, impartial artists." Rather, Milton's "narrowness" is here defined as his salient feature and chief strength.[9]

My own chapter is a meditation on Milton criticism in the last decades of the seventeenth century and in the last decade both of the twentieth century and of the second millennium. But don't be deceived: though I'm thinking about the past and especially the present, my interest is in what Tennessee Williams calls "the perhaps"[10] and involves a wish to nudge Milton criticism into the future tense. I sense not an ending but a new beginning. This chapter, necessarily selective, will bring under scrutiny from the seventeenth century just three receptions afforded by John Dryden, Sir Allen Apsley, and Jane Lead – and affording a fix on where Milton criticism once was and hence on how far, if far at all, it has come today. Turning to the twentieth century, I will look at representations of Milton by all sides within the culture wars. Then and now the questions are: would Milton liberate women or keep them in subjection? are women subordinate to men or their equals? is Milton an ancient or a modern, a poet of imagination or of reason? is he a revolutionary or a conservative by temperament? This last question, especially, points to the base line for the very earliest receptions, for those initial critiques of *Paradise Lost*, wherein heresies and schisms emerge as marks of rebellious independence, occasions for scandal, and evidence of blasphemy; where transgressions, perceived as tokens of error, seem to figure a poet " 'too full of the Devill' " and a poem whose dwelling places are conflict, controversy, and indeterminacy.[11] Custom, tradition, indeed all the common glosses of theologians, are, for Milton, enemies of truth whereas constant labor, tireless seeking, and continual interrogation are, again for Milton, a means of moving beyond the unthinking distortions of orthodoxy into the realm of truth. Milton's "contradictions and inconsistencies" are both a hallmark of his poetry and, as George Saintsbury remarks, a cause for much of the "thrust and parry" in the criticism that poetry has elicited.[12]

Milton's seventeenth-century readership, particularly telling in its observations on *Paradise Lost*, raises other important questions: why did some
men like Sir Allen Apsley apparently feel threatened by the poem and thus
refuse what they perceived to be its realities by hurling (as did John
Dunton) the supposed misogyny of *Samson Agonistes* against it? why were
others like John Dryden applying correctives to Milton's epic-prophecy, or
to then current interpretations of it, by raising their own poems against it?
Such correctives and revisions, almost always bringing *Paradise Lost* into
line with orthodoxy, imply that Milton's poem, not ideologically innocent,
is an insufficient carrier of the patriarchal tradition, unsupportive of its
structures of thought, unsettling (even unsafe) in the challenges it poses to
masculinist assumptions. In a poem that exalts Eve and indicts Adam,
Paradise Lost is seen (by Barbara Lewalski) "turn[ing] into an Eviad," while
Milton is seen (by John Shawcross) as "reject[ing] some masculinist infer-
ences, just as numerous other masculinist positions are rejected."[13] Such
suppositions are authenticated in Milton's own century by the writings of
Jane Lead.

   Like its epic precursors, Milton's poem depicts a man's world but with
the alarming sense that such a world may be finished; that certain forms of
masculinity stand as a wall between this world and the promised paradise.
What is it about *this* narrative of creation and fall that, in Milton's own
century, caused some men like Dryden and Apsley to feel marginalized
and, alternatively, some women like Jane Lead to think they were being
centered in history and privileged by this particular account of their history? Witness, first, the examples of Dryden and Apsley who, like critics
ever since, seem to discern an unbearable collision of values in *Paradise
Lost*. Like Roger L'Estrange, they would replace Milton's "*Plurality* of
Truths" with one truth on the grounds that "*Christianity* is a *Religion* of Order,
not of Confusion; nor of *variance with it self*" and on the grounds, too, that
"Rebellion is as bad as false Doctrine."[14] An apostate bard, they all seem to
think, Milton is of the devil's party and speaks with the devil's voice.[15]

   The example of Dryden is especially complicated; for quite apart from
the fact that he marched with Marvell and Milton in Cromwell's funeral
procession, in one signal instance he seems, at least initially, to be
affiliating with Milton and, by interlacing his poem with *Paradise Lost*, to be
exalting woman and promoting her cause.[16] Nevertheless, Dryden's *The
State of Innocence, and Fall of Man* (1677) is a remarkably "curious affair"[17]
with just one of its many curiosities being the radically altered inflections of
the poem once we consider the title of the published work in relation to the

title of the "dramatic transversion" of *Paradise Lost* announced for publication in 1674: *The Fall of Angels and man in innocence*.[18] The topic foregrounded in 1674 is merely alluded to, first in a headnote appended to the edition of 1677 (p. 1) and then in the text of the poem itself (pp. 2, 7, 26), where the accent is placed (emphatically so) on Man's fall, not Satan's or his cohorts'. By Dryden, then, Milton's failings are located in his terrestrial representations, which are themselves so conflicted that, according to one report, Dryden can only clear *Paradise Lost* of its contradictions by writing his own poem as a contradiction of Milton's contradictions.

In a conversation imagined by Thomas Brown, Mr. Bays (who is Dryden) explains his poem, an "*Opera* of *Adam*" (apparently in contradistinction to Milton's epic of Eve) – and explains it thus:

the very same Spirit of Contradiction ... seiz'd me when I undertook to clear *Miltons* Paradice of Weeds, and garnish that noble Poem with the additional beauty and softness of Rhyme. He, like a blind buzzard as he was, makes *Adam* perform his addresses so ungracefully, introduces him discoursing so unlike a Gentleman, with that negligence of Language, and stupidity of Spirit, that I'gad, you'd pitty his condition. And then for Eve, as he has drawn her Character, she talks so like an insipid Country House-keeper, whose knowledge goes no farther than the Still or the Dairy, who is as little acquainted with the tenderness of passion, as the management of an Intreague, that one cannot choose but wonder at it. Now when I came to fall upon this work, I was resolved to bestow a little good breeding upon our first Parents.[19]

It would appear from the front matter to *The State of Innocence* that Dryden will overgo his precursor by revealing the oracle concerning women that Milton, however well intentioned, has left shrouded in mystery [A4]. What Dryden says of himself apparently applies equally to Milton: "the Priest was always unequal to the Oracle: The God within him was too mighty for his Breast: He labour'd with the Sacred Revelation, and there was more of the Mystery left behind than Divinity it self could inable him to express" [A2v]. What Dryden, in turn, chooses to emphasize, at least here in his dedicatory epistle, is that woman, at least *this* woman, "Beauty ... in ... its Supreme Perfection" [A2v], is "a Paradise" [A3], "the most perfect Workmanship of Heaven" [A2], in her beauty excelling both her own and the other sex; and her beauty (as portrayed here) is both inward and spiritual: "Moral perfections are rais'd higher by you in the softer Sex; as if Men were of too course a mould for Heaven to work on, and that the Image of Divinity could not be cast to likeness in so harsh a Metall" [A3]. What Milton seems merely to hint at is that to which Dryden will give full utterance – but only *here*. The accompanying poem, in contrast to the dedicatory epistle, displays a Dryden who craftily reverses Milton's studied advances, thereby silencing bold transgressions and with them the feminism that Milton, however guardedly, seems to sponsor.

Dryden's strategy is always, it seems, to cancel Miltonic ambiguity: in Hell where Satan and his cohorts have completely lost their original glory – "how chang'd from him . . . / How faded all thy Glories are!" (p. 2) – that in *Paradise Lost* they still retain; and in Eden where, reverting to Genesis 2, Dryden represents woman as last created (p. 34) and therefore secondary to Adam, a *servant* to him as the angels are "Servants" to God (p. 9), and as man's "softer part" and weak subject (pp. 13, 27). Dryden's Raphael is emphatic: Eve, "An equal, yet thy subject, is design'd" (p. 9), according to which logic Adam's greatest mistake is surrendering his "boasted Soveraignty" to Eve (pp. 13, 38), who, as Satan insists, is "The weaker . . . and . . . my easier prey" (p. 19). Here, the division between the sexes is marked by *his* perfection, *her* power, with *her* fall receiving preponderant attention, a consequence of which is that Adam's misogyny is now so fully justified that his "did I sollicite thee . . ." speech in *Paradise Lost* (10.744ff.) is, by Dryden, given to Eve – "Did we solicite Heav'n to mould our clay?" (p. 41) – thus allowing Adam to rebuke Eve for accusing her Maker: "Seek not, in vain, our maker to accuse" (p. 41). Dryden conveniently forgets that in thus adhering to scripture Milton reinforces its point of presenting "a liuely image of our corrupt nature . . . *in Adam*, after the time of his fall,"[20] in his forgetfulness hiding the possibility that in Milton's poem patriarchy, misogyny, even blasphemy become manifestations of such corruption. In Dryden's poem, man is the consoler and woman, the complainer: "Th' unhappiest of creation is a wife," says Eve, who as nature's "defect" is "Made lowest, in the highest rank of life" (p. 39). In her concluding speech of the poem, Eve's farewell to Eden – "Farewell, you happy shades! . . . / Farewell, you flow'rs" (p. 44) – is made to echo Satan's "Farewel happy Fields / Where Joy for ever dwells" (*Paradise Lost* 1.249–50), with the final speech of the poem now given over to Raphael whose last words are of a "*Paradise* within" (p. 45).[21]

It is as if, knowing that Milton has by this time abandoned the Eve/Satan typology, Dryden must restore it and, aware of Milton's giving Eve privilege of place by assigning her the last speaking part in *Paradise Lost* (see 12.610–23), Dryden must reassign the concluding speech if not to Adam, then to an angel. It is as if Dryden, in anticipation of one of his later defenders, is here saying: Milton is no Christian, at least no orthodox Christian, thus authorizing my own translation of his poetic fictions into revered orthodoxies and thereby saving me from the obligation of imitating anything but Milton's superior literary qualities.[22] The "new and brilliant meaning" that Dryden allegedly fixes to "Milton's wonderful phrase 'Paradise within'," might be construed, with reference to the dedicatory preface, as Dryden's making of woman herself a paradise but can only be construed, with reference to the accompanying poem, in the defining terms of Bruce King: "Paradise within has come to represent those virtues of temperance and self-regulation that Dryden felt were necessary if man was to avoid life's unrest,"[23] and that Dryden in his poem represents as the attributes of gender-specific man.

Writing in the aftermath of Dryden's poem and in concert with it, Sir Allen Apsley brings the emerging lines of Milton criticism into sharper focus. And perhaps even more so than Dryden, Apsley is Milton's opposite. We do not know from the preface to *Order and Disorder* (1679) that Apsley read *Paradise Lost*, although even the preface raises certain suspicions.[24] We only know that Apsley read poems like *Paradise Lost* and worried over the fact that poets, even "the best" like Milton, were re-presenting the biblical account of creation "blasphemously . . . and bruitishly . . . erroniously, imperfectly, and uncertainly" [A1]: "the wisest of mankind," Apsley writes, have "walk'd in the dim light of corrupted nature and defective Traditions," with a few of the supposedly wise having produced a "vain, foolish, atheistical Poesie," thus "turning Scripture into a Romance" [A1, A1v, A2]. Moreover, aware that some think scripture is "prophan'd by being descanted on in numbers" but also aware that "a great part of the Scripture was originally written in verse" [A2], Apsley writes *Order and Disorder* with the obvious intention of ordering the current disorder and of remaking what other poets have unmade in a poem that, as John Shawcross has noted, bears marks of "Influence from *Paradise Lost*, passim."[25] As with Dryden, however, the "influence" generates a revisioning of Milton with Apsley, like Dryden (but altogether more conspicuously), meaning to reclaim minds now made to wander in a maze of fancies, figments, and other human inventions. Apsley attempts to do so by eradicating the false impressions and by exposing the lies still perpetrated by inspired poets and divine philosophers. Both these objections obviously comprehend Milton, who in Apsley's Preface is nameless but whose poem, from the perspective established by that Preface, is regarded as a manifestation of atheistical and apostatizing tendencies in an age where false poetry and prophecy abound.

For Apsley, clearly, what has been undone can be redone in poetry so long as, with no mincing of words, it holds fast to the following propositions: that the coeternity and coequality of the Father and Son are not replicated in the earthly creation; that man and woman are not, in the same way God and his Son are, "joynt actor[s]" in creation (p. 5); that man himself "cannot be / Refin'd enough for angels company" (p. 33) but also is sufficiently refined in *his* creation that, while needing "sweetness of so-cietie," he is not given "an equal mate" (p. 31). Man (gender-specific man) is the last created but also "the noblest creature," the world's epitome, the "root / ... whence all ... graces shoot" (p. 25). Words that in Milton's poem apply to man and woman alike – "such grace / The hand that formd them on thir shape hath pourd" (*Paradise Lost* 4.364–65) – and to woman quite specifically – "Grace was in all her steps" (8.488) – in Apsley's poem apply to man alone: "Let us ... / Make man after our own similitude, / Let *him* our sacred imprest image bear / Ruling o're all in earth, and sea, and air" (p. 24). The weak and apostate side of Creation relating to Adam rather as the church relates to Christ (p. 38), Eve is here faulted for the fall or "first and easier overthrow" (p. 50), hence enjoined to "Subjection" by a husband (64) who, perceiving her to be a "foolish woman" (as is made evi-dent by her whimpering laments), asserts his obvious superiority by taking the lead (Milton had given to Eve) in consolation and reconciliation (pp. 70, 72–73).[26]

In a poem evading anything that might be construed as controversial or as transgressing the wisdom of the ages, Apsley marks the difference between the sexes, as well as their hierarchical relationship, by envisioning woman complaining and man consoling. Knowing that Apsley actually read and was conversant with *Paradise Lost* is of crucial importance; for his poem is close enough to Milton's in time, as well as concern, that we can use it (rather as we have used Dryden's) to discriminate between male voices articulating comparable themes and, given Apsley's commitment to the commonplaces of tradition, to measure the nature and extent of what those like Apsley perceived as Milton's disturbing transgressions. From a simple juxtaposition of their poems, it is clear that Aspley would turn right-side-up the world he thinks Milton has turned upside down.

As we have seen, point by point, item by item, Apsley undoes what Milton has done in *Paradise Lost*: the paralleling of the relationship between Adam and Eve with that between the Father and the Son, of things on earth with things in heaven; the assertion (some of the time) that humankind shares in the divine resemblance; Milton's allowing Adam and Eve to converse with angels; his insinuation of their equality, at least his having Adam ask for a mate equal to him and then having God reassure Adam that he has been given just what he asked for; the representation of Eve as consoler and comforter, as the immediate agent in man's redemption and in history's restoration; the admission of Eve to the company of prophets and exaltation of her as bearer of both the seed and the word; Milton's representation of her as mother of all the living. Augmentations of the scriptural text Apsley repeatedly opposes: "circumstances that we cannot know . . . / We will not dare t' invent, nor will we take / Guesses" (p. 46) about matters into which we should not "too far enquire" (p. 54). Apsley will not do what, by implication, Milton has done, thus producing "gross poetick fables" in which "some truths . . . [are] wrapt up in many lies" (p. 46).

Apparently what makes *Paradise Lost* so disruptive a text for Apsley, one so problematical in its transgressions, is not its insistences but its insinuations, not its claims or disclaimers but its hesitancies and uncertainties, its often bewilderingly ambiguous language, its planned contradictions, its narrative gaps, its calculated omissions, frustrations, entrapments, its conflicted and conflicting narratives. For Apsley, it seems, *Paradise Lost* is defective and imperfect because, quite apart from inscribing Christian clichés, it allows for their interrogation and contains not one but competing systems of interpretation – is no reservoir of received opinion or harbor for Christian orthodoxies but a challenge to both through its surface of contradictions and basement of subversions. Resistant to Milton's project, Apsley nevertheless defines, unapprovingly to be sure, the procedures through which patriarchy is being undermined from the inside, the entire system needing shoring up if it is not, under the weight of *Paradise Lost*, going to topple. But then *Paradise Lost* is just like its biblical counterpart, as a secular scripture is written in perfect analogy with the sacred text: it exhibits a critical consciousness, it contains a summons for critical interpretation and an invitation to make interpretive choices – and not always the common ones. Unlike Dryden and Apsley, Milton exchanges the safety of paraphrasing for the risks attendant upon reconfiguring and reinterpreting biblical stories. Milton's early readers were as sensitive as Dayton Haskin has made us to the fact that "as an interpreter," Milton "was liberated . . . from an obsession with certainty and closure . . . to glimpse in imagination new interpretive possibilities."[27] It is just that these early readers are sometimes appalled by what today we often applaud. We see the same strategies but value them differently. What happens in these early receptions of *Paradise Lost*, where they run amuck so to speak, is identical with what goes wrong with the history of the reception of the very biblical stories in which Milton's last poems are centered (Adam and Eve falling, Jesus wandering, and Sampson and Delilah sparring) – in the words of Mieke Bal, "the repression of the problem" through which process "the heterogeneous ideology of the text," whether it be *Paradise*

Lost, Paradise Regained, or *Samson Agonistes,* gets "turned into a monolithic one" only to be reproblematized at a later and crucial stage in the reception history of each of these poems.[28]

Witness now the example of Jane Lead, visionary and dissenter, whose altering eye sees differently than Dryden or Apsley. For Lead, as for Milton, the celestial battle is internalized with *"Michael* in thee . . . Fight[ing] against the Dragon [in thee]"; and, again like Milton, Lead would replace formalized, institutionized religion with a sect of one.[29] The crucial text for our purposes is *A Fountain of Gardens,* a spiritual diary recording Lead's visions from 1670 onward, and then her poem introductory to these meditations, "Solomon's PORCH: Or The Beautiful Gate of Wisdom's Temple. A Poem; Introductory to the Philadelphian Age."[30] If Milton transposed end-time to explain origins, Lead reverses his strategy, employing the vision of Milton's last books to envision time in the moments just before the millennium. Man and woman who have "Travel[ed] *hand in hand* thro' every Age" (vol. I, Ev; my italics) are restored to the divine resemblance they had lost, Christ now "in ev'ry Feature, ev'ry line, / Appearing" (vol. I, E2): their "New Senses open flye; / They see" as "The Glorious Aera, *Now, Now, Now,* begins" (vol. I, E2v–E3; see also G2). This is a time of heroines who once again "in Visionary Dreams . . . *See*" (vol. I, F3v) and who in the new world are finally enlightened, unfettered, free. Lead, echoing Milton throughout, openly appeals to her prophetic precursor:

> Now Mighty Bard sing out thy Sonnet free,
>   Nor doubt, it true shall be.
>   Come Thou and joyn
> Thy loud Prophetick Voice with mine.

At which point Milton's song becomes her own:

> "Ring out ye Chrystal Sphears,
> "Now bless our Humane Ears:
> *For ye have* Power to touch our Senses so:
> "Now *shall* your Silver Chime
> "Move in Melodious time;
> And the *deep* Base of Heav'ns great *Orb* shall Blow.
>
>   (vol. I, F4v)

Barak and Deborah, David and Mary, are the biblical types for Milton and Lead who are the singers, the proclaimers of the millennium then at hand (vol. I: G2–G2v, [G3v]; vol. II, p. 500). Achieving a paradise within, what Lead describes as "the inward ground of a Renewed Mind,"[31] singing together, Lead and Milton will cause morning to break in England; will, in their symbolic reintegration of the sexes becoming a new Eve and Adam, repossess the paradise from which the old Eve and Adam were long ago expelled. Together, Milton and Lead figure forth "the Paradisical Male and Female."[32]

Only the exactness with which Lead replicates, but in reverse, the vision of the final books of *Paradise Lost* makes it seem inevitable that, like Eve's triumph song, her own will invoke "the Divine Illustrious *Deborah*" (vol. I, G2). If in its political aspect *Paradise Lost* could be translated into England lost, Lead insists that her own vision of paradise regained be similarly translated though the injunction of her coda, *England is now restored* (vol. I, Hv). And it is no small matter, given Milton's trilogy of last poems, that in Lead's vision England is restored by those who find their countertypes in Delilah and Sampson (vol. I, pp. 42–47) and their prototypes in Deborah and Barak, Mary and David, or Jesus, in visions where now the "True *Phinix* ... in Heav'nly Flames *Revives*" (vol. I, G2v) and now the true "Eagle-Bird" is a hatching (vol. I, p. 428).[33]

Wisdom, in the figure of Eve, may have led the way out of paradise; but here, joining with Eve and breaking the head of the serpent, leaving it dead in the path, wisdom now leads the way back into paradise (vol. II, pp. 111–15).[34] If Eve and Adam were one before the fall, they become one again in their restoration at the end of time (vol. II, p. 118). What Lead has inferred from Milton is that Eve, whose birth had filled so many with disgust, in her life after the fall becomes a new "Center of Vision and Revelation" (vol. II, p. 138). After Adam's fall, she writes, "the Eternal Word ... did incorporate with *Eve*, whereby power and ability were given to bring forth wholly after the spirit" (vol. II, pp. 172–73); and she reached such conclusions, one supposes, because she had read the last books of *Paradise Lost* as untrapping the senses and opening the doors of perception; as articulating a recurring experience through which the mind is refined and the people transformed into a nation of visionaries. "Where there is no Vision the People perish."[35] Blind like Milton, Lead could also *see*. It is noteworthy that, when the Lord comes to Lead in vision, he speaks to her in Miltonic idiom, telling her that though her "'corporeal Eyes be Dim'" she possesses a spiritual eye with which to see and tell what is "hidden" to "mortal sight."[36] Lead merely brings out of concealment what precursor poet-critics like Dryden and Apsley sought to hide.

Lead's invocation and echo of Milton are interesting in their own right but also illustrate a common device through which women of the seventeenth century impose censure and imply praise: they will arraign male authors like Sophocles and Euripides, while admitting others like Spenser and Milton to their company. Their objective is to rid the world of conventional precepts concerning the sexes, which often entails their conflating custom and tradition and associating both with error. The credit they give to male authors – as when one of them declares, "The feminine sex is exceedingly honoured by poets in their writings"[37] – depends, predictably, upon how well this or that writer's views accord with their own and how effective such allies may be in furthering their different agendas.

Given Milton's essentially subversive agenda in *Paradise Lost*, together with the critique of culture his poem inscribes, and given the supposition of many that poets are the unacknowledged legislators of the world, that empire follows art, we might expect in the aftermath of the publication of Milton's poem seismic shifts in the values of Western culture and, attendant upon those shifts, an emerging understanding and by now a full acceptance of Milton as a revolutionary thinker and artist. Yet over three centuries the topics of Milton criticism as well as its commonplaces, no less than the comprehension of Milton by the culture at large, instead of shifting radically, have stayed surprisingly and sometimes stubbornly the same. In its own century caught up within the war of the sexes, *Paradise Lost* now figures, if parenthetically nonetheless pointedly, in the still larger context of the culture wars where Milton, when cited, is often used as a metaphor for those being cast aside to make space for new voices. Milton is perceived as *the* canonical poet, *the* patriarch, within a long line of patriarchal poets; and his timeliness seems increasingly in importance to override his timelessness.

A culture war, in its ideal form, is "a conversation the culture has with itself, on behalf of the country," says A. Bartlett Giamatti; but in its current form, "that conversation . . . is stymied" by those who insist "there is only one Truth, and it is complete."[38] It is a war, from the contrary perspective of William Bennett, that in its current form derives from "an all-out assault on the great works and ideas of western civilization"[39] and that, we will discover, engages – or in the case of Bennett, *disengages* – Milton in unexpected ways. Although Bennett himself is silent about Milton, Bennett's perennial questions come into focus and then achieve specificity in the writings of his allies. As the topics of patriarchy and misogyny are broached, as the debate between the sexes then comes into play, Milton's name does appear, but in discussions where representations of his positions, even if differently understood, are unconflicted, uncontested. Typically, Bennett's allies presume that Milton's values are identical with their own, though occasionally a voice is heard saying that, whatever enlightened values may be today, Milton's were the values of yesterday. In this latter regard, especially when the issue is Milton's alleged misogyny, both sides in the debate (as represented, let us say, by Allan Bloom and Gerald Graff) can agree.

What does a poet like Milton have to do with solving our problems, asks Allan Bloom, particularly when, in looking to Milton, we have too often discovered that he is a repository for "the elitist, sexist, nationalist prejudices we are trying to overcome";[40] a repository, that is, for a politics we think is outmoded and for values we no longer find congenial. His critics today are displacing Milton's essentially conservative politics, this argument goes, with their own vulgar radicalism, turning Milton the misogynist into a feminist or, more often, excoriating Milton for the misogyny that, indigenous to his times, was a mark of this poem's authenticity as a token of its own culture. For some, in any event, present-day criticism is stilling the voice and values of an earlier civilization with the noise and inanities of its own. And Alvin Kernan argues similarly, that there is no question that the old canonical literature (by which he means the triumvirate of Chaucer, Shakespeare, and Milton) was "thoroughly politicized" and "often treated women in at times a contemptuous, and nearly always a patronizing fashion."[41] As if by sleight of hand, Milton's failings are being used, it seems, to mask present-day failures.

When Milton figures in the current academic debate, all too often it is by way of saying directly or obliquely that his excellence is his irrelevance and thereupon complaining, as Bloom does, about the "apolitical character of the humanities," their "habitual deformation or suppression of the political content in the classic literature," which is true to its own time, if not to our own. "The humanities are embarrassed by the political content of many of the literary works belonging to them" and, unhesitatingly, have moved "to alter their contents" by way of exchanging "their truth" for *our* values, and by way of surrendering, says Bloom, "their contents" to the imperatives of modern cultures, thus forcing a book's relevance.[42] A poet like Milton is thus seen as being hijacked by the multiculturalists, then transformed into one of their barbarians, and thereupon deployed (in one dramatic instance) by Ice-T's studio to defend him.[43]

Otherwise, Milton's name appears in the culture debate for the purpose of illustrating through him a standard of "cultural literacy"[44] – a standard established by safe texts and met when, matching authors with titles, people are able to pair with Milton's name *not* Sonnet 18 ("Avenge O Lord thy slaughter'd Saints") and *Samson Agonistes* but Sonnet 23 ("Mee thought I saw my late espoused saint") and *Paradise Lost*;[45] when thereupon they learn from these representative works not only a cultural vocabulary but the significance of its key terms. *Paradise Lost* is thus a defining poem when it comes to knowing about – and fixing an understanding to – such figures as Adam, Eve, and Satan; to such concepts as "equal" and "more equal," patriarchy and God's justice, the Renaissance and Renaissance man; to books like Genesis, and genres like epic and pastoral, and places like the Garden of Eden, and phrases like "justifie the wayes of God to men."

Additionally, Milton's name appears within this debate by way of illustrating the alliance of plagiarism and poetics within a tradition where writings we designate as classics are, in Alvin Kernan's reckoning, merely vehicles for "received ideas" – a culture's commonplaces – and where, in Roger Kimball's elaboration of such a proposition, "received doctrines" get elided with "the truth" as Kimball, quoting Werner Gundersheimer, wonders what else to call them.[46] In effect, a point of view is accepted as the reality; and that reality, in turn, is acknowledged as the truth. Once the classics of a culture have been equated with the truth and once humanists have been declared the custodians of those truths, the classics can be used to argue, in the face of any challenge to their status, that in championing canonical change humanists are "cut[ting] themselves off from both their foundations and their ideals," in the process eroding the base of "a common culture" that the canon – that writers like Milton – are meant to uphold.[47]

Both sides agree that the canon is a commonplace book of our culture. Yet, if from the one side, the classics safeguard the *status quo*, from another, as participants in a canonical tradition that includes loss, recovery, and new accommodations, the classics contain "a wide variety of opinions, often clashing with one another," and, not necessarily endorsing received values, may afford what Irving Howe (after Robert Frost) calls "counter-speech."[48] *Paradise Lost* is an enduring monument to the proposition that "we are all committed to truths" but most of all to those truths which are "perpetually in dispute."[49] The truths over which we wrangle are those, we learn from Milton, that really matter.

Not only does Milton's name show up in this debate as a way of targeting feminism but as an attack on theory generally, the oppressive ideologies of which are seen as tyrannizing canonical texts. From one side of the debate, we hear repeatedly that the facts will eventually kill all our theories; that if we are to reclaim our culture, we must reclaim its inheritance (the canon), as well as its institutions (the universities). We must reclaim Milton and his *Paradise Lost* as reservoirs of traditional values and doing so demonstrate, again through Milton's example, that, in Bloom's words, "The latest enemy of the vitality of classic texts is feminism," which forgets that "*all* literature up to today is sexist," that God himself "was once a sexist," and that the "Muses never sang to the poets about liberated women."[50] In this debate, even commentators like Gerald Graff, who are otherwise conspicuously to the left of Bloom and Kernan, sometimes concur as evidenced by Graff for whom the politics of *Paradise Lost* lies in "what is taken for granted." Thus for Graff it goes without saying "that Eve is mentally inferior to Adam."[51] Exasperation is the obvious response, and obviously evident in Louis Menand's observation: "Milton is not responsible for the historical subjugation of women – only an English professor would believe otherwise."[52]

Not just most of the participants in the culture wars, but some feminists have forgotten that a patriarchal Milton, a bruisingly misogynistic Milton, is an early invention of Milton's male readership; that such conceptualizations figure, in the inaugural phase of Milton criticism, as part of a challenge to and devaluation of feminism itself. And some historians, both literary and cultural, have forgotten Wilde's pronouncement that our only obligation to history is to rewrite it – to keep rewriting it. John Searle looks back to the good old days when Christian gentlemen (like his grandfather) set off for life with Milton's *Paradise Lost* and the Bible in their saddlebags.[53] He does so, however, without ever acknowledging the ideology, or interpretation of texts, implicit in an anecdote that makes *Paradise Lost* a companion of the text it would often correct and a mere echo of a text it would supplement.

In our own time, *Paradise Lost* will be the text the Hell's Angels pack away in their hip pockets; that Malcolm X will read in prison and in which he will then discover the fundamental teachings of the Muslim religion; that will appear on a departmental citation for Officer Hicks, gay cop of San Francisco; that will enable a *Washington Post* editorialist to wax eloquently on the *whys* of the Iranian hostage crisis and a *New York Times* correspondent to wonder "What kind of God is this?"; that will be cited by Joan Blythe as reinforcement for her views on the "cons" of the new sex bans on college campuses; that will allow a *Newsweek* writer to reflect upon the now defunct fairy-tale marriage of Charles and Princess Di; and that never gets so much as a mention in a *New York Post* column on "The lost canon of English literature."[54]

The issue, finally, is whether *Paradise Lost* is a vehicle of timeless or timely truths and, more largely, whether the standards of permanent interest and steady value are typically met by canonical authors. Michael Berube asks the right question and responds incisively to it:

what are these spiritual lessons, these timeless truths? Lately we've noticed that our antagonists get uncharacteristically tongue-tied when we ask them what specific truths they have in mind: Is *Paradise Lost* a 10,000 word version of 'just say no'? Likewise they begin to bluster when we ask them who they mean by us, and they get downright sullen when we ask whether these great works say the same thing every time they speak.

That's why nothing outrages the Right quite like the current academic interest in attempting to understand what literary works did and didn't say to their contemporary readers and audiences, and for what reasons. From the Right's perspective, inquiring into the historical production and reception of cultural artifacts is the most subversive enterprise of all, for it threatens to undo the very notion of artistic autonomy and timelessness . . .

Generally, when the Right complains that we're reading ideologically, it means that we're reading historically.[55]

And to read historically, Berube makes clear, means that we are reading critically, attuned to complexity and both alert to, and appreciative of, conflict and contradiction, the conspicuous features of Milton's poems and the very features the Right worries are there to impel history toward a revolutionary outcome. For anyone troubled by collapsing hierarchies and by subversive maneuvers, or by notions of oppressive traditions and political transformations, Milton's last poems are bound to be a disruptive presence. This is so in part because, within the boundaries of canonical literature, Milton's last poems are the surest reminder that texts used to serve elitist ideologies (let us say imperialism, racism, and sexism) are not necessarily based upon, much less biased toward, such attitudes; that religious poems are not necessarily possessed of coherent creeds.

The lesson learned from studying *Paradise Lost* in relation to the Bible and its hermeneutic traditions is virtually identical with the one to be garnered from reading the same poem within the context of poetic imitations inspired by *Paradise Lost* or within the context of the poem's emerging interpretive traditions. In the simple formulation of Christopher Hill: Milton is "not an orthodox reader"[56] – or interpreter – of scripture, his project involving less the reproduction of biblical tales than the reimagining of their myths in the light of current politics and contemporary history. Moreover, not only *Paradise Lost* (and here one can easily add *Samson Agonistes*), but also its scriptural subtexts, are inspired with contradictions sufficiently unsettling that the typical tendency in criticism, as well as the enterprise of both poet-imitators and book-illustrators, is to contradict both texts (biblical no less than Miltonic) out of their contradictions. In fact, not contradictions *within* the Bible or Milton's poem, only contradictions *of* them, are heresies in a critical tradition that, ever since Dryden, has risen up against *Paradise Lost* "to regularize . . . thought" in a poem that, in the eloquent formulation of William Kerrigan, "seems forever beyond us, unsettled and in process."[57] No one more – or better – than the Milton of *de doctrina Christiana* so fully authorizes our challenges to those critical alignments of his writings with orthodoxy, with "an unproblematic, centrist orthodoxy"[58] that Milton habitually associates with custom and error as he also alerts us to the fact that "many" of his "views . . . are at odds with . . . conventional opinions" and thereupon chastizes those who "condemn anything they consider inconsistent with conventional beliefs . . . [with the] invidious title – 'heretic' or 'heresy'" (*CP* VI: 121, 123).

Finally, rather than fogging over the meaning(s) of *Paradise Lost*, the spirit of contradiction in Milton's poem, together with its clashing perspectives and different arenas of conflict, are the transmitters of meanings – not easy but subtle, sophisticated, often stinging consciousness into a new kind of awareness. Itself a field of contending forces and competing paradigms, Milton's poem contains – but is not contained by – frustrating tensions and ambiguities that, a goad to truth, are also the poem's most distinctive defining features. If, as Gerald Graff contends, "the most influential tradition in today's politically oriented academic criticism is to see works of art not as simple ideological statements but as swords of ideological and psychological conflict,"[59] then *Paradise Lost*, a battleground for its culture's contending viewpoints and ideologies, testifies to the lasting value of discussion, debate, dispute, dissent. To move from Milton's prose writings to his last poems is to move not from politics to poetry but from the writings of a feisty polemicist to those of a wily politician who knows that inscribing contradictions leads to debating alternatives – a debate, in turn, that witnesses to the positive potentiality of controversy.

Milton's poetry is marked, not marred, by such inconsistencies and contradictions; they inhabit its very center where competing Genesis hermeneutics vie with one another, but also competing Revelation hermeneutics: which version has priority, Genesis 1 or 2? where there are contradictions, which version prevails? who leads the angels in battle – Michael or Christ? and is the battle itself actual or imaginary, carnal or spiritual? And at the poem's center are contending images of Christ the tiger and Christ the lamb; and contrary cosmologies – Ptolemaic and Copernican – which find their counterparts in conflicting theologies. In Milton's poetic universe, Copernican cosmology subtends a Christocentric religion. The contradictions within Milton's poems, that is, find their parallels in conflicts both within the scriptural texts and hermeneutic traditions on which they are based and within the critical tradition they found.

Transported from Milton's sources, some of these contradictions inhabit *Paradise Lost* as mere complexities, but others continue to exist in the poem as contradictions – a point worth insisting upon just because the understanding of Milton criticism, especially of late, has been paralyzed, indeed impoverished, by the suppression of such conflicts or just plain avoidance of them. To set the critical understanding free again we may have to reclaim *Paradise Lost* as a poem of proliferating contradictions, restore a conflict model to its criticism, and then remember this poem for what, historically, it has always been: the battleground for competing intellectual paradigms and clashing critical methodologies. More than signaling a move against existing traditions and interpretations, contradictions are a means of complicating and reconstituting both. By dislodging commonplaces and effecting dislocations, contradictions open seemingly closed systems, or enlarge those needlessly constricted, and, admitting to the possibility of coexisting meanings and rival interpretations, stimulate the pursuit of truth even as they keep all notions of truth tentative, contingent, perspectival.

As with Milton's poetry, so with Milton criticism generally and so with Milton in the culture wars today; the temptation is always to choose sides when the wiser recourse, on occasion, may be to choose not to choose, thus locating significance in the conflicts and wresting meaning from the contradictions. That may also be the wiser course for a new Milton criticism, which instead of confronting opposing points of view in order to silence one of them, might be empowered and emboldened by competing interpretations to produce finer honings of its own (not always fully nuanced) readings. Criticism of the highest order unfetters – it does not constrain – the mind; it may correct but does not coerce. When it cries up liberty, it means liberty, testing the values it posits, tolerating unavoidable ambiguities as well as differences of opinion, and as a matter of course, hosting conflicting systems of thought. Such criticism, rather like Milton's poetry, makes space for thinking the unthinkable, for speaking the unspeakable, and for challenging what for too long has gone unchallenged. Like A. Bartlett Giamatti's ideal university, *Paradise Lost* is a place where competing systems of thought collide; where they are "tested, debated ... freely, openly,"[60] and, even if hotly, usually civilly. It is a poem that allows its readers to dwell in possibilities, which multiply, as its interpretive traditions, over time repressed, are now recuperated and as those traditions, in turn, identify Milton's poem with the broadest possible – not narrowest – cultural history.

While *Paradise Lost* may not settle, it nonetheless brings and keeps under scrutiny the nagging questions, the thorny issues of theology and politics, through its sexual politics and gender trouble reminding us of the enormous barriers to changing entrenched structures and ideas as well as the

JOSEPH WITTREICH

imminent dangers in remaining sexually and culturally blind. As much about what unites as about what divides us; acutely sensitive to the interconnectedness of science and religion, of politics and poetry – their interdependence and mutuality; in its global reach uniquely poised for global challenges and in its vast learning seemingly addressed to knowledge-based societies still in our future; here threatened by the Right and there scorned by the Left – in all these ways, *Paradise Lost* is at once a harbinger of cultural transformations and preparation for them. From its perspectives of history, *Paradise Lost* forms a perspective on history – on the politics as well as the poetry of a history seething with contradictions, yet rife with possibilities. A poet of the seventeenth century, Milton with his future gaze may prove to be (singularly among the triumverate of Chaucer, Shakespeare, and Milton) the poet *for* the new millennium – the poet *for* the twenty-first century.

The eye altering alters all: at the dawn of the twentieth century Milton seemed indubitably the poet of the past – a monument to dead ideas. Yet in the still dark hours before the dawn of the twenty-first century, it appears as if Milton may be the poet for the future of which his last poems are an embodiment. But let it not be said of the New Age as Margaret Fuller said of the last, that "the Father is still far beyond the understanding of his child."[61] Instead, let it continue to be said that, still a champion of its freedoms and an exponent of its ethics and ideas, Milton agitates the world from sleep; that by Milton the dark clouds of ignorance are again being rolled into the distance.

NOTES

1. The research for this essay was completed with the generous support of The PSC-CUNY Research Foundation. The epigraphs are from Jonathan Richardson, Sr., "The Life of the Author," *Explanatory Notes and Remarks on Milton's Paradise Lost* (London, 1734), p. xxxix, and Harold Bloom from an interview with Robert Moynihan, *A Recent Imagining* (Hamden, CN, 1986), p. 21. All quotations of Milton's poetry are from *The Complete Poetry of John Milton*, ed. John T. Shawcross, rev. edn. (New York, 1971).
2. Richard Corum, "In White Ink: *Paradise Lost* and Milton's Ideas of Women," in Julia Walker, eds., *Milton and the Idea of Woman* (Urbana and Chicago, 1988), p. 142.
3. Louis Menand, "What Are Universities For?", *Harper's Magazine* 283 (December 1991), 48.
4. Walter Raleigh, *Milton* (1900; rpt. New York, 1967), p. 85.
5. Himmelfarb's position is thus summarized by Roger Kimball, *Tenured Radicals:*

How Politics Has Corrupted Our Higher Education (1990; rpt. New York, 1991), p. 179.

6. William B. Hunter, "Animadversions upon the Remonstrants' Defenses against Burgess and Hunter," *SEL* 34 (Winter 1994), 195, 198, 202.

7. I borrow this phrase from, and here sketch the argument of, William Kolbrener, "Those Grand Whigs, Bentley and Fish," in *Milton's Warring Angels: A Study of Critical Engagements* (Cambridge, 1997), pp. 107–32.

8. Barbara Lewalski, "Milton on Women – Yet Again," in Sally Minogue, ed., *Problems in Feminist Criticism* (London and New York, 1990), p. 50.

9. Henry A. Beers, *Milton's Tercentenary* (New Haven, 1910), pp. 32, 37.

10. See Williams's preface to *Orpheus Descending*, "The Past, the Present and the Perhaps," in *Orpheus Descending with Battle of Angels* (New York, 1958), pp. v–x.

11. John Beale quoted by Nicholas von Maltzahn, "The First Reception of *Paradise Lost*," *Review of English Studies* 47 (1996), 495.

12. George Saintsbury, "Milton," *The Cambridge History of English Literature*, 15 vols. (1917; rpt. New York, 1932), vol. VII, p. 137.

13. Lewalski, "Milton on Women – Yet Again," p. 58, and Shawcross, *John Milton: The Self and the World* (Lexington, KY, 1993), p. 7 (see also p. 12).

14. Roger L'Estrange, *The Observator*, No. 283, February 3, 1682[3], [1].

15. I tell this story and document it in "'Under the Seal of Silence': Repressions, Receptions, and the Politics of *Paradise Lost*," in Peter E. Medine and Joseph Wittreich, eds., *Soundings of Things Done: Essays on Early Modern Literature in Honor of S. K. Heninger, Jr.* (Newark, 1997), pp. 302–03.

16. For a reading contrary to my own, see Jean Gagen, "Anomalies in Eden: Adam and Eve in Dryden's *The State of Innocence*," in Albert C. Labriola and Edward Sichi, Jr., *Milton's Legacy in the Arts* (University Park and London, 1988), pp. 135–50.

17. See Bruce King, *Dryden's Major Plays* (Edinburgh and London, 1966), p. 95.

18. See R. G. Moyles, *The Text of Paradise Lost: A Study in Editorial Procedure* (Toronto, 1985), pp. 22, 156; and see also Dryden's published work, *The State of Innocence, And Fall of Man* (London, 1677). All quotations from Dryden's text are cited parenthetically within the text.

19. Thomas Brown, *The Reasons of Mr. Bays Changing his Religion* (London, 1688), pp. 18–19, 21.

20. John Calvin, *A Commentarie ... vpon the first booke of Moses called Genesis*, trans. Thomas Tymme (London, 1578), p. 103 (my italics).

21. What were Eve's last words in *Paradise Lost* are here transferred to a prelapsarian scene where Eve says, "With thee to live, is Paradise alone: / Without the pleasure of thy sight is none" (p. 17). Adam, in turn, is a practitioner of the same kind of false rhetoric that Dryden displays in his dedicatory epistle: "Thee, Goddess, thee th' Eternal did ordain / His softer Substitute on Earth to Reign" (p. 13). If woman is "softer" and "better," she is also "weak," hence less perfect: "thou art weak ... More perfect I," Adam says to Eve (p. 27, 28). Even in her first waking moments, Eve is depicted as a coy mistress who will make Adam beg for an embrace (pp. 14). Less finely drawn, less complicated than Milton's characters, those of Dryden are far more stereotypical.

22. See *Dryden: The Dramatic Works*, ed. Montague Summers, 6 vols. (London, 1931–32), vol. III, p. 409.

23. King, *Dryden's Major Plays*, pp. 99, 115.

24. See Apsley's *Order and Disorder* (London, 1679). All quotations from Apsley are cited parenthetically within the text. Apsley's son is one of the subscribers to the 1688 edition of *Paradise Lost*.

25. Shawcross, *Milton: A Bibliography for the Years 1624–1700* (Binghamton, 1984), p. 251, no. 795.

26. See also Apsley, *Order and Disorder*, p. 33, where it is remarked of Adam, still alone in paradise, that "Whether he beg'd a mate it is not known."

27. Dayton Haskin, *Milton's Burden of Interpretation* (Philadelphia, 1994), p. 148.

28. Mieke Bal, *Lethal Love: Feminist Literary Readings of Biblical Love Stories* (Bloomington, 1987).

29. See Lead, *The Laws of Paradise Given forth by Wisdom to a Translated Spirit* (London, 1695), p. 45 (see also p. 51); and *The Tree of Faith* (London, 1696), [A3].

30. See Lead, *A Fountain of Gardens Watered by the Rivers of Divine Pleasure*, 3 vols. (London, 1696–1701). Volume II is dated 1697, and volume III (in two parts) is dated 1700 (part 1) and 1701 (part 2). The British Library has a second copy of volume I dated 1697. This collection, though now rare, was reprinted four times. All quotations of Lead are cited parenthetically within the text and are taken from this edition.

31. Lead, *The Wonders of God's Creation Manifested, In the Variety Of Eight Worlds* (London, 1700), p. 21.

32. See Lead, *The Signs of the Times: Forerunning the Kingdom of Christ, And Evidencing When It Is Come* (London, 1699), p. 15.

33. Lead looks for a faithful Delilah and a "true *Nazarite*," "the true *Sampson*" (vol. I, pp. 42–45), an "untouched and free *Nazarite*" whose cause is defined by the biblical David, not the Sampson of The Book of Judges (vol. I, pp. 159–61). The true Sampson is, for Lead, to be distinguished from the figurative, if not false, imperfect Sampson (vol. I, p. 43). Moreover, the true eagle bird is not one who as in *Samson Agonistes*, a bird of prey (1695–96), attacks with fury but one who fends off such attacks (see Lead, *Tree of Faith*, pp. 8–9; see also pp. 15–16).

34. See also III, ii, [a]. Also relevant here are Lead, *Signs of the Times*, pp. 13–14, 15; *Laws of Paradise*, A3v–A4; *The Revelation of Revelations* (London, 1683), pp. 38–39; and *The Wars of David* (1700; rpt. London, 1816), pp. 121–25, 134.

35. These words furnish the epigraph for Lead's *The Ascent of the Mount of Vision* (London, 1699), and, within the context of this paragraph, see especially pp. 3–4.

36. See also *Signs of the Times*, p. 1. In the knowledge that Lead knew Milton's poetry, readers may find *The Ascent of the Mount of Vision* relevant as well (see n. 35 above).

37. See Ester Sowernam, "Ester hath hang'd Haman," in Simon Shepherd, ed., *The Woman's Sharp Revenge: Five Women's Pamphlets from the Renaissance* (London, 1985), p. 99.

38. A. Barlett Giamatti, *A Free and Ordered Space: The Real World of the University* (New York, 1990), pp. 24–25.

39. William Bennett, *The De-Valuing of America: The Fight for Our Culture and Our Children* (New York and London, 1992), p. 156.
40. Allan Bloom, *The Closing of the American Mind* (New York, 1987), p. 353.
41. Alvin Kernan, *The Death of Literature* (New Haven and London, 1990), pp. 32, 212.
42. Bloom, *Closing of the American Mind*, pp. 353, 373.
43. See the account as given by Robert Hughes, *Culture of Complaint: The Fraying of America* (New York and Oxford, 1993), p. 79.
44. I borrow the phrase from E. D. Hirsch, Jr., *Cultural Literacy: What Every American Needs to Know* (1987; rpt. New York, 1988). For Milton's relevance in this context, see pp. 106–07, 153, 169, 170, 174, 182, 188. Even as I write this chapter, a piece by Bob Herbert on "How Budget Cuts May Thwart an Upstate Revival as Illustated by Milton, New York," appears on the Op-Ed page of *The New York Times*, June 21, 1995, A19, under the title "Paradise Lost."
45. It is not that *Samson Agonistes* is unknown, but in point of fact this poem is more likely to be cited with reference to natural rather than political phenomenon (see, e.g., *The New York Times* editorial, "Dark Amid the Blaze of Noon," July 11, 1991, A20). Or if the poem (or its master-myth) *is* cited within a political context, the context typically invokes Samson as a negative example: see, e.g., the anecdote concerning Adlai Stevenson, brute force, and failed leadership reported by Joseph Wittreich, *Interpreting Samson Agonistes* (Princeton, 1986), p. xxvii; the remark by Richard Nixon reported in "Tape Shows Nixon Feared Hoover," *The New York Times*, June 5, 1991, A20, in which Nixon fears Hoover as the man "who will pull down the temple with him, including me"; the warning, in connection with the O. J. Simpson trial, that tabloids will report "exclusives" on *Simpson Agonistes* ("Of Course Race Is a Factor in the O. J. Case," *The New York Times*, July 7, 1994, F1.
46. See Kernan, *Death of Literature*, p. 110.
47. Kimball, *Tenured Radicals*, pp. 187, 194.
48. Irving Howe, "The Value of the Canon," in Paul Berman, ed., *Debating P. C.: The Controversy over Political Correctness on College Campuses* (New York, 1992), p. 161.
49. If traces of Milton's voice are heard in this debate, they are probably to be found in observations like this one by Stanley Fish, *There's No Such Thing as Free Speech* (New York and Oxford, 1994), p. 79.
50. Bloom, *Closing of the American Mind*, pp. 65, 66.
51. Gerald Graff, *Beyond the Culture Wars: How Teaching the Conflicts Can Revitalize American Education* (New York and London, 1992), p. 164.
52. Louis Menand, "Illiberalisms," *The New Yorker*, May 20, 1991, 106.
53. John Searle, "The Storm Over the University," in Berman, ed., *Debating P. C.*, p. 120.
54. See Wittreich, *Feminist Milton* (Ithaca, New York and London, 1987), pp. 1–2, as well as Peter Steinfels, "Beliefs," *The New York Times*, July 24, 1993, A7; Joan Blythe et al., "New Rules About Sex on Campus," *Harper's Magazine*, September 1993, 33–42, plus "Sex with the Professor, Part II," *Harper's*

266   JOSEPH WITTREICH

Magazine, January 1994, 6, 85, as well as her remarks quoted by Bob Sipchen in "A Lesson in Love? The Latest Campus Debate is Whether Student-Professor Romances Are About Power or Passion," *The Los Angeles Times*, September 16, 1994, E6; Karine Ames with Kendall Hamilton, "For Better, for Worse," *Newsweek*, February 15, 1993, 67; and Steven Lewis, "The Lost Canon of English Literature," *The New York Post*, June 24, 1993.

55. Michael Berube, "Public Image Limited: Political Correctness and the Media's Big Lie," in Berman, ed., *Debating P. C.*, pp. 147–48.

56. Hill, *The English Bible and the Seventeenth-Century Revolution* (London, 1993), p. 373. See also Wittreich, " 'He Ever Was a Dissenter': Milton's Transgresive Maneuvers in *Paradise Lost*," in *Arenas of Conflict: Milton and the Unfettered Mind* (Selinsgrove, PA, 1997), pp. 293–323.

57. William Kerrigan, "Milton's Place in Intellectual History," *The Cambridge Companion to Milton*, ed. Dennis Danielson (Cambridge and New York, 1989), pp. 272, 273.

58. I borrow the phrase from John Rumrich, *Milton Unbound: Controversy and Reinterpretation* (Cambridge, 1996), p. 3.

59. Graff, *Beyond the Culture Wars*, p. 159.

60. Giamatti, *A Free and Ordered Space*, pp. 29–30.

61. S. Margaret Fuller, "The Prose Works of Milton," *Papers on Literature and Art*, 2 vols. (London, 1846), vol. I, p. 39.

Index

Mercurius Politicus, 139, 140, 143, 151–52
Michael, 190, 223–24
Miller, Leo, 150
Millington, Gilbert, 142
Milton, John
  Arianism, 13, 76–89
  Arminianism, 4, 5, 13, 41–44, 93–110, 160
  authorship, construction of, 139–41, 145–54
  authorship of *de doctrina Christiana*, 1, 6–11,
    75–77, 97
  blasphemy and, 176–92
  culture wars and, 15–16, 255–62
  early political and religious beliefs, 49–67
  feminist reaction to, 257–58, *see also Paradise
    Lost*, sexual politics of
  heresy, usage of the word, 21–36
  marriage, attitudes toward, 118–19, 127–32
  monism, 13, 75, 83, 117, 129, 133
  neo-Christian interpretation of, 2–3, 204
  New Historicist interpretation of, 49
  postmodern interpretation of, 49
  PROSE WORKS
  Animadversions, 27, 46
  *Apology Against a Pamphlet (Apology for
    Smectymnuus)*, 45, 61, 152, 164, 177, 190
  Areopagitica, 98, 107, 183, 199, 222: freedom
    of publication, 5, 46, 63–64, 139, 144–47,
    149, 151–52, heresy, use of the word in, 22,
    28–30, 35, interpretive communities and,
    200–01, pursuit of knowledge, 4, 16
  artis logicae (Art of Logic), 8–10, 84
  Colasterion, 30, 159
  de doctrina Christiana (Christian Doctrine), 64,
    188, 225, 260: antitrinitarianism, 142,
    Arianism in, 76–85, 89, Arminianism in,
    13, 94, 96–110, authorship of, 1, 6–11, 64,
    75–85, 88–89, 245, heresy in, 32–33, 34,
    64, relation to *Paradise Lost*, 11, 75–77, 94,
    96–110
  defensio secunda (Second Defence), 22, 31–32, 59,
    150, 152, 179, 181, 187
  Doctrine and Discipline of Divorce, 61–63, 78,
    95, 98, 108, 109
  Eikonoklastes, 22, 150, 153, 190, 202
  Judgment of Martin Bucer, The, 63
  Observations upon the Articles of Peace, 31, 184
  Of Education, 51, 63, 151
  Of Reformation, 40, 41–42, 45, 46, 151
  Of True Religion, 22, 33–34, 36, 77
  Prelatical Episcopacy, 46
  Prolusions, 170
  *pro populo Anglicano defensio (Defence of the
    English People)*, 14, 22, 30–31, 152, 159, 190,
    208, 226, 227: insulting in, 161–73
  Ready and Easy Way, The, 106, 163, 221, 222

Reason of Church-Government, The, 22, 28, 30,
  42, 44–47, 51, 59, 60, 67, 108, 152
Tenure of Kings and Magistrates, The, 22, 30, 152
Treatise of Civil Power, A, 31, 33, 176, 179, 183,
  186, 192, 227, heresy in, 22–27
  publication licenser, 5, 139–54
  relation to Calvinism, 93–110
  Socinianism, 77
  VERSE WORKS
  Ad Patrem (To his Father), 59
  Arcades, 55, 60
  Comus (A Maske Presented at Ludlow Castle), 43,
    56–57, 60, 67
  Elegy I, 51
  Elegy IV, 53
  Elegy V, 51
  Elegy VI, 51
  Elegy VII, 51
  Il Penseroso, 54
  L'Allegro, 54
  Lycidas, 44, 57–58, 67, 118
  Methought I Saw, 256
  Nativity Ode, 53–54
  On the Late Massacre in Piemont, 256
  *On the New Forcers of Conscience under the Long
    Parliament*, 2
  Paradise Lost: animate materialism, 13,
    117–18, 129, 133, Arianism, 76–77, 79,
    81–83, 85–86, Arminianism, 43–44,
    93–97, 100–10, blasphemy in, 178,
    181–92, critical reception, 2, 244–62,
    see also interpretive communities *and*
    readers and readership, culture wars,
    15–16, 244–62, eroticism in, 117, 127–32,
    insulting in, 159, kissing in, 13, 117–18,
    129, 133, Providence and political
    action, 223–25, readers' responses,
    15–16, 76–77, relation of God the Father
    to the Son, 81–83, 85–86, relation to *de
    doctrina Christiana*, 11, 75–77, 94, 96–110,
    sexual politics, 244–62, Socinianism in,
    142
  Paradise Regained, 15, 128, 189, 199, 209,
    219–20, 226–30, 231, 234, 236
  Poems of Mr. John Milton, 49, 65–67, 118, 152,
    153
  Samson Agonistes, 15, 159, 219–20, 230–35,
    237–39, 247, 265n.45, as closet drama,
    199, 201, 204–11
  monism, 13, 83, 117, 129, 133
  Montaigne, Michel de, 203
  Morrill, John, 39, 47
  Moseley, Humphrey, 65–66, 204
  Mueller, Janel, 1, 12
  Mueller, Martin, 233